MCA
Modern Desktop
Administrator Practice Tests

MCA
Modern Desktop
Administrator Practice Tests
Exam MD-100 and MD-101

Crystal Panek

A Wiley Brand

This book is dedicated to my loving husband, William Panek, and to my two wonderful daughters, Alexandria and Paige. Thank you all for your love and support. I love you all more than anything!

Acknowledgments

I would like to thank my husband and best friend, Will, because without him I would not be where I am today—Thank you! I would also like to express my love to my two daughters, Alexandria and Paige, who have always shown me nothing but love and support. Thank you all!

I would like to thank everyone on the Sybex team, especially my Associate Acquisitions Editor, Devon Lewis, who always helps me to make the best books possible, and Jon Buhagiar, who is the Technical Editor. It's important to have the best technical expert supporting you, and he did an amazing job. I would like to thank Barath Kumar Rajasekaran, the Production Editor, and Gary Schwartz, the Project Editor.

Finally, I also want to thank everyone behind the scenes that helped make this book possible. Thank you all for your hard work and dedication.

—Crystal Panek

About the Author

 **Crystal Panek** holds these certifications: MCP, MCP+I, MCSA, MCSA+ Security and Messaging, MCSE-NT (3.51 & 4.0), MCSE 2000, 2003, 2012/2012 R2, 2016, MCSE+ Security and Messaging, MCDBA, MCTS, and MCITP.

For many years, Crystal trained as a contract instructor, teaching at locations such as MicroC, Stellacon Corporation, and the University of New Hampshire. She then became the vice president for a large IT training company, and for 15 years, she developed training materials and courseware to help thousands of students get through their certification exams. She currently works on a contract basis creating courseware for several large IT training facilities.

She currently resides in New Hampshire with her husband and two daughters. In her spare time, she likes to camp, hike, shoot trap and skeet, golf, bowl, and go snowmobiling.

About the Technical Editor

Jon Buhagiar, BS/ITM, MCSE, CCNA, A+, N+, Project+, is an information technology professional with two decades of experience in higher education and the private sector.

Jon currently serves as supervisor of network operations at Pittsburgh Technical College. In this role, he manages data center and network infrastructure operations and IT operations, and he is involved in project management of projects supporting the quality of education at the college. He also serves as an adjunct instructor in the college's School of Information Technology department, where he has taught courses on Microsoft and Cisco certifications. Jon has been an instructor for 20+ years with several colleges in the Pittsburgh area, since the introduction of the Windows NT MCSE in 1998.

Jon earned a BS degree in information technology management from Western Governors University. He also achieved an associate degree in business management from Pittsburgh Technical College. He has recently become a Windows Server 2016 Microsoft Certified Solutions Expert (MCSE) and earned the Cisco Certified Network Associate (CCNA) certification. Other certifications include CompTIA Network+, CompTIA A+, and CompTIA Project+.

In addition to his professional and teaching roles, he has authored *CCNA Routing and Switching Practice Tests: Exam 100-105, Exam 200-105,* and *Exam 200-125; CompTIA Network+ Review Guide: Exam N10-007, 4th Edition; CompTIA A+ Deluxe Study Guide: Exam 220-1002* (all Sybex, 2016); and *CCNA Certification Practice Tests: Exam 200-301* (Sybex, 2020). He has also served as the technical editor for the second edition of the *CompTIA Cloud+ Study Guide* (Sybex, 2016), *CCNA Security Study Guide: Exam 210-260* (Sybex, 2018), *CCNA Cloud Complete Study Guide: Exam 210-451 and Exam 210-455* (Sybex, 2018), *CCNP Enterprise Certification Study Guide: Implementing* (Sybex, 2018), *Operating Cisco Enterprise Network Core Technologies: Exam 300-401* (Sybex, 2020), and *MCA Modern Desktop Administrator Complete Study Guide: Exam MD-100 and Exam MD-101* (Sybex, 2020).

Jon has spoken at several conferences about spam and email systems. He is an active radio electronics hobbyist and has held a ham radio license for the past 18 years, KB3KGS. He experiments with electronics and has a strong focus on the Internet of Things (IoT).

Contents at a Glance

Contents at a Glance

Contents

Contents

Introduction

This book can be used as a companion book to William Panek's *MCA Microsoft 365 Certified Associate Modern Desktop Administrator Complete Study Guide: Exam MD-100 and Exam MD-101* (Sybex, 2020). Use this book as a guide to help you test your knowledge before you take Microsoft exams MD-100 and MD-101. This book provides you with about 1,000 questions that cover all of the concepts and exam objects for the Microsoft 365 Certified: Modern Desktop Administrator Associate certification exams.

Use this book as a training tool to determine which areas you may need to focus more on before sitting for these exams. Microsoft recommends that candidates who take these two exams be IT professionals who will deploy, configure, secure, manage, and monitor devices and client applications in an enterprise environment. Candidates should also be familiar with managing identity, access, policies, updates, and apps. Candidates should have an understanding of enterprise scenarios, cloud-integrated services, and Microsoft 365 workloads, and they must be experienced in deploying, configuring, and maintaining Windows 10 and non-Windows devices and technologies.

The Microsoft Certification Program

Having a Microsoft certification on your résumé will make it stand out to a perspective employer by showing them that you are ready to succeed. In this day and age of technology, I tell students that having industry certifications is almost as important as having a college degree. Most companies looking to hire someone in the IT field are almost certainly going to look for someone who has achieved certification.

According to Microsoft, individuals should get certified to "give you a professional edge by providing globally recognized industry endorsed evidence of skills mastery, demonstrating your abilities and willingness to embrace new technologies. Verify your skills—and unlock your opportunities."

Since the start of its certification program, Microsoft has certified more than two million people. As the computer network industry continues to increase in both size and complexity, this number is sure to grow—and the need for proven ability will also increase. Certifications can help companies verify the skills of prospective employees.

There are a large number of certifications available through Microsoft. These certifications change occasionally. To see the list of certifications currently offered by Microsoft, check out its website at www.microsoft.com/en-us/learning/browse-all-certifications.aspx.

Microsoft 365 Certified: Modern Desktop Administrator Associate Exam Requirements

Candidates must pass these two exams:

MD-100: Windows 10

MD-101: Managing Modern Desktops

Microsoft has certification paths for many different technical job roles. Each of these certifications consists of passing a series of exams to earn certification. Certifications fall into three categories.

- Fundamentals Certifications

- Role-Based Certifications

- Additional/Specialty Certifications

The Microsoft 365 Certified: Modern Desktop Administrator Associate falls under the Role-Based Certification category.

Exam MD-100

Exam MD-100 measures your ability to undertake these technical tasks: deploy Windows, manage devices and data, configure connectivity, and maintain Windows.

Exam MD-101

Exam MD-101 measures your ability to undertake these technical tasks: deploy and update operating systems, manage policies and profiles, manage and protect devices, and manage apps and data.

For more information regarding the Microsoft 365 Certified: Modern Desktop Administrator Associate certification, go to Microsoft's website at docs.microsoft.com/ en-us/learn/certifications/m365-modern-desktop.

Types of Exam Questions

To protect exam security, Microsoft does not identify exam formats or question types prior to taking an exam. Microsoft is always introducing new and state-of-the-art testing technologies and question types. Microsoft reserves the right to integrate new technologies into exams at any time without advance notice. Microsoft exams may contain any of the following:

- Active screen

- Best answer

- Build list

- Case studies/scenarios

- Drag and drop

- Exam and questions samples

- Hot area

- Labs

- Multiple choice

- Repeated answer choices
- Short answer

Tips for Taking the Windows 10 Exams

Here are some general tips for achieving success on your certification exam:

- Arrive early at the exam center so that you can relax and review your study materials. During this final review, you can look over tables and lists of exam-related information.

- Read the questions carefully. Do not be tempted to jump to an early conclusion. Make sure that you know *exactly* what the question is asking.

- Answer all questions. If you are unsure about a question, mark it for review and come back to it at a later time.

- On simulations, do not change settings that are not directly related to the question. Also, assume default settings if the question does not specify or imply which settings are used.

- For questions that you're not sure about, use a process of elimination to get rid of the obviously incorrect answers first. This improves your odds of selecting the correct answer when you need to make an educated guess.

Exam Registration

As of the release date of this book, Microsoft exams are offered at more than 1,000 Authorized VUE Testing Centers around the world. For the location of a testing center near you, go to VUE's website at www.vue.com. If you are outside of the United States and Canada, contact your local VUE registration center.

Find out the number of the exam that you want to take and then register with the VUE center nearest to you. At this point, you will be asked for advance payment for the exam. The exams are $165 each, and you must take them within one year of payment. You can schedule exams up to six weeks in advance or as late as one working day prior to the date of the exam. You can cancel or reschedule your exam if you contact the center at least two working days prior to the exam. Same-day registration is available in some locations, subject to space availability. Where same-day registration is available, you must register a minimum of two hours before test time.

When you schedule the exam, you will be provided with instructions regarding appointment and cancellation procedures, ID requirements, and information about the testing center location. In addition, you will receive a registration and payment confirmation letter from VUE.

Microsoft requires certification candidates to accept the terms of a nondisclosure agreement before taking certification exams.

Who Should Read This Book?

This book is intended for individuals who want to earn their Microsoft 365 Certified: Modern Desktop Administrator Associate: Windows 10 certification by passing exams MD-100 and MD-101.

Use this book as a study guide to help you pass the Microsoft exams. It will also help anyone who wants to learn the real ins and outs of the Windows 10 operating system using the question explanations.

What's Inside?

Here is a glance at what's contained in each chapter:

Part I: Modern Desktop Admin, Exam MD-100

Chapter 1: Deploy Windows   In the first chapter, we cover questions on how to deploy Windows 10 and how to perform post-installation configurations. This is a partial list, but some of the questions will cover subjects such as configuring language packs, migrating user data, performing a clean installation, performing an in-place upgrade, specifying mobility settings, and customizing the Windows desktop.

Chapter 2: Manage Devices and Data   This chapter asks questions on how to manage local users, local groups, and devices. It covers questions regarding configuring data access and protection, configuring devices by using local policies, and managing Windows security. Questions will cover subjects such as configuring permissions, configuring the local registry, troubleshooting group policies, configuring user account control (UAC), and implementing encryption.

Chapter 3: Configure Connectivity   This chapter asks questions on how to configure networking and configuring remote connectivity. It covers questions regarding configuring IP settings, configuring VPN clients, troubleshooting networking, and configuring Wi-Fi profile and remote management, as well as PowerShell remoting.

Chapter 4: Maintain Windows   This chapter asks questions on configuring system and data recovery, managing updates, and monitoring and managing Windows. It covers questions regarding performing file recovery, using OneDrive, recovering Windows 10, checking and troubleshooting updates, selecting the appropriate servicing channel, analyzing event logs, and managing the Windows 10 environment.

Part II: Modern Desktop Admin, Exam MD-101

Chapter 5: Deploy and Update Operating Systems   This chapter asks questions on how to plan and implement Windows 10 by using dynamic deployment, planning and implementing Windows 10 by using Windows Autopilot, upgrading devices to Windows 10, managing updates, and managing device authentication. It covers questions regarding managing and troubleshooting provisioning packages, evaluating and selecting an appropriate deployment option, assigning deployment profiles, identifying upgrade and downgrade paths, migrating user profiles, optimizing Windows 10 delivery, using Desktop Analytics, configuring Windows Update for Business, and more.

Chapter 6: Manage Policies and Profiles   This chapter asks questions on planning and implementing co-management, implementing conditional access and compliance policies for devices, configuring device profiles, and managing user profiles. It covers questions regarding implementing co-management precedence, migrating group policies to mobility device management (MDM) policies, conditional access policies, device compliance policies, device profiles, user profiles, Enterprise State Roaming, and Folder Redirection.

Chapter 7: Manage and Protect Devices   This chapter asks questions on how to manage Microsoft Defender and managing Intune device enrollment and inventory. It covers questions regarding implementing and managing Microsoft Defender tools, Microsoft Defender Advanced Threat Protection, and Microsoft Defender Antivirus; configuring enrollment settings and Intune automatic enrollment, enrolling devices; and monitoring device health using different tools.

Chapter 8: Manage Apps and Data   This chapter asks questions on how to deploy and update applications and how to implement Mobile Application Management (MAM). This chapter covers questions pertaining to assigning apps to groups, deploying apps, enabling sideloading, gathering readiness data, configuring and implementing kiosks, using MAM policies, using Windows Information Protection (WIP) policies, and using Azure Information Protection templates.

Chapter 9: Practice Exam 1: MD-100   This is a series of review questions on what you learned when going through Chapters 1–4.

Chapter 10: Practice Exam 2: MD-101   This is a series of review questions on what you learned when going through Chapters 5–8.

How to Contact Wiley or the Author

You can contact the author at authorcrystalpanek@hotmail.com.

If you believe that you have found an error in this book and it is not listed on the book's page at www.wiley.com, you can report the issue to our customer technical support team at support.wiley.com.

NOTE You can access the Sybex Interactive Online Test Bank at www.wiley.com/go/Sybextestprep.

Exam MD-100 and Exam MD-101 Certification Objectives

This book has been written to cover the MCA Modern Desktop Administrator exam MD-100 and exam MD-101 objectives. The following table lists the domains measured by these exams and the extent to which they are represented:

Exam Objective	Percentage of Exam
Part 1 - MD-100 Objectives	
1.0 Deploy Windows 10	15–20%
2.0 Manage Devices and Data	35–40%
3.0 Configure Connectivity	15–20%
4.0 Maintain Windows	25–30%
Total	100%
Part 2 - MD-101 Objectives	
5.0 Deploy and Update Operating Systems	35–40%
6.0 Manage Policies and Profiles	25–30%
7.0 Manage and Protect Devices	20–25%
8.0 Manage Apps and Data	10–15%
Total	100%

Objectives Map for Exam MD-100 and Exam MD-101

The following is the objective map for the MCA Modern Desktop Administrator certification exams. This will enable you to find the location where each objective is covered in the book.

Part 1: MD-100	
1.0 Deploy Windows	
1.1 Deploy Windows 10	Chapter 1
▪ Configure language packs ▪ Migrate user data ▪ Perform a clean installation ▪ Perform an in-place upgrade (using tools such as MDT, WDS, ADK, etc.) ▪ Select the appropriate Windows edition ▪ Troubleshoot activation issues	
1.2 Perform Post-Installation Configuration	Chapter 1
▪ Configure Edge and Internet Explorer ▪ Configure mobility settings ▪ Configure sign-in options ▪ Customize the Windows desktop	
2.0 Manage Devices and Data	
2.1 Manage Local users, Local Groups, and Devices	Chapter 2
▪ Manage devices in directories ▪ Manage local groups ▪ Manage local users	
2.2 Configure Data Access and Protection	Chapter 2
▪ Configure NTFS permissions ▪ Configure shared permissions	
2.3 Configure Devices by Using Local Policies	Chapter 2
▪ Configure local registry ▪ Implement local policy ▪ Troubleshoot group policies on devices	
2.4 Manage Windows Security	Chapter 2
▪ Configure User Account Control (UAC) ▪ Configure Microsoft Defender Firewall ▪ Implement encryption	

6.0 Manage Policies and Profiles	
6.1 Plan and Implement Co-Management	Chapter 6
• Implement co-management precedence • Migrate group policy to MDM policies • Recommend a co-management strategy	
6.2 Implement Conditional Access and Compliance Policies for Devices	Chapter 6
• Implement conditional access policies • Manage conditional access policies • Plan conditional access policies • Implement device compliance policies • Manage device compliance policies • Plan device compliance policies	
6.3 Configure Device Profiles	Chapter 6
• Implement device profiles • Manage device profiles • Plan device profiles	
6.4 Manage User Profiles	Chapter 6
• Configure user profiles • Configure Enterprise State Roaming in Azure AD • Configure sync settings • Implement Folder Redirection, including OneDrive	
7.0 Manage and Protect Devices	
7.1 Manage Microsoft Defender	Chapter 7
• Implement and manage Microsoft Defender Application Guard • Implement and manage Microsoft Defender Credential Guard • Implement and manage Microsoft Defender Exploit Guard • Implement Microsoft Defender Advanced Threat Protection • Integrate Microsoft Defender Application Control • Manage Microsoft Defender Antivirus	

7.2 Manage Intune Device Enrollment and Inventory	Chapter 7
▪ Configure enrollment settings ▪ Configure Intune automatic enrollment ▪ Enable device enrollment ▪ Enroll non-Windows devices ▪ Enroll Windows devices ▪ Generate custom device inventory reports' Review device inventory	
7.3 Monitor Devices	Chapter 7
▪ Monitor device health (e.g., log analytics, Desktop Analytics, or other cloud-based tools, etc.) ▪ Monitor device security	
8.0 Manage Apps and Data	
8.1 Deploy and Update Applications	Chapter 8
▪ Assign apps to groups ▪ Deploy apps by using Intune ▪ Deploy apps by using Microsoft Store for Business ▪ Deploy O365 ProPlus ▪ Enable sideloading of apps into images ▪ Gather Office readiness data ▪ Configure and implement kiosk (assigned access) or public devices	
8.2 Implement Mobile Application Management (MAM)	Chapter 8
▪ Implement MAM policies ▪ Manage MAM policies ▪ Plan MAM ▪ Configure Windows Information Protection ▪ Implement Azure Information Protection templates ▪ Securing data by using Intune	

Modern Desktop Admin, Exam MD-100

Chapter

1

Deploy Windows

---

1. You are the administrator for your company network. You just bought a new computer with a preinstalled version of Windows 10. You need to migrate your existing users from a previous computer that was running an earlier version of Windows. Using the User State Migration Tool, which commands should you use to manage this process? (Choose two.)

   A. `loadstate.exe`

   B. `scanstate.exe`

   C. `usmt.exe`

   D. `windowsmigrate.exe`

2. You are the administrator for your company network. You have a computer named Computer1 that runs Windows 10 Enterprise. This machine is configured with multiple shared print queues. You are planning on migrating the print queues to a new computer called Computer2. What should you do?

   A. Using the Print Management Console, use the Migrate Printers utility.

   B. Using the Control Panel, use the Migrate Printers utility.

   C. Using the Printers & Scanners utility, use the Migrate Printers utility.

   D. Using the Print Management tool, use the Export Printers tool.

3. You are the administrator for your company network. You are currently using Windows 10 Professional, and you have a hardware component that you no longer want to use. You do not want to delete the driver—you just plan to deactivate it. Using Device Manager, what can you do to the drivers to meet your needs?

   A. Disable the drivers.

   B. Remove the drivers.

   C. Roll back the drivers.

   D. Upgrade the drivers.

4. You are the administrator for your company network. You are planning to deploy Windows 10 to a large number of secure computers. You want to select the version of Windows 10 that meets these requirements:

   - Must use the default browser, Microsoft Edge

   - Minimizes the attack surface on the computer

   - Supports joining Microsoft Azure Active Directory (Azure AD)

   - Only allows the installation of applications by using the Microsoft Store

   Which version of Microsoft 10 should you install?

   A. Windows 10 Pro

   B. Windows 10 Enterprise

   C. Windows 10 Pro in S mode

   D. Windows 10 Home in S mode

5. You are the administrator for your company network. Your organization is moving over to Windows 10. You are looking for a way to run multiple storage commands by using a scripting tool. What tool should you use to meet your needs?

    A.   AD FS for scripting

    B.   Disk Administrator for scripting

    C.   Windows PowerShell for scripting

    D.   SCCM for scripting

6. You are the administrator for your company network. You are planning on installing a new driver for a video card, but you are not sure if the driver you are about to install is the correct one. If you install the new driver and it's not correct, which of the following is the easiest way to allow you to return your computer to the previous state?

    A.   Use the Roll Back Driver.

    B.   Reboot in Safe Mode.

    C.   Use the Startup Repair tool.

    D.   Use the System Restore utility.

7. You are the administrator for your company network. You are planning to start a new installation by using the command line. You decide to use the `setup.exe` command-line setup utility with an answer file. Which command-line switch should you use to implement the installation in this format?

    A.   You should use `/apply`.

    B.   You should use `/generalize`.

    C.   You should use `/noreboot`.

    D.   You should use `/unattend`.

8. You are the administrator for your company network. You have a system that runs both Windows 7 and Windows 10. Each operating system is installed on a separate partition. What action should you perform to ensure that the computer always starts using Windows 7 by default?

    A.   In the root of the Windows 7 partition, create a `boot.ini` file.

    B.   In the root of the Windows 10 partition, create a `boot.ini` file.

    C.   Run `bcdedit.exe` with the `/bootcd` parameter.

    D.   Run `bcdedit.exe` with the `/default` parameter.

9. You are the administrator for your company network. You are deploying Windows 10 to several new laptop computers. These laptops are to be used by employees when working at client locations. Each employee will be assigned one laptop and one Android device. You want to ensure that the employees lock their laptops when they leave them for an extended period of time. What should you recommend that they do?

    A.   Configure the Dynamic Lock settings from the Settings app.

    B.   Configure the Lock Screen settings and the Screen Timeout settings from the Settings app.

C.   Configure the Windows Hello settings from Sign-in options.

D.   Enable Bluetooth discovery, and pair the Android device to the laptop.

10.   You are the administrator for your company network. A Windows 10 user has requested that their Start Menu options be modified to meet their needs. Where do you go to make the modifications that the user would like?

A.   Ease of Access Tool

B.   Personalization

C.   Snipping Tool

D.   Time and Language

11.   You are the administrator for your company network. You are configuring the power settings for an employee's laptop. You are configuring the laptop to go into sleep mode after a certain amount of time of inactivity. What happens when the laptop enters sleep mode?

A.   All data will be saved to the hard disk.

B.   The laptop will shut down.

C.   The monitor and hard disk turn off, but the computer will remain in an active state.

D.   When you resume activity on the laptop, the user session will not be available.

12.   You are the administrator for your company network. An employee calls to tell you that they accidentally just deleted an important file on their computer. What is the easiest way for this file to be restored?

A.   Instruct the user to go to Folder Options and click the Show Deleted Files option.

B.   Instruct the user to click the Recycle Bin icon on their desktop and restore the deleted file.

C.   Instruct the user to go to Folder Options and click the Undo Deleted Files option.

D.   Instruct the user that you will restore the file from the most recent tape backup.

13.   You are the administrator for your company network. You have a computer that currently runs Windows 7. This machine has a local user with a customized profile. You want to perform a clean installation of Windows 10 without formatting the drives. You plan to migrate the settings of the users to the new Windows 10 machine. You run `scanstate.exe` and specify the `C:\Users` subfolder. What do you do next?

A.   Run `loadstate.exe` and specify the `C:\Windows.old` subfolder.

B.   Run `usmtuils.exe` and specify the `C:\Users` subfolder.

C.   Run `loadstate.exe` and specify the `C:\Users` subfolder.

D.   Run `scanstate.exe` and specify the `C:\Windows.old.` subfolder.

14. You are the administrator for your company network. You are using Windows Deployment Services (WDS) to install several hundred Windows 10 employee computers. When the employees attempt to use WDS, they are unable to finish the unattended installation. You believe that the WDS server has not been configured to respond to the employee's requests. What utility should you configure on the WDS server so that it responds to the requests?

A. Active Directory Sites and Services

B. Active Directory Users and Computers

C. Active Directory Users and Groups

D. Windows Deployment Services MMC snap-in

15. You are the administrator for your company network. You have a mounted Windows 10 Windows Image (.wim). What should you do if you want to view the list of third-party drivers installed on the WIM?

A. Open the mount folder using Windows Explorer.

B. Run dism with the /get-drivers parameter.

C. Run driverquery.exe with the /si parameter.

D. View all hidden drivers using Device Manager.

16. You are the administrator for your company network. You want to edit the Registry without using the Control Panel. What are the two utilities that are supported by Windows 10 to edit the Registry manually? (Choose two.)

A. regedit

B. regedt32

C. regeditor

D. registryeditor

17. You are the administrator for your company network. A user is using Windows 10 on their laptop computer and wants to change the desktop background. What do you suggest the user do to change the background on the laptop?

A. Right-click My Computer and choose Manage from the context menu.

B. Right-click My Computer and choose Properties from the context menu.

C. Right-click the empty space on the desktop and choose Personalize from the context menu.

D. Select Control Panel ➢ System.

18. You are the administrator for your company network. You have a large number of computers running Windows 10 in a workgroup. These computers have low-bandwidth metered Internet connections. What should you configure if you need to reduce the amount of Internet bandwidth that is being consumed when updates are being downloaded?

A. Use Background Intelligent Transfer Service (BITS).

B. Use Delivery Optimization.

C. Use distributed cache mode in BranchCache.

D. Use hosted mode in BranchCache.

19. You are the administrator for your company network. You have just performed a clean installation of Windows 10 on a computer. Which of the following Windows 10 utilities could you use if you want to create an image of the installation to be used as a template for remote install?

    A. Deployment Image Servicing and Management (DISM)

    B. Distributed File System (DFS)

    C. System Preparation Tool (Sysprep)

    D. Windows System Image Manager (Windows SIM)

20. You are the administrator for your company network. On a Windows 10 computer, you are configuring the services. You need to ensure that if a service fails to load, it will attempt to restart. Using the service's Properties dialog box, which tab should you go to?

    A. The Dependencies tab

    B. The General tab

    C. The Log On tab

    D. The Recovery tab

21. You are the administrator for your company network. You are planning on deploying a large number of new computers within your network, each with the same configuration. You are looking to create a reference image that will be applied to all of the new machines. Which utility will you use to accomplish this goal?

    A. You should use the `dism.exe` utility.

    B. You should use the `setup.exe` utility.

    C. You should use the `wdsutil.exe` utility.

    D. You should use the Windows SIM utility.

22. You are the administrator for your company network. You have a Windows 10 computer that will be used as a reference. You plan to create and deploy an image of this Windows 10 computer. You create an answer file named `answer.xml`. You want to ensure that the installation applies the answer file after the image has been deployed. Which command should you run prior to capturing the image?

    A. `dism.exe /append answer.xml /check`

    B. `dism.exe /mount answer.xml /verify`

    C. `sysprep.exe /generalize /oobe /unattend:answer.xml`

    D. `sysprep.exe /reboot /audit /unattend:answer.xml`

23. You are the administrator for your company network. You are planning to use the System Preparation tool to install Windows 10 using images. You are going to create an image from a reference computer and then copy the image to all of the new machines. However, you do not want to create a security identifier (SID) on the destination computer when you use the image. To achieve this goal, what `sysprep.exe` command should you use?

    A. `/generalize`

    B. `/oobe`

C. /quiet

D. /specialize

24. You are the administrator for your company network. You have an isolated network that you are using for testing. This testing environment contains multiple computers that are running Windows 10 and are part of a workgroup. When testing, these machines remain as part of the workgroup. You notice that none of the computers are being activated. What should you do if you want to activate these computers without connecting the testing environment to the Internet?

A. Use Active Directory–based activation.

B. Use the Get-WindowsDeveloperLicense cmdlet.

C. Use Key Management Service (KMS).

D. Use the Volume Activation Management Tool (VAMT).

25. You are the administrator for your company network. One of your employees is not happy with how the mouse and keyboard respond when they are trying to work. Which utility would you recommend to the user so that they can configure the mouse pointer rate and the keyboard speed to meet their needs?

A. Computer Management

B. Control Panel

C. Microsoft Management Console

D. Registry Editor

26. You are the administrator for your company network. An employee has a laptop computer that uses Advanced Configuration and Power Interface (ACPI), and they want to see how much battery power is available. The user also wants to see whether the laptop has been configured to hibernate. What utility should you recommend the user use to answer their questions?

A. Battery Meter

B. Computer Manager

C. Device Manager

D. Microsoft Management Console (MMC)

27. You are the administrator for your company network. You have an employee with limited vision. You want to set up their computer with the ability to read the screen text aloud as well as any text, menus, and buttons. What accessibility app should you implement?

A. You should implement Dialog Manager.

B. You should implement Narrator.

C. You should implement Orator.

D. You should implement Read-Aloud Text.

28. You are the administrator for your company network. An employee has a laptop that is running Windows 10 Home Edition. What should you do first if you want to synchronize the files from the laptop to their network folder?

A. Configure all of the files on the laptop as read-only.

B. Enable one-way synchronization.

C. Enable two-way synchronization.

D. Upgrade the laptop to Windows 10 Enterprise.

29. You are the administrator for your company network. You are planning on creating a deployment plan that will automate about 100 new Windows 10 computers. You want to use WDS to perform the installations. You plan to create an answer file to automate the installation; however, you do not want to use a text editor. What program can you use if you want to create an unattended answer file using a GUI interface?

A. Microsoft BitLocker Administration and Monitoring (MBAM)

B. Deployment Image Servicing and Management (DISM)

C. System Preparation Tool (Sysprep)

D. Windows System Image Manager (SIM)

30. You are the administrator for your company network. You have a dual-boot machine, but you'd like the primary operating system to be Windows 10. What file do you need to configure?

A. bcboot.ini

B. bcdboot

C. bcdedit

D. boot.ini

31. You are the administrator for your company network. Your company uses an app from the Microsoft Store for Business. There are several computers that are not allowed to access the Internet; however, you want to distribute the application to these computers. How do you distribute the application to the machines that don't have Internet access? (Choose all that apply.)

A. Use a Microsoft Intune deployment.

B. Use a WDS deployment.

C. Using DISM, deploy an AppX package.

D. Using ICD, create a provisioning package.

E. Using Windows SIM, create an answer file.

32. You are the administrator for your company network. You need to create a script that will verify the activation status of a large number of computers. What should you include in the script?

A. Run the sfc.exe command with the /scannow parameter.

B. Run the sfc.exe command with the /verifyonly parameter.

C. Run the slmgr.vbs script with the /dli parameter.

D. Run the slmgr.vbs script with the /ipk parameter.

33. You are the administrator for your company network. A user has recently come up to you and asked for your assistance. They accidentally saved the wrong username and password when logging into an application, and they'd like your assistance in fixing it. Where should you go on the user's machine to make that change?

    A. Credential Manager

    B. Password Manager

    C. Username Manager

    D. Website Manager

34. You are the administrator for your company network. You have a Windows 10 domain that contains two computers: Computer1 and Computer2. What should you use if you are on Computer1 and want to view the installed devices and the drivers that are on Computer2?

    A. You should use the `driverquery.exe` command.

    B. You should use the `Get-OdbcDriver` cmdlet.

    C. You should use the `Get-PnpDevice` cmdlet.

    D. You should use the `Get-WindowsDriver` cmdlet.

35. You are the administrator for your company network. You want to prepare a system for imaging, and you are planning to use Sysprep. Which switch should you use if you want to reset the security ID (SID) and clear the event logs?

    A. You should use `/audit`.

    B. You should use `/generalize`.

    C. You should use `/oobe`.

    D. You should use `/unattend`.

36. You are the administrator for your company network. You have a system in your network that is currently running Windows 7 Enterprise. This system has a 32-bit legacy application that has some issues when working with Windows 10 Enterprise. For authentication, this application uses a domain single sign-on (SSO). The vendor of the application recently released a version of the application that is fully compatible with Windows 10 Enterprise. However, it cannot be installed to the Windows 7 computer because of some registry setting conflicts found at `HKEY_CURRENT_USER`. You plan to migrate this computer to Windows 10 Enterprise. However, there are a few requirements that must be met.

    ▪ The employees still need to be able to use the original version of the application while the new version is being validated.

    ▪ The old version needs to be removed once the new version is validated.

    ▪ The employees will authenticate only once to use the application.

    What should you use to meet these requirements?

    A. You should use Hyper-V.

    B. You should use the Microsoft Application Compatibility Toolkit (ACT).

    C. You should use Microsoft Application Virtualization (App-V).

    D. You should use User Experience Virtualization (UE-V).

37. You are the administrator for your company network. You have several computers on your network that still run Windows 7. These machines run a custom application. This application is compatible with Windows 10 Enterprise. You are planning on migrating the Windows 7 computers to newly purchased computers with Windows 10 already preinstalled. On a USB flash drive, you add the User State Migration Tool (USMT). You want to ensure that when you migrate to the Windows 10 machines, the custom application settings are applied. What should you do first to migrate these machines?

A. On the Windows 10 Enterprise computers, install the custom application.

B. On the Windows 10 Enterprise computers, run the loadstate.exe command.

C. On the Windows 7 computers, run the scanstate.exe command.

D. On the Windows 10 computers, run the scanstate.exe command.

38. You are the administrator for your company network. You have a Windows 10 computer with a microphone attached. You want a hands-free way to ask your system a question. You want to use Microsoft's digital assistant. What is the name of this application?

A. Alexa

B. Cortana

C. Google Assistant

D. Siri

39. You are the administrator for your company network. You have several Windows 10 Enterprise tablets. What should you do if you want to minimize power usage whenever a user presses the sleep button?

A. Configure the sleep button setting to Hibernate using Power Options.

B. Configure the sleep button setting to Sleep using Power Options.

C. In the tablet's BIOS, disable the C-State control.

D. Set the system cooling policy to passive by configuring the active power plan.

40. You are the administrator for your company network. You have a Windows 10 Enterprise with a workgroup environment. You want to stop the computers in the IT department from sleeping. However, you still want the screens to shut off after a certain amount of time when the computer is not being used. What should you do if you want to configure and apply a standard power configuration scheme to the IT department's computers? (Choose all that apply.)

A. On one of the computers in the IT department, use powercfg /S to modify the power scheme. Then, run powercfg /export to export the power scheme.

B. On one of the computers in the IT department, use powercfg /X to modify the power scheme. Then, run powercfg /export to export the power scheme to the rest of the computers in the IT department.

C. Use powercfg /import to import the power scheme to the rest of the IT department's computers. Then, run powercfg /s to set the power scheme to Active.

D. Use powercfg /import to import the power scheme to the rest of the IT department's computers. Then run powercfg /x to set the power scheme to Active.

41. You are the administrator for your company network. You have a Windows 10 Enterprise computer named Computer1, which is a member of an Active Directory domain. You have a line-of-business (LOB) universal app named App1, which was developed internally. You need to ensure that you can run the application on Computer1. You have been tasked to meet the following requirements:

- You need to minimize the cost to deploy the application.

- You need to minimize the attack surface on the computer.

What should you do?

A. Certify the application by using the Microsoft Store.

B. Enable the Sideload apps setting using the Update & Security setting on Computer1.

C. Run the `Add-AppxProvisionedPackage` cmdlet.

D. With a certificate issued by a third-party certificate authority, sign the application.

42. You are the administrator for your company network. You are preparing a system for imaging by using Sysprep. You want to allow the end users to be able to customize their Windows operating systems, create user accounts, name their computer, and perform other tasks. To allow this, what Sysprep setting should you utilize?

A. You should use `/audit`.

B. You should use `/generalize`.

C. You should use `/oobe`.

D. You should use `/unattend`.

43. You are the administrator for your company network. You have a new laptop computer that is running Windows 10 and is a member of a workgroup that is connected to a Wi-Fi network. You discover that the active network location on the computer is set to public. You want to change the network location to a private network. What should you do? (Choose all that apply.)

A. You should use the Network Troubleshooting Tool.

B. You should use Settings ➢ Network And Internet ➢ Wi-Fi.

C. You should use System ➢ Network And Internet ➢ Wi-Fi.

D. You should use Windows Firewall.

44. You are the administrator for your company network. You have a Windows 10 laptop computer. A user reports that their battery seems to be having issues. You want to generate a report to review the battery life of the laptop that lists the expected battery life after a full charge. You'd also like to see the history of the battery life. What should you use to generate this report?

A. From the command prompt, use the `powercfg` command.

B. In the Control Panel, use the Power Options settings.

C. In the Settings app, use the Power & Sleep setting.

D. Use Performance Monitor.

45. You are the administrator for your company network. Your network contains a single Active Directory domain that has a Key Management Service (KMS) host. You plan on deploying Windows 10 to several new laptop computers. What command should you run if you want to ensure that Windows 10 will attempt to activate on the laptops?

A. You should run `ospp.vbs /act`.

B. You should run `ospp.vbs /dstatus`.

C. You should run `slmgr.vbs /ato`.

D. You should run `slmgr.vbs /dli`.

46. You are the administrator for your company network. You have a computer on your network that is running a 32-bit version of Windows 7 Professional. You are planning on performing an in-place upgrade to Windows 10. Which two editions of Windows 10 can you upgrade this computer to? (Choose two.)

A. You can upgrade to the 32-bit version of Windows 10 Enterprise.

B. You can upgrade to the 64-bit version of Windows 10 Enterprise.

C. You can upgrade to the 32-bit version of Windows 10 Home.

D. You can upgrade to the 32-bit version of Windows 10 Professional.

E. You can upgrade to the 64-bit version of Windows 10 Professional.

47. You are the administrator for your company network. You have a Windows 10 computer that acts as an administrative workstation and the Key Management Service (KMS) host. This machine is named Computer1. What should you run from Computer1 if you want to verify the activation status on a computer named Computer2?

A. You should run `Get-RDLicenseConfiguration computer2`.

B. You should run `ospp.vbs /tokact:computer2`.

C. You should run `slmgr.vbs computer2 /dlv`.

D. You should run `winrs.exe -r:computer2 netdom.exe`.

48. You are the administrator for your company network. You have a 64-bit version of Windows 10 Professional installed on a new computer. You obtain a new driver for this machine. This driver is not digitally signed. What should you do first if you want to test the installation of the driver?

A. Run `dism.exe` and specify the `/add-driver` and `/force-unsigned` parameters.

B. Configure the Driver Installation settings from Computer Configuration in Group Policy.

C. Configure the Driver Installation settings from User Configuration in Group Policy.

D. Restart the computer by using the Advanced Boot Menu.

49. You are the administrator for your company network. You have a user on your network using a Windows 10 computer. This user reports that Cortana displays news topics that the user doesn't want to see. How do you stop the news topics from displaying on this user's computer?

A. You should modify the Location settings.

B. You should modify the News app settings.

    C. You should modify the Notebook.

    D. You should modify Reminders.

50. You are the administrator for your company network. You are discussing some of the features of Windows 10. One of the features is the ability to project a Windows 10 laptop or mobile device to a projector or television. What is the name of this feature?

    A. Mirrorcast

    B. Miracast

    C. Projectme

    D. ScreenProjector

51. You are the administrator for your company network. You are having a discussion with a user regarding a feature that Microsoft brought back with Windows 10. What is the name of this feature that was on Windows 7 and brought back with Windows 10?

    A. Device Guard

    B. Microsoft Passport

    C. Start Menu

    D. Windows Hello

52. You are the administrator for your company network. You and a colleague are discussing Microsoft's Mobility Center and which versions of Windows 10 it's available on. On which versions of Windows 10 is the Mobility Center available? (Choose all that apply.)

    A. Windows 10 Enterprise.

    B. Windows 10 Home.

    C. Windows 10 Professional.

    D. The Mobility Center is no longer available with Windows 10.

53. You are the administrator for your company network. You are planning on installing Windows 10 on a computer that has a 1 GHz CPU, 2 GB RAM, and an 18 GB hard drive. Which version of Windows 10 can you install?

    A. You can install the 32-bit version of Windows 10 Enterprise.

    B. You can install the 64-bit version of Windows 10 Enterprise.

    C. You can install the 64-bit version of Windows 10 Home.

    D. You can install the 64-bit version of Windows 10 Professional.

54. You are the administrator for your company network. You have a Windows 10 laptop that is currently running a 64-bit application. The application fails to launch and generates an error message. The message indicates that the application is not supported on the current version of Windows. What should you do if you need to ensure that the application can run successfully?

    A. Use the Application Compatibility Manager (ACM) to create an inventory package.

    B. Use the Compatibility Administrator tool to create a fix.

    C. Use the Standard User Analyzer (SUA) to run the application.

    D. Use the Windows Imaging and Configuration Designer (Windows ICD) to create a package that includes the application.

55. You are the administrator for your company network. You and a colleague are discussing upgrade and installation options. If you have a machine that is currently running Windows 2000, what must you do?

   A. You must perform a clean installation.

   B. You must perform an upgrade.

   C. You cannot perform either an upgrade or a clean installation.

   D. You would need to perform a clean installation and then perform an upgrade.

56. You are the administrator for your company network. You and a colleague are discussing the three phases of performing a clean install of Windows 10. What are the three phases? (Choose three.)

   A. Collecting Information

   B. Gathering Hardware

   C. Installing Windows

   D. Setting Up Windows

57. You are the administrator for your company network. You have just installed Windows 10, and you'd like to review the error log that was created during the installation process. What is the name of this log file, and where is it stored?

   A. C:\Windows\setupact.log

   B. C:\Windows\setuperr.log

   C. C:\Windows\error.log

   D. C:\Windows\setuperror.log

58. You are the administrator for your company network. You and a colleague are discussing the different ways in which Microsoft allows an administrator to perform automated deployment of Windows 10. Which are ways in which an administrator can automate the deployment of Windows 10? (Choose all that apply.)

   A. Microsoft Deployment Toolkit (MDT)

   B. Windows Automated Installation Kit (AIK)

   C. Windows Deployment Services (WDS)

   D. System Preparation Tool (Sysprep)

   E. Device Manager

59. You are the administrator for your company network. You have a system that is configured to dual boot. Each operating system is installed on separate partitions. What command should you run if you want to specify the amount of time used before the system will boot into the default operating system?

   A. You should run bcdedit /default.

   B. You should run bcdedit /displayorder.

   C. You should run bcdedit /timeout.

   D. You should run bcdedit /timeset.

60. You are the administrator for your company network. You are planning on creating an answer file. What should you name the answer file that will work with unattended installations?

    A. `autounattend.txt`

    B. `autounattend.xls`

    C. `autounattend.xml`

    D. `autounattend.docx`

61. You are the administrator for your company network. You are planning on using Windows Deployment Services (WDS) to install a Windows operating system without using an installation disk. What is the first step that you need to take when preparing the WDS server?

    A. Configure and start WDS.

    B. Configure the WDS server to respond to client computers.

    C. Install WDS.

    D. Make sure that the server meets the requirements of running WDS.

62. You are the administrator for your company network. You are planning on performing an unattended installation for a large number of computers. What are some of the advantages of using an unattended installation? (Choose all that apply.)

    A. Can be configured to provide automated responses.

    B. Can be expanded to include installation instructions.

    C. Can be used to install clean copies or upgrade existing operating systems.

    D. Saves time and money.

    E. The physical media must be distributed to all of the computers.

63. You are the administrator for your company network. You are planning on using Windows Deployment Services (WDS) to install a Windows operating system without using an installation disk. There are some requirements for using WDS. One of the requirements states that at least one of the partitions must be formatted as what type of file system?

    A. FAT

    B. FAT32

    C. NTFS

    D. ReFS

64. You are the administrator for your company network. You are using `sysprep.exe` to prepare a system for imaging. What Sysprep option should you use if you want to restart the computer?

    A. `/generalize`

    B. `/reboot`

    C. `/restart`

    D. `/start`

65. You are the administrator for your company network. You are planning on using the Sysprep utility to create images. Where can you find the `sysprep.exe` file?

   A. `C:\Windows\Setup\Sysprep`

   B. `C:\Windows\Boot\Sysprep`

   C. `C:\Windows\System\Sysprep`

   D. `C:\Windows\System32\Sysprep`

66. You are the administrator for your company network. You are planning on using Windows Deployment Services (WDS). What is one component that you must pay attention to when using WDS?

   A. The boot firmware

   B. The Preboot Execution Environment (PXE) network devices

   C. The creation of the image using the `imgcrt.exe` tool

   D. The type of data storage used on the computer

67. You are the administrator for your company network. You are using the Deployment Image Servicing and Management (DISM) tool to manipulate an image. What DISM option should you use if you want to display information about images?

   A. `/Apply-Image`

   B. `/Capture-Image`

   C. `/Get-ImageInfo`

   D. `/List-Image`

68. You are the administrator for your company network. You are planning on using Sysprep to set up images. You remember that the Windows activation clock starts to decrease as soon as Windows starts for the first time. However, you have the ability to restart the clock. How many times are you allowed to restart the activation clock using Sysprep?

   A. One

   B. Two

   C. Three

   D. Four

69. You are the administrator for your company network. You and a colleague are discussing the default Windows 10 desktop. When a user logs onto the computer for the first time, what are some of the items that are included on the desktop? (Choose all that apply.)

   A. Control Panel

   B. Icons

   C. Recycle Bin

   D. Start Menu

   E. Tiles

   F. Wallpaper

70. You are the administrator for your company network. You have a new hire coming into the company who has a sight impairment. This new employee can see but needs to be able to magnify the screen when needed. What Windows 10 accessory can this new employee use?

A. Ease of Access tools

B. Personalization

C. Snipping Tool

D. Time and Language

71. You are the administrator for your company network. Some employees want to change the wallpaper picture on their computers. What setting should you direct them to?

A. Background

B. Colors

C. Theme

D. Wallpaper

72. You are the administrator for your company network. Some employees want to change the screensaver on their computer. What setting should you direct them to?

A. Background

B. Lock Screen

C. Screensaver

D. Theme

73. You are the administrator for your company network. You want to use Windows Power-Shell to create a service. What is the cmdlet that you will run?

A. `Get-Service`

B. `New-Service`

C. `Restart-Service`

D. `Start-Service`

74. You are the administrator for your company network. You support several Windows 10 Enterprise laptops. You have been tasked to configure these laptops to support offline file access. What is the first step needed to configure the laptops to meet your needs?

A. Select Enable Offline Files.

B. Select Manage Offline Files.

C. Select Offline Files and then select Set Up.

D. Select Set Up New Sync Partnerships.

75. You are the administrator for your company network. You and a colleague are discussing the differences between the various Internet browsers that are available for Windows 10. One of the browsers available provides users with a new way to find pages and read and write on the web; plus, they can get assistance from Cortana when needed. What is the name of the Internet browser that you are discussing?

   A. Chrome

   B. Edge

   C. Firefox

   D. Internet Explorer

76. You are the administrator for your company network. A user has reached out to you and informed you that they'd like to use their favorite photo as a password. Where do you set this up on the user's computer?

   A. Windows Hello

   B. Password

   C. Sign-in Options

   D. Your Info

77. You are the administrator for your company network. You are planning on deploying a new Windows 10 Enterprise image to a large number of client computers that are all similarly configured. You are planning on using the Windows SIM tool to create an answer file that will be used to automate the installation. You want each computer to contain two partitions: one for the system partition and one as a data partition. What component of the answer file do you need to modify to support this configuration?

   A. auditSystem

   B. oobeSystem

   C. specialize

   D. Windows PE

78. You are the administrator for your company network. You have an employee who has just transferred from France. Even though the employee speaks perfect English, they have asked if you can configure their work computer to be in French. Where do you go to configure this request?

   A. Accounts

   B. Personalization

   C. System

   D. Time & Language

79. You are the administrator for your company network. You are planning on using the `wdsutil` command-line utility to configure your Windows Deployment Services (WDS) server. What switch would you use if you wanted to initialize the configuration of the WDS?

   A. You should use `/copy-image`.

   B. You should use `/enable`.

C. You should use `/initialize-server`.

D. You should use `/modify-server`.

80. You are the administrator for your company network. You are trying to decide whether you'd like to use Windows Deployment Services (WDS) as a method of installing Windows 10. Which of the following options is *not* an advantage to using a WDS automated installation?

A. It can deploy multiple images for mixed environments.

B. It can create reference images using the Image Capture Wizard.

C. It can standardize the installations throughout a group or organization.

D. The physical media needs to be distributed to all computers that will be installed.

81. You are the administrator for your company network. You have just completed the installation of the operating system on a new Windows 10 machine. Once the installation is complete, what is the next step needed to ensure that the new machine is ready to use?

A. You will want to check Microsoft's website for all updates and patches.

B. You will want to configure the `sethc.exe` file.

C. You will want to install Microsoft 365.

D. You will want to set the computer to dual boot.

82. You are the administrator for your company network. You and a colleague are discussing how to configure Windows Update. Where would you need to go to configure Windows Update?

A. You will go to Personalization to make changes.

B. You will go to Restore Hidden Updates to make changes.

C. You will go to Settings to make changes.

D. You will go to View Update History to make changes.

83. You are the administrator for your company network. You have a division within your company that requires that the same software be installed from scratch each week on their training computers. You decide to utilize the tool called Image Capture Wizard to deploy the disk images. Which Windows 10 utility can you use along with Image Capture Wizard to create these images for the training computers?

A. Answer Manager

B. Setup Manager

C. System Preparation Tool (Sysprep)

D. User Account Control (UAC)

84. You are the administrator for your company network. You have recently heard that some of the Microsoft operating systems within the organization may have a loophole that may allow an attacker to gain access onto the network. What type of updates do you need to install to help resolve this issue?

A. You should install critical updates.

B. You should install definition updates.

C.   You should install security updates.

D.   You should install software updates.

85.   You are the administrator for your company network. You need to deploy Windows 10 to multiple computers. You are planning on automating the installation so that there will be no required user interaction during the installation process. Which of the following should you use?

A.   You should use the Image Capture Wizard.

B.   You should use the System Preparation Tool (Sysprep).

C.   You should use the `wdsutil` command-line utility.

D.   You should use Windows System Image Manager (SIM).

86.   You are the administrator for your company network. You are planning on updating all your Windows 10 machines with all of the current updates that are available for Windows 10. What type of update will you be installing to get everything updated in one installation versus installing each patch individually?

A.   You will be installing definition updates.

B.   You will be installing security updates.

C.   You will be installing a service pack.

D.   You will be installing software updates.

87.   You are the administrator for your company network. You have recently installed Windows 10 on a new computer, and you want to check to see whether there are any updates available. What is one way that you can perform this task?

A.   Click the Check For Updates button.

B.   Click the Does My Computer Need To Be Updated button.

C.   Click the Restore Hidden Updates button.

D.   Click the View Update History button.

88.   You are the administrator for your company network. You have a Windows To Go workspace on a USB memory drive. You are attempting to start a computer using the drive, and you receive an error message that states, "Your PC/Device needs to be repaired. The application or operating system couldn't be loaded because a required file is missing or contains errors." What should you do to repair the Windows To Go workspace?

A.   On the USB memory drive, reapply the Windows To Go image.

B.   Restart the computer using a recovery disk and then perform a system restore.

C.   Restart the computer and then select the Last Known Good Configuration.

D.   Restart the computer in safe mode and then perform a system restore.

89. You are the administrator for your company network. You and a colleague are discussing how Microsoft processes updates and when they are released to the public for download. Updates are normally released on a particular day of the week. What is the nickname of this day of the week when updates are released?

A. Maintenance Mondays

B. Patch Tuesdays

C. Update Wednesdays

D. Fixed Fridays

90. You are the administrator for your company network. You have asked a junior administrator to perform some tasks on a user's computer that will modify some Registry settings. However, you do not want this junior administrator to open the Registry directly. What utility should this junior administrator use to perform the tasks?

A. Control Panel

B. Microsoft Management Console (MMC)

C. Sync Center

D. Windows to Go

91. You are the administrator for your company network. You are upgrading a computer to Windows 10 and fear that there may have been some issues with the installation. You plan to check the log files that were created during the installation. What files should you review if you want to see what actions were taken and whether there were any errors? (Choose all that apply.)

A. You should check `installerr.log`.

B. You should check `setupact.log`.

C. You should check `setuperr.log`.

D. You should check `wininstall.log`.

92. You are the administrator for your company network. You plan on upgrading a computer to Windows 10, 32-bit. You need to determine whether you have enough RAM on the machine. What is minimum requirement for memory for the 32-bit version of Windows?

A. 128 MB

B. 256 MB

C. 512 MB

D. 1,024 MB

93. You are the administrator for your company network. You and a colleague are discussing a tool that shows which computers and components have been verified to work with Windows 10. What is the name of this tool that an administrator can use to see whether certain devices will work with Windows 10?

A. Windows Compatible Products List

B. Microsoft Compatibility List

C. Windows 10 Help and Support

D. Windows 10 Hardware Tool

94. You are the administrator for your company network. You currently have a computer that is still running Windows XP Professional. You plan to install Windows 10. Which of the following installation options should you choose?

A. You must perform a clean installation to Windows 10.

B. You must perform a promotion to Windows 10.

C. You must perform a renovation to Windows 10.

D. You must perform an upgrade to Windows 10.

95. You are the administrator for your company network. You and a colleague are discussing the clean installation process. If you are performing a clean installation of Windows 10 to the same partition as an existing Windows installation, the contents of the original Windows directory will be placed in which directory?

A. The C:\Windows directory

B. The C:\Windows.old directory

C. The C:\Windows\old directory

D. The C:\WindowsOS directory

Chapter

2

Manage Devices and Data

THE MD-100 EXAM TOPICS COVERED IN THIS CHAPTER INCLUDE:

✓ **Domain 2: Manage Devices and Data 10**

- 2.1: Manage local users, local groups, and devices
    - Manage devices in directories
    - Manage local groups
    - Manage local users
- 2.2: Configure data access and protection
    - Configure NTFS permissions
    - Configure shared permissions
- 2.3: Configure devices by using local policies
    - Configure local registry
    - Implement local policy
    - Troubleshoot group policies on devices
- 2.4: Manage Windows Security
    - Configure User Account Control (UAC)
    - Configure Microsoft Defender Firewall
    - Implement encryption

1. You are the administrator for your company network. A department within the organization has a new custom application. For the application to run properly, you need to make some changes to the computer policy. You make changes through a Local Group Policy setting; however, you suspect that the policy is not being applied properly because of a conflict with another Local Group Policy setting. What utility should you run to see a list of how the group policies are being applied to the computer and the user?

    A. gpaudit

    B. gpinfo

    C. gporesult

    D. gpresult

2. You are the administrator for your company network. You need to track the usage of a Windows 10 computer. You plan to record user logon and logoff events. What auditing policy should you enable?

    A. You should enable Audit Account Logon Events.

    B. You should enable Audit Account Management.

    C. You should enable Audit Process Tracking.

    D. You should enable Audit System Events.

3. You are the administrator for your company network. You have a user who needs to perform some administrative tasks. You want to require that this user enter an administrator password to perform these tasks. What type of account should you create for this user?

    A. You should create an Administrator user account.

    B. You should create an Authenticated user account.

    C. You should create a Power user account.

    D. You should create a Standard user account.

4. You are the administrator for your company network. You have several Windows 10 computers that are part of a workgroup and have BitLocker Drive Encryption (BitLocker) enabled. You add these computers to the Microsoft Azure Active Directory (Azure AD). What should you do first if you need to make sure you can recover the BitLocker recovery key for the computers from Azure AD?

    A. You should add a BitLocker key protector.

    B. You should disable BitLocker.

    C. You should disable the TMP chip.

    D. You should suspend BitLocker.

5. You are the administrator for your company network. You have a Windows 10 computer that has a network folder that resides on an NTFS partition. Both NTFS permissions and share permissions have been applied. Which statement best describes how NTFS permissions and share permissions work together when applied to the same folder?

    A. NTFS permissions will always take priority over the share permissions.

    B. Share permissions will always take priority over the NTFS permissions.

C. The system will look at the combined share permissions and the combined NTFS permissions. Whichever set is least restrictive will be applied.

D. The system will look at the combined share permissions and the combined NTFS permissions. Whichever set is most restrictive will be applied.

6. You are the administrator for your company network. You have a Windows 10 computer. You need to configure User Account Control (UAC) to prompt you for your credentials. Which setting should you modify so that you will be prompted for your credentials?

A. You should modify the Administrators Properties in Local Users And Groups.

B. You should modify the Security Options in Local Group Policy Editor.

C. You should modify the User Account Control Settings in Control Panel.

D. You should modify the User Rights Assignment in Local Group Policy Editor.

7. You are the administrator for your company network. What port should you open on your firewall if you want to use Device Health Attestation on your network or in the cloud?

A. You should open port 25.

B. You should open port 110.

C. You should open port 443.

D. You should open port 995.

8. You are the administrator for your company network. You have a Windows 10 computer named Computer1 that has a service named App1, which is configured to log on as an account named Service1. You find out that a user has used the Service1 account to sign into the computer and delete some files. You need to ensure that the account that is used by App1 cannot be used by a user to sign into the computer. Using the principle of least privilege, what should you do?

A. On Computer1, configure App1 to sign in as a Local System account and then select the Allow Service To Interact With Desktop checkbox. Then, you should delete the Service1 account.

B. On Computer1, assign the Service1 account the Deny Log On Locally user right.

C. On Computer1, assign the Service1 account the Deny Log On As A Service user right.

D. On Computer1, configure App1 to sign in as a Guest account and then select the Allow Service To Interact With Desktop checkbox. Then, you should delete the Service1 account.

9. You are the administrator for your company network. You want to create a new local user account on Windows 10 by using Windows PowerShell. Which command do you use?

A. Use Add-LocalUser.

B. Use Add-WindowsUser.

C. Use New-LocalUser.

D. Use New-WindowsUser.

10. You are the administrator for your company network. Your network has an Active Directory domain that contains hundreds of Windows 10 computers. You find out that every day when users are on their Lock screen, they will see a different background image. They also see tips on using different features of Windows 10. What Group Policy setting should you change to disable the daily background image and tips from appearing on all of the Windows 10 computers?

   A. You should select Do Not Suggest Third-Party Content in Windows Spotlight.

   B. You should turn off all Windows Spotlight features.

   C. You should turn off Windows Spotlight in Settings.

   D. You should turn off the Windows Welcome Experience.

11. You are the administrator for your company network. You have a Windows 10 computer, and you'd like to prevent standard users from changing the wireless network settings on this machine. What should you use that will allow the administrator to modify the wireless settings while the standard user cannot?

   A. Use the Control Panel to go to Network And Internet Settings, then go to the Network And Sharing Center, and then click View Network Connections.

   B. Use the Local Group Policy Editor (gpedit.msc).

   C. Use the System Configuration Utility (msconfig.exe).

   D. Use the Windows Configuration Designer.

12. You are the administrator for your company network. You want to view and control all of the hardware that is attached to a computer. What tool should you use to see this?

   A. File Explorer

   B. Device Manager

   C. Disk Management

   D. Task Manager

13. You are the administrator for your company network. You have a Windows 10 computer that you are looking to expand the disk space on. You are thinking of using spanned volumes. Which statements are true regarding spanned volumes? (Choose all that apply.)

   A. They can contain space from 2 to 24 physical drives.

   B. They can contain space from 2 to 32 physical drives.

   C. They can be formatted as FAT32 or NTFS partitions.

   D. They can be formatted only as NTFS partitions.

14. You are the administrator for your company network. You have a new computer that has been installed with the 64-bit version of Windows 10 Professional. You have a new driver for a device on this computer; however, the driver is not digitally signed. What should you do first if you want to test the installation of the driver on the computer?

   A. Configure the Driver Installation settings from Computer Configuration in Group Policy.

   B. Configure the Driver Installation settings from User Configuration in Group Policy.

C. Restart the computer by using the advanced startup options.

D. Run `dism.exe` and specify the `/add-driver` and `/force-unsigned` parameters.

15. You are the administrator for your company network. You have a Windows 10 computer that contains a folder named `MyFolder`. Which action(s) should you take to log any users who take ownership of the files within the folder? (Choose all that apply.)

A. Configure the Audit File System setting from a Group Policy object (GPO).

B. Configure the Audit Sensitive Privilege Use setting from a Group Policy object (GPO).

C. Install the Remote Server Administration Tools (RSAT).

D. On `MyFolder`, modify the Advanced Security Settings.

E. On `MyFolder`, modify the folder attributes.

16. You are the administrator for your company network. You have recently hired an assistant, and you want them to perform some administrative duties. You'd like this new admin assistant to be able to restore files on Windows 10 computers, but you don't want to allow them to perform backups. What should you assign to the new admin assistant?

A. Add the admin assistant to the Administrators group.

B. Add the admin assistant to the Backup Operators group.

C. Grant the admin assistant the Read right to the root of each volume to be backed up.

D. Grant the admin assistant the user right Restore Files And Directories.

17. You are the administrator for your company network. You are worried that your network's security may have been compromised. You want to set up a policy that will not allow hackers to be able to continuously attempt user logons using different passwords. What Local Security Policy should you set to accomplish this goal?

A. You should configure an Account Lockout Policy.

B. You should configure an Audit Policy.

C. You should set a Password Policy.

D. You should set Security Options.

18. You are the administrator for your company network. You have a Windows 10 computer that needs to have security so that if the drive is stolen, the data will be prevented from being accessed. What should you to do prevent the data from being accessed from a stolen hard drive?

A. Set the BitLocker Drive Encryption using the Device Manager icon in Control Panel.

B. Set the BitLocker Drive Encryption using the Hardware icon in Control Panel.

C. Set the BitLocker Drive Encryption using a Local Group Policy.

D. Set the BitLocker Drive Encryption using the System icon in Control Panel.

19. You are the administrator for your company network. You have a computer that is configured to dual boot with 64-bit Windows 10 Enterprise installed on the local disk and 64-bit Windows 10 Professional installed in a VHDX file named `Disk1.vhdx`. You start the computer in Windows 10 Enterprise. What utility should you use if you want to install an unsigned driver to Windows 10 Professional when the computer starts in Windows 10 Professional?

A. `Add-Windows Image`

B. `bcdboot.exe`

C. `bootcfg.exe`

D. `bcdedit.exe`

20. You are the administrator for your company network. Management has tasked you to create and implement a new security policy. You have configured password policies so that the employees must change their passwords every 30 days. You want to prevent them from reusing passwords that they have recently used. Which password policy should you implement?

A. You should implement Enforce Password History.

B. You should implement Passwords Must Be Advanced.

C. You should implement Passwords Must Be Unique.

D. You should implement Passwords Must Meet Complexity Requirements.

21. You are the administrator for your company network. You and a colleague are discussing rules that use IPsec to secure traffic while it crosses the network. These rules can be used to specify the connections between two computers that must be authenticated or encrypted. What is the name for the rules being discussed?

A. Connection security rules

B. DHCP rules

C. Firewall rules

D. TCP rules

22. You are the administrator for your company network. You have several Windows 10 computers that are part of a workgroup. You want to prevent the employees from using Microsoft Store apps on their computers. How should you achieve this task?

A. Configure the Security Options from Security Settings in the Local Group Policy.

B. Configure the Software Restriction Policies from Security Settings in the Local Group Policy.

C. Configure the Store settings from Administrative Templates in the Local Group Policy.

D. Configure the Store Restriction Policies from Security Settings in the Local Group Policy.

23. You are the administrator for your company network. You have been tasked to implement a form of two-factor authentication. What should you implement to meet this request?

A. Implement and install fingerprint scanners.

B. Implement and install retina scanners.

C. Implement passwords and usernames.

D. Implement smart cards.

24. You are the administrator for your company network. You have about 25 Windows 10 computers. You have configured the computers to forward all events to a computer named Computer1. When you log into Computer1, you do not see any of the security events from the other computers. What should you do to ensure that the security events are forwarded to Computer1?

A. Add the account of Computer1 to the Event Log Readers group on Computer1.

B. Add the Network Service account to the Event Log Readers group on each computer.

C. Run `wecutil ac /q` on each computer.

D. Run `winrm qc -q` on each computer.

25. You are the administrator for your company network. You have several Windows 10 Enterprise desktop computers that are members of an Active Directory domain. The standard domain user accounts are configured with mandatory user profiles. What should you do if you have several users who have been transferred into a different department and you need to modify their profiles?

A. Change the extension of the `NTuser.man` file in the user profile directory to `NTuser.dat`.

B. Configure the user's document library to include folders from network shares.

C. Remove the `.man` extension from the user profile name.

D. Use Group Policy to configure Folder Redirection.

26. You are the administrator for your company network. You have an Active Directory Domain Services (AD DS) domain with Windows 10 Enterprise client computers. You have several laptop computers that you want to configure so that after 20 minutes of running on battery power, they will go to sleep. What actions should you perform to complete this task? (Choose two.)

A. Configure the Power Management settings by creating a Group Policy object (GPO).

B. Configure the Sleep Management settings by creating a Group Policy object (GPO).

C. Configure the Power Management settings by editing the local Group Policy.

D. Configure the Shut Down options by editing the local Group Policy.

E. Link the Group Policy object (GPO) to the organizational unit (OU) that contains the laptop computers.

27. You are the administrator for your company network. You have an Active Directory domain that contains Windows 10 Enterprise client computers. Employees sometimes will use USB drives to store sensitive files that are stored on several computers. However, the corporate security policy states that all removable storage drives must be encrypted, and this includes the USB drives. What should you do if you need to ensure that if an employee forgets their passwords for their encrypted BitLocker to Go USB device, that the employee can resolve the situation themselves?

A. Create a USB startup key for each computer.

B. Implement the BitLocker Network Unlock feature.

    C.   Instruct the user to open BitLocker Drive Encryption, select Back Up Recovery Key, and then select Save To A File.

    D.   Instruct the user to run `manage-bde -forcerecovery` from an elevated command prompt.

28. You are the administrator for your company network. The network consists of an Active Directory domain that has a Windows 10 computer named Computer1. What command should you run if you want to view the settings of the Group Policy objects (GPOs) in the domain and the local Group Policies that are applied to Computer1?

    A.   You should run the `gpfixup` command.

    B.   You should run the `gpresult` command.

    C.   You should run the `gpupdate` command.

    D.   You should run the `secedit` command.

29. You are the administrator for your company network. Your network contains an Active Directory domain and Windows 10 computers. To which group would you add a user if you wanted them to be able to create and modify the shares remotely on the computers?

    A.   You would add the user to the Administrators group.

    B.   You would add the user to the Network Configuration Operators group.

    C.   You would add the user to the Power Users group.

    D.   You would add the user to the Remote Management Users group.

30. You are the administrator for your company network. The company uses an application that confirms a network connection to a server by sending a ping request to the IPv6 address of the server. If the server replies, then the application loads. An employee contacts you that they cannot open the application. You go to the user's computer and send a ping request to the server. The request fails. You go back to your computer and send a ping request, and the server replies. You need to make sure that the ping request from the user's computer works when contacting the server. What Microsoft Defender Firewall rule could be the possible cause of the problem?

    A.   File and Printer Sharing (Echo Request ICMPv6-In)

    B.   File and Printer Sharing (Echo request ICMPv6-Out)

    C.   File and Printer Sharing (NB-Datagram-In)

    D.   File and Printer Sharing (NB-Datagram-Out)

31. You are the administrator for your company network. You have a Windows 10 computer that is part of a workgroup. You run the following commands on the computer:

```
New-LocalUser -Name NewUser -NoPassword
Add-LocalGroupMember User -Member NewUser
```

What does this do to the computer configuration?

    A.   NewUser appears on the sign-in screen and can log in without a password.

    B.   NewUser appears on the sign-in screen but must set a new password on the first login attempt.

C. NewUser is prevented from logging in until an administrator manually sets a password for the user.

D. NewUser is prevented from logging in until the user is assigned additional user rights.

32. You are the administrator for your company network. You have a Windows 10 computer that is joined to Azure Active Directory (Azure AD). When you try to open the Control Panel, you receive an error message that states, "This operation has been cancelled due to restrictions in effect on this computer. Please contact your system administrator." What should you do if you need to be able to access the Control Panel from this computer?

A. Check the Group policy preferences.

B. Check the Local Group Policy.

C. Check the PowerShell execution policy.

D. Check the Settings app.

33. You are the administrator for your company network. You have a Windows 10 computer that contains a folder named Folder1. You need to provide a user with the ability to modify the permissions on the folder. Keeping in mind the principle of least privilege, what NTFS permissions should you assign the user?

A. Assign the Full Control permission.

B. Assign the Modify permission.

C. Assign the Read & Execute permission.

D. Assign the Write permission.

34. You are the administrator for your company network. You have an Azure Active Directory (Azure AD) tenant that contains a user named user1@mysite.com. You have a Windows 10 computer named Computer1. You join this computer to the Azure AD and enable Remote Desktop. By using Remote Desktop, user1@mysite.com tries to connect to Computer1 and receives an error message that says, "The logon attempt failed." What should you do first to ensure that the user can connect to Computer1?

A. Assign user1@mysite.com the Cloud device administrator role in Azure AD.

B. Assign user1@mysite.com the Security administrator role in Azure AD.

C. Create a local user and add the new user to the Remote Desktop Users group on Computer1.

D. Modify the Allow Log On Through Remote Desktop Services user right from the local Group Policy.

35. You are the administrator for your company network. You have several Windows 10 computers that have BitLocker Drive Encryption (BitLocker) enabled. You need to update the firmware on the computers. What cmdlet should you run if you want to make sure that you are not prompted for the BitLocker recovery key when you restart the computers but you want the drives to be protected by BitLocker upon subsequent restarts?

A. You should run Add-BitLockerKeyProtector.

B. You should run Disable-BitLocker.

C. You should run Unlock-BitLocker.

D. You should run Suspend-BitLocker.

36. You are the administrator for your company network. You network contains several Windows 10 machines on which you are planning to configure some Local Group Policy objects (LGPOs). Which of the following can you *not* configure using LGPOs?

A. You cannot configure administrative templates.

B. You cannot configure Folder Redirection.

C. You cannot configure Internet Explorer settings.

D. You cannot configure Windows Update settings.

37. You are the administrator for your company network. You have a file that was created on a Windows 10 computer. The file is called `mytext.txt`. You need to change the file extension from `.txt` to `.vbx`. When you go to change the extension, you do not see the extension types. What should you do to see the extension types?

A. Check Show Extensions For Files.

B. Check Unhide Extensions For Files.

C. Uncheck Hide All File Types.

D. Uncheck Hide Extensions For Known File Types.

38. You are the administrator for your company network. Your network is made up of several Windows 10 client machines. What should you implement if you are looking to implement another form of security on these machines to prevent unauthorized users from accessing them?

A. You should implement Windows Data Protection.

B. You should implement Microsoft Defender Firewall.

C. You should implement Windows Encryption Protection.

D. You should implement Windows Secure Data Protocol.

39. You are the administrator for your company network. A new corporate security policy was issued, and you must configure the Password Must Meet Complexity Requirements policy. Since you made the change, a few users are indicating that they are having issues when changing their passwords. Given the following password options, which passwords meet the Password Must Meet Complexity Requirements policy? (Choose all that apply.)

A. `!@#$%^&*(-[]+`

B. `1587365Ab`

C. `aBC-1`

D. `ABCde!`

40. You are the administrator for your company network. You recently had an employee resign, and another user has been hired to take over their position. This new user has been assigned the old user's laptop. You want the new user to have access to all of the same resources as the old employee. What is the easiest way to handle the new employee's transition into the position?

A. Copy the old employee's account and name the new copied account with the name of the new hire.

B. Do a search in the Registry and replace all of the old employee's entries with the new hire's name.

C. Rename the old employee's account to the new hire's name.

D. Take ownership of all of the old employee's resources and assign the new hire Full Control to the resources.

41. You are the administrator for your company network. You have a Windows 10 computer that contains a folder with sensitive data. What should you do if you need to log which users read the contents of the folder and which users modify and/or delete files within the folder?

A. From the properties of the folder, configure the Auditing settings, and from the Audit Policy in the local Group Policy, configure Audit Directory Service Access.

B. From the properties of the folder, configure the Auditing settings, and from the Audit Policy in the local Group Policy, configure Audit Logon Events.

C. From the properties of the folder, configure the Auditing settings, and from the Audit Policy in the local Group Policy, configure Audit Object Access.

D. From the properties of the folder, configure the Auditing settings, and from the Audit Policy in the local Group Policy, configure Audit System Events.

42. You are the administrator for your company network. You are planning to enable BitLocker Drive Encryption (BitLocker) on your network. In which version(s) of Windows 10 can BitLocker be enabled? (Choose all that apply.)

A. Windows 10 Basic Edition

B. Windows 10 Education Edition

C. Windows 10 Enterprise Edition

D. Windows 10 Professional Edition

43. You are the administrator for your company network. You are setting up a computer for an employee who works from an office in their home. This user is not familiar with computers. You do not want this user to be made a local administrator, but you do want the user to be given the rights to manually change Windows Updates. What should you do to configure this for the home user?

A. Modify the Local Group Policy object (LGPO) for Windows Update to allow the user to make changes manually.

B. Set Windows Update modifications to Anyone.

C. Tell the home user how to log into the Administrator account.

D. This configuration cannot be done. Only administrators can change Windows Update.

44. You are the administrator for your company network. New company policy states that all hardware on the network must use BitLocker and BitLocker To Go. What utility will help you manage and maintain BitLocker and BitLocker to Go?

A. You should utilize the Microsoft Administration and Access Monitor (MAAM) utility.

B. You should utilize the Microsoft BitLocker Configuration Manager (MBCM) utility.

C. You should utilize the Microsoft BitLocker Administration and Monitoring (MBAM) utility.

D. You should utilize the Microsoft BitLocker Monitoring and Administration (MBMA) utility.

45. You are the administrator for your company network. You have a Windows 10 Enterprise computer that has File History enabled. You create a folder named `C:\Data`. You want to ensure that this new folder is protected by File History. What are two possible methods to achieve the goal? (Choose two.)

    A. Create a new library that contains the new folder using File Explorer.

    B. From the File History Control Panel app, modify the Advanced settings.

    C. Include the new folder in an existing library using File Explorer.

    D. Modify the system attributes of the new folder using File Explorer.

46. You are the administrator for your company network. You are creating a custom console for the Microsoft Management Console (MMC). What will the filename extension be by default?

    A. The custom console will have the `.con` file extension.

    B. The custom console will have the `.mcn` file extension.

    C. The custom console will have the `.mmc` file extension.

    D. The custom console will have the `.msc` file extension.

47. You are the administrator for your company network. You have been tasked with creating groups. Which statements are true with regard to creating groups in Windows 10? (Choose all that apply.)

    A. Group names can contain spaces.

    B. Group names can have up to 64 characters.

    C. Group names can utilize the same name as a username, but they may not be the same name as another group on that computer.

    D. In order to create groups, you must be a member of the Administrators group.

48. You are the administrator for your company network. Your network computers are using Windows 10 Enterprise. What command should you run if you want to run the Print Management tools using the command prompt?

    A. You should run the `printbrm.exe` command.

    B. You should run the `printmgmt.exe` command.

    C. You should run the `printmig.exe` command.

    D. You should run the `prtmgmt.exe` command.

49. You are the administrator for your company network. You have been tasked with creating roaming profiles for users in the Marketing department. You want these profiles to be both mandatory and roaming. On Windows 10 computers, who is able to maintain these mandatory profiles?

    A. The Administrators group can maintain the profiles.

    B. The Power Users group can maintain the profiles.

    C. The Server Operators group can maintain the profiles.

    D. The user who uses the profile can maintain the profile.

50. You are the administrator for your company network. You have a Windows 10 computer that will be used by children who are visiting the office. You want to configure access restriction by using Parental Controls. When configuring Parental Controls, what can be configured? (Choose all that apply.)

A. You can configure when the children can access the computer.

B. You can configure which websites the children can visit.

C. You can configure which programs the children can access.

D. You can configure which other computers on the network the children can access.

51. You are the administrator for your company network. You have an 8 MB file that you have compressed into a 4 MB file on a partition that has an NTFS file system. You now need to copy this file to the partition on another computer that has FAT32. You want to ensure that the file remains compressed. What should you do?

A. Copy the file using the xcopy /comp command.

B. In the folder's properties on the destination computer, ensure you set the option Compress Contents To Save Disk Space.

C. This cannot be done. You cannot preserve disk compression on a non-NTFS partition.

D. Use the Windows Explorer utility to copy the file and specify the option Keep Existing Attributes.

52. You are the administrator for your company network. You have a Windows 10 Enterprise computer named PrntSvr1 that is configured with multiple shared print queues. What should you do if you've been tasked with migrating these queues to a new computer named PrntSvr2?

A. In the Control Panel, use the Migrate Printers utility.

B. In the Print Management tool, use the Export Printers tool.

C. In the Print Management tool, use the Migrate Printers utility.

D. In the Printers & Scanners utility, use the Migrate Printers utility.

53. You are the administrator for your company network. You have three computers that each run different versions of Windows 10. They are as follows:

Name	TPM Version	Operating System
Computer1	None	Windows 10 Enterprise
Computer2	2.0	Windows 10 Professional
Computer3	1.2	Windows 10 Enterprise

All of the computers have both C:\ and D:\ volumes. All of the computers have the Require Additional Authentication At Startup Group Policy settings disabled. You have been tasked to encrypt the C:\ volume on the machines using BitLocker Drive Encryption (BitLocker). On which computers can you encrypt using BitLocker? (Choose all that apply.)

A. Computer1

B. Computer2

C. Computer3

D. None of the computers

54. You are the administrator for your company network. One of your employees reaches out to you and explains that they believe they are having an issue with their network card. What tool can you use to see if there are any issues with this device?

A. You can use Device Configuration.

B. You can use Device Hardware.

C. You can use Device Manager.

D. You can use Manage Hardware.

55. You are the administrator for your company network. New corporate policy states that all installed drivers must be signed. You need to verify that all of the drivers installed on the network Windows 10 computers are signed. What should you do?

A. From the command prompt, run `drivers.exe`.

B. From the command prompt, run `sigverif.exe`.

C. From the command prompt, run `verify.exe`.

D. From Device Manager, run a scan.

56. You are the administrator for your company network. You have a Windows 10 machine that has two NTFS volumes, `C:\` and `D:\`. What should you do if you've been tasked with disabling previous versions from the `D:\` volume?

A. Convert the hard drive that contains the `D:\` volume to Dynamic from the Disk Management snap-in.

B. Modify the Quota settings from the properties of the `D:\` volume.

C. Modify the Sharing settings from the properties of the `D:\` volume.

D. Modify the System Protection settings from System Properties.

57. You are the administrator for your company network. You have a Windows 10 computer named Computer1 that has four folders in separate volumes. The folders are as follows:

- `C:\Folder1`: This folder has the NTFS file system, and BitLocker is disabled.

- `D:\Folder2`: This folder has the NTFS file system, and BitLocker is enabled.

- `E:\Folder3`: This folder has the FAT32 file system, and BitLocker is disabled.

- `F:\Folder4`: This folder has the FAT32 file system, and BitLocker is disabled.

You include all four folders in the Documents library and configure File History to run every 15 minutes. You then turn on File History. Which folders will be protected by File History? (Choose all that apply.)

A. `Folder1`

B. `Folder2`

C. `Folder3`

D. `Folder4`

58. You are the administrator for your company network. You have an Active Directory domain with a Windows 10 computer named Computer1. On this computer, you create an NTFS folder and assign it Full Control to Everyone. You share this folder as Share1 and assign permissions. You assign User1 Full Control, and you assign User2 Change. Given the assigned permissions to the share, what can be performed by User1 and not by User2?

A. User1 can copy a file created by another user to a subfolder.

B. User1 can delete a file created by another user.

C. User1 can rename a file created by another user.

D. User1 can set the permissions for a file and take ownership of files.

59. You are the administrator for your company network. A new corporate policy has been initiated where the company wants to start using virtual smart cards on the Windows 10 Enterprise laptops and tablets. Before you implement any changes, you want to ensure that the systems can support the virtual smart cards. What should you do to verify that the systems can support the virtual smart cards?

A. Ensure that BitLocker Drive Encryption is enabled on a system drive.

B. Ensure that the laptops and tablets are running Windows 10 Enterprise Edition.

C. Ensure that each laptop and tablet can read a physical smart card.

D. Ensure that each laptop and tablet has a Trusted Platform Module (TPM) chip.

60. You are the administrator for your company network. You have several Windows 10 Enterprise computers that are part of an Active Directory domain. Recently, you have configured several users with super-mandatory profiles. One of the users reports that they have lost all of their personal data after the computer restarted. What should you do if you need to configure the user's computer to prevent possible data loss in the future?

A. Add the .dat extension to the user profile name.

B. Configure the user's Documents library to include folders from network shares.

C. Remove the .man extension from the user profile name.

D. Using the domain group policy, configure Folder Redirection.

61. You are the administrator for your company network. You have a Windows 10 Enterprise computer that has a shared folder named C:\Sales on an NTFS volume. The current NTFS and share permissions are as follows:

- Everyone has Read and Execute NTFS permissions and Read Shared folder permissions.

- Sales has Modify NTFS permission and Full Control Shared folder permission.

A user is a member of both the Everyone and Sales groups. This user must be able to access C:\Sales from across the network. What will the effective permissions of this user be to the C:\Sales folder?

A. Full Control

B. Modify

C. Read

D. Read and Execute

62. You are the administrator for your company network. You have been asked to assign the Admin group the rights to Read, Change, and Assign Permissions to documents in the Documents folder. The current permissions on the Documents shared folder are as follows:

Group/User	NTFS Permission	Shared Permission
Sales	Read	Change
Marketing	Modify	Change
R & D	Deny	Full Control
Finance	Read	Read
Admin	Change	Change

What do you need to do to give the Admin group the rights to perform their job? (Choose all that apply.)

A. Assign the Admin group Full Control to Shared permissions.

B. Assign the Sales group Full Control to Shared permissions.

C. Assign the Sales group Full Control to NTFS permissions.

D. Assign the Finance group Modify to NTFS permissions.

E. Assign the Admin group Full Control to NTFS permissions.

63. You are the administrator for your company network. You deploy an application to all of the computers within the domain. What should you do if you need to use Group Policy to restrict certain groups from running the new application?

A. You should configure AppLocker.

B. You should disable BitLocker.

C. You should set up DirectAccess.

D. You should run the User State Management Tool (USMT).

64. You are the administrator for your company network. You have a Windows 10 Enterprise computer that has File History and system protection turned on for the C: drive. You accidentally press Shift+Delete on the keyboard, deleting a folder on the C: drive. What should you do to restore the most recent version of this folder to its original location?

A. Use a manually selected restore point.

B. Use File History.

C. Use the latest restore point.

D. Use the Recycle Bin

65. You are the administrator for your company network. You have a new Windows 10 computer. You download a new driver for a device that is installed on this computer. The driver package is stored in C:\Drivers and includes these files:

- driver.inf
- driver.dll

- `driver.sys`
- `driver.cat`

You are using File Explorer, and you want to install the new driver onto the computer. What file should you use to start the installation process?

A. Select the `driver.cat` file.

B. Select the `driver.dll` file.

C. Select the `driver.inf` file.

D. Select the `driver.sys` file.

66. You are the administrator for your company network. You and a colleague are discussing that when Windows 10 is installed as part of a workgroup environment, Windows 10 will add several built-in accounts. These accounts are created automatically when you install the operating system. One of the following accounts is disabled by default. Which one is it?

A. Administrator

B. DefaultAccount

C. Guest

D. Initial User

67. You are the administrator for your company network. You and a colleague are discussing User Access Control (UAC). You are planning on enabling UAC, but you are not sure which level you should select on the slider. Which level is the default level?

A. Always Notify Me

B. Notify Me Only When Applications Try To Make Changes

C. Notify Me Only When Applications Try To Make Changes (Do Not Dim My Desktop)

D. Never Notify Me

68. You are the administrator for your company network. You and a colleague are discussing the creation of user accounts; more specifically, the item that gets generated automatically whenever a user account is created. What is the item that is being discussed?

A. Access Control

B. Password

C. Security Identifier

D. Username

69. You are the administrator for your company network. You have a Windows 10 Enterprise computer. You add a 1 TB hard drive and create a new volume that you've assigned as the D: drive letter. You format this new drive with NTFS. What should you do if you want to limit the amount of space that each user can use on this new drive? (Choose all that apply.)

A. Select the default quota limit for new users on this volume by setting the Limit Disk Space To option.

B. Run `convert d: /fs:ntfsNTFS`.

C. Select the checkbox Enable Quota Management.

D. Select the checkbox Deny Disk Space To Users Exceeding Quota Limit.

70. You are the administrator for your company network. You and a colleague are discussing a Windows 10 feature that, when configured, will lock down a device so that it can only run trusted applications that are defined in your code integrity policies. What is this feature called?

A. Credential Guard

B. Device Guard

C. Local Security Authority (LSA)

D. Virtualization-Based Security (VBS)

71. You are the administrator for your company network. You are planning on using Device Guard. You'd like to use Windows PowerShell to set it up. Which PowerShell command should you use if you'd like to allow an administrator to create a Code Integrity policy as an XML file?

A. `Get-GIPolicy`

B. `Merge-CIPolicy`

C. `New-CIPolicy`

D. `Set-GIPolicy`

72. You are the administrator for your company network. You want to protect your systems from common malware hacks that use executable files and scripts that attack applications such as Microsoft 365. Which Microsoft tool should you use to accomplish this goal?

A. You should use Microsoft Defender Application Control.

B. You should use Microsoft Defender Credential Guard.

C. You should use Microsoft Defender Exploit Guard.

D. You should use Microsoft Defender Firewall with Advanced Security.

73. You are the administrator for your company network. You are attempting to set up Microsoft Defender Firewall to allow FTP traffic. What two port numbers should you set up?

A. You should set up ports 20 and 21.

B. You should set up ports 25 and 53.

C. You should set up ports 53 and 80.

D. You should set up ports 80 and 443.

74. You are the administrator for your company network. You are considering upgrading a basic disk to a dynamic disk on a Windows 10 computer. A colleague has asked you to describe the function of a dynamic disk. Which statement best describes this?

A. Dynamic disks are the only hard drive configuration used by Windows 10.

B. Dynamic disks support features such as simple partitions, extended partitions, spanned partitions, and striped partitions.

C. Dynamic disks can be recognized by older, legacy operating systems such as Windows NT 4.

D. Dynamic disks support features such as simple volumes, extended volumes, spanned volumes, mirrored volumes, and striped volumes.

75. You are the administrator for your company network. An employee with a Windows 10 computer informs you that they have been noticing that the larger a file gets, the longer it takes to access it. They have been having issues with a lot of their larger files. You suspect that the problem is possibly related to the files being spread across the disk. What utility can you use to store the file sequentially across the disk?

   A. You should utilize Disk Administrator.

   B. You should utilize Disk Cleanup.

   C. You should utilize Disk Defragmenter.

   D. You should utilize Disk Manager.

76. You are the administrator for your company network. You are attempting to set up Microsoft Defender Firewall to allow SMTP inbound and outbound rules. What port number should you set up?

   A. You should set up port 20.

   B. You should set up port 25.

   C. You should set up port 53.

   D. You should set up port 80.

77. You are the administrator for your company network. All of your system computers are running Windows 10. You want to make sure that all of the applications that are installed on the computers have been company approved. What should you use to ensure this?

   A. You should use Microsoft Defender Antivirus.

   B. You should use Microsoft Defender Application Control.

   C. You should use Microsoft Defender Credential Guard.

   D. You should use Microsoft Defender Exploit Guard.

78. You are the administrator for your company network. You are planning on setting up inbound and outbound rules on your Windows 10 machines. What should you use to accomplish this?

   A. You should implement Microsoft Defender Application Control.

   B. You should implement Microsoft Defender Credential Guard.

   C. You should implement Microsoft Defender Exploit Guard.

   D. You should implement Microsoft Defender Firewall with Advanced Security.

79. You are the administrator for your company network. You are attempting to set up Microsoft Defender Firewall to allow DNS inbound and outbound rules. What port number should you set up?

   A. You should set up port 20.

   B. You should set up port 25.

   C. You should set up port 53.

   D. You should set up port 80.

80. You are the administrator for your company network. You have a Windows 10 Enterprise computer. This computer does not have a Trusted Platform Module (TPM) chip installed. You want to configure BitLocker Drive Encryption (BitLocker) on this machine. What Group Policy object (GPO) setting should you configure?

A. You should configure the Allow Access To BitLocker-Protected Fixed Data Drives From Earlier Version Of Windows setting.

B. You should configure the Allow Network Unlock At Startup setting.

C. You should configure the Require Additional Authentication At Startup setting.

D. You should configure the Use Of Hardware-Based Encryption For Operating System Drives setting.

81. You are the administrator for your company network. You have been tasked with assigning a user, User1, the rights to Read and Change a document in the C:\Documents folder. Here are the current permissions on the shared folder:

Group/User	NTFS Permission	Shared Permission
Sales	Read	Change
Marketing	Modify	Change
Research	Deny	Full Control
Finance	Read	Read
User1	Read	Change

User1 is also a member of the Sales and Finance groups. When accessing the C:\Documents folder, User1 can read all the files but is unable to change or delete files. What should you do to give User1 the minimum amount of rights to perform their job?

A. You should assign Finance Change Shared permission.

B. You should assign Finance Modify NTFS permission.

C. You should assign Sales Full Control Shared permission.

D. You should assign User1 Full Control NTFS permission.

E. You should assign User1 Modify NTFS permission.

82. You are the administrator for your company network. Your network contains an Active Directory domain that contains a group called Group1. All of the computers in this domain are running Windows 10. Every computer has a folder named C:\Documents that has the default NTFS permissions assigned. You add a folder named Templates to the C:\Documents directory on all of the computers. You have to configure the NTFS permissions to meet the requirements for a new company policy, which states that all domain users must be able to open the files within the Templates folder but that only the members of Group1 can edit the files within it. How should you configure the NTFS settings on the Templates folder with regard to inheritance?

A. You should disable inheritance and copy explicit permissions.

B. You should disable inheritance and remove permissions.

C. You should enable inheritance.

D. You should enable inheritance and remove permissions.

83. You are the administrator for your company network. Your network contains an Active Directory domain that contains a group called Group1. All of the computers in this domain are running Windows 10. Every computer has a folder named C:\Documents that has the default NTFS permissions assigned. You add a folder named Templates to the C:\Documents directory on all of the computers. You have to configure the NTFS permissions to meet the requirements for a new company policy. The requirements are that all domain users must be able to open the files within the Templates folder but that only the members of Group1 can edit the files within the Templates folder. How should you configure the NTFS settings for the Templates folder in regard to permissions for the domain users?

A. You should assign the Allow Modify permission.

B. You should assign the Allow Read & Execute permission.

C. You should assign the Deny Modify permission.

D. You should assign the Deny Read & Execute permission.

84. You are the administrator for your company network. Your network contains an Active Directory domain that includes a group called Group1. All of the computers in this domain are running Windows 10. Every computer has a folder named C:\Documents that has the default NTFS permissions assigned. You add a folder named Templates to the C:\Documents directory on all of the computers. You have to configure the NTFS permissions to meet the requirements for a new company policy. The requirements are that all domain users must be able to open the files within the Templates folder but that only the members of Group1 can edit the files within the Templates folder. How should you configure the NTFS settings on the Templates folder in regard to permissions for Group1?

A. You should assign the Allow Modify permission.

B. You should assign the Allow Read & Execute permission.

C. You should assign the Deny Modify permission.

D. You should assign the Deny Read & Execute permission.

85. You are the administrator for your company network. You have a Windows 10 Enterprise computer. Using the Microsoft Defender Firewall with Advanced Security tool, you change settings on a reference computer. You want to apply the same settings to all of the other company computers. You want to save the Microsoft Defender Firewall with Advanced Security configuration settings from the reference computer and import the configuration settings into a Group Policy object (GPO) at a later time. What should you do to implement this?

A. You should open Local Group Policy Editor, select the Windows Firewall with Advanced Security node, and then select the Export Policy action.

B. You should run the netsh advfirewall export c:\settings.wfw command.

C. You should run the netsh advfirewall export c:\settings.xml command.

D. You should run the netsh firewall export c:\settings.xml command.

86. You are the administrator for your company network. You have created a custom Microsoft Management Console (MMC) that contains several snap-ins. You have named this MyConsole1. Users use the custom MMC to manage specific computer settings. Users report that whenever they close the custom MMC, they are prompted to save it. What should you do if you want to prevent the custom MMC from prompting to save every time the users close it?

A. From the File menu, click Add/Remove Snap-in and then click Edit Extensions.

B. From the File menu, click Options and then modify the console mode.

C. Modify the Authors property from the Details settings of the MMC file.

D. Modify the permissions from the Security settings of the MMC file.

87. You are the administrator for your company network. You have a Windows 10 computer that has two volumes. The volumes are named C:\ and D:\. Volume C:\ is formatted with NTFS, and volume D:\ is formatted with exFAT. What should you use if you need to ensure that you can recover files stored in D:\Data?

A. You should use File History.

B. You should use Backup and Restore (Windows 7).

C. You should use System Restore points.

D. You should use wbadmin.exe.

88. You are the administrator for your company network. On a Windows 10 computer, you are reconfiguring the storage. You have an existing storage pool, and you need to add an existing disk to it. What PowerShell command should you use to add this disk to the storage pool?

A. You should use the Add-PhysicalDisk cmdlet.

B. You should use Diskpart.

C. You should use the Resize-StorageTier cmdlet.

D. You should use the Set-StoragePool cmdlet.

89. You are the administrator for your company network. You have a Windows 10 computer with File History enabled. The user of this computer states that a previous version of a file, D:\Folder1\File1.docx, is unavailable from the Previous Versions tab. What should you do if you need to ensure that the previous version of the file is created? (Choose all that apply.)

A. You should add D:\Folder1\ to the Documents library.

B. You should create a backup of drive D:\ using Backup and Restore (Windows 7).

C. You should modify the Backup settings in Settings.

D. You should turn on System Protection for the D:\ drive.

90. You are the administrator for your company network. You have a computer that runs Windows 10. You have been tasked to configure Windows Hello. You want to configure the PIN complexity rules for this computer. You should modify which policy setting?

A. You should modify Biometrics.

B. You should modify Credential User Interface.

C. You should modify Smart Cards.

D. You should modify Windows Hello for Business.

91. You are the administrator for your company network. The network consist of a workgroup that uses Windows 10 Enterprise computers. You have been tasked to assign the users Read and Write permissions to a company shared folder. You add each user to a group named `CompanyNetworkUsers`. You need to grant permissions to the share. You must meet the following requirements:

- All users must have Read and Write access to existing files.

- Any new files must allow the creator to modify the new file's permissions.

What actions should you take? (Choose two.)

- **A.** You should assign Full Control permissions to the Creator Owner group on the shared folder.

- **B.** You should assign Full Control permissions to the Domain Admins group on the shared folder.

- **C.** You should assign Modify permissions to the `CompanyNetworkUsers` group on the shared folder.

- **D.** You should assign List and Execute permissions to the `CompanyNetworkUsers` group on the shared folder.

92. You are the administrator for your company network. You and a colleague are discussing an option that allows you to seize control over a resource. Some scenarios might be that there are files or folders that were created by a deleted user account or you are reusing a hard drive that came from another computer. What is this called when you seize control over a resource?

- **A.** Acquire Ownership

- **B.** Relinquish Ownership

- **C.** Seize Ownership

- **D.** Take Ownership

93. You are the administrator for your company network. You and a colleague are discussing Microsoft Defender Exploit Guard and some of the features it includes. One feature is the ability to protect files, folders, and memory areas on a computer from unauthorized changes by unfriendly applications, such as ransomware. What is the name of this feature of Microsoft Defender Exploit Guard?

- **A.** Account protection

- **B.** Controlled folder access

- **C.** Device Guard

- **D.** Windows Guard

94. You are the administrator for your company network. You are installing a new hard disk drive onto a computer. This disk has not been formatted. What is a step you must take first to be able to use the hard disk drive?

- **A.** You must format the disk using `convert`.

- **B.** You must defragment the disk.

    C. You must initialize the disk.

    D. You must partition the disk.

95. You are the administrator for your company network. You want to set up Home Folders for a user. You open the user's Properties dialog box by accessing the Local Users And Groups utility, opening the User's folder, and then double-clicking the user account. What tab should you go to in order to set up the Home Folder?

    A. You should go to the General tab.

    B. You should go to the Member Of tab.

    C. You should go to the Home Folder tab.

    D. You should go to the Profile tab.

96. You are the administrator for your company network. You have a user who is a member of both the R & D and Marketing groups. There is a shared folder called MyShare that everyone uses. The current shared folder permissions for the folder are as follows:

Group/User	NTFS Permission	Shared Permission
Sales	Read	Deny
Marketing	Modify	Full Control
R & D	Read	Read
HR	Full Control	Deny
Admin	Full Control	Change

What will the user's local and remote permissions be when the user logs into the MyShare folder?

    A. The user's local permission will be Full Control, and their remote permission will be Deny.

    B. The user's local permission will be Modify, and their remote permission will be Full Control.

    C. The user's local permission will be Read, and their remote permission will be Change.

    D. The user's local permission will be Read, and their remote permission will be Deny.

97. You are the administrator for your company network. You have a computer that runs Windows 10 and is used by several users. The computer is joined to an Active Directory domain. All of the users are members of the Administrators group. Each user has an Active Directory account. You have a confidential Microsoft Word document. You need to ensure that you are the only user who can open this confidential document. What should you configure?

    A. You should configure the account policies.

    B. You should configure the Encrypting File System (EFS) settings.

    C. You should configure the NTFS permissions.

    D. You should configure the Share permissions.

98. You are the administrator for your company network. You and a colleague are discussing data deduplication on Windows 10. Where does data deduplication get enabled?

   A. You enable this on the files.

   B. You enable this on the folders.

   C. You enable this on the partitions.

   D. You enable this on the volumes.

99. You are the administrator for your company network. You and a colleague are discussing Windows 10 platforms. Windows 10 supports several types of file systems. What are the most common file systems used with Windows 10? (Choose two.)

   A. File Allocation Table (FAT)

   B. File Allocation Table 32 (FAT32)

   C. Windows NT File System (NTFS)

   D. Resilient File System (ReFS)

100. You are the administrator for your company network. You and a colleague are discussing the convert command. What does the command convert d: /fs:ntfs do?

   A. The command will convert the D: drive from FAT to NTFS.

   B. The command will convert the D: drive from NTFS to FAT.

   C. The command will format the D: drive to FAT.

   D. This command will scan the D: drive for errors.

101. You are the administrator for your company network. You and a colleague are discussing Shared folder permissions. Which of the following are true regarding Shared folder permissions? (Choose all that apply.)

   A. Shared folder permissions apply to files.

   B. Shared folder permissions apply to folders.

   C. Shared folder permissions apply locally to the data.

   D. Shared folder permissions apply remotely to the data.

102. You are the administrator for your company network. You and a colleague are discussing the NTFS file system. What is an advantage to using the NTFS file system?

   A. Compression

   B. Encryption

   C. Quotas

   D. Security

   E. All of the above

103. You are the administrator for your company network. You and a colleague are discussing the benefits of the NTFS file system. You are thinking about setting up disk quotas. By default, Windows 10 supports disk quota restrictions, but at what level?

A. The drive level is the default.

B. The folder level is the default.

C. The partition level is the default.

D. The volume level is the default.

104. You are the administrator for your company network. You and a colleague are discussing the benefits of using the NTFS file system. One of the benefits allows you to move occasionally used files to external hard drives. What is the name of the benefit that you are discussing?

A. You are discussing dynamic volumes.

B. You are discussing mounted drives.

C. You are discussing remote storage.

D. You are discussing self-healing NTFS.

105. You are the administrator for your company network. You and a colleague are discussing using BitLocker. You know that there is a requirement for the number of partitions that are needed. What is the minimum number of partitions that are needed to use BitLocker?

A. One

B. Two

C. Three

D. Four

106. You are the administrator for your company network. You and a colleague are discussing managing volumes. What type of volume are we discussing when we say that it is a simple volume that spreads data across multiple disks?

A. Mirrored volume

B. RAID-5 volume

C. Spanned volume

D. Striped volume

107. You are the administrator for your company network. You have a user who is a member of both the HR and Marketing groups. There is a shared folder called MyShare that everyone uses. The current shared folder permissions for the folder are as follows:

Group/User	NTFS Permission	Shared Permission
Sales	Read	Deny
Marketing	Modify	Full Control
R & D	Read	Read
HR	Full Control	Deny
Admin	Full Control	Change

What will the user's local and remote permissions be when they log into the MyShare folder?

- **A.** The user's local permission will be Full Control, and their remote permission will be Deny.
- **B.** The user's local permission will be Deny, and their remote permission will be Deny.
- **C.** The user's local permission will be Full Control, and their remote will be Change.
- **D.** The user's local permission will be Change, and their remote permission will be Read.

108. You are the administrator for your company network. You and a colleague are discussing that when Windows 10 is installed as part of a workgroup environment, Windows 10 will add some built-in accounts. These accounts are created automatically when you install the operating system. One of these accounts uses the name of the registered user. Which one is it?

- **A.** Administrator
- **B.** DefaultAccount
- **C.** Guest
- **D.** Initial User

109. You are the administrator for your company network. You have a computer that has the following four hard disk drives installed:

- Drive A: 500 GB operating system volume
- Drive B: 400 GB data volume
- Drive C: 400 GB empty volume
- Drive D: 500 GB empty volume

You want to create a two-way mirror by using Storage Spaces. What drives should you use, while at the same time minimizing data loss?

- **A.** You should use drive A: and drive B:.
- **B.** You should use drive A: and drive D:.
- **C.** You should use drive B: and drive C:.
- **D.** You should use drive C: and drive D:.

110. You are the administrator for your company network. A user wants to use a picture to log into the system. Windows 10 provides the ability to use a picture to be used for logon along with gestures. How many gestures do you add to a photo for logon?

- **A.** One
- **B.** Two
- **C.** Three
- **D.** Four

111. You are the administrator for your company network. You and a colleague are discussing an authentication and encryption communication method that contains a set of security protocols that provide identity authentication and secure, private communication through encryption. What is the name of this communication method?

    A. Automatic Private IP Addressing (APIPA)

    B. Microsoft Deployment Toolkit (MDT)

    C. Secure Channel (Schannel)

    D. Trusted Platform Module (TPM)

112. You are the administrator for your company network. You and a colleague are discussing the ever-increasing demands of storage. Which of the following are used to surpass the limitation of 26 drive letters and to join two volumes into a folder on a separate physical disk drive?

    A. Data points

    B. Drive points

    C. Mount points

    D. Volume points

113. You are the administrator for your company network. You are using the `Diskpart` command-line utility. You want to use the switch that will allow you to make a partition on a disk, a volume on one or more disks, or a virtual hard disk (VHD). What switch command do you use?

    A. You should use `diskpart /assign`.

    B. You should use `diskpart /create`.

    C. You should use `diskpart /convert`.

    D. You should use `diskpart /reduce`.

114. You are the administrator for your company network. You have decided to take advantage of the security provided by the NTFS file system. Which of the following is the default security permission for Users on new folders and shares?

    A. Change

    B. Full Control

    C. Read

    D. Write

115. You are the administrator for your company network. You have a user who is a member of both the Sales and R & D groups. There is a shared folder called MyShare that everyone uses. The current shared folder permissions for the folder are as follows:

Group/User	NTFS Permission	Shared Permission
Sales	Full Control	Read
Marketing	Modify	Full Control
R & D	Modify	Change
HR	Full Control	Deny
Admin	Full Control	Read

The user is trying to make changes to a document in the shared folder and is unable to make the necessary changes. What permission will you need to change to allow the user to make the changes?

A. The Sales folder shared permission will need to be changed to Change.

B. The Sales folder shared permission will need to be changed to Modify.

C. The R & D NTFS permission will need to be changed to Change.

D. Nothing. The Sales folder shared permission meets the user's requirements.

116. You are the administrator for your company network. You have a user who is a member of the Sales, R & D, and HR groups. There is a folder called MyShare on the server. The current permissions of the folder are as follows:

Group/User	NTFS Permission
Sales	Read
Marketing	Modify
R & D	Modify
HR	Full Control
Admin	Full Control

What is this user's effective NTFS permission?

A. The user's effective permission will be Deny.

B. The user's effective permission will be Full Control.

C. The user's effective permission will be Modify.

D. The user's effective permission will be Read.

117. You are the administrator for your company network. You have a user who is a member of the Sales, R & D, and HR groups. There is a folder called MyShare on the server. The current permissions of the folder are as follows:

Group/User	NTFS Permission
Sales	Read
Marketing	Modify
R & D	Modify
HR	Deny
Admin	Full Control

What is this user's effective NTFS permission?

A. The user's effective permission will be Deny.

B. The user's effective permission will be Full Control.

C. The user's effective permission will be Modify.

D. The user's effective permission will be Read.

118. You are the administrator for your company network. You have decided to take advantage of the security provided by shared permissions. The default shared permission for Administrators on new folders is which of the following?

A. Change

B. Full Control

C. Read

D. Write

119. You are the administrator for your company network. You and a colleague are discussing disk quotas. You know that there are a few options available when setting up disk quotas. What type of quota is a predefined way to set up quotas?

A. Quotas by volume

B. Quotas by user

C. Specifying quota entries

D. Quota templates

120. You are the administrator for your company network. You have a Windows 10 computer that has a printer installed. You need to configure the settings of the printer remotely using another computer. While on the remote computer, what tool should you use?

A. From the Administrative Tools, use Print Management.

B. From the Control Panel, use Device Manager.

C. From the Control Panel, use Devices And Printers.

D. From the Settings App, use Printers & Scanners.

121. You are the administrator for your company network. Your company has issued a new security policy. They would like all users to be issued a security ID badge that will have that user's group and rights assigned using the badge. How should you go about implementing the new corporate policy?

A. You should implement BitLocker To Go on the ID badges.

B. You should implement folder permissions only.

C. You should implement smart cards.

D. You should implement the use of key fobs with built-in user rights.

122. You are the administrator for your company network. You and a colleague are discussing using BitLocker on the network. What operating systems can support the use of BitLocker? (Choose all that apply.)

A. Windows 7 Home

B. Windows 8.1 Enterprise Edition

C. Windows 10 Education Edition

D. Windows 10 Professional Edition

123. You are the administrator for your company network. You and a colleague are discussing whether you want to implement BitLocker onto your corporate network. Which statement is true regarding BitLocker?

   A. BitLocker uses Remote Lock and Wipe.

   B. BitLocker uses Network Unlock.

   C. BitLocker can't protect against a stolen server drive.

   D. BitLocker has to be associated with a corporate SAN.

124. You are the administrator for your company network. You have a computer that dual boots between Windows 10 and Windows 7. You need to install a new hard drive. This drive will be used for storing large files and classified data. You will need to be able to access these files from either operating system. With what file system should you format the new hard drive to meet your requirements?

   A. You should use the CDFS file system.

   B. You should use the FAT16 file system.

   C. You should use the FAT32 file system.

   D. You should use the NTFS file system.

125. You are the administrator for your company network. You have a Windows 10 computer on your network that has classified, sensitive data stored on it. You need to prevent users from copying files from this machine to any removable disk. What should you do to ensure that files cannot be copied to a USB device?

   A. This can't be done; the files can still be copied onto a USB device.

   B. Set the BitLocker Drive Encryption using the Hardware icon in Control Panel.

   C. Set the BitLocker Drive Encryption using the Device Manager icon in Control Panel.

   D. Set the BitLocker Drive Encryption using a Local Group Policy.

Chapter

3

Configure Connectivity

THE MD-100 EXAM TOPICS COVERED IN THIS CHAPTER INCLUDE:

✓ **Domain 3: Configure Connectivity**

- 3.1 Configure networking

    - Configure client IP settings

    - Configure mobile networking

    - Configure VPN client

    - Troubleshoot networking

    - Configure Wi-Fi profiles

- 3.2 Configure remote connectivity

    - Configure remote management

    - Enable PowerShell Remoting

    - Configure remote desktop access

1. You are the administrator for your company network. You notice that you cannot access any of the computers on the remote subnet by IP address after configuring a new machine and connecting it to the network. You can still access the computers on the local subnet by using their IP addresses. What is the most likely cause of this issue?

   A. You have incorrectly defined the default gateway.

   B. You have incorrectly defined the DNS server.

   C. You have incorrectly defined the IP address.

   D. You have incorrectly defined the subnet mask.

2. You are the administrator for your company network. You have two DHCP servers on your network. One of the DHCP servers was accidentally misconfigured and has sent your computer the wrong IP and DNS server configuration information. You have disabled the misconfigured DHCP server. You need to update your computer's IPv4 DHCP configuration information. What commands should you run on your computer? (Choose two.)

   A. You should run the `ipconfig /flushdhcp` command.

   B. You should run the `ipconfig /registerdhcp` command.

   C. You should run the `ipconfig /release` command.

   D. You should run the `ipconfig /renew` command.

3. You are the administrator for your company network. The network contains an Active Directory domain. The domain contains several computers that run Windows 10. Users in the Sales department use these computers. You have a Windows 10 computer named Computer1. From this computer, you are planning on running a script that will execute a Windows PowerShell command on the Sales department computers. You need to ensure that you can run the PowerShell commands on the Sales department from Computer1. What should you do first?

   A. Enable the Allow Remote Shell Access setting from the Local Group Policy.

   B. Enable the Turn On Script Execution setting from the Local Group Policy.

   C. Run the `Enable-MMAgent` cmdlet using Windows PowerShell.

   D. Run the `Enable-PSRemoting` cmdlet using Windows PowerShell.

4. You are the administrator for your company network. Your corporate Internet Service Provider (ISP) has assigned you a network address of 192.168.154.0. You have been given the entire range to use. What address class have you been assigned?

   A. You have been assigned a Class A address.

   B. You have been assigned a Class B address.

   C. You have been assigned a Class C address.

   D. You have been assigned a Class D address.

5. You are the administrator for your company network. You are deploying several Windows 10 computers. Every computer has both a cellular connection and a Wi-Fi connection capability. What should you do if you want to prevent the computers from using the cellular connection unless the user manually connects to it?

   A. For the cellular connection, clear the Let Windows Manage This Connection checkbox.

   B. For the Wi-Fi connection, select the Let Windows Manage This Connection checkbox.

   C. Run the command `netsh wlan set hostednetwork mode=disallow`.

   D. For the cellular connection, set the Use Cellular Instead Of Wi-Fi setting to Never.

6. You are the administrator for your company network. Your company is looking at rebuilding its entire network. There are currently only 150 employees. There are plans for hiring more than 500 new employees. The company is currently using the IPv4 192.168.x.x class; however, the company does not want to purchase a new TCP/IP class. What IP address should you use to accommodate the new network? (Choose all that apply.)

   A. You can change the network to 10.0.0.0/8.

   B. You can change the network to 172.16.0.0/16.

   C. You can change the network to 192.10.0.0/24.

   D. You can change the network to 223.10.0.0/24.

7. You are the administrator for your company network. When traveling, an employee needs to be able to use Remote Desktop and VPN on their laptop to access a Windows 10 Enterprise desktop computer. What should you do if you need to set up a secure Remote Desktop connection on the desktop computer? (Choose two).

   A. You should allow remote connections.

   B. You should disable Remote Assistance connections.

   C. You should make the user account a standard user.

   D. You should require Network Level Authentication.

8. You are the administrator for your company network. You have several Windows 10 computers. Each computer has two network interfaces named Interface1 and Interface2. What should you do if you want to ensure that all network traffic uses Interface1 when available?

   A. You should modify the provider order from Network Connections in Control Panel.

   B. You should run the `Set-NetAdapterBinding -Name Interface2 -Enabled $true -ComponentID ms_tcpip -TThrottleLimit 0` command.

   C. You should run the `Set-NetIPInterface -InterfaceAlias Interface1 -InterfaceMetric 1` command.

   D. You should set a static IP address on Interface1.

9. You are the administrator for your company network. This is a small network with only five employees. The company does not have the finances available to purchase a server and all the client access licenses for every employee. What type of network should you set up?

   A. You should create a HomeGroup.

   B. You should load Windows Server onto a Windows 10 computer.

C.   You should set up an Azure Active Directory.

D.   You should set up all Windows 10 clients onto a workgroup.

10. You are the administrator for your company network. You have a Windows 10 machine that needs to have a static TCP/IP address. What should you do after you have assigned an IP address to the machine and you now need to list the computer with the DNS server?

A.   You should run `ipconfig /dns`.

B.   You should run `ipconfig /flushdns`.

C.   You should run `ipconfig /registerdns`.

D.   You should run `ipconfig /renewdns`.

11. You are the administrator for your company network. A user on the network has a Windows 10 computer. While using Remote Desktop, the user connects to a Microsoft Azure virtual machine named VM1. The user creates a virtual private network (VPN) connection to a sister company. When the VPN connection is established, the user cannot connect to VM1; however, when they disconnect from the VPN, they can connect to VM1. What should you do if you need to ensure that the user can connect to the virtual machine when connected to the VPN?

A.   Add the IP address of the virtual machine to the bypass list to bypass the proxy from the proxy settings.

B.   Clear the Use Default Gateway On Remote Network checkbox from the properties of the virtual private network.

C.   Configure a static default gateway address from the properties of the virtual private network.

D.   Specify a Remote Desktop Gateway (RD Gateway) from the properties of the Remote Desktop connection to the virtual machine.

12. You are the administrator for your company network. You and a colleague are discussing configuring a VPN client. Which tab of the Connection Properties dialog box is where you would want to enter the VPN server address or hostname?

A.   The General tab

B.   The Networking tab

C.   The Options tab

D.   The Security tab

13. You are the administrator for your company network. Many of your users travel and utilize laptop computers. Corporate notifies you that they'd like to move away from connecting to the corporate network by using a VPN connection and would like to switch to using the cloud. What version of Active Directory do you want to start utilizing?

A.   You should utilize Azure Active Directory.

B.   You should utilize DirectAccess.

C.   You should utilize OneDrive.

D.   You should utilize Windows Server Active Directory.

14. You are the administrator for your company network. The company has an Active Directory Domain Services (AD DS) domain that uses Windows 10 Enterprise machines. The network uses a Dynamic Host Configuration Protocol (DHCP) server. You want to assign a static DHCP reservation to a client computer. You need to obtain the media access control (MAC) address of the client computer. What command should you run to find this information?

A. You should run the `ipconfig` command.

B. You should run the `ipconfig /all` command.

C. You should run the `ipconfig /allcompartments` command.

D. You should run the `ipconfig /flushdns` command.

15. You are the administrator for your company network. You and a colleague are discussing subnet masks and how to determine the Classless Inter-Domain Routing (CIDR) number. Given the subnet mask 255.255.224.0, what would the CIDR equivalent be?

A. /17

B. /18

C. /19

D. /20

16. You are the administrator for your company network. You and a colleague are discussing subnet masks and how to determine the Classless Inter-Domain Routing (CIDR) number. Given the subnet mask 255.255.255.224, what would the CIDR equivalent be?

A. /24

B. /25

C. /26

D. /27

17. You are the administrator for your company network. Your network consists of a large number of Windows 10 computers. You want to assign static IP addresses rather than utilizing a DHCP server. You want these computers to be configured to use the 192.168.10.0 network. What subnet mask should you use for this network address?

A. You should use the subnet mask of 255.0.0.0.

B. You should use the subnet mask of 255.255.0.0.

C. You should use the subnet mask of 255.255.255.0.

D. You should use the subnet mask of 255.255.255.255.

18. You are the administrator for your company network. Your network contains an Active Directory domain. All computers run Windows 10. You enable Windows PowerShell remoting on the computers. You need to ensure that a particular user can establish remote PowerShell connections to the computers. What group should you add this user to?

A. The user should be a member of the Access Control Assistance Operators group.

B. The user should be a member of the Power Users group.

C. The user should be a member of the Remote Desktop Users group.

D. The user should be a member of the Remote Management Users group.

19. You are the administrator for your company network. You and a colleague are discussing enabling Remote Desktop. You open Control Panel. Where do you go from here to enable Remote Desktop on a computer?

A. Device Manager

B. Network And Sharing Center

C. System

D. Sync Center

20. You are the administrator for your company network. The company has several Windows 10 Enterprise client computers. The organization is configured for IPv4 and IPv6. What should you do on the client computers if you want to disable Media Sensing for IPv6 without affecting the IPv4 communications?

A. You should run the `Disable-NetAdapter` Windows PowerShell cmdlet.

B. You should run the `Disable-NetAdapterBinding` Windows PowerShell cmdlet.

C. You should run the `Set-NetIPv4Protrocol` Windows PowerShell cmdlet.

D. You should run the `Set-NetIPv6Protocol` Windows PowerShell cmdlet.

21. You are the administrator for your company network. You have a user who is unable to access a server within the domain. After you perform some troubleshooting, you figure out that the user cannot access the server by its name, but you can access it by using its IP address. What is most likely the cause of the problem?

A. An incorrectly defined DHCP server

B. An incorrectly defined DNS server

C. An incorrectly defined IP address

D. An incorrectly defined subnet mask

22. You are the administrator for your company network. Your network contains an Active Directory domain that has more than 1,000 Windows 10 computers. What should you do if you want to prevent the computers from one department from appearing in the Network in File Explorer?

A. You should configure DNS to use an external provider.

B. You should disable the Network List Service.

C. You should modify the file in the `%systemroot%\system32\drivers\etc\networks` directory.

D. You should turn off Network Discovery.

23. You are the administrator for your company network. Your network contains an Active Directory domain that has two computers, named Computer1 and Computer2. Both computers run Windows 10. On Computer1, you need to run the `Invoke-Command` cmdlet to execute several PowerShell commands on Computer2. What should you do first?

A. Add Computer1 to the Remote Management Users group on Computer2.

B. Configure the Trusted For Delegation setting for the computer account of Computer2 from Active Directory.

    C.   Run the `Enable-PSRemoting` cmdlet on Computer2.

    D.   Run the `New-PSSession` cmdlet on Computer1.

24. You are the administrator for your company network. Your network has a DNS server that contained corrupted data. You fix the issues on the server. One of the users in the network is complaining that they are still unable to access Internet resources. You check to see whether things are working on another computer on the same subnet. What command should you run to fix the issue?

    A.   You should run the `DNS /flushdns` command.

    B.   You should run the `ipconfig /flush` command.

    C.   You should run the `ipconfig /flushdns` command.

    D.   You should run the `ping /flush` command.

25. You are the administrator for your company network. Your network contains an Active Directory domain. The domain contains a user named User1. The user creates a Microsoft account. The user needs to sign into a cloud resource by using the Microsoft account without being prompted for credentials. What setting should be configured so that the user is not prompted?

    A.   In Active Directory Users And Computers, modify the Users setting.

    B.   In Computer Management, modify the Users setting.

    C.   In the Control Panel, modify the User Accounts setting.

    D.   In the Settings app, modify the Email & App Accounts setting.

26. You are the administrator for your company network. All of your network users use laptop computers. Windows 10 has a built-in feature that allows a user, when using a wireless network adapter, to choose the wireless network that they want to connect to. What is this feature called?

    A.   It is called Available Network Finder (ANF).

    B.   It is called Network Availability Viewer (NAV).

    C.   It is called View Available Networks (VAN).

    D.   It is called View Networks (VN).

27. You are the administrator for your company network. You and a colleague are discussing Classless Inter-Domain Routing (CIDR). Which of the following subnet masks represents the CIDR of /27?

    A.   255.255.255.224

    B.   255.255.255.240

    C.   255.255.255.248

    D.   255.255.255.254

28. You are the administrator for your company network. You and a colleague are discussing IP address classes. Which of the following addresses would be Class B addresses? (Choose all that apply.)

   A. 10.14.100.240

   B. 131.107.10.150

   C. 189.10.14.1

   D. 198.102.17.9

29. You are the administrator for your company network. You have a computer that runs Windows 10. You need to troubleshoot connectivity problems on this computer. What tool should you use if you want to view the remote addresses and see the active TCP connections on this machine?

   A. Performance Monitor

   B. Resource Monitor

   C. Task Manager

   D. Microsoft Defender Firewall with Advanced Security

30. You are the administrator for your company network. You have a computer that runs Windows 10. This computer connects to several wireless networks. What tool should you use if you want to see the wireless networks that this computer can connect to?

   A. You should use the Details tab for the wireless adapter in Device Manager.

   B. You should use the Event Viewer System log.

   C. You should use the properties of the wireless adapter in Network Connections in Control Panel.

   D. You should use Wi-Fi in the Settings app.

31. You are the administrator for your company network. Your company has a Remote Desktop Gateway (RD Gateway). You have a server that is accessed by using Remote Desktop Services (RDS) through the RD Gateway. What setting should you use if you want to configure a Remote Desktop connection to connect through the gateway?

   A. You should configure the Connect From Anywhere settings.

   B. You should configure the Connection settings.

   C. You should configure the Local Devices And Resources settings.

   D. You should configure the Server Authentication settings.

32. You are the administrator for your company network. You have a laptop computer that is running Windows 10. This computer will automatically connect to a Wi-Fi network called MyWireless when it is in range. What should you do if you want to prevent your laptop from automatically connecting to the Wi-Fi network?

   A. Disable the Link-Layer Topology Discovery Mapper service from the Services console.

   B. Disable Link-Layer Topology Discovery Responder from the properties of the Wi-Fi adapter.

   C. Run `netsh wlan delete profile name="MyWireless"` from a command prompt.

   D. Run `netsh wlan profile delete name="MyWireless"` from a command prompt.

33. You are the administrator for your company network. You have a laptop computer that is running Windows 10. This computer will automatically connect to a Wi-Fi network called MyWireless when it is in range. What should you do if you want to prevent your laptop from automatically connecting to the Wi-Fi network?

   A. Disable the Link-Layer Topology Discovery Mapper service from the Services console.

   B. Disable Link-Layer Topology Discovery Responder from the properties of the Wi-Fi adapter.

   C. On the Connection tab, check the Connect Automatically When This Network Is In Range option.

   D. On the Connection tab, uncheck the Connect Automatically When This Network Is In Range option.

34. You are the administrator for your company network. Your company has several portable client computers that run Windows 10 Enterprise. The client computers have the following network connections:

Network Name	Connection Type	Network Profile
Wired1	Wired	Private
WiFi1	Wireless	Public
HotSpot1	Public Hotspot	Public

None of the client computers can discover other computer or devices regardless of the type of connection they use. What should you do on the client computers if you want to configure the connections so that the computers can discover other devices and computers only when connected to the Wired1 or WiFi1 connections? (Choose two.)

   A. For the HotSpot1 connection, select No, Don't Turn On Sharing Or Connect To Devices.

   B. For the WiFi1 connection, select Yes to turn on sharing and connect to devices. For the Public profile, turn on Network Discovery.

   C. For the Wired1 connection, change the network profile connection to Public and then turn on Network Discovery for the Public profile.

   D. For the Wired1 connection, select Yes to turn on sharing and connect to devices. For the Private profile, turn on Network Discovery.

35. You are the administrator for your company network. Your company has Windows 10 Enterprise client computers that are connected to a corporate private network. Users are unable to connect using Remote Desktop from their home computers to their work computers. What setting should you configure on the home computers so that the users can remotely connect to the office computers by using Remote Desktop and that they are unable to access any other corporate network resources?

   A. You should configure the DirectAccess connection.

   B. You should configure the Remote Desktop Gateway (RD Gateway) IP address.

    C. You should configure the Remote Desktop local resources.

    D. You should configure the virtual private network (VPN) connection.

36. You are the administrator for your company network. The network contains a single Active Directory domain with a computer that runs Windows 10. An administrator creates a custom Microsoft Management Console (MMC) that uses the Active Directory Users And Computer snap-in on the Windows 10 machine. You use this computer to perform management tasks. You copy the custom MMC to another computer. What should you do on the Windows 10 computer so that you can use the custom MMC and all of the features offered by the MMC?

    A. You should enable the Side Load Apps developer feature.

    B. You should disable User Account Control (UAC).

    C. You should install the Microsoft Application Compatibility Toolkit (ACT).

    D. You should install the Remote Server Administration Tools (RSAT).

37. You are the administrator for your company network. You and a colleague are discussing troubleshooting methods for checking network connectivity. One method that you are discussing is by pinging the loopback address at the command prompt. What is the IPv4 diagnostic loopback address?

    A. You should ping 127.0.0.0.

    B. You should ping 127.0.0.1.

    C. You should ping 127.0.1.0.

    D. You should ping 127.1.0.0.

38. You are the administrator for your company network. You and a colleague are discussing troubleshooting methods for checking network connectivity. One method that you are discussing is pinging the loopback address at command prompt. What is the IPv6 diagnostic loopback address?

    A. You should ping ::1.

    B. You should ping ::01.

    C. You should ping 0:0:0:0:0:0:0:1111.

    D. You should ping 1:0:0:0:0:0:0:0011.

39. You are the administrator for your company network. You have two computers, Computer1 and Computer2, on your workgroup that run Windows 10. On Computer1, you perform the following configurations:

    ▪ Create a user named User1.

    ▪ Add User1 to the Remote Desktop Users group.

On Computer2, you perform the following configurations:

    ▪ Create a user named User1 and specify the same user password as the one set on Computer1.

    ▪ Create a share named Share2 and grant User1 Full Control access to Share2.

    ▪ Enable Remote Desktop.

What are the effects of the configuration if User1 attempts to access Share2 from Computer1?

A. The user will be able to access Share2 without a prompt.

B. The user will be prompted for credentials.

C. The user will be denied access to Share2.

D. The user will be prompted for credentials but will not be able to access Share2.

40. You are the administrator for your company network. You have two computers, Computer1 and Computer2, on your workgroup that run Windows 10. On Computer1, you perform the following configurations:

- Create a user named User1.
- Add User1 to the Remote Desktop Users group.

On Computer2, you perform the following configurations:

- Create a user named User1 and specify the same user password as the one set on Computer1.
- Create a share named Share2 and grant User1 Full Control access to Share2.
- Enable Remote Desktop.

What are the effects of the configuration if User1 attempts to sign into Remote Desktop on Computer2 from Computer1?

A. The user will be able to sign into Remote Desktop without a prompt.

B. The user will be prompted for credentials and be able to sign in as User1.

C. The user will be prompted for credentials and be prevented from signing in as User1.

D. The user will be prompted for credentials but will not be able to sign in as User1.

41. You are the administrator for your company network. A user is using a computer running Windows 10. When this user connects to the corporate network, they are unable to access the internal company servers but can access the servers on the Internet. You run the `ipconfig /all` command and receive the following:

```
Connection-specific DNS Suffix . :
Description . . . . . . . . . . : Ethernet 1
Physical Address . . . . . . . . : 00-50-B6-7B-E4-81
DHCP Enabled . . . . . . . . . . : Yes
Autoconfiguration Enabled . . . : Yes
Link-local IPv6 Address . . . . : fe80::5d56:3419:eB3b:3c46%17 (Preferred)
IPv4 Address . . . . . . . . . . : 192.168.0.121(Preferred)
Subnet Mask . . . . . . . . . . : 255.255.255.0
Lease Obtained . . . . . . . . . : Friday, March 27, 2020 11:38:12 AM
Lease Expires . . . . . . . . . : Friday, March 27, 2020 11:38:12 PM
Default Gateway . . . . . . . . : 192.168.0.1
DHCP Server . . . . . . . . . . : 192.168.0.2
```

```
DHCPv6 IAID . . . . . . . . . . : 536891574
DHCPv6 Client DUID . . . . . . . : 00-01-00-01-22-AC-5F-64-00-50-B6-7B-E4-81
DNS Servers . . . . . . . . . . : 131.107.10.60
                                  192.168.0.3
NetBIOS over Tcpip . . . . . . . : Enabled
```

You send a ping request and can ping the default gateway, the DNS servers, and the DHCP server successfully. What configuration could be causing the issue?

A. The issue is with the default gateway address.

B. The issue is with the DNS servers.

C. The issue is with the IPv4 address.

D. The issue is with the subnet mask.

42. You are the administrator for your company network. You have a computer that is running Windows 10. You go to the Settings app and view the connection properties. It shows the following:

   ▪ The Network profile is set to Public.

   ▪ The Metered connection is set to On.

   You want to enable Windows Remote Management (WinRM) on this computer. What must you do first?

   A. You must first run `winrm qc` at the command prompt.

   B. You must first set up Microsoft OneDrive syncs.

   C. You must first set the Network profile to Private.

   D. You must first turn off Metered connection.

43. You are the administrator for your company network. You have a Remote Desktop Session Host (RD Session Host) server that is available from the internal network. You must connect to a Remote Desktop Gateway (RD Gateway) server to access this server remotely. You configure a Remote Desktop connection successfully from a laptop computer. You use this laptop to access the RD Session Host server from the internal network. While at home, you try to connect to the RD Session Host server using the Remote Desktop connection, but the connection fails. What should you configure on the laptop if you want to connect to the RD Session Host server?

   A. You should configure the Connect From Anywhere settings in Remote Desktop Connection.

   B. You should configure the Performance settings in Remote Desktop Connection.

   C. You should configure the Remote Assistance settings in System Properties.

   D. You should configure the Remote Desktop settings in System Properties.

44. You are the administrator for your company network. You have a desktop computer and a tablet that both run Windows 10 Enterprise. The desktop computer is located in the office and is a member of an Active Directory domain. The network contains an Application Virtualization (App-V) infrastructure, and there are several App-V applications deployed to all desktop computers. The tablet is used at your house and is a member of a workgroup. Both the home and corporate locations have Internet connectivity. You need to be able to access all of the applications that run on the desktop computer from the tablet. What should you do from the desktop computer?

    A. Enable Remote Assistance on the desktop computer.

    B. Enable Remote Desktop on the desktop computer.

    C. Run the Remote Desktop Client on the desktop computer.

    D. Deploy Application Virtualization (App-V) packages on the desktop computer.

45. You are the administrator for your company network. You have a desktop computer and a tablet that both run Windows 10 Enterprise. The desktop computer is located in the office and is a member of an Active Directory domain. The network contains an Application Virtualization (App-V) infrastructure, and there are several App-V applications deployed to all desktop computers. The tablet is used at your house and is a member of a workgroup. Both the home and corporate locations have Internet connectivity. You need to be able to access all of the applications that run on the desktop computer from the tablet. What should you do from the tablet?

    A. Enable Remote Assistance on the tablet.

    B. Enable Remote Desktop on the tablet.

    C. Run the Remote Desktop Client on the tablet.

    D. Deploy Application Virtualization (App-V) packages on the tablet.

46. You are the administrator for your company network. A user on the network is having an issue with their computer, and when they call you, you are unable to figure out what they are trying to tell you. You want to be able to view the user's computer remotely and have the user show you exactly what the issue is. What tool should you use?

    A. You should utilize Device Assistance.

    B. You should utilize Device Manager.

    C. You should utilize Quick Assist.

    D. You should utilize Remote Manager.

47. You are the administrator for your company network. You and a colleague are discussing Remote Assistance and a specific technology that is integrated into it. This technology uses Peer Name Resolution Protocol (PNRP) to set up direct peer-to-peer transfers using a central machine on the Internet. What is the name of this tool that is integrated into Remote Assistance?

    A. Connection Wizard

    B. Easy Connect

    C. Network Manager

    D. Remote Assistance Manager

48. You are the administrator for your company network. You are connecting to the remote Windows host using by Remote Desktop Protocol (RDP) client, and you want to save your login credentials. What tab do you use to save your login credentials?

A. The Advanced tab

B. The Display tab

C. The General tab

D. The Programs tab

49. You are the administrator for your company network. On a Windows 10 computer, you enable Windows PowerShell remoting. However, you want to limit what PowerShell cmdlets can be used on a remote session. What should you do first?

A. Run the Enter-PSSession cmdlet.

B. Run the New-PSSession cmdlet.

C. Run the New-PSSessionConfigurationFile cmdlet.

D. Run the Register-PSSessionConfiguration cmdlet.

50. You are the administrator for your company network. You have a Windows 10 machine that will be used as a virtual private network (VPN). What VPN protocol should you use if you need to configure the machine to support VPN Reconnect?

A. You should use Internet Key Exchange Protocol Version 2 (IKEv2).

B. You should use Layer 2 Tunneling Protocol (L2TP).

C. You should use Point-to-Point Tunneling Protocol (PPTP).

D. You should use Secure Socket Tunneling Protocol (SSTP).

51. You are the administrator for your company network. You have decided to use DHCP for IPv6. You want all the computers running Windows 10 IPv6 to obtain their TCP/IP information through DHCP. How would you set up the network?

A. You should set Active Directory Static IP addresses.

B. You should set up DNS to use DHCP.

C. You should set up a Stateful network.

D. You should set up a Stateless network.

52. You are the administrator for your company network. You have a Windows 10 machine that is located on a perimeter network and only uses inbound TCP port 443 to connect from the Internet. You install the Remote Access server role on the computer. You need to configure the computer to accept virtual private network (VPN) connections over port 443. What VPN protocol should you use?

A. You should use Internet Key Exchange Protocol Version 2 (IKEv2).

B. You should use Layer 2 Tunneling Protocol (L2TP).

C. You should use Point-to-Point Tunneling Protocol (PPTP).

D. You should use Secure Socket Tunneling Protocol (SSTP).

53. You are the administrator for your company network. You and a colleague are discussing the different `ipconfig` switches. Which of the following options will allow you to purge the DNS resolver cache?

   A. You should run `ipconfig /flushdns`.

   B. You should run `ipconfig /killdns`.

   C. You should run `ipconfig /purgedns`.

   D. You should run `ipconfig /removedns`.

54. You are the administrator for your company network. You and a colleague are discussing virtual private network (VPN) connections and how to connect to a VPN on Windows 10. What must you have first before a Windows 10 machine can connect to a VPN?

   A. You must have a VPN certificate.

   B. You must have a VPN encryption key.

   C. You must have a VPN profile.

   D. You must have a VPN username.

55. You are the administrator for your company network. You and a colleague are discussing Remote Desktop connection speeds. What tab would you use in Remote Desktop Connection that would allow you to set the connection speeds?

   A. The General tab

   B. The Display tab

   C. The Experience tab

   D. The Advanced tab

56. You are the administrator for your company network. You and a colleague are discussing virtual private networks (VPNs). When you're setting up a VPN, where does it sit?

   A. A VPN sits between the external network and the Internet, accepting connections from clients in the outside world.

   B. A VPN sits between the internal network and the Internet, accepting connections from clients in the outside world.

   C. A VPN sits between behind the firewall on the internal network and the Internet, rejecting connections from clients in the outside world.

   D. A VPN sits between behind the firewall on the external network and the Internet, rejecting connections from clients in the outside world.

57. You are the administrator for your company network. You want to enable your Routing and Remote Access Service (RRAS) server to act as a virtual private network (VPN). Where do you modify the properties to specify whether your RRAS server is a router, a Remote Access server, or both?

   A. On the General tab of the server's Properties dialog box

   B. On the Logging tab of the server's Properties dialog box

   C. On the PPP tab of the server's Properties dialog box

   D. On the Security tab of the server's Properties dialog box

58. You are the administrator for your company network. You and a colleague are discussing the ping command-line utility. Which of the following addresses would you use with ping to test the loopback address of the local IPv4 computer?

A. 1.1.1.1

B. 127.0.0.1

C. 256.0.0.1

D. 255.255.255.255

59. You are the administrator for your company network. You receive a phone call at 1 a.m. informing you that one of the servers is not working properly. There is currently no one in the office to fix the issue. How can you connect to the server to fix it?

A. Use Hyper-V.

B. Use Remote Assistance.

C. Use Remote Desktop.

D. Use Virtual PC.

60. You are the administrator for your company network. You want to view the TCP/IP details of a Windows 10 Enterprise system to make sure that a user is using DHCP and that the IP address is correct. What command-line utility and switch should you use?

A. ipconfig /all

B. ipconfig /flushdns

C. route add

D. tracert

61. You are the administrator for your company network. You run ipconfig /all on a network computer. You see an IP address of 169.254.0.136 with a subnet mask of 255.255.0.0. You are not using DHCP. What does this indicate?

A. It indicates that you are using APIPA.

B. It indicates that you are using DHCP.

C. It indicates that you are using DNS.

D. It indicates that you are using WINS.

62. You are the administrator for your company network. Your company has decided on using 255.255.255.240 as its new subnet mask. What is the increment for subnet ranges in a 240 subnet mask?

A. 4

B. 8

C. 16

D. 32

63. You are the administrator for your company network. You and a colleague are discussing troubleshooting a virtual private network (VPN). What should you check first when troubleshooting a VPN connection?

A. Check that the authentication settings in the server's policies (if any) match the supported set of authentication protocols.

B. Check that the clients can connect to the Internet Service Provider (ISP).

C. Check that the username and password are correct.

D. Check that the VPN protocol used by the client is enabled.

64. You are the administrator for your company network. You and a colleague are discussing subnet mask ranges. Which subnet mask has ranges of 32?

A. 255.255.240.0

B. 255.255.224.0

C. 255.255.248.0

D. 255.255.252.0

65. You are the administrator for your company network. You and a colleague are discussing a Windows 10 feature that helps reduce the time needed for retrieving shared files and folders. What is this feature called?

A. Broadband tethering

B. Transparent tethering

C. Broadband caching

D. Transparent caching

66. You are the administrator for your company network. You and a colleague are discussing an advantage to using Windows 10 and mobility. This ability allows at least 10 devices to connect to an Internet connection on a machine. They can then use the Internet. What is this feature called?

A. Broadband tethering

B. Transparent tethering

C. Broadband caching

D. Transparent caching

67. You are the administrator for your company network. You and a colleague are discussing the networking models used by Microsoft. What are the models called? (Choose all that apply.)

A. Domain-based networks

B. Home-based networks

C. HomeGroups

D. Workgroups

68. You are the administrator for your company network. You and a colleague are discussing trusts. What kind of trust is set up between one domain and another domain in the same forest?

A. Domain trust

B. External trust

C. Forest trust

D. Shortcut trust

69. You are the administrator for your company network. You and a colleague are discussing Wi-Fi profiles. What tool do you use to create a Wi-Fi profile?

A. App Manager

B. Configuration Manager

C. Device Manager

D. W-Fi Manager

70. You are the administrator for your company network. Your users use Windows tablets to access the network. The company tablets use a broadband Wi-Fi connection. The company wants you to watch how much data the users are using on this connection. How do you do that?

A. You should configure the broadband connection as a metered network.

B. You should enable Performance Monitor.

C. You should enable tablet metering in the tablet's settings.

D. You should turn on network resource monitoring.

71. You are the administrator for your company network. You have a single subnet with 1,600 client computers. You need to select a subnet mask that will support all of the client computers. You need to minimize the number of unused addresses. Which subnet mask should you choose?

A. 255.255.240.0

B. 255.255.248.0

C. 255.255.252.0

D. 255.255.254.0

72. You are the administrator for your company network. A user has called to inform you that they are having an issue with their computer. This user is a novice and does not really know their way around a computer. You want to use Quick Assist to take control of the computer remotely to troubleshoot the issue. What should you send to the user to initiate the remote session?

A. A connection file

B. An Easy Connect request

C. A numeric security code

D. A password

73. You are the administrator for your company network. The company uses Windows 10 Enterprise client computers. Users are currently unable to connect to the office from their home computers by using Remote Desktop. You need to make sure that the users can remotely connect from their home offices. What setting should you configure on the home computers so that the users won't be able to access other corporate network resources from their home computers?

A. You should configure the DirectAccess connection.

B. You should configure the Remote Desktop Gateway IP address.

C. You should configure the Remote Desktop local resources.

D. You should configure the virtual private network connection.

74. You are the administrator for your company network. You have two Windows 10 computers, named Computer1 and Computer2. You have an Azure Active Directory (Azure AD) user account named admin@mysite.com that is in the local Administrators group on each computer. You sign onto Computer1 by using the admin account. You need to ensure that you can use Event Viewer on Computer1 to connect to the event logs on Computer2. What should you do to be able to access those event logs?

A. Run the `Enable-PSRemoting` cmdlet on Computer1.

B. Run the `Enable-PSRemoting` cmdlet on Computer2.

C. Run the `winrm quickconfig` command on Computer1.

D. Run the `winrm quickconfig` command on Computer2.

75. You are the administrator for your company network. You and a colleague are discussing how to establish a Remote Assistance session using the command prompt. What command opens Windows Remote Assistance?

A. `connectnow.exe`

B. `mrsa.exe`

C. `msra.exe`

D. `remoteassist.exe`

76. You are the administrator for your company network. You are connecting to a router that has the IP address of 192.168.1.1 on a standard, default Class C network using a subnet mask of 255.255.255.0. Which of the following is a valid IP address for the network adapter?

A. 192.168.0.1

B. 192.168.1.1

C. 192.168.100.1

D. 192.168.1.100

77. You are the administrator for your company network. You and a colleague are discussing a setting that determines whether a Windows 10 system can locate other computers and devices on a network. What is this setting called?

A. Discovery

B. Network Detection

    C. Network Discovery

    D. Windows Locator

78. You are the administrator for your company network. You and a colleague are discussing using the ping command. Which of the following commands enables pinging your own computer to see whether it is operational?

    A. `ping 128.0.0.1`

    B. `ping localclient`

    C. `ping localhost`

    D. `ping network adapter`

79. You are the administrator for your company network. You and colleague are discussing the steps on how to connect a Windows 10 machine to a domain. What must be set up first to connect a computer to a network?

    A. Firewall

    B. Network access point

    C. Network interface card (NIC)

    D. Router

80. You are the administrator for your company network. You and a colleague are discussing configuring a network adapter. You open the network adapter properties to view and change configuration parameters of the adapter. Which tab lists the resource settings for the network adapter?

    A. The Advanced tab

    B. The Details tab

    C. The Driver tab

    D. The General tab

    E. The Resources tab

81. You are the administrator for your company network. You want to view a list of all the MAC addresses that a computer has connected to in the past. Which command should you use to view this list?

    A. `arp -a`

    B. `arp -s`

    C. `netstat -a`

    D. `ping 127.0.0.1`

82. You are the administrator for your company network. You and a colleague are discussing the different types of wireless network standards. When connecting 802.11a, 802.11b, and 802.11n wireless networks together, which wireless device will guarantee connectivity between these networks?

    A. A wireless bridge

    B. A wireless hub

C. A wireless network adapter

D. A wireless router

83. You are the administrator for your company network. You and a colleague are discussing troubleshooting a network adapter. What are some reasons why a network adapter may not be functioning properly? (Choose all that apply.)

   A. The network adapter is on the Hardware Compatibility List (HCL).

   B. The network adapter has outdated drivers.

   C. The network adapter is not recognized by Windows 10.

   D. The network adapter has been correctly configured.

84. You are the administrator for your company network. You and a colleague are discussing a Windows 10 feature that allows you to turn a computer into a wireless hotspot. What is this feature called?

   A. Hosted Network

   B. Mobile Hotspot

   C. Wi-Fi Network

   D. Wireless Spot

85. You are the administrator for your company network. You have several Windows 10 computers and laptops that have been connected to a wireless network. To make the wireless local area network (WLAN) more secure, which of the following tasks disallows additional client access to the wireless access point (WAP)?

   A. You should disable SSID broadcasting.

   B. You should disable WPA2.

   C. You should enable the channel bonding.

   D. You should enable the frame aggregation.

86. You are the administrator for your company network. You and a colleague are discussing a technology that allows you to run multiple operating systems concurrently on one computer. What is this technology called?

   A. It is called remote access.

   B. It is called a Terminal Server.

   C. It is called a virtual directory.

   D. It is called virtualization.

87. You are the administrator for your company network. You are setting up several computers on a classful network with a default subnet mask of 255.0.0.0. What class would be using this subnet mask?

   A. You are using a Class A subnet mask.

   B. You are using a Class B subnet mask.

   C. You are using a Class C subnet mask.

   D. You are using a Class D subnet mask.

88. You are the administrator for your company network. You want to set up 100 computers on a private Class A network. Which of the following IP network numbers meets all the criteria for a private Class A network?

A. 128.10.1.0

B. 192.168.1.0

C. 172.16.0.0

D. 10.0.0.0

89. You are the administrator for your company network. You and a colleague are discussing the different ways that you can access a computer on a network to fix an issue remotely. One of these ways allows you to take control of a computer's keyboard, video, and mouse. It does not require someone to be available on the remote machine, and any actions that are performed remotely will not be visible to the monitor. What is this tool called?

A. Easy Connect

B. PC Anywhere

C. Remote Assistance

D. Remote Desktop

90. You are the administrator for your company network. You and a colleague are discussing how to run Windows PowerShell commands on a remote computer. What is it called when you have the ability to run PowerShell on a remote machine?

A. PowerShell RemoteAccess

B. PowerShell Remoting

C. PowerShell Connection

D. Terminal Services

91. You are the administrator for your company network. You and a colleague are discussing an IPv6 link-state address. Which of the following represents the beginning of an IPv6 link-state address?

A. 127

B. 172

C. 2001

D. fe80

92. You are the administrator for your company network. A user contacts you to let you know that they cannot connect to the Internet. You examine the `ipconfig` results as shown here:

```
IPv4 Address. . . . . . . .: 10.254.254.1
Subnet Mask . . . . . . . : 255.255.255.0
Default Gateway . . . . . .: 10.254.254.255
```

What is most likely the cause of the issue given the `ipconfig` results?

A. The subnet mask is incorrect.

B. The IP address is incorrect.

    C. The default gateway is incorrect.

    D. The subnet mask and the IP address are incorrect.

93. You are the administrator for your company network. A user cannot connect to any websites. You examine the `ipconfig` results as shown here:

```
Windows IP Configuration
  Host Name . . . . . . . . . . : Computer1
  Primary Dns Suffix  . . . . . :
  Node Type . . . . . . . . . . : Hybrid
  IP Routing Enabled. . . . . . : No
  WINS Proxy Enabled. . . . . . : No
Ethernet adapter lan:
  Connection-specific DNS Suffix. :
  Description . . . . . . . . . : Intel(R) 82566DC-2 Gigabit Network
Connection
  Physical Address. . . . . . . : 00-1C-C0-A1-55-16
  DHCP Enabled. . . . . . . . . : No
  Autoconfiguration Enabled . . . : Yes
  IPv4 Address. . . . . . . . . : 10.254.254.105(Preferred)
  Subnet Mask . . . . . . . . . : 255.255.255.0
  Default Gateway . . . . . . . : 10.254.254.1
  DNS Servers . . . . . . . . . : 10.255.254.1
```

What could be the reason why this user cannot access the Internet?

    A. The computer has no IP address.

    B. The default gateway address is incorrect.

    C. The DNS server address is incorrect.

    D. The MAC address is incorrect.

94. You are the administrator for your company network. You and a colleague are discussing virtual private networks (VPNs). When you're configuring a VPN, L2TP uses what protocol for encryption?

    A. Internet Protocol Security (IPsec)

    B. Multi Protocol Encapsulation (MPE)

    C. Point-to-Point Tunneling Protocol (PPTP)

    D. Secure Socket Tunneling Protocol (SSTP)

95. You are the administrator for your company network. You are troubleshooting a network connectivity problem. A command is run, and the following results appear:

```
Request timed out.
Request timed out.
```

103. You are the administrator for your company network. You and a colleague are discussing Remote Desktop Connection. Which tab in the Remote Desktop Connection options is used to access local drives on the remote computer?

   A.   The General tab

   B.   The Display tab

   C.   The Local Resources tab

   D.   The Advanced tab

104. You are the administrator for your company network. The network is using the address 137.25.0.0; it is composed of 20 subnets, with a maximum of 300 hosts on each subnet. The company is on a merger-and-acquisitions spree, and your manager has told you to prepare for an increase to 50 subnets with some containing more than 600 hosts. Using the existing network address, which of the following subnet masks would work for this requirement?

   A.   255.255.240.0

   B.   255.255.248.0

   C.   255.255.252.0

   D.   255.255.254.0

105. You are the administrator for your company network. You have a Windows 10 machine that needs to be able to communicate with all computers on the internal network. The company decides to add 15 new segments to its IPv6 network. How should you configure the IPv6 address so that the server can communicate with all of the segments?

   A.   Configure the address as `fd00::2b0:e0ff:dee9:4143/8`.

   B.   Configure the address as `fe80::2b0:e0ff:dee9:4143/32`.

   C.   Configure the address as `ff80::2b0:e0ff:dee9:4143/64`.

   D.   Configure the address as `fe80::2b0:e0ff:dee9:4143/64`.

Chapter

4

Maintain Windows

THE MD-100 EXAM TOPICS COVERED IN THIS CHAPTER INCLUDE:

✓ **Domain 4: Maintain Windows**

- 4.1 Configure system and data recovery

    - Perform file recovery (including OneDrive)

    - Recover Windows 10

    - Troubleshoot startup/boot process

- 4.2 Manage updates

    - Check for updates

    - Troubleshoot updates

    - Validate and test updates

    - Select the appropriate servicing channel

    - Configure Windows update options

- 4.3 Monitor and manage Windows

    - Configure and analyze event logs

    - Manage performance

    - Manage Windows 10 environment

1. You are the administrator for your company network. You have a Windows 10 computer. What should you do if you want to use Windows Update but want to be able to change the settings manually?

    A. Modify the Windows Update settings from the Local Group Policy.

    B. On the Windows 10 computer, log on as a member of the Administrators group.

    C. Right-click the command prompt, select Run As Administrator, and then run Wuapp.exe.

    D. Right-click Windows Update and select Run As Administrator.

2. You are the administrator for your company network. You and a colleague are discussing the Advanced Boot Options menu in Windows 10 during the boot process. How do you access the Advanced Boot Options menu?

    A. Hold the Alt key down and click the Restart option.

    B. Hold the Shift key down and click the Restart option.

    C. Press F8.

    D. Press F10.

3. You are the administrator for your company network. You have a Windows 10 computer that has an application running. You want to collect data about the processor utilization used by the application. You decide to use Performance Monitor. You should monitor what performance object?

    A. You should monitor the Process performance object.

    B. You should monitor the Processor Performance performance object.

    C. You should monitor the Processor Information performance object.

    D. You should monitor the Processor performance object.

4. You are the administrator for your company network. You have a Windows 10 computer. You use Windows Backup and Restore to create a backup image. You need to perform a complete restore of the computer. What is one way to begin the restore?

    A. Open the Windows Backup and Restore Center and click Advanced Restore.

    B. Open the Windows Backup and Restore Center and click Restore Computer.

    C. Start your computer. From the Advanced Boot Options menu, select Last Known Good Configuration.

    D. Start the computer by using the Windows 10 installation media. Select Repair Your Computer.

5. You are the administrator for your company network. You are installing Windows 10 on a new computer. You update the video card driver and restart the computer. When the computer starts, the screen flickers and then goes blank. You restart the computer, and the screen goes blank again. What should you do first if you need to configure the video card driver?

    A. You should insert the Windows 10 installation media into the computer, restart the computer, and use System Recovery to perform a startup repair.

    B. You should restart the computer in Debugging Mode.

C. You should restart the computer in low-resolution video mode.

D. You should restart the computer in Safe Mode.

6. You are the administrator for your company network. A user is attempting to start a Windows 10 computer and receives an error message indicating that the "BOOTMGR is missing." You want to fix this issue. You start the computer in recovery mode. What command should you run next?

   A. Bootrec /RebuiltBcd

   B. Bootrec /ScanNow

   C. Diskpart /FixMbr

   D. Sfc /ScanNow

7. You are the administrator for your company network. The company has a main office and a branch office that are connected using a WAN link. The main office provides access to the Internet. The branch office has about 30 Windows 10 computers that contain small hard drives with little free space left. What should you do to prevent the branch office computers from downloading updates from peers on the network?

   A. You should configure the computers to use BranchCache in hosted cache mode.

   B. You should configure the network connections as metered connections.

   C. You should configure the updates to use the Semi-Annual Channel (Targeted) channel.

   D. You should modify the Delivery Optimizations settings from the Settings app.

8. You are the administrator for your company network. You want to make sure that you can recover system configuration and data if a computer's hard disk fails. What should you do?

   A. You should create a backup of all file categories.

   B. You should create a Backup and Restore image.

   C. You should create a system restore point.

   D. You should perform an Automated System Recovery (ASR) backup.

9. You are the administrator for your company network. You have a Windows 10 computer that has been working fine; however, there is a newer version of a network adapter driver available. You download and install the newer driver. After you load the driver, the network device stops working correctly. What tool can you use to help fix the computer?

   A. You can use the Driver Repair utility.

   B. You can use the Driver Rollback utility.

   C. You can use the Reverse Driver application.

   D. You can use the Windows 10 Driver Compatibility tool.

10. You are the administrator for your company network. You have a Windows 10 computer that has BitLocker Drive Encryption (BitLocker) enabled on all volumes. You start the computer from the Windows Recovery Environment (WinRE). What should you do if you need to read the data on the system drive?

   A. You should run cipher with the /adduser parameter.

   B. You should run cipher with the /rekey parameter.

    C.   You should run `manange-bde` with the `-off` parameter.

    D.   You should run `manage-bde` with the `-unlock` parameter.

11. You are the administrator for your company network. You and a colleague are discussing data recovery strategies. You want to be able to back up all data files and folders in the `C:\Data` folder, to restore individual files and folders in `C:\Data`, and to ensure that data is backed up to and restored from external media. What utility should you use to meet your requirements?

    A.   You should use the Backup and Restore utility to back up and restore files.

    B.   You should use the NTBackup utility to back up and restore individual files and folders.

    C.   You should use the Previous Versions tab to restore the files and folders.

    D.   You should use the System Restore feature to perform backup and restore operations.

12. You are the administrator for your company network. Your company purchases several new laptop computers that use a new hardware platform. You install Windows 10 onto the new laptops while in a testing environment. Some of these computers are frequently generating stop errors. What should you use to identify what is causing the stop errors?

    A.   You should use Performance Monitor.

    B.   You should use Reliability Monitor.

    C.   You should use System Configuration.

    D.   You should use Task Manager.

13. You are the administrator for your company network. You are planning on migrating the network to Windows 10. What Windows 10 application should you use if you'd like to perform the following tasks?

    ▪   Be able to collect data from local or remote Windows 10 computers on the network. You can collect data from a single computer or multiple computers at the same time.

    ▪   Be able to view the data as it is being collected in real time or historically.

    A.   You should use Computer Monitor.

    B.   You should use Event Viewer.

    C.   You should use Performance Monitor.

    D.   You should use Windows Monitor.

14. You are the administrator for your company network. You have a Windows 10 computer. You can start the computer, but you cannot log in. What should you do if you need to start the computer using the Windows Recovery Environment (WinRE)?

    A.   From the login screen, hold down the Shift key and then click Restart.

    B.   Hold down the Ctrl+Alt+Delete keys for 10 seconds.

C. Turn off the computer. Then turn the computer back on and press F8.

D. Turn off the computer. Then turn the computer back on and press F10.

15. You are the administrator for your company network. You have a Windows 10 computer. You have a full backup of this computer on an external USB drive that is stored off-site. Using File Explorer, you deleted several files from your personal Microsoft OneDrive account. You then emptied the Recycle Bin on the computer. What should you use if you want to be able to recover files two months after you deleted them using the least amount of time possible?

A. You should use the OneDrive Recycle Bin.

B. You should use the full backup on the external USB drive.

C. You should use Recovery in the Settings app.

D. The files cannot be recovered.

16. You are the administrator for your company network. Your domain contains several Windows 10 computers. On one computer, named Computer1, you are planning on creating a collector-initiated subscription to collect the event logs from the Windows 10 computers. You want to configure the environment to support the event log collection. What should you do? (Choose two.)

A. On Computer1, add Computer1 to the Event Log Readers group.

B. On Computer1, enable Windows Remote Management (WinRM).

C. On the Windows 10 computers, add Computer1 to the Event Log Readers group.

D. On the Windows 10 computers, change the Startup Type setting of Windows Event Collector to Automatic.

E. On the Windows 10 computers, enable Windows Remote Management (WinRM).

17. You are the administrator for your company network. Your users use Windows 10 devices. Your Marketing users travel to locations where there may be limited, expensive bandwidth for extended periods of time. What should you do if you want to prevent all Windows updates from downloading while the Marketing users are on the road, while at the same time not interrupting their ability to receive emails or access the Internet?

A. Set a data limit from Network & Internet in the Settings app.

B. Set the network connections as metered connections from Network & Internet in the Settings app.

C. Turn on Pause Updates from Update & Security in the Settings app.

D. You cannot stop the Windows updates from running.

18. You are the administrator for your company network. You have a Windows 10 machine, and you want to update the video drivers. What should you do to update the video drivers?

A. You should install new drivers using Device Manager.

B. You should install new drivers using Driver Manager.

C. You should upgrade the drivers using Device Manager.

D. You should upgrade the drivers using Driver Manager.

19. You are the administrator for your company network. A Windows 10 Enterprise client machine has a system drive and a data drive. You are getting ready to back up the computer before installing new software. You must meet the following requirements:

- From within Windows, the system disk from the backup must be mountable.
- The system disk from the backup must be bootable.
- The backup must be able to be restored in the event of a hard disk failure.
- The backup must contain data from both hard disk drives.

What backup method should you implement to meet your requirements?

A. You should implement File History.

B. You should implement a storage pool.

C. You should implement a system image.

D. You should implement a system repair disk.

20. You are the administrator for your company network. You have a Windows 10 computer that you enable File History on. What should you do if you want to protect a folder named D:\MyFolder using File History?

A. Add D:\MyFolder to the Documents folder from File Explorer.

B. Configure the Recovery settings from the Settings app.

C. Configure the Select Drive settings from File History in Control Panel.

D. Modify the Security settings of D:\MyFolder from File Explorer.

21. You are the administrator for your company network. You and a colleague are discussing a Microsoft utility that allows you to collect information in a log and analyze the data in real time. What is this utility called?

A. Disk Cleanup

B. Event Viewer

C. Performance Monitor

D. Resource Monitor

22. You are the administrator for your company network. You have a Windows 10 computer. You test Windows updates on the computer before making the updates available to all of the other corporate users. One of the updates has a conflict with a device driver. What should you do if you need to remove the update from the computer?

A. Revert the system state to a restore point that was created before the update was installed using System Restore.

B. Run the vmic qfe delete command from an elevated command prompt.

C. Run the wusa.exe command with the /uninstall parameter from an elevated command prompt.

D. Nothing can be done to remove the update.

23. You are the administrator for your company network. You deploy Windows 10 onto a computer that contains a folder named C:\MyFolder. The folder contains several documents. What should you do so that you can recover the files in the folder by using the Previous Versions tab?

A. Enable File History and add the folder to File History.

B. Enable File History and add the folder to the Documents folder.

C. Set up Backup and Restore (Windows 7) and add the folder to the backup.

D. You cannot recover documents using the Previous Version tab.

24. You are the administrator for your company network. A computer uses a SCSI adapter that supports a SCSI drive. This drive contains the Windows 10 system and the boot partition. After updating the SCSI driver, you restart the computer, but it loads with errors. What should you do first if you need to get this computer running properly without errors?

A. You should restore the computer's configuration with the last backup.

B. You should boot the computer with the System Image reload.

C. You should boot the computer and perform a driver rollback.

D. You should boot the computer to the Recovery Console and manually copy the old driver back to the computer.

25. You are the administrator for your company network. You and a colleague are discussing the output modes for Performance Monitor. What are the three output modes for Performance Monitor? (Choose three.)

A. Graph View

B. Histogram View

C. Line View

D. Report View

26. You are the administrator for your company network. You have several Windows 10 computers. You have a Windows Server Update Services (WSUS) server. What settings should you do if you want to configure the computers to install the updates using WSUS?

A. Configure Automatic Updates.

B. Configure auto-restart reminder notifications for updates.

C. Specify Engaged Restart Transition And Notification Schedule For Updates.

D. Specify the intranet Microsoft update service location.

27. You are the administrator for your company network. You have a Windows 10 computer that has two volumes, C: and D:. Both of the volumes are formatted using the NTFS file system. What should you do if you need to disable Previous Versions on the D: volume?

A. Convert the hard disk drive that contains the D: volume from the Disk Management snap-in volume to Dynamic.

B. Modify the Quota settings from the properties of the D: volume.

C. Modify the Sharing settings from the properties of the D: volume.

D. Modify the System Protection settings from System Properties.

28. You are the administrator for your company network. You have a Windows 10 computer that is used to test new Windows features. You want to configure this computer to receive preview builds of Windows 10 as soon as they are available. In the Settings app, what should you configure from Update & Security to set this up?

A. You should configure Delivery Optimization.

B. You should configure For Developers.

C. You should configure Windows Insider Program.

D. You should configure Windows Update.

29. You are the administrator for your company network. You have a computer that runs Windows 10. On this computer, you discover that Windows updates are failing to install. You want to generate a log file that contains detailed information regarding the failures. What cmdlet should you run?

A. You should run the `Get-LogProperties` cmdlet.

B. You should run the `Get-WindowsErrorReporting` cmdlet.

C. You should run the `Get-WinEvent` cmdlet.

D. You should run the `Get-WindowsUpdateLog` cmdlet.

30. You are the administrator for your company network. You have a Microsoft Azure Active Directory (Azure AD) tenant. Some of the users use Windows Hello for Business to sign in to their computers. You purchase a new computer and join the computer to the Azure AD. When the new user attempts to configure the sign-in options, they receive an error message stating that "Some settings are hidden or managed by your organization." You open Device Manager and confirm that all of the hardware is working correctly. What should you do first if you need to ensure that the user can use Windows Hello for Business facial recognition to sign in to the computer?

A. You should purchase an infrared (IR) camera.

B. You should upgrade the computer to Windows 10 Enterprise.

C. You should enable UEFI Secure Boot.

D. You should install a virtual TPM driver.

31. You are the administrator for your company network. You have a Windows 10 computer that has File History turned on. You have files that are located in a folder called D:\ Photos. What should you do if you want to ensure that you can recover previous versions of the files in the folder?

A. Add the folder, D:\Photos, to the Pictures folder.

B. Enable sharing for the folder, D:\Photos.

C. Modify the Recovery settings in the Settings app.

D. Turn on System Protection for drive D:.

32. You are the administrator for your company network. You and a colleague are discussing the creation of restore points. Which of the following are times when a restore point should be created? (Choose all that apply.)

A. Before installing applications or drivers

B. Before significant system events

C. Before System Restore is used to restore files, in the event that the changes need to be undone

D. Manually upon request

33. You are the administrator for your company network. You have a Windows 10 computer that is configured to install updates using Windows Server Update Services (WSUS). Microsoft releases a new update that is not approved in WSUS. What should you do if you want to install this update onto the computer?

A. Clear the Defer Upgrades checkbox and then Check For Updates.

B. From Microsoft Updates, click Check Online For Updates and then Check For Updates.

C. Run `gpupdate /force /sync` from a command prompt.

D. Using Windows PowerShell, run the `Get-WindowsUpdateLog` cmdlet and then run the `Update-Module` cmdlet.

34. You are the administrator for your company network. You and a colleague are discussing the creation of restore points. Restore points are created automatically every how many days?

A. 2

B. 5

C. 7

D. 14

35. You are the administrator for your company network. You are planning on installing a new application. Prior to installing the new application, you want to back up the existing data on the computer. You also need to make sure that you are able to recover individual files that are replaced or deleted during the installation. What should you do?

A. In the Backup And Restore Center window, click the Back Up Now button.

B. In the Backup And Restore Center window, click the Back Up Computer button.

C. You should create a system restore point.

D. You should perform an Automated System Recovery (ASR) backup and restore.

36. You are the administrator for your company network. You have a Windows 10 Enterprise computer that has File History and System Protection turned on for the C: drive. You accidentally press the Delete key on the keyboard, deleting a folder on the C: drive. What is the easiest way to recover this folder?

A. Use a manually selected restore point

B. Use File History

C. Use the latest restore point

D. Use the Recycle Bin

37. You are the administrator for your company network. You have a Windows 10 computer. You decide to install a second hard drive on the computer and create a new volume. What should you use if you want to enable System Protection for the new volume?

A. You should use the Settings app.

B. You should use System Properties.

C. You should use the wbadmin command.

D. You should use the Windows PowerShell Set-Volume cmdlet.

38. You are the administrator for your company network. On a USB memory drive, you have a Windows To Go workspace. When you attempt to start a computer using the USB, you receive an error message that states, "Your PC/Device needs to be repaired. The application or operating system couldn't be loaded because a required file is missing or contains errors." What should you do to repair the Windows To Go workspace?

A. On the USB memory drive, reapply the Windows To Go image.

B. Using a recovery disk, restart the computer and perform a system restore.

C. Restart the computer and then select the Last Known Good Configuration.

D. Restart the computer in Safe Mode and then perform a system restore.

39. You are the administrator for your company network. You are performing maintenance on a computer. You open Indexing Options and then click Pause. You then finish the maintenance. What should you do to resume indexing?

A. From the Services console, restart the Indexing Options service.

B. From the Services console, restart the Storage Service service.

C. From the Services console, restart the Windows Search service.

D. Sign out of Windows and then sign back in.

40. You are the administrator for your company network. You have a Windows 10 computer that has a 1 TB volume. What tool should you use if you want to receive a notification when the volume has less than 100 GB of free space left?

A. You should use Event Viewer.

B. You should use Performance Monitor.

C. You should use Resource Monitor.

D. You should use System Configuration.

41. You are the administrator for your company network. You have a Windows 10 computer that has the following local users:

User1: Administrators

User2: Event Log Readers

User3: Device Owners

User4: Power Users

User5: Users

Which users can analyze the security event logs? (Choose all that apply.)

- **A.** User1
- **B.** User2
- **C.** User3
- **D.** User4
- **E.** User5

42. You are the administrator for your company network. You have a Windows 10 computer that has the following local users:

User1: Administrators

User2: Event Log Readers

User3: Device Owners

User4: Power Users

User5: Users

Which users can analyze the system event logs? (Choose all that apply.)

- **A.** User1
- **B.** User2
- **C.** User3
- **D.** User4
- **E.** User5

43. You are the administrator for your company network. You have a Windows 10 computer that has File History turned on. You create a new folder on the D: drive. What should you do to protect a new folder using File History?

- **A.** You should configure the Backup settings using the Settings app.
- **B.** You should configure the Recovery settings using the Settings app.
- **C.** You should configure the Select drive settings using File History in Control Panel.
- **D.** You should modify the General settings of the folder using File Explorer.

44. You are the administrator for your company network. A user, User1, is a member of the local Administrators group on two computers, Computer1 and Computer2. The user cannot access the Event Viewer logs on Computer2 from Computer1. However, using Computer Management, the user can connect to Computer2 remotely. What should you do if you need to make sure that the user can use Event Viewer on Computer1 to remotely view the event logs on Computer2?

A. You should modify the Microsoft Defender Firewall settings on Computer2.

B. You should start the Remote Registry services on Computer2.

C. Run the `Enable-PSRemoting` cmdlet on Computer1.

D. You should run `winrm quick config` on Computer2.

45. You are the administrator for your company network. You have a Windows 10 computer for which you have just upgraded the network adapter driver. You notice that after the upgrade, you cannot access network resources. You open Device Manager and see a warning symbol next to the network adapter. What should you do if you need to restore access to the network resources?

A. You should assign a static IP address to the network adapter.

B. You should disable the network adapter and scan for hardware changes.

C. You should roll back the network adapter driver.

D. You should uninstall the network adapter and scan for hardware changes.

46. You are the administrator for your company network. An employee reports that during the past week his computer has been running slower than usual. What tool should you use if you want to identify any application failures that have occurred during the past week?

A. You should use Performance Monitor.

B. You should use Reliability Monitor.

C. You should use Resource Monitor.

D. You should use Task Manager.

47. You are the administrator for your company network. You have an application running that is causing issues. You open Task Manager and want to stop the application from running. What tab do you use in Task Manager to stop the application from running?

A. The Details tab

B. The Options tab

C. The Performance tab

D. The Users tab

48. You are the administrator for your company network. You have a new Windows 10 computer. You have a document that is stored on Microsoft OneDrive. Using File Explorer, you try to open the document but discover that the file is corrupt. What should you use if you need to access a previous version of the document?

A. Backup and Restore (Windows 7)

B. File History

   C. OneDrive online

   D. The Recycle Bin

49. You are the administrator for your company network. You have a Windows 10 Professional computer. You receive a SMART alert that the hard disk on this computer will soon be failing. You connect an external hard disk to the computer. What should you use if you need to create a backup that you can use to restore the operating system and the user documents from the external drive?

   A. `Start-OB Backup`

   B. `Start-WB Backup`

   C. `vssadmin.exe`

   D. `wbadmin.exe`

50. You are the administrator for your company network. Your company has a shared OneDrive for Business location that has video files that are used for training purposes. When a user attends a training session, they synchronize the files from the OneDrive location to their computers. A user is fired and in retaliation deletes all of the files that were located on the local machine, causing all of the files on OneDrive for Business and synchronized files for all users to be deleted. The user also emptied out the Recycle Bin on the local machine. What should you do to restore all the deleted video files?

   A. You should restore the files from another computer's Recycle Bin.

   B. You should restore the files from the OneDrive for Business Recycle Bin.

   C. You should restore the files from the second-stage OneDrive for Business Recycle Bin.

   D. You should restore the files by using the `Clear-RecycleBin` Windows PowerShell cmdlet.

51. You are the administrator for your company network. You are trying out an application on your computer. However, you decide that it's not exactly what you were looking for, so you attempt to uninstall the application. The application fails to uninstall. What should you do if you want to remove the unwanted application from the computer while preserving the user data and other installed applications?

   A. You should perform a driver rollback.

   B. You should use the Reset This PC option.

   C. You should perform a restore by using File History.

   D. You should restore from a System Restore point.

52. You are the administrator for your company network. You have a Windows 10 Enterprise computer that has a OneDrive synchronized folder that contains .pdf files. What should you do if you need to ensure that you can restore previous versions of these files?

   A. You should configure the computer as a trusted computer.

   B. You should configure System Restore.

   C. You should enable File History.

   D. You should enable Sync Your Settings on the computer.

53. You are the administrator for your company network. You are running Windows 10 machines and a few Windows Server 2019 machines throughout the network. You want to use Event Viewer to review event logs for Critical and Error events only. What should you do if you need to see all of these events from the logs?

  A. Use the Administrative Events view.

  B. Create a custom view and choose Administrative Events.

  C. Create a custom view and select Critical, Error, and Verbose for all logs.

  D. Perform a search on the system log for all of the required events.

54. You are the administrator for your company network. You have a Windows 10 computer that is taking a long time to start. What tool should you use if you want to identify what applications might be causing the greatest delays when starting this computer?

  A. You should use Performance Monitor.

  B. You should use Resource Monitor.

  C. You should use System Configuration.

  D. You should use Task Manager.

55. You are the administrator for your company network. You are running Windows 10 machines and a few Windows Server 2019 machines throughout the network. On a Windows 10 machine, you want to collect performance data for a specified period of three weeks. In the data collected, you want the CPU utilization, disk utilization, and memory utilization included. What should you do to accomplish this?

  A. You should create a custom performance set.

  B. You should create a session Data Collector Set.

  C. You should create a Trace event.

  D. You should create a User-Defined Data Collector Set.

56. You are the administrator for your company network. A few users have indicated that a particular application is taking too long to load. You use Performance Monitor to create a baseline report for one of the computers. You monitor the processor, the disk subsystem, and the network subsystem. You notice that the disk subsystem has a high load of activity. What other subsystem should you also monitor prior to knowing for sure if there is a disk subsystem bottleneck?

  A. You should also monitor the Application counters.

  B. You should also monitor the Memory counters.

  C. You should also monitor the Network counters.

  D. You should also monitor the Processor counters.

57. You are the administrator for your company network. You and a colleague are discussing the best ways to monitor performance. What is it called when you monitor performance over a given period of time?

  A. A baseline

  B. A computer precedent

C. An event criterion

D. A paradigm

58. You are the administrator for your company network. You have a computer that is running Windows 10. This system is used within the corporate network. You go to the Settings app and view the connection properties. It shows the following:

- The Network profile is set to Public.

- The Metered connection is set to On.

What must you do first if you want to ensure that Microsoft OneDrive syncs on this computer?

A. Set the Network profile to Private.

B. Run `winrm qc` at the command prompt.

C. Turn off the metered connection.

D. Set up Microsoft OneDrive syncs.

59. You are the administrator for your company network. You and a colleague are discussing Event Viewer. You open Event Viewer and notice that you have an informational event. What is the icon representing an information event?

A. Red circle with a white "i" in it

B. Red circle with a white "x" in it

C. Yellow triangle with a black "!" in it

D. White circle with a blue "i" in it

60. You are the administrator for your company network. You have a large number of Windows 10 computers. All of the computers in the network are joined to Microsoft Azure Active Directory (Azure AD). All of the computers are configured differently in terms of update settings. Some of the computers are configured for manual updates. You want to configure Windows Update for these machines. You must meet the following requirements:

- The computers must be managed from a central location.

- You must minimize traffic across the Internet.

- You must keep costs to a minimum.

What Windows Update technology should you use to meet your requirements?

A. Microsoft System Center Configuration Manager (SCCM)

B. Windows Server Update Service (WSUS)

C. Windows Update for Business

D. Windows Update Management Center

61. You are the administrator for your company network. You have a large number of Windows 10 computers. All of the computers in the network are joined to Microsoft Azure Active Directory (Azure AD). All of the computers are configured differently in terms of update settings. Some of the computers are configured for manual updates. You want to configure Windows Update for these machines. You must meet the following requirements:

- The computers must be managed from a central location.

- You must minimize traffic across the Internet.

- You must keep costs to a minimum.

You are setting up Windows Update. How should you manage the traffic?

A. You should use BranchCache.

B. You should use Client Peer Cache.

C. You should use Delivery Optimization.

D. You should use Peer Cache.

62. You are the administrator for your company network. You have a Windows 10 computer that has four disk drives installed. They are as follows:

- Drive1 is a 500 GB OS volume.

- Drive2 is a 400 GB data volume.

- Drive3 is a 400 GB empty volume.

- Drive4 is a 500 GB empty volume.

Using Storage Spaces, you want to minimize data loss by creating a two-way mirror. What drives should you incorporate?

A. You should use Drive1 and Drive2.

B. You should use Drive1 and Drive4.

C. You should use Drive2 and Drive3.

D. You should use Drive3 and Drive4.

63. You are the administrator for your company network. You have a Windows 10 computer. You create a task named MyTask, which is attached to the following event:

Log: System

Source: Kernel-General

Event ID: 16

The task is not showing the results you want. What tool do you use if you want to modify the settings of the task?

A. You should use the Event Viewer.

B. You should use the Settings app.

C. You should use System Configuration.

D. You should use the Task Scheduler.

64. You are the administrator for your company network. You and a colleague are discussing the output modes for Performance Monitor. You view the output mode, as shown in the following graphic.

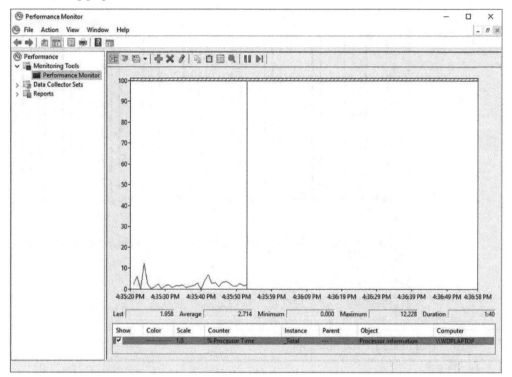

What output mode are you observing?

A. Graph view

B. Histogram Bar view

C. Line view

D. Report view

65. You are the administrator for your company network. You and a colleague are discussing the output modes for Performance Monitor. You view the output mode, as shown in the following graphic.

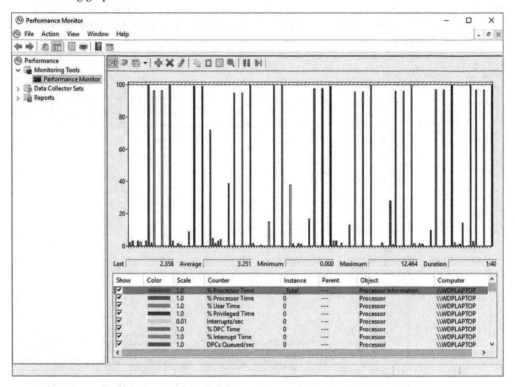

What output mode are you observing?

A. Graph view

B. Histogram Bar view

C. Line view

D. Report view

66. You are the administrator for your company network. You and a colleague are discussing offline OneDrive files and folders statuses. You open File Explorer and see an icon showing two blue arrows forming a circle. What does this symbol represent?

A. It is in sync with the online version.

B. It is syncing.

C. It is out of sync.

D. This icon is not used with OneDrive.

67. You are the administrator for your company network. You and a colleague are discussing offline OneDrive files and folders statuses. You open File Explorer and see an icon showing a green circle with a green check mark inside of it. What does this symbol represent?

A. It is in sync with the online version.

B. It is syncing.

C. It is out of sync.

D. This icon is not used with OneDrive.

68. You are the administrator for your company network. You and a colleague are discussing offline OneDrive files and folders statuses. You open File Explorer and see an icon showing a red circle with a red X inside of it. What does this symbol represent?

A. It is in sync with the online version.

B. It is syncing.

C. It is out of sync.

D. This icon is not used with OneDrive.

69. You are the administrator for your company network. You and a colleague are discussing services. You want to determine what action to take if a service fails to load. What tab would you use to set this up?

A. The Dependencies tab

B. The General tab

C. The Log On tab

D. The Recovery tab

70. You are the administrator for your company network. You have a Windows 10 computer that is infected by a virus. You are trying to access the Settings app, but unfortunately you cannot access it due to the virus. You want to restart the computer and ensure that the computer can display the advanced startup options when the computer restarts. What are two possible ways to achieve this goal? (Choose two.)

A. From the Start menu, using Power On, hold down the Shift key while selecting Restart.

B. Run `shutdown /r /o` from a command prompt.

C. Using System Configuration, select Safe Boot, select minimal, and then click Restart from the Start menu.

D. Using System Configuration, select Selective Startup and then click Restart from the Start menu.

71. You are the administrator for your company network. You have a Windows 10 Enterprise computer. You are planning to install the most recent updates to this computer. You want to ensure that you can revert to the current state in the event that the computer becomes unresponsive after the update. What should you do?

A. From the Accounts section of the Settings app, use the Sync Your Settings option.

B. From the Computer Settings, use the Refresh Your Computer option.

C. From the Control Panel, use the Backup And Restore (Windows 7) option.

D. From the Recovery section of the Settings app, use the Reset This Computer option.

72. You are the administrator for your company network. You have a Windows 10 computer that has File History enabled. You notice that the previous versions of a particular document is unavailable in the Previous Versions tab. You need to make sure that previous versions of the file are created. What can you do? (Choose all that apply.)

    A. Add the folder in which the file is located to the Documents folder.

    B. Create a backup of the drive in which the file is located by using Backup and Restore (Windows 7).

    C. Turn on system protection for the drive in which the file is located.

    D. Using the Settings app, modify the Backup settings.

73. You are the administrator for your company network. You have a Windows 10 computer that has two volumes named C and D. The C volume is formatted as NTFS, and the D volume is formatted with exFAT. What should you use if you want to ensure that you can recover files stored in a folder on the D drive?

    A. You should use Backup and Restore (Windows 7).

    B. You should use File History.

    C. You should use System Restore points.

    D. You should use wbadmin.exe.

74. You are the administrator for your company network. Your network contains an Active Directory domain that contains a Windows Server 2016 server, named Server1, and a Windows 10 computer, named Computer1. The server contains a share called Backup. All of the network users can read and write data to the share. At 13:00 on Monday, you configure Backup and Restore (Windows 7) on Computer1 with the following settings:

    ▪ Backup Destination: \\Server1\Backup

    ▪ What do you want to back up? Local Disk (D:)

    ▪ Include a system image of drives: System Reserved (C:)

    ▪ Schedule: Daily at 23:00

    You want to identify how many backups will be available on Thursday at 17:00. How many backups will be created for the Local Disk (D:) drive?

    A. One backup that uses ZIP files

    B. One backup that uses VHDX files

    C. Three backups that use ZIP files

    D. Three backups that use VHDX files

75. You are the administrator for your company network. Your network contains an Active Directory domain that contains a Windows Server 2016 server, named Server1, and a Windows 10 computer, named Computer1. The server contains a share called Backup. All of the network users can read and write data to the share. At 13:00 on Monday, you configure Backup and Restore (Windows 7) on Computer1 with the following settings:

    ▪ Backup Destination: \\Server1\Backup

    ▪ What do you want to back up? Local Disk (D:)

- Include a system image of drives: System Reserved (C:)
- Schedule: Daily at 23:00

You want to identify how many backups will be available on Thursday at 17:00. How many system image backups of the C drive?

A. One backup that uses ZIP files

B. One backup that uses VHDX files

C. Three backups that use ZIP files

D. Three backups that use VHDX files

76. You are the administrator for your company network. During the boot process, you want to see what is being loaded. Using the Advanced Boot Options menu, you have enabled boot logging. Where will the log file be stored?

A. The log file will be stored as \Windows\Bootlog.txt.

B. The log file will be stored as \Windows\Logging.txt.

C. The log file will be stored as \Windows\Ntbtlog.txt.

D. The log file will be stored as \Windows\Startup.txt.

77. You are the administrator for your company network. You and a colleague are discussing Safe Mode. Safe Mode runs at what screen resolution?

A. It runs at 640 × 480.

B. It runs at 800 × 600.

C. It runs at 1024 × 768.

D. It runs at 1280 × 1024.

78. You are the administrator for your company network. You and a colleague are discussing system protection. What should you do if you want a Windows 10 machine to retain only the last System Protection snapshot?

A. Disable Shadow Copies and then run System Protection.

B. Run Disk Cleanup For System Restore and then run Shadow Copies.

C. Enable Shadow Copies and set the Keep Only Last Shadow Copy option.

D. In System Protection, set the Keep Only Last Shadow Copy option.

79. You are the administrator for your company network. You have a Windows 10 computer. You configure a backup job to back up all the files and folders onto an external NTFS hard drive. The backup fails to back up all of the files that have the encryption attribute set. What should you do if you want to back up all encrypted files while keeping the files encrypted?

A. Add the certificate of the local administrator account to the list of users who can transparently access the files and schedule the backup.

B. Enable Volume Shadow Copy on the external drive and schedule the backup.

    C. Manually copy the encrypted files to the external hard disk drive.

    D. Schedule the backup to occur when you are not logged on to the computer.

80. You are the administrator for your company network. A user has informed you that their Windows 10 computer will not boot because of missing or corrupted system files. The machine is not able to boot into Safe Mode. What tool can you use to replace the corrupted system file?

    A. System Restore

    B. Startup Repair

    C. System Image Recovery

    D. Uninstall Updates

81. You are the administrator for your company network. You have a several hundred Windows 10 computers. These computers use low-bandwidth metered Internet connections. When downloading updates, you want to decrease the amount of Internet usage that these machines utilize. What should you configure?

    A. You should configure Delivery Optimization.

    B. You should configure distributed cache mode in BranchCache.

    C. You should configure hosted mode in BranchCache.

    D. You should configure Privacy Settings.

82. You are the administrator for your company network. You and a colleague are discussing configuring Windows Update. What app do you utilize to configure Windows Update?

    A. Use Personalization to configure Windows Update.

    B. Use Restore Hidden Updates to configure Windows Update.

    C. Use Settings to configure Windows Update.

    D. Use View Update History to configure Windows Update.

83. You are the administrator for your company network. You and a colleague are discussing the different update types available from Microsoft. One update affects the Microsoft operating systems and the possibility of allowing an attacker to gain access onto the network through a loophole. What type of updates should you install to help prevent this type of attack?

    A. Critical Updates

    B. Definition Updates

    C. Security Updates

    D. Software Updates

84. You are the administrator for your company network. You and a colleague are discussing the Windows Startup settings. What function key will launch Enable Safe Mode with Command Prompt?

    A. F2

    B. F4

C. F6

D. F8

85. You are the administrator for your company network. You have a new computer that you have recently installed Windows 10 onto. What is one method to use if you want to check to see whether there are any available updates that need to be installed?

    A. The Check For Updates option

    B. The Does My Computer Need To Be Updated option

    C. The Restore Hidden Updates option

    D. The View Update History option

86. You are the administrator for your company network. You and a colleague are conferring about how Microsoft processes updates and when they become available to be released to the public. Updates are typically released on a certain day of the week. What is this day of the week referred to when updates are released?

    A. Maintenance Mondays

    B. Patch Tuesdays

    C. Update Wednesdays

    D. Fixed Fridays

87. You are the administrator for your company network. You have an application running that is causing issues. You open Task Manager and want to see what services are currently running on the computer. What tab do you use in Task Manager to stop a service from running?

    A. The Details tab

    B. The Services tab

    C. The Performance tab

    D. The Users tab

88. You are the administrator for your company network. You and a colleague are discussing Windows built-in utilities. Which utility will help delete unnecessary files from a computer?

    A. Disk Cleanup

    B. Disk Defragmenter

    C. Registry Editor

    D. Task Scheduler

89. You are the administrator for your company network. You and a colleague are discussing the Windows 10 Security And Maintenance screen. Which of the following is not a part of the Maintenance section?

    A. Check for solutions to problem reports

    B. Drive status

    C. HomeGroup

    D. Virus protection

90. You are the administrator for your company network. You and a colleague are discussing the Windows 10 Security And Maintenance screen. If the Security and Maintenance section discovers an issue that requires immediate attention, what does the icon display?

   A. A green box

   B. An orange flashing triangle

   C. A red circle with a white X

   D. A yellow triangle with a black exclamation point

91. You are the administrator for your company network. You and a colleague are discussing a built-in utility in Windows 10 that helps improve a computer's performance by moving sectors of data on the hard disk. What is this utility called?

   A. Disk Cleanup

   B. Disk Defragmenter

   C. Registry Editor

   D. Task Scheduler

92. You are the administrator for your company network. You and a colleague are discussing the Windows 10 built-in utility called Disk Defragmenter. By default, how often is this utility set to run?

   A. Biweekly

   B. Every day

   C. Once a month

   D. Once a week

93. You are the administrator for your company network. You and a colleague are discussing viruses and how they affect computer systems. You want to check your systems for malicious software without using a third-party tool. Windows 10 provides a utility that helps remove malicious components from Windows 10 systems. What is this utility called?

   A. Malicious Software Removal Tool (MSRT)

   B. Virus Software Removal Tool (VSRT)

   C. Microsoft Defender

   D. Windows Firewall

94. You are the administrator for your company network. You and a colleague are discussing the Windows 10 Task Scheduler. When using this tool, which command will create a task by using a wizard?

   A. Create Basic Task

   B. Create Scheduled Task

   C. Create Task

   D. Create Task Automatically

95. You are the administrator for your company network. You and a colleague are discussing Windows 10 Servicing options. One of these servicing options receives updates once Microsoft makes them available to the public. Which option is it?

    A. Long-Term Servicing Channel

    B. Semi-Annual Channel (Targeted)

    C. Semi-Annual Channel

    D. Short-Term Servicing Channel

96. You are the administrator for your company network. You and colleague are discussing Microsoft's Patch Tuesdays. There is one program that is typically updated the second Tuesday of every month. Which program is updated frequently?

    A. Microsoft Defender

    B. The Microsoft website

    C. The Windows Firewall

    D. The Malicious Software Removal Tool

97. You are the administrator for your company network. You and a colleague are discussing backups. Backups can be stored on which of the following devices or media? (Choose all that apply.)

    A. On a CD/DVD

    B. On the same drive on which you are backing up

    C. On a USB

    D. On external hard drives

    E. On the network

98. You are the administrator for your company network. You and a colleague are discussing System Protection and restore points. By default, how often does Windows 10 automatically create restore points?

    A. Restore points are created every day.

    B. Restore points are created once every three days.

    C. Restore points are created once every seven days.

    D. Restore points are created once every 30 days.

99. You are the administrator for your company network. You have a new piece of software that you'd like to install. However, you want to take precautions in case there is an issue. What can you do to protect your system if something goes wrong?

    A. Create an image with the recovery disk.

    B. Create a restore point.

    C. Install the application in Safe Mode.

    D. Perform a Windows 7 backup.

100. You are the administrator for your company network. You have discovered a virus on a computer. The virus is causing issues with the computer and preventing it from booting properly. Which of the following recovery boot options should be avoided?

A. Booting into Safe Mode

B. Booting into Safe Mode with Networking

C. The Repair Your Computer option

D. Booting into Safe Mode with Command Prompt

101. You are the administrator for your company network. You and a colleague are discussing performing standard backups. Which backup utility includes the System Image tool?

A. Backup and Restore (Windows 7)

B. File History

C. Windows 10 File Recovery drive

D. Windows 10 Restore

102. You are the administrator for your company network. You have performed a System Restore on a Windows 10 machine. However, there is an issue with the restore point, and now the computer will not boot. What should you do to try to resolve the issue?

A. There is nothing that can be done—it's too late.

B. You should manually delete all of the files that changed.

C. You should restart the computer.

D. You should undo the System Restore.

103. You are the administrator for your company network. You and a colleague are discussing ways to protect personal files. Windows 10 has a feature that allows you to protect personal files by automatically backing up the files. What is this feature called?

A. Backup and Restore (Windows 7)

B. File History

C. File Recovery

D. System Restore

104. You are the administrator for your company network. You and a colleague are discussing ways to repair unbootable operating systems. What can you use to assist you with an unbootable operating system?

A. Backup and Restore (Windows 7)

B. Device Manager

C. File History

D. Windows Recovery Environment (WinRE)

105. You are the administrator for your company network. You and a colleague are discussing how to bring a system back to a previous point in time. Which of the following is a representation of the state of a computer's system files and settings from a particular period of time?

  A. A File History backup

  B. A restore point

  C. A Windows 10 File Recovery drive

  D. A Windows Recovery Environment

106. You are the administrator for your company network. You and a colleague are discussing the Windows Recovery Environment (WinRE). What is the WinRE based on?

  A. WinRE is based on Backup and Restore (Windows 7).

  B. WinRE is based on DOS boot disk.

  C. WinRE is based on Windows installation ISO.

  D. WinRE is based on Windows PE.

107. You are the administrator for your company network. You and a colleague are discussing a way to view system information to see what hardware and software is loaded on a Windows 10 machine. You'd like to use Windows PowerShell to show that information. What command should you run?

  A. `Get-ControlPanelItem`

  B. `Get-ComputerInfo`

  C. `Get-EventLog`

  D. `Get-MyInformation`

108. You are the administrator for your company network. You and a colleague are discussing how to look at system performance and processes. What program gives you a quick look at system performances and the processes that are running?

  A. Performance Monitor

  B. Resource Monitor

  C. System Information

  D. Task Manager

109. You are the administrator for your company network. You and a colleague are discussing the different ways to access the Control Panel. You'd like to access the Control Panel by using Windows PowerShell. What command do you run?

  A. `Get-ControlPanel`

  B. `Get-ControlPanelItem`

  C. `Get-EventLog`

  D. `Get-MyInformation`

110. You are the administrator for your company network. You and a colleague are discussing a tool that can allow a user to access shared files and folders on a network at any time—even when not connected to the network. What is this tool called?

A. Disk Management

B. Remote Desktop Connection

C. Sync Center

D. Windows Remote Assistance

111. You are the administrator for your company network. You and a colleague are discussing the different utilities used by Microsoft. One of these utilities uses a PS prefix at a command prompt to indicate the session about to be run. Which of the following utilities would use a PS prefix?

A. Computer Management

B. MS-DOS command window

C. Windows PowerShell

D. Windows Remote Assistance

112. You are the administrator for your company network. You and a colleague are discussing services. You want to change the service startup type, which can be set to automatic, manual, or disabled. What tab would you use to set this up?

A. The Dependencies tab

B. The General tab

C. The Log On tab

D. The Recovery tab

113. You are the administrator for your company network. You and a colleague are discussing the wide variety of Windows 10 recovery techniques that Microsoft provides. One of these techniques shows a log of application and system messages including errors, informational messages, and warnings. What is this recovery technique called?

A. Backup and Restore

B. Driver Rollback

C. Event Viewer

D. Safe Mode

E. Startup Repair Tool

F. System Restore

114. You are the administrator for your company network. You and a colleague are discussing the wide variety of Windows 10 advanced boot options. One of these techniques is an exact copy of the Windows 10 drive. What is this advanced boot option called?

A. System Restore

B. System Image Recovery

C. Startup Repair

D. Command Prompt

E. Startup Settings

F. Go back to previous build

115. You are the administrator for your company network. You and a colleague are discussing the wide variety of Windows 10 advanced boot options. One of these techniques can help restore missing or corrupted system files. What is this advanced boot option called?

A. System Restore

B. System Image Recovery

C. Startup Repair

D. Command Prompt

E. Startup Settings

F. Go back to previous build

116. You are the administrator for your company network. You and a colleague are discussing the wide variety of Windows 10 recovery techniques that Microsoft provides. One of these techniques can be used if a computer will not boot into Safe Mode and can be used to replace corrupted system files. What is this recovery technique called?

A. Backup and Restore

B. Driver Rollback

C. Event Viewer

D. Safe Mode

E. Startup Repair Tool

F. System Restore

117. You are the administrator for your company network. You and a colleague are discussing Microsoft's subscription-based storage system called OneDrive. OneDrive allows users to use up to a certain amount of cloud storage for free without a subscription. How much cloud storage is provided for free?

A. 3 GB

B. 5 GB

C. 8 GB

D. 10 GB

118. You are the administrator for your company network. You and a colleague are discussing Microsoft's subscription-based storage system called OneDrive. To use OneDrive, you must first have which of the following?

A. Administrator account

B. Local User account

C. Microsoft account

D. OneDrive account

Modern Desktop Admin, Exam MD-101

PART

II

Chapter

5

Deploy and Update Operating Systems

THE MD-101 EXAM TOPICS COVERED IN THIS CHAPTER INCLUDE:

✓ **Domain 5: Deploy and Update Operating Systems**

- 5.1: Plan and Implement Windows 10 by Using Dynamic Deployment
  - Evaluate and select an appropriate deployment options
  - Pilot deployment
  - Manage and troubleshoot provisioning packages
- 5.2: Plan and Implement Windows 10 by Using Windows Autopilot
  - Evaluate and select an appropriate deployment options
  - Pilot deployment
  - Create, validate, and assign deployment profile
  - Extract device HW information to CSV file
  - Import device HW information to cloud service
  - Troubleshoot deployment
- 5.3: Upgrade Devices to Windows 10
  - Identify upgrade and downgrade paths
  - Manage in-place upgrades
  - Configure a Windows analytics environment
  - Perform Upgrade Readiness assessment
  - Migrate user profiles
- 5.4: Manage Updates
  - Configure Windows 10 delivery optimization
  - Configure Windows Update for Business
  - Deploy Windows updates
  - Implement feature updates
  - Monitor Windows 10 updates
- 5.5: Manage Device Authentication
  - Manage authentication policies
  - Manage sign-on options
  - Perform Azure AD join

1. You are the administrator for your company network. You use Windows Autopilot to configure the computer settings of computers that are issued to employees. An employee has been using an issued Windows 10 computer and then leaves the company. You'd like to transfer that computer to a new user. You need to make sure that when the new user first starts the computer, they will be prompted to select the language settings and to agree to the license agreement. What should you do?

   A. You should create a new Windows Autopilot self-deploying deployment profile.

   B. You should create a new Windows Autopilot user-driven deployment profile.

   C. You should perform a local Windows Autopilot Reset.

   D. You should perform a remote Windows Autopilot Reset.

2. You are the administrator for your company network. Your company infrastructure is comprised of the following:

   - A Microsoft 365 tenant

   - An Active Directory forest

   - A Microsoft Store for Business

   - A Key Management Service (KMS) server

   - A Windows Deployment Services (WDS) server

   - A Microsoft Azure Active Directory (Azure AD) Premium tenant

   You purchase 100 new Windows 10 computers, and you want to make sure that the new computers are automatically joined to the Azure AD by using Windows Autopilot. What management tool should you use?

   A. You should use the Azure Active Directory Admin Center.

   B. You should use Microsoft Intune.

   C. You should use the Volume Activation Management Tool console.

   D. You should use the Windows Deployment Services console.

3. You are the administrator for your company network. Your company infrastructure is comprised of the following:

   - A Microsoft 365 tenant

   - An Active Directory forest

   - A Microsoft Store for Business

   - A Key Management Service (KMS) server

   - A Windows Deployment Services (WDS) server

   - A Microsoft Azure Active Directory (Azure AD) Premium tenant

   You purchase 100 new Windows 10 computers, and you want to make sure that the new computers are automatically joined to the Azure AD by using Windows Autopilot. What information will be required from each computer?

    A. You will need the device serial number and hardware hash.

    B. You will need the MAC address and computer name.

    C. You will need the volume license key and computer name.

    D. No additional information will be needed.

4. You are the administrator for your company network. You have a reference computer that runs Windows 10 that will be used to create and deploy an image. You create an answer file named myanswers.xml. You want to ensure that the installation applies the answer file after the image is deployed. What command should you run before you capture the image?

    A. You should run dism.exe/append myanswers.xml/check.

    B. You should run dism.exe/mount myanswers.xml/verify.

    C. You should run sysprep.exe/generalize/oobe/unattend:myanswers.xml.

    D. You should run sysprep.exe/reboot/audit/unattend:myanswers.xml.

5. You are the administrator for your company network. You have the following computers:

Name	Operating System	Memory	BitLocker
Computer1	32-bit version of Windows 7 (SP1)	1 GB	Enabled
Computer2	64-bit version of Windows 7 (SP1)	4 GB	Enabled
Computer3	32-bit version of Windows 8.1	2 GB	Enabled
Computer4	64-bit version of Windows 8.1	4 GB	Disabled

You are planning to perform an in-place upgrade to the 64-bit version of Windows 10. Given their current state, which computers can you upgrade to the 64-bit version of Windows 10?

    A. You can upgrade Computer1, Computer2, Computer3, and Computer4.

    B. You can upgrade Computer2 and Computer4 only.

    C. You can upgrade Computer4 only.

    D. You can upgrade Computer3 and Computer4 only.

6. You are the administrator for your company network. You are using Windows Deployment Service (WDS) to install a number of Windows 10 computers. When users attempt to use WDS, they are not able to complete the unattended installation. You suspect that the WDS server has not been configured to respond to user requests. To respond to user requests, which one of the following utilities should you use to configure the WDS server?

    A. You should use Active Directory Users and Computers.

    B. You should use Active Directory Users and Groups.

    C. You should use the Windows Deployment Service (WDS) MMC snap-in.

    D. You should use the WDSMAN utility.

7. You are the administrator for your company network. You want to ensure that your systems automatically deploy software updates during a maintenance window. What should you do?

   A. Configure Automatic Maintenance Activation Boundary from the Maintenance Scheduler settings.

   B. Configure Automatic Maintenance Random Delay from the Maintenance Scheduler settings.

   C. From the Windows Update settings, enable Configure Automatic Updates, select 3-Auto Download And Notify For Install, and then enter a time.

   D. From the Windows Update settings, enable Configure Automatic Updates, select 4-Auto Download And Schedule The Install, and then enter a time.

8. You are the administrator for your company network. You have a Microsoft 365 subscription, and all machines are running Windows 10. You want to prevent your users from enrolling their devices in the Windows Insider Program. Using Microsoft 365 Device Management, what should you configure?

   A. You should configure an app configuration policy.

   B. You should configure a custom device configuration profile.

   C. You should configure a Windows 10 security baseline.

   D. You should configure a Windows 10 update ring.

9. You are the administrator for your company network. You want to create a new Azure Active Directory policy for your users. What PowerShell command should you use to accomplish this?

   A. `New-AzureActiveDirectoryPolicy`

   B. `New-AzureADPolicy`

   C. `New-AzurePolicy`

   D. `Set-AzurePolicy`

10. You are the administrator for your company network. The network has an Active Directory domain. The domain contains several thousand Windows 10 computers. You implement hybrid Microsoft Azure Active Directory (Azure AD) and Microsoft Intune. You have to register all of the existing computers automatically to Azure AD and enroll the computers in Intune. What should you do while using the least amount of administrative effort?

   A. You should configure an Autodiscover address record.

   B. You should configure an Autodiscover service connection point (SCP).

   C. You should configure a Group Policy object (GPO).

   D. You should configure a Windows Autopilot deployment profile.

11. You are the administrator for your company network. Your network contains an Active Directory domain that is synced to Microsoft Azure Active Directory (Azure AD). All the network computers are enrolled in Microsoft Intune. The domain contains the following computers:

Name	Operating System
Computer1	Windows 8.1 Enterprise
Computer2	Windows 10 Enterprise without the latest feature update
Computer3	Windows 10 Enterprise without the latest feature update

You are evaluating which Intune actions you can use to reset the computers to run Windows 10 Enterprise with the latest update. On which computers do you perform the Fresh Start action?

- **A.** Computer1 only
- **B.** Computer2 only
- **C.** Computer3 only
- **D.** Computer2 and Computer3 only
- **E.** Computer1, Computer2, and Computer3

12. You are the administrator for your company network. Your network contains an Active Directory domain that is synced to Microsoft Azure Active Directory (Azure AD). All of the network computers are enrolled in Microsoft Intune. The domain contains the following computers:

Name	Operating System
Computer1	Windows 8.1 Enterprise
Computer2	Windows 10 Enterprise without the latest feature update
Computer3	Windows 10 Enterprise without the latest feature update

You are evaluating which Intune actions you can use to reset the computers to run Windows 10 Enterprise with the latest update. On which computers do you perform a Clean Wipe action?

- **A.** Computer1 only
- **B.** Computer2 only
- **C.** Computer3 only
- **D.** Computer2 and Computer3 only
- **E.** Computer1, Computer2, and Computer3

13. You are the administrator for your company network. Your company purchases several new Windows 10 computers. The computers have cameras that support Windows Hello for Business. You configure the Windows Hello for Business Group Policy settings as shown in the following table:

Setting	State	Comment
Allow enumeration of emulated smart card for all users	Not configured	No
Turn off smart card emulation	Not configured	No
Use PIN recovery	Not configured	No
Use a hardware security device	Not configured	No
Use biometrics	Enabled	No
Configure device unlock factors	Not configured	No
Configure dynamic lock factors	Enabled	No
Use Windows Hello for Business	Enabled	No
Use certificate on-premises authentication	Not configured	No

What are the valid methods that a user can use to sign in? (Choose two.)

A. The user can use facial recognition.

B. The user can use a PIN.

C. The user can use a smart watch that is Bluetooth-enabled.

D. The user can use a USB key.

14. You are the administrator for your company network. You and a colleague are discussing Windows Autopilot error codes. Which of the following codes shows `Error code: ERROR_NOT_SUPPORTED` when you have used Windows Autopilot Reset?

A. `0x800705B4`

B. `0x801c0003`

C. `0x80180018`

D. `0x80070032`

15. You are the administrator for your company network. You have about 20 computers that are currently running Windows 7. These computers have the following configurations:

- The TPM chip is disabled.
- A single MBR disk.
- Hardware virtualization is disabled.
- Data Execution Prevention (DEP) is enabled.
- UEFI firmware is running in BIOS mode.

You are planning to upgrade the computers to Windows 10. You want to ensure that the computers can use Secure Boot. What actions should you perform? (Choose two.)

A. You should convert the firmware from BIOS to UEFI.

B. You should convert the MBR disk to a GPT disk.

C. You should disable Data Execution Prevention (DEP).

D. You should enable hardware virtualization.

E. You should enable the TPM chip.

16. You are the administrator for your company network. You have a Windows 10 computer. You create a Windows PowerShell script named `config.ps1`. After feature updates are installed on the computer, you want to run the PowerShell script. What file should you modify on the computer?

A. `litetouch.wsf`

B. `setupconfig.ini`

C. `unattend.bat`

D. `unattend.xml`

17. You are the administrator for your company network. You have several computers that are running Windows 10 and have been configured by using Windows Autopilot. A user performs the following tasks on one of the computers:

- Creates a VPN connection to the corporate network

- Installs a Microsoft Store app named App1

- Connects to a Wi-Fi network

You perform a Windows Autopilot Reset on the computer. What will be the state of the Wi-Fi connection on the computer when the user signs in?

A. The Wi-Fi connection will be removed.

B. The Wi-Fi connection will be retained, and the passphrase will be retained.

C. The Wi-Fi connection will be retained, but the passphrase will be reset.

D. The Wi-Fi connection will be removed, but the passphrase will be retained.

18. You are the administrator for your company network. You have several computers that are running Windows 10 and have been configured using Windows Autopilot. A user performs the following tasks on one of the computers:

- Creates a VPN connection to the corporate network

- Installs a Microsoft Store app named App1

- Connects to a Wi-Fi network

You perform a Windows Autopilot Reset on the computer. What will be the state of App1 on the computer when the user signs in?

A. The app will be reinstalled at sign-in.

B. The app will be removed.

C. The app will be retained.

D. Nothing will happen; it can't be done.

19. You are the administrator for your company network. You have several computers that are running Windows 10 and have been configured by using Windows Autopilot. A user performs the following tasks on one of the computers:

- Creates a VPN connection to the corporate network

- Installs a Microsoft Store app named App1

- Connects to a Wi-Fi network

You perform a Windows Autopilot Reset on the computer. What will be the state of the VPN connection on the computer when the user signs in?

A. The VPN connection will be removed.

B. The VPN connection will be retained, and the credentials will be cached.

C. The VPN connection will be retained, but the credentials will be reset.

D. The VPN connection will be removed, but the credentials will be cached.

20. You are the administrator for your company network. Your company has a Microsoft Azure Active Directory (Azure AD) tenant. You have a volume licensing agreement and use product keys to activate Windows 10. You are planning on deploying Window 10 Professional to several hundred new computers by using the Microsoft Deployment Toolkit (MDT) and Windows Deployment Services (WDS). What should you configure if you need to make sure the new computers will be configured with the correct product keys during the installation?

A. The Device settings in Azure AD

B. An MDT task sequence

C. A WDS boot image

D. A Windows Autopilot deployment profile

21. You are the administrator for your company network. You and a colleague are discussing some security features that are built into Windows 10. One feature helps defend against data theft and offline tampering by providing drive encryption. What is this Windows 10 feature called?

A. BitLocker

B. Device Health Attestation (DHA)

C. Multifactor Authentication (MFA)

D. Secure Boot

22. You are the administrator for your company network. You and a colleague are discussing the different deployment scenarios and the categories into which certain scenarios fall. You are discussing Subscription Activation. Which category does this fall into in regard to deployment scenarios?

A. Contemporary deployment category

B. Dynamic deployment category

C. Modern deployment category

D. Traditional deployment category

23. You are the administrator for your company network. Your network has an Active Directory domain that runs Windows 10 computers that are enrolled in Microsoft Intune. Updates are deployed by using Windows Update for Business. Users in a group must meet the following requirements:

- Update installations can happen any day, but only between 00:00 and 05:00.

- Updates must be downloaded from Microsoft and from other company computers that have already downloaded the updates.

What settings should you modify if you need to configure the Windows 10 update rings in Intune to meet the requirements? (Choose two.)

   A. Update Settings ➤ Quality Update Deferral Period (Days)

   B. Update Settings ➤ Servicing Channel

   C. User Experience Settings ➤ Automatic Update Behavior

   D. User Experience Settings ➤ Delivery Optimization Download Mode

24. You are the administrator for your company network. Your company has several hundred Windows 10 computers that are managed by using Microsoft Intune. Windows updates are currently being downloaded without using Delivery Optimization. What should you do in Intune if you'd like to configure the computers to use Delivery Optimization?

   A. Configure an app protection policy.

   B. Create a device configuration profile.

   C. Configure a device compliance policy.

   D. Configure a Windows 10 update ring.

25. You are the administrator for your company network. You and a colleague are discussing Autopilot and what needs to be done if a device has not downloaded the Autopilot profile. You first reboot the device during an Out of Box Experience (OOBE) to allow the device to try to retrieve the profile, but that doesn't work. What should you do next?

   A. At the start of the OOBE, you should press Shift+F10 to open a command prompt and then enter **shutdown /r /t 0**.

   B. At the start of the OOBE, you should press Shift+F10 to open a command prompt and then enter **shutdown /s /t 0**.

   C. At the start of the OOBE, you should press Shift+F8 to open a command prompt and then enter **shutdown /h /t 60**.

   D. At the start of the OOBE, you should press Shift+F8 to open a command prompt and then enter **shutdown /o /t 60**.

26. You are the administrator for your company network. You have 200 Windows 10 computers that are joined to Microsoft Azure Active Directory (Azure AD) and enrolled in Microsoft Intune. You want to set a custom image as the wallpaper and sign-in screen. What two settings should you configure in Device Restrictions? (Choose two.)

   A. You should configure the General settings.

   B. You should configure the Display settings.

C. You should configure the Locked Screen Experience settings.

D. You should configure the Personalization settings

27. You are the administrator for your company network. Your company is using Windows Update for Business. The Research department has several Windows 10 computers that use specialized hardware and software. What should you do if you need to prevent the video drivers from being updated automatically by using Windows Update? (Choose two.)

   A. From the Device Installation And Restrictions settings in a Group Policy object (GPO), enable Prevent Installation Of Devices Using Drivers That Match These Device Setup Classes and then type the device GUID.

   B. From the Settings app, clear the Give Me Updates For Other Microsoft Products When I Update Windows checkbox.

   C. From the Device Installation settings in a Group Policy object (GPO), enable Specify Search Order For Device Driver Source Locations and then select Do Not Search Windows Update.

   D. From the Windows Update settings in a Group Policy object (GPO), enable Do Not Include Drivers With Windows Updates.

28. You are the administrator for your company network. You are planning to install several hundred Windows 10 computers into your company's data center. You decide to use Windows Deployment Services (WDS). You are currently using a Windows Server 2012 R2 domain and have verified that the network meets the requirements for using WDS. You'd like to use the command-line utility to configure the WDS server. What is this utility called?

   A. `dism.exe`

   B. `wdsutil.exe`

   C. `setup.exe`

   D. `sysprep.exe`

29. You are the administrator for your company network. You and a colleague are discussing a service that will identify compatibility issues and receive mitigation suggestions based on cloud-enabled data insights. What is this service called?

   A. Configuration Associate

   B. Desktop Analytics

   C. Windows Analytics

   D. Windows Services Manager

30. You are the administrator for your company network. You and a colleague are discussing downgrade capabilities in Windows 10 and who can downgrade. Who can downgrade their current version of Windows 10?

   A. Volume license customers whose licenses have not expired and do not have an edition of Windows 10 with an active license.

   B. Volume license customers whose licenses have expired who do not have an edition of Windows 10 with an active license.

   C. Volume license customers whose licenses have expired who have an edition of Windows 10 with an active license.

   D. It cannot be done. Downgrades are not possible.

31. You are the administrator for your company network. You have several computers that run Windows 10 Professional. The computers are joined to Microsoft Azure Active Directory (Azure AD) and enrolled in Microsoft Intune. You need to upgrade the computers to Windows 10 Enterprise. What should you configure in Intune?

   A. You should configure a device enrollment policy.

   B. You should configure a device cleanup rule.

   C. You should configure a device compliance policy.

   D. You should configure a device configuration profile.

32. You are the administrator for your company network. The network contains an Active Directory domain that is synced to Microsoft Azure Active Directory (Azure AD). The domain contains 100 laptops that run Windows 8.1 Professional. The users of the laptops work from home. The company uses Microsoft Intune, the Microsoft Deployment Toolkit (MDT), and Windows Configuration Designer to manage client computers. You purchase new Windows 10 Enterprise licenses for the laptops. You verify that the hardware and applications on the laptops are compatible with Windows 10. The users will be bringing their laptop computers into the office, where IT will deploy Windows 10 to the laptops while the users wait. You want to recommend a deployment process for the laptops so that they will retain their installed applications. The solution must minimize the time it takes to perform this process. What should you recommend?

   A. A clean installation using a Windows Configuration Designer provisioning package

   B. A clean installation and the User State Migration Tool (USMT)

   C. An in-place upgrade

   D. Windows Autopilot

33. You are the administrator for your company network. Your network contains an Active Directory domain that contains several hundred Windows 10 computers. You have both an onsite Active Directory network and a Microsoft Azure Active Directory (Azure AD) with Microsoft Intune. What should you use if you want to register all the existing computers automatically to the Azure AD network and also enroll all of the computers in Intune?

   A. You should use an Autodiscover service connection point (SCP).

   B. You should use a DNS Autodiscover address record.

   C. You should set up a Group Policy object (GPO).

   D. You should use a Windows Autopilot deployment profile.

34. You are the administrator for your company network. You install a feature update on a Windows 10 computer. You are worried about how the update will affect a specific application. How many days do you have to roll back the update?

   A. 5 days

   B. 10 days

C. 14 days

D. 30 days

35. You are the administrator for your company network. You have two Windows 10 computers that are enrolled in Microsoft Intune. They are as follows:

   ■ Computer1 is a member of Group1.

   ■ Computer2 is a member of Group1 and Group2.

   In Intune, Windows 10 update rings are defined as shown:

Name	Quality Deferral (Days)	Assigned
Ring1	3	Yes
Ring2	10	Yes

   You assign the update rings as shown:

Name	Include	Exclude
Ring1	Group1	Group2
Ring2	Group2	Group1

   What will the quality deferral (days) be on Computer1?

   A. 3 days

   B. 7 days

   C. 10 days

   D. 13 days

36. You are the administrator for your company network. You have two Windows 10 computers that are enrolled in Microsoft Intune. They are as follows:

   ■ Computer1 is a member of Group1.

   ■ Computer2 is a member of Group1 and Group2.

   In Intune, Windows 10 update rings are defined as follows:

Name	Quality Deferral (Days)	Assigned
Ring1	3	Yes
Ring2	10	Yes

You assign the update rings as follows:

Name	Include	Exclude
Ring1	Group1	Group2
Ring2	Group2	Group1

What will the quality deferral be on Computer2?

A. 3 days

B. 7 days

C. 10 days

D. 13 days

37. You are the administrator for your company network. Your network contains an Active Directory forest with a single domain and three sites named SiteA, SiteB, and SiteC. All of the client computers in the forest run Windows 10. Each site is associated with two subnets. SiteA contains two subnets named Subnet1 and Subnet2. Delivery Optimization is enabled. You have a computer, Computer1, which is on Subnet1. From which hosts will Computer1 download updates?

A. Any computer in the domain

B. Any computer on the network

C. The computers in SiteA only

D. The computers in Subnet1 only

38. You are the administrator for your company network. You have standardized that all users run Windows 10 Enterprise. A few users purchase their own computers that run Windows 10 Professional. You want to recommend a solution that will upgrade the computers to Windows 10 Enterprise, join the computers to Microsoft Azure Active Directory (Azure AD), and install several Microsoft Store apps. You want to meet the following requirements:

- You need to make sure that any applications installed by the users are retained.

- You need to minimize user intervention.

What should you recommend be used?

A. You should recommend using Microsoft Deployment Toolkit (MDT).

B. You cannot upgrade these systems since they are already running Windows 10.

C. You should recommend using a Windows Configuration Designer provisioning package.

D. You should recommend using Windows Deployment Services (WDS).

39. You are the administrator for your company network. The company has a Microsoft 365 subscription. A remote user buys a new laptop that has Windows 10 Professional installed. They will be using this laptop for corporate business. You need to configure the laptop as follows:

- You must modify the layout of the Start menu.

- You must upgrade Windows 10 Professional to Windows 10 Enterprise.

- You must join the laptop to the Microsoft Azure Active Directory (Azure AD) scorporate domain.

What should you do?

A. You should create a custom Windows image (.wim) file that contains an image of Windows 10 Enterprise and upload the file to a Microsoft user.

B. You should create a provisioning package (.ppkg) file and email the file to the user.

C. You should create a Sysprep Unattend (.xml) file and email the file to the user.

D. You should create a Windows To Go workspace and ship the workspace to the user.

40. You are the administrator for your company network. You want to look at an Azure Active Directory policy for the corporate users. What PowerShell command should you use to accomplish this?

A. Get-AzurePolicy

B. Get-AzureADPolicy

C. View-AzureADPolicy

D. View-AzurePolicy

41. You are the administrator for your company network. You have several hundred Windows 10 computers. You need to create a provisioning package that performs the following tasks:

- Adds a VPN connection to the corporate network

- Removes the Microsoft News and the Xbox Microsoft Store apps

What customization settings should you configure? (Choose two.)

A. The ConnectivityProfiles settings

B. The Personalization settings

C. The Policies settings

D. The ProvisioningCommands settings

42. You are the administrator for your company network. Using Windows Autopilot, you need to assign the same deployment profile to all of the corporate computers. What actions should you perform? (Choose two.)

A. You should assign a Windows Autopilot deployment profile to a group.

B. You should create a Group Policy object (GPO) that is linked to a domain.

C. You should create a Microsoft Azure Active Directory (Azure AD) group that has dynamic membership rules and uses the OperatingSystem tag.

D. You should create a Microsoft Azure Active Directory (Azure AD) group that has dynamic membership rules and uses the ZTDId tag.

E. You should join the computers to Microsoft Azure Active Directory (Azure AD).

F. You should join the computers to an on-premises Active Directory domain.

43. You are the administrator for your company network. Your network contains an Active Directory domain that contains several hundred Windows 7 computers. Some of these computers are used by multiple users. You are planning to refresh the operating system of the computers to Windows 10, but you need to retain the personalization settings to applications before you refresh the computers. Your solution must minimize network bandwidth and network storage space. What command should you run on the computers?

A. dism.exe /i myapp.xml /genconfig:myfile1.xml /nocompress /ui :mysite*

B. scandisk /i myapp.xml /genconfig:myfile1.xml /nocompress /ui :mysite*

C. scanstate /i myapp.xml /genconfig:myfile1.xml /nocompress /ui :mysite*

D. usmtutils.exe /i myapp.xml /genconfig:myfile1.xml /nocompress /ui :mysite*

44. You are the administrator for your company network. You are planning on deploying Windows 10 devices. Some of the devices will be configured for English, and others will be configured for Japanese. You need to create a single multivariant provisioning package for the devices. You create the provisioning package. What should you do next to add the language settings to the package?

A. Create a file named languages.xml that contains a header for English.

B. Create a file named languages.xml that contains a header for Japanese.

C. Modify the customizations.xml file.

D. Modify the .ppkg file.

45. You are the administrator for your company network. You have a Windows 10 Windows Image (WIM) that is mounted. What should you do if you need to view the list of third-party drivers installed on the WIM?

A. Open the mount folder from File Explorer.

B. Run dism and specify the /get-drivers parameter.

C. Run driverquery.exe and use the /si parameter.

D. View all hidden drivers using Device Manager.

46. You are the administrator for your company network. Your network contains an Active Directory domain. You create a provisioning package named Package1 that has the following configurations:

Enter device name: Comp%RAND1%

Share devices: No

Remove pre-installed software: No

Network: Wired

Domain name: mysite.com

Domain user name: mysite\administrator

Domain user password: *******

What is the maximum number of devices that can run the package successfully?

A. 1 device

B. 10 devices

C. 25 devices

D. Unlimited devices

47. You are the administrator for your company network. You have subscribed to a new Azure AD subscription. You want the users to be able to reset passwords by themselves. What Azure AD feature allows users to reset their own passwords?

A. The Azure password reset feature

B. The password reset service

C. The self-service password reset

D. The user-enabled password reset

48. You are the administrator for your company network. Your company has an Azure Active Directory (Azure AD) domain name of CrystalPanek.onmicrosoft.com. You and a colleague are discussing the default domain name. You want you to change the default domain name to Panek.onmicrosoft.com. How can you change the initial domain name?

A. You can use the Custom Domain Names section of Azure AD and change the name.

B. You can use Azure AD, go to default directories, and change the domain name.

C. You can use PowerShell to change the default domain name.

D. This can't be done.

49. You are the administrator for your company network. You want to create a new installation of Windows 10 using the command line. You plan to accomplish this by using the setup.exe command-line setup utility. What command-line option should you use if you want to use an answer file with this command-line utility?

A. /apply

B. /generalize

C. /noreboot

D. /unattend

50. You are the administrator for your company network. You have a computer that is currently loaded with Windows 7, and you also want to load it with Windows 10. You'd like this machine to be able to dual-boot between the two operating system versions. You install Windows 10 on a new partition on the computer. What should you do if you want the computer to start in Windows 7 by default?

A. Change the boot.ini file so that Windows 7 is the default.

B. Edit the bcdedit.exe with the /default parameter to set Windows 7 as the default.

C. Delete the Windows 10 boot.ini file so that the machine reverts to Windows 7 by default.

D. Edit the bcdedit.exe with the /order parameter to set Windows 7 as the default.

51. You are the administrator for your company network. You have a hybrid Microsoft Azure Active Directory (Azure AD) tenant. You configure a Windows Autopilot deployment profile. The deployment profile is configured as follows:

Name: Autopilot1

Convert all targeted devices to Autopilot: No

Deployment Mode: User-Driven

Join to Azure AD as: Azure AD joined

You want to apply the profile to a new computer. What should you do first?

- **A.** Assign a user to a specific Autopilot device.
- **B.** Enroll the device in Microsoft Intune.
- **C.** Import a CSV file into Windows Autopilot.
- **D.** Join the device to Azure AD.

52. You are the administrator for your company network. You have a hybrid Microsoft Azure Active Directory (Azure AD) tenant. You configure a Windows Autopilot deployment profile. The deployment profile is configured as follows:

Name: Autopilot1

Convert all targeted devices to Autopilot: No

Deployment Mode: User-Driven

Join to Azure AD as: Azure AD joined

When the Windows Autopilot profile is applied to the computer, the computer will be which of the following?

- **A.** Joined to Active Directory only
- **B.** Joined to Azure AD only
- **C.** Registered in Azure AD only
- **D.** Joined to Active Directory and registered in Azure AD

53. You are the administrator for your company network. You have a Microsoft Intune subscription. You configure a Windows Autopilot deployment profile. The deployment profile is configured as follows:

Name: Profile1

Convert all targeted devices to Autopilot: No

Deployment Mode: User-Driven

Out-of-box experience (OOBE): Defaults configured

End user license agreement (EULA): Hide

Privacy settings: Hide

Hide change account settings: Hide

User account type: Standard

Apply computer name template (Windows Insider only): No

Users who deploy Autopilot using Profile1 can perform which of the following?

A. Users can create additional local users on the device.

B. Users can modify the desktop settings for all device users.

C. Users can modify the desktop settings only for themselves.

D. Users are prevented from modifying any desktop settings.

54. You are the administrator for your company network. You have a Microsoft Intune subscription. You configure a Windows Autopilot deployment profile. The deployment profile is configured as follows:

Name: Profile1

Convert all targeted devices to Autopilot: No

Deployment Mode: User-Driven

Out-of-box experience (OOBE): Defaults configured

End user license agreement (EULA): Hide

Privacy settings: Hide

Hide change account settings: Hide

User account type: Standard

Apply computer name template (Windows Insider only): No

During the deployment, users can configure which of the following?

A. Users can configure the computer name.

B. Users can configure the Cortana settings.

C. Users can configure the keyboard layout.

D. Users can configure the wallpaper settings.

55. You are the administrator for your company network. You have a couple of Windows 7 computers named Computer1 and Computer2. Computer1 has a 32-bit CPU that runs of Windows 7 Enterprise. Computer2 has a 64-bit CPU that runs Windows 7 Enterprise. You are planning to perform an in-place upgrade on both computers to the 64-bit version of Windows 10. Which computers can you upgrade to the 64-bit version of Windows 10?

A. You can only upgrade Computer1.

B. You can only upgrade Computer2.

C. You can upgrade both Computer1 and Computer2.

D. Neither one can be upgraded to Windows 10.

56. You are the administrator for your company network. You have decided to create a Windows 10 image that you will copy to a DVD and deploy to several new Windows 10 computers. To automate the setup process, you want to use an answer file. Where should the answer file be located so that you can use it during installation?

   A. On a network share

   B. On the root of the DVD

   C. On a separate DVD

   D. On a WDS server

57. You are the administrator for your company network. You have been tasked with creating a deployment plan to automate installations for 100 computers that need to have Windows 10 installed. You plan to use Windows Deployment Services (WDS) for the installations. To automate the installations fully, you need to create an answer file. You don't want to create the answer file by using a text editor. What other program should you use to create the unattended answer files using a GUI interface?

   A. Answer Manager

   B. Deployment Image Servicing and Management (DISM)

   C. System Preparation Tool (Sysprep)

   D. Windows System Image Manager (SIM)

58. You are the administrator for your company network. You want to install a group of 25 computers using disk images to be used in conjunction with the System Preparation Tool. You plan to create an image using a reference computer and then copy the image to the rest of the machines. You want to create a new unique Security Identifier (SID) on the destination computer when you use the image and when it is added to the domain. What `sysprep .exe` command-line option should you use?

   A. `/generalize`

   B. `/oobe`

   C. `/quiet`

   D. `/specialize`

59. You are the administrator for your company network. What tool can you use if your company wants to set up a way to integrate their onsite Active Directory (AD) with Azure Active Directory (Azure AD)?

   A. You should use Active Directory Replicator.

   B. You should use Azure AD Connect.

   C. You should use Azure AD Replication.

   D. You should use Site-to-Site VPN Gateway Connectors.

60. You are the administrator for your company network. You want to look at an Azure Active Directory application policy for your user's applications. What PowerShell command should you use?

   A. `Add-AzureADPolicy`

   B. `Get-AzureADApplicationPolicy`

    C. `Create-AzurePolicy`

    D. `Install-AzureADPolicy`

61. You are the administrator for your company network. You want to view your Azure AD directory settings for an Azure AD subscription. What PowerShell command should you use?

    A. `Add-AzureADDirectorySetting`

    B. `Get-AzureADDirectorySetting`

    C. `Set-AzureADDirectorySetting`

    D. `View-AzureADDirectorySetting`

62. You are the administrator for your company network. You must complete the installation of a Windows 10 machine. After the Window 10 install is complete, what should you do next to make sure that the computer is ready to be used?

    A. Check Microsoft's website for all updates and patches.

    B. Configure the `sethc.exe` file.

    C. Install Microsoft 365.

    D. Set up the machine to dual-boot.

63. You are the administrator for your company network. There is a Microsoft tool that allows a Windows 10 computer to be set up with all applications and operating systems automatically without any administrator intervention. What is this called?

    A. Deployment Image Servicing and Management (DISM)

    B. Windows 10 Admin setup

    C. Windows Autopilot

    D. Windows Internal Database (WID) Server

64. You are the administrator for your company network. You and a colleague are discussing Windows Update. Which of the following options can be configured in Windows Update? (Choose all that apply.)

    A. Change Active Hours

    B. Check For Updates

    C. Restore Hidden Updates

    D. View Update History

65. You are the administrator for your company network. You need to deploy Windows 10 to multiple computers. You decide to automate the installation so that no user interaction is required during the installation process. Which one of the following utilities should you use?

    A. Image Capture Wizard

    B. System Preparation Tool

    C. `wdsutil.exe` utility

    D. Windows SIM

66. You are the administrator for your company network. You have recently decided to add an Azure Active Directory (Azure AD) subscription. You and a colleague are discussing Azure security and how to make sure that user logins are secure. What feature allows an Intune administrator to control the Windows Hello for Business experience on Windows 10 and Windows 10 Mobile devices?

   A. Azure Identity Protection

   B. Azure AD Identity Protection

   C. Azure AD Security add-on

   D. Azure AD User Security

67. You are the administrator for your company network. You have two computers named Computer1 and Computer2 that run Windows 10. You create a provisioning package named `Package1` on Computer1. What file must be applied to Computer2 if you plan to apply the provisioning package to Computer2?

   A. `Customizations.xml`

   B. `Package1.cat`

   C. `Package1.icdproj.xml`

   D. `Package1.ppkg`

68. You are the administrator for your company network. Your company uses a Microsoft Store for Business that contains an application that you need to install. You have three computers that cannot access the Internet. Given the following options, how do you distribute the application to the three computers?

   A. Create an answer file using Windows System Image Manager (Windows SIM).

   B. Create a deployment using Microsoft Intune.

   C. Create a deployment from Windows Deployment Services (WDS).

   D. Create a provisioning package using Windows Configuration Designer (WCD).

69. You are the administrator for your company network. You and a colleague are discussing a two-factor biometric authentication method that also allows users to authenticate to Azure AD. What is the name of the authentication method being discussed?

   A. SecurePass

   B. Windows Authenticator

   C. Windows Hello

   D. Windows Hello for Business

70. You are the administrator for your company network. You and a colleague are discussing the ways in which to apply a provisioning package. You'd like to use Windows PowerShell. What command should you use to apply a provisioning package using PowerShell?

   A. The `Add-ProvisioningPackage` command

   B. The `Export-ProvisioningPackage` command

   C. The `Get-ProvisioningPackage` command

   D. The `Install-ProvisioningPackage` command

71. You are the administrator for your company network. You and a colleague are discussing Windows 10 Subscription Activation methods. One of the methods is to use volume activation. One of these services is an automated service that is hosted on a computer in a domain-based network, and all volume editions of Windows 10 intermittently connect to the host to request activation. What is this service called?

A. Active Directory–based activation

B. Key Management Service (KMS)

C. Multiple Activation Key (MAK)

D. Windows Multi-Activation Tool

72. You are the administrator for your company network. You have a Windows 10 image that is mounted to C:\MyMount. You create a provisioning package that is stored in C:\MyFolder. What command-line command should you run if you want to customize the image by using the provisioning package?

A. DISM.exe /Image=C:\MyMount /Add-ProvisioningPackage /Packagepath:C:\MyFolder\ Custom.exe

B. DISM.exe /Image=C:\MyMount /Add-ProvisioningPackage /Packagepath:C:\MyFolder\ Custom.ppkg

C. DISM.exe /Image=C:\MyMount\Windows /Add-ProvisioningPackage Packagepath:C:\ MyFolder\Custom.exe

D. DISM.exe /Image=C:\MyMount\Windows /Add-ProvisioningPackage Packagepath:C:\ MyFolder\Custom.msu

73. You are the administrator for your company network. You have four computers that are configured as follows:

Computer Name	Trusted Platform Module (TPM) Version	Wi-Fi Direct Support	Second-Level Address Translation (SLAT)-Capable Processor Support	Camera Type
Computer1	None	No	Yes	Webcam and illuminated infrared camera
Computer2	1.2	Yes	Yes	Illuminated infrared camera
Computer3	2.0	No	Yes	Webcam
Computer4	2.0	Yes	No	Webcam

You need to deploy Windows 10 Enterprise. The deployment must support Miracast, BitLocker Drive Encryption (BitLocker), and Windows Hello with facial recognition. On which computer should you install Windows 10 to meet your deployment requirements?

A. Install Windows 10 on Computer1.

B. Install Windows 10 on Computer2.

C. Install Windows 10 on Computer3.

D. Install Windows 10 on Computer4.

74. You are the administrator for your company network. You have a computer that runs the 32-bit version of Windows 7 Professional. Which editions of Windows 10 can you upgrade this computer with if you want to perform an in-place upgrade to Windows 10? (Choose two.)

A. The 32-bit version of Windows 10 Professional

B. The 64-bit version of Windows 10 Professional

C. The 32-bit version of Windows 10 Enterprise

D. The 64-bit version of Windows 10 Enterprise

75. You are the administrator for your company network. You have five computers that are currently running Windows 8. You need to perform an upgrade installation to Windows 10 on these computers. Given the following options, what is one possible way to upgrade the Windows 8 machines to Windows 10?

A. You should apply an image of Windows 10 by running `imagex.exe`.

B. You should start the computers from Windows PE and then run `setup.exe` from a network share that contains the Windows 10 installation source files.

C. While signed in to Windows 8, you should run `setup.exe` from a network share that contains the Windows 10 installation source files.

D. You should apply updates by using Windows Update.

76. You are the administrator for your company network. You and a colleague are discussing Windows Update for Business and the different types of updates that it provides. One of the update types is typically released on the second Tuesday of each month and includes security, critical, and driver updates. What type of update is being discussed?

A. Feature Updates

B. Non-Deferrable Updates

C. Pilot Updates

D. Quality Updates

77. You are the administrator for your company network. You and a colleague are discussing troubleshooting Windows Autopilot. One important aspect to check when troubleshooting Windows Autopilot is to check the network connectivity to see whether the device can access the Windows Autopilot services. Which method falls into the checking network connectivity process?

A. Ensure that device hardware IDs have been synchronized to the Windows Autopilot deployment service.

B. Ensure that the deployment profile has been assigned to the device.

C. Ensure that the users have not surpassed the device enrollment limits.

D. Ensure that the Windows Autopilot has Internet access.

78. You are the administrator for your company network. You and a colleague are discussing Windows Autopilot. There are several different deployment scenarios available with Windows Autopilot. One of the available scenarios is used to redeploy a Windows 10 device. This process will remove any personal files, applications, and settings. This process returns a device to its original settings. What deployment scenario is being discussed?

A. Windows Autopilot for existing devices

B. Windows Autopilot self-deploying mode

C. Windows Autopilot user-driven mode

D. Windows Autopilot Reset

79. You are the administrator for your company network. You purchase licenses for several apps from the Microsoft Store, and you list the apps in your Microsoft Store for Business. You need to inform the users on how to install the apps. What should you have them use?

A. The Microsoft Store app and a Microsoft account

B. The Microsoft Store app and a Microsoft Azure Active Directory (Azure AD) account

C. A web browser and a Microsoft Azure Active Directory (Azure AD) account

D. A web browser and a Microsoft account

80. You are the administrator for your company network. You and a colleague are discussing provisioning packages and what they are used for. Given the following options, what is the one item that a provisioning package cannot do?

A. Add computers onto a domain.

B. Configure the Windows user interface.

C. Remove installed software.

D. Downgrade a Windows 10 version from the Enterprise to Home.

81. You are the administrator for your company network. You want to update an Azure Active Directory (Azure AD) application policy for a user's applications. What Windows PowerShell command can you use to accomplish this task?

A. `Add-AzureADPolicy`

B. `Add-AzureADApplicationPolicy`

C. `Create-AzurePolicy`

D. `Set-AzureADPolicy`

82. You are the administrator for your company network. You want to create an Azure Active Directory (Azure AD) policy for your users. What PowerShell command would you use to accomplish this task?

A. `Create-AzureADPolicy`

B. `Edit-AzureADPolicy`

C. `New-AzurePolicy`

D. `New-AzureADPolicy`

83. You are the administrator for your company network. You have a training department that needs the same software installed from scratch on the training computers each week. You determine that you'd like to use Deployment Image Servicing and Management (DISM) to capture the images. What Windows 10 utility can you use in conjunction with DISM to create the images?

- **A.** Answer Manager
- **B.** Setup Manager
- **C.** System Preparation Tool (Sysprep)
- **D.** Universal Authentication Factor (UAF)

84. You are the administrator for your company network. Your company has an Azure Active Directory (Azure AD) domain name of CrystalPanek.onmicrosoft.com. You want to add a new domain name for Panek.onmicrosoft.com. How can you add the new domain name to the existing domain?

- **A.** You can use the Custom Domain Names section of Azure AD and change the name.
- **B.** You can use Azure AD, go to default directories, and change the domain name.
- **C.** You can use PowerShell to change the default domain name.
- **D.** This can't be done.

85. You are the administrator for your company network. You and a colleague are discussing the logs used by the Configuration Manager client. There are many logs available, but one log type records policy changes. What is the name of this log?

- **A.** PolicyAgent.log
- **B.** PolicyAgentProvider.log
- **C.** PolicyEvaluator.log
- **D.** PolicyPlatformClient.log

86. You are the administrator for your company network. You and a colleague are discussing Windows Configuration Designer (WCD) and some of the limitations. Given the following options, which one of the following is not a true statement about the limitations of WCD?

- **A.** You can run only one instance of Windows Configuration Designer (WCD) on a computer at a time.
- **B.** You can run multiple instances of Windows Configuration Designer (WCD) on a computer at a time.
- **C.** You can open multiple projects at the same time within Windows Configuration Designer (WCD), but you can build only one project at a time.
- **D.** You can add apps and drivers. When adding apps and drivers, all files stored in the same folder will be imported.

87. You are the administrator for your company network. You and a colleague are discussing Windows Update for Business and how you can configure Windows Update to control the distribution and deployment of Windows updates to devices. One feature of Windows Update for Business is that you can assign Windows 10 devices into groups to identify the order in which groups will receive their updates. What is this feature of Windows Update for Business called?

A. External Deployment Groups

B. Internal Deployment Groups

C. Peer-to-Peer Delivery

D. Support for Semi-Annual Channel

88. You are the administrator for your company network. You are planning on installing Windows 10 on a computer that has a 1 GHz CPU, 2 GB RAM, and a 15 GB hard drive. Which version of Windows 10 can you install?

A. The 32-bit version of Windows 10 Enterprise

B. The 64-bit version of Windows 10 Enterprise

C. The 64-bit version of Windows 10 Home

D. The 64-bit version of Windows 10 Professional

89. You are the administrator for your company network. You and a colleague are discussing the User State Migration Tool (USMT). The USMT can be used to automate migration. Which statement is not true regarding the USMT?

A. You can migrate the ACL information for specified files and folders.

B. You can migrate folders from the Public profiles.

C. You can migrate local and domain-based user accounts and folders from each user profile.

D. You can migrate passwords.

90. You are the administrator for your company network. You and a colleague are discussing Windows Update for Business and the different types of updates that it provides. One of the update types includes anti-malware and anti-spyware definition updates that are used by Windows Security components, such as Microsoft Defender. What type of update is being discussed?

A. Feature Updates

B. Non-Deferrable Updates

C. Pilot Updates

D. Quality Updates

91. You are the administrator for your company network. You need to create the Upgrade Readiness report. Which Group Policy object (GPO) setting should you configure?

A. The Diagnostics: Configure Scenario Execution Level

B. The Specify Intranet Microsoft Update Service Location

C. The CommercialID

D. Forwarder Resource Usage

E. Audit Other Account Logon Events

92. You are the administrator for your company network. You and a colleague are discussing the use of dynamic deployments. Which of the following is considered a dynamic deployment?

A. Bare-metal install

B. In-place upgrade

C. Subscription Activation

D. Wipe-and-load upgrade

93. You are the administrator for your company network. You and a colleague are discussing the types of transformations that are currently available by using dynamic provisioning. One of these types is created by using the Windows Configuration Designer (WCD) and can be used to send one or more configurations to apps and settings on a device. Which transformation type is being discussed?

A. Answer Files

B. Azure AD Join with Automatic MDM Enrollment

C. Provisioning Package

D. Subscription Activation

94. You are the administrator for your company network. You and a colleague are discussing ways in which to deploy a provisioning package. There are several methods available; however, you'd like to use Windows PowerShell. Which PowerShell cmdlet will allow you to apply a provisioning package?

A. `Add-ProvisioningPackage`

B. `Export-ProvisioningPackage`

C. `Get-ProvisioningPackage`

D. `Import-ProvisioningPackage`

95. You are the administrator for your company network. You and a colleague are discussing deployment options. After you have tested an installation in your test lab environment, what should the next step be?

A. Build a test lab.

B. Perform a full rollout.

C. Perform a pilot deployment.

D. Don't bother with testing; just add the new software to the corporate systems.

96. You are the administrator for your company network. You and a colleague are discussing the benefits of using Desktop Analytics. One of the benefits allows for using collected market data along with data from your environment. The service will then predict potential issues and suggests potential mitigations. What benefit is being discussed?

A. Configuration Manager integration

B. Device and software inventory

C. Issue identification

D. Pilot identification

97. You are the administrator for your company network. You and a colleague are discussing troubleshooting provisioning packages. One issue that you may encounter is possible configuration errors or missing customizations. You want to review the provisioning package using Windows Configuration Designer (WCD). What file should you open to review it for proper configuration?

   A. package1.xml

   B. package1.cat

   C. package1.icdproj.xml

   D. package1.ppkg

98. You are the administrator for your company network. You and a colleague are discussing Windows Autopilot. There are several different deployment scenarios available with Windows Autopilot. One of the available scenarios is used for transforming Windows 10 devices that will be automatically configured for use as a kiosk terminal, as a shared computer, or as a digital signage device. What deployment scenario is being discussed?

   A. Windows Autopilot for existing devices

   B. Windows Autopilot user-driven mode

   C. Windows Autopilot self-deploying mode

   D. Windows Autopilot Reset

99. You are the administrator for your company network. You and a colleague are discussing using Windows Autopilot. You understand that there are some networking configuration requirements and prerequisites that are needed to utilize Windows Autopilot. Which statement regarding Windows Autopilot is true?

   A. The devices must have access to the Internet.

   B. The devices do not need to have access to the Internet.

   C. The devices should use DHCP for name resolution.

   D. The devices should have firewall access for port 80 for HTTPS traffic.

100. You are the administrator for your company network. You and a colleague are discussing how to collect the hardware ID from existing devices using PowerShell. What command should you use?

   A. Add-WindowsAutoPilotInfo.ps1

   B. Get-WindowsAutoPilotInfo.ps1

   C. Install-WindowsAutoPilotInfo.ps1

   D. Set-WindowsAutoPilotInfo.ps1

101. You are the administrator for your company network. You and a colleague are discussing how to extract hash information from Configuration Manager. What file extension must be used to extract this information?

   A. .csv

   B. .docx

C. .exe

D. .txt

102. You are the administrator for your company network. You and a colleague are discussing Windows Autopilot error codes. Which code states "Something went wrong. This user is not authorized to enroll. You can try to do this again or contact your system administrator with the error code"?

A. 0x800705B4

B. 0x801c0003

C. 0x80180018

D. 0x80070032

103. You are the administrator for your company network. You and a colleague are discussing a way to create an inventory of apps that are running within the organization. What service that works in conjunction with Configuration Manager will allow you to create an inventory of apps?

A. Delivery Optimization

B. Desktop Analytics

C. Upgrade Readiness

D. Windows Analytics

104. You are the administrator for your company network. You and a colleague are discussing Upgrade Readiness. Microsoft has recently retired Windows Analytics, and Upgrade Readiness was part of this service. You want to switch to the newer product called Desktop Analytics. What should you do?

A. Demote the Upgrade Readiness connection.

B. Promote the Upgrade Readiness connection.

C. Remove the Upgrade Readiness connection.

D. Upgrade the Upgrade Readiness connection.

105. You are the administrator for your company network. You and a colleague are discussing using the User State Migration Tool (USMT) to migrate user profiles. Several migration types are available. One such migration is used when the source and destination computers for the upgrade are different machines. What is this type of migration called?

A. It is called an in-place migration.

B. It is called an inline migration.

C. It is called a side-by-side migration.

D. it is called a wipe-and-load migration.

106. You are the administrator for your company network. You and a colleague are discussing files that can be used with the User State Migration Tool (USMT). What file extension is used with the migration files?

A. .csv

B. .docx

    C.   .txt

    D.   .xml

107. You are the administrator for your company network. You and a colleague are discussing
User State Migration components. One of the components is used to compress, encrypt,
and validate the migration store files. What is this component called?

    A.   config.xml

    B.   loadstate.exe

    C.   scanstate.exe

    D.   usmtutils.exe

108. You are the administrator for your company network. You and a colleague are discussing
using the User State Migration Tool (USMT) to migrate user profiles. Several migration
types are available. One such migration is used when the source and destination computers
for the upgrade are the same machine. What is this type of migration called?

    A.   It is called an in-place migration.

    B.   It is called an inline migration.

    C.   It is called a side-by-side migration.

    D.   It is called a wipe-and-load migration.

109. You are the administrator for your company network. You and a colleague are discussing
configuring Delivery Optimization settings using Group Policy download mode. Which
download mode is being discussed if it is described as HTTP downloading and peering in
the same private group on a local LAN?

    A.   Group

    B.   HTTP Only

    C.   Internet

    D.   Simple

110. You are the administrator for your company network. You and a colleague are discussing
Windows Update for Business. There are several applicable features of Windows Update.
One feature allows you to specify when updates will be applied to devices. What is this
feature called?

    A.   Integration with existing tools

    B.   Internal deployment groups

    C.   Maintenance windows

    D.   Peer-to-peer delivery

111. You are the administrator for your company network. You and a colleague are discussing
Windows Update for Business and the different types of updates that it provides. One of
the update types includes all previous security and quality updates and introduces new
operating system feature additions and changes. What type of update is being discussed?

    A.   Feature Updates

    B.   Non-Deferrable Updates

C. Pilot Updates

D. Quality Updates

112. You are the administrator for your company network. You and a colleague are discussing Windows Update for Business and how it can be configured by using Group Policy settings. There are several important GPO settings for Windows Update for Business. One of these settings allows an administrator to specify when to receive quality updates or to defer receiving quality updates. What Windows Update for Business group policy is being discussed?

A. The Manage Preview Updates setting

B. The Manage Windows Diagnostics setting

C. The Select When Preview Builds And Feature Updates Are Received setting

D. The Select When Quality Updates Are Received setting

113. You are the administrator for your company network. You and a colleague are discussing the retirement of Windows Analytics. One component, however, has been continued through the Azure Portal. What is the name of this feature?

A. Device Health

B. Device Strength

C. Update Compliance

D. Upgrade Readiness

114. You are the administrator for your company network. You and a colleague are discussing Update Compliance solutions. Within the Update Compliance solution, an administrator can view the diagnostic data relating to devices. The data is split into different sections. What is the name of the default section of the Update Compliance workspace?

A. Feature Update Status

B. Need Attention!

C. Security Update Status

D. Microsoft Defender AV Status

115. You are the administrator for your company network. You and a colleague are discussing different authentication methods. Which one of the following tools allows for the use of security questions?

A. Azure AD Self-Service Password Reset (SSPR).

B. Azure Multifactor Authentication (Azure MFA).

C. Password Manager (PassMgr).

D. This can't be done.

116. You are the administrator for your company network. You and a colleague are discussing multifactor authentication. Your colleague asks you for an example of multifactor authentication. What do you tell your colleague?

A. Multifactor authentication is using biometric fingerprints and voice recognition.

B. Multifactor authentication is using smart cards and PINs.

C. Multifactor authentication is using retina scans and voice recognition.

D. Multifactor authentication is using usernames, PINs, and employee ID numbers.

117. You are the administrator for your company network. You and a colleague are discussing the different multifactor authentication categories. One example is when an employee is using a key fob that has authentication tokens that generate a one-time password that must be used at login. What multifactor authentication category would this scenario fall under?

A. Something you are

B. Something you have

C. Something you know

D. Something you need

118. You are the administrator for your company network. You and a colleague are discussing Azure Multifactor Authentication (Azure MFA) and the methods that can be enabled. One of these methods uses a risk policy to enforce two-step verification for signing into all cloud applications. What method is being discussed?

A. Azure AD Identity Protection

B. Changing device state

C. Changing user state

D. Conditional access policy

119. You are the administrator for your company network. You and a colleague are discussing the use of Microsoft Accounts within the organization. You'd like to limit the use of Microsoft accounts. If you're using a Group Policy object (GPO), which policy can prevent users from using Microsoft accounts for authentication for applications or services?

A. Account: Block Certain Microsoft Accounts

B. Accounts: Block Microsoft Accounts

C. Block All Consumer Microsoft Account User Authentication

D. Block Certain Consumer Microsoft Account User Authentication

120. You are the administrator for your company network. You have a Microsoft Azure Active Directory (Azure AD) tenant. Some of the users use Windows Hello for Business to sign in to their computers. You purchase a new computer and join the computer to the Azure AD. When the new user attempts to configure the sign-in options, they receive an error message that states that "Some settings are hidden or managed by your organization." You open Device Manager and confirm that all of the hardware is working correctly. What should you do first if you need to ensure that the user can use Windows Hello for Business facial recognition to sign in to the computer?

A. You should enable UEFI Secure Boot.

B. You should install a virtual TPM driver.

C. You should purchase an infrared (IR) camera.

D. You should upgrade the computer to Windows 10 Enterprise.

121. You are the administrator for your company network. A user has reached out and informed you that they'd like to use their favorite photo as a password. Where do you set this up on the user's computer?

- **A.** Password
- **B.** Sign-in options
- **C.** Windows Hello
- **D.** Your Info

122. You are the administrator for your company network. You have a computer that runs Windows 10. You have been tasked to configure Windows Hello. You want to configure the PIN complexity rules for this computer. Which policy setting should you modify?

- **A.** Biometrics
- **B.** Credential User Interface
- **C.** Smart Cards
- **D.** Windows Hello for Business

123. You are the administrator for your company network. A user wants to use a picture to log in to the system. Windows 10 provides the ability to use a picture along with gestures for logon. How many gestures do you add to a photo for logon?

- **A.** One
- **B.** Two
- **C.** Three
- **D.** Four

124. You are the administrator for your company network. You and a colleague are discussing the use of complex Windows Hello personal identification numbers (PINs). You know that a PIN can require or block special characters, uppercase characters, lowercase characters, and digits. What is the maximum length of a PIN in characters?

- **A.** 8
- **B.** 32
- **C.** 69
- **D.** 127

125. You are the administrator for your company network. You and a colleague are discussing Windows 10 sign-in options and privacy. One method allows for automatically locking your computer when you walk away from it. What is this method called?

- **A.** Active lock
- **B.** Dynamic lock
- **C.** Picture password
- **D.** Security key

Chapter

6

Manage Policies and Profiles

THE MD-101 EXAM TOPICS COVERED IN THIS CHAPTER INCLUDE:

✓ **Domain 6: Manage Policies and Profiles**

- 6.1: Plan and implement co-management
  - Implement co-management precedence
  - Migrate group policy to MDM policies
  - Recommend a co-management strategy
- 6.2: Implement conditional access and compliance policies for devices
  - Implement conditional access policies
  - Manage conditional access policies
  - Plan conditional access policies
  - Implement device compliance policies
  - Manage device compliance policies
  - Plan device compliance policies
- 6.3: Configure device profiles
  - Implement device profiles
  - Manage device profiles
  - Plan device profiles
- 6.4: Manage user profiles
  - Configure user profiles
  - Configure Enterprise State Roaming in Azure AD
  - Configure sync settings
  - Implement Folder Redirection, including OneDrive

1. You are the administrator for your company network. You are creating a device configuration profile in Microsoft Intune. What profile type should you use if you want to implement an ADMX-backed policy?

    A. A custom policy

    B. A device restrictions policy

    C. A device restrictions (Windows 10 Team) policy

    D. An identity protection policy

2. You are the administrator for your company network. You have a Microsoft 365 subscription, and all of the computers are enrolled in Microsoft Intune. You have certain requirements that you need to meet to secure your Windows 10 environment. These requirements are shown here:

Requirement	Detail
Requirement1	Ensure that Microsoft Exchange Online can be accessed from known locations only.
Requirement2	Lock a device that has a high Windows Defender Advanced Threat Protection (Windows Defender ATP) risk score.

    What should you implement to meet Requirement1?

    A. A conditional access policy.

    B. A device compliance policy.

    C. A device configuration profile.

    D. It can't be done.

3. You are the administrator for your company network. You have a Microsoft 365 subscription, and all the computers are enrolled in Microsoft Intune. You have certain requirements that you need to meet to secure your Windows 10 environment. These requirements are shown here:

Requirement	Detail
Requirement1	Ensure that Microsoft Exchange Online can be accessed from known locations only.
Requirement2	Lock a device that has a high Windows Defender Advanced Threat Protection (Windows Defender ATP) risk score.

    What should you implement to meet Requirement2?

    A. A conditional access policy.

    B. A device compliance policy.

    C. A device configuration profile.

    D. It can't be done.

4. You are the administrator for your company network. You and a colleague are discussing using hybrid mobile device management (MDM). You are planning to create a new hybrid connection. What should you do to complete the migration?

A. Add a device enrollment manager (DEM) in Intune.

B. Assign all users Intune licenses.

C. Change the tenant MDM authority to Intune.

D. This cannot be done.

5. You are the administrator for your company network. Your company has a Microsoft 365 subscription. You manage all devices using Microsoft Intune. The company uses conditional access to restrict access to Microsoft 365 services for devices that do not comply with the company's security policies. What should you use if you need to identify which devices will be prevented from accessing Microsoft 365 services?

A. The Conditional Access blade in the Azure Active Directory admin center

B. The Device Compliance blade in the Intune admin center

C. The Device Health solution in Desktop Analytics

D. The Windows Defender Security Center

6. You are the administrator for your company network. You have several hundred Windows 10 computers that are joined to Microsoft Azure Active Directory (Azure AD) and enrolled in Microsoft Intune. What folder should you include if you want to redirect Windows known folders to Microsoft OneDrive for Business?

A. You should include the Desktop folder.

B. You should include the Downloads folder.

C. You should include the Music folder.

D. You should include the Saved Games folder.

7. You are the administrator for your company network. You have a Microsoft Azure Active Directory (Azure AD) tenant. All corporate devices are enrolled in Microsoft Intune. You have a web-based application that uses Azure AD to authenticate. What should you configure if you need to prompt all users of the application to agree to the protection of corporate data when they access the app from both corporate and noncorporate devices?

A. You should configure notifications in Device Compliance.

B. You should configure Terms and Conditions in Device Enrollment.

C. You should configure Terms of Use in Conditional Access.

D. You should configure an Endpoint Protection Profile in Device Configuration.

8. You are the administrator for your company network. You have the following unrooted devices enrolled in Microsoft Intune:

Name	Platform	IP Address
DeviceA	Windows	192.168.10.35
DeviceB	Android	10.10.10.40
DeviceC	Android	192.168.10.10

The devices are members of a group named GroupA. You create a device compliance location in Intune that has the following configurations:

Name: NetworkA

IPv4 range: 192.168.10.0/24

You create a device compliance policy for the Android platform in Intune. The policy has following configurations:

Name: PolicyA

Device health: Rooted devices: Block

Locations: NetworkA

Mark device noncompliant: Immediately

Assigned: GroupA

In Intune, the device compliance policy has the following configurations:

Mark devices with no compliance policy assigned as: Compliant

Enhanced jailbreak detection: Enabled

Compliance status validity period (days): 20

Which of the following statements is not true?

A. DeviceA is marked as complaint.

B. DeviceB is marked as compliant.

C. DeviceC is marked as compliant.

D. All of the devices are marked as compliant.

9. You are the administrator for your company network. Your network contains an Active Directory that has two Windows 10 computers named Computer1 and Computer2. Folder Redirection is configured for a domain user. The AppData\Roaming folder and the Desktop folder are redirected to a network share. The user signs into Computer1 and performs the following:

- The screen saver is configured to start after 5 minutes of inactivity.
- The default save location for Microsoft Word is modified.
- A file named File1.docx is created on the desktop.
- The desktop background is modified.

You need to identify what will be retained when the user signs into Computer2. What will the user see when they log into the computer?

A. The user will only see `File1.docx` and the desktop background.

B. The user will see `File1.docx`, the screen saver settings, the desktop background, and the default save location for Word.

C. The user will see `File1.docx` only.

D. The user will see `File1.docx`, the desktop background, and the default save location for Word only.

10. You are the administrator for your company network. You and a colleague are discussing dynamic disks. You are planning on upgrading a basic disk to a dynamic disk on a Windows 10 computer. Which of the following statements is true regarding dynamic disks on Windows 10?

    A. Dynamic disks can be recognized by older operating systems such as Windows NT 4 in addition to new operating systems such as Windows 10.

    B. Dynamic disks are supported only by Windows 2000 Server and Windows Server 2003.

    C. Dynamic disks support features such as simple partitions, extended partitions, spanned partitions, and striped partitions.

    D. Dynamic disks support features such as simple volumes, extended volumes, spanned volumes, mirrored volumes, and striped volumes.

11. You are the administrator for your company network. Your network contains an Active Directory domain that contains 200 Windows 10 computers. Folder Redirection for a Desktop folder has the following properties configured:

    ▪ Grant The User Exclusive Rights To Desktop is enabled.

    ▪ Move The Content Of Desktop To The New Location is enabled.

    ▪ The Policy Removal setting is set to Leave The Folder In The New Location When Policy Is Removed.

    A server is set to be the target. You are planning to use known folder redirection in Microsoft OneDrive for Business. When you implement known folder redirection, you need to ensure that the user's desktop content remains on their desktop. What actions should you perform? (Choose two.)

    A. Clear the Grant The User Exclusive Rights To Desktop checkbox.

    B. Change the Policy Removal setting.

    C. Disable Folder Redirection.

    D. Clear the Move The Contents Of Desktop To The New Location checkbox.

12. You are the administrator for your company network. Your company has computers that run Windows 8.1, Windows 10, and macOS. You are using Microsoft Intune to manage the computers. You need to create an Intune profile to configure Windows Hello for Business on the computers that support it. What platform type should you use?

    A. You should use macOS.

    B. You should use Windows 10 or later.

   C. You should use Windows 8.1.

   D. You should change the operating systems to a legacy operating system that supports Windows Hello for Business.

13. You are the administrator for your company network. Your company has computers that run Windows 8.1, Windows 10, and macOS. You are using Microsoft Intune to manage the computers. You need to create an Intune profile to configure Windows Hello for Business on the computers that support it. What profile type should you use?

   A. Device restrictions

   B. Device restrictions (Windows 10 Team)

   C. Endpoint protection

   D. Threat protection

14. You are the administrator for your company network. Your network contains an Active Directory domain that is synced to Microsoft Azure Active Directory (Azure AD). You have a Microsoft 365 subscription. You decide to create a conditional access policy for Microsoft Exchange Online. What setting should you configure if you want to configure the policy to prevent access to Exchange Online unless connected from a device that is hybrid Azure AD joined?

   A. The Device Platforms setting

   B. The Device State setting

   C. The Locations setting

   D. The Sign-In Risk setting

15. You are the administrator for your company network. You have 20 Windows 10 computers that are joined to Microsoft Azure Active Directory (Azure AD). You have a Microsoft 365 subscription. You are planning to replace these computers with new computers that also run Windows 10. The new computers will be joined to Azure AD. What should you configure if you need to ensure that the desktop background, the Favorites, and the browsing history are available on the new computers?

   A. You should configure Enterprise State Roaming.

   B. You should configure Folder Redirection.

   C. You should configure system settings.

   D. You should configure roaming user profiles.

16. You are the administrator for your company network. Your network contains an Active Directory domain that syncs to Azure Active Directory (Azure AD). Your existing onsite computers are managed using Microsoft System Center Configuration Manager (Current Branch). You configure the domain for co-management. You plan on deploying 100 new Windows 10 devices. The devices will be joined to Azure AD and enrolled in Microsoft Intune. What should you create in Intune first so that you can ensure that the devices are co-managed?

   A. An app configuration policy

   B. An app for the Configuration Manager client

   C. A conditional access policy

   D. A device compliance policy

   E. A device configuration profile

17. You are the administrator for your company network. Your network contains an Active Directory domain that syncs to Azure Active Directory (Azure AD). The Active Directory domain contains several hundred Windows 10 computers. The computers are managed by using Microsoft System Center Configuration Manager (Current Branch). What should you configure first if you need to pilot co-management for only five of the computers?

A. A device collection in Configuration Manager

B. A domain local distribution group in Active Directory

C. A dynamic device group in Azure AD

D. An Intune Connector for Active Directory

18. You are the administrator for your company network. You are planning on setting up a device configuration profile in Intune that will allow your users to be able to reset their own passwords. Using Intune, what device configuration profile option should you configure?

A. A custom option

B. The endpoint protection option

C. The identity protection option

D. The kiosk option

19. You are the administrator for your company network. Your company has a Microsoft 365 subscription. You have a new junior administrator who is responsible for deploying Windows 10 to computers and joining the computers to Microsoft Azure Active Directory (Azure AD). The new administrator can successfully join computers to Azure AD. However, within a few days, the junior administrator receives an error message that states, "This user is not authorized to enroll. You can try to do this again or contact your system administrator. Error code (0x801c0003)." You need to ensure that the junior administrator can join computers to Azure AD. What should you do while following the principle of least amount of privilege?

A. Assign the Cloud Device Administrator role to the junior administrator.

B. Assign the Global Administrator role to the junior administrator.

C. Modify the Device settings in Azure AD.

D. Modify the User settings in Azure AD.

20. You are the administrator for your company network. All computers are enrolled in Microsoft Intune, and you have a Microsoft 365 subscription. You must meet corporate requirements for securing Windows 10 devices. What device configuration profile type should you use if you need to lock devices that have a high Windows Defender Advanced Threat Protection (Windows Defender ATP) risk score?

A. A device restrictions profile type

B. An endpoint protection profile type

C. An identity protection profile type

D. A kiosk profile type

21. You are the administrator for your company network. You manage a Microsoft 365 environment that has co-management enabled. All computers run Windows 10 and are deployed using the Microsoft Deployment Toolkit (MDT). You need to suggest a solution to deploy Microsoft Office 365 ProPlus to new computers. The latest version must always be installed. Your solution must also follow the principle of least amount of privilege. What is the best command-line tool to use for the deployment?

A. A Group Policy object (GPO)

B. Microsoft Deployment Toolkit (MDT)

C. Microsoft Intune

D. Microsoft System Center Configuration Manager

E. Office Deployment Toolkit (ODT)

22. You are the administrator for your company network. You have installed Windows 10 on a Windows XP Professional computer. The computer is capable of dual-booting. The Windows XP machine is using the FAT32 file system, and the Windows 10 machine is using NTFS. You boot the computer to Windows XP for testing the compatibility of the application using both operating systems. Which of the following file systems will be seen by both operating systems?

A. Only the FAT32 partition will be seen by both.

B. Only the NTFS partition will be seen by both.

C. Neither the FAT32 nor the NTFS partition will be seen.

D. Both the FAT32 and the NTFS partition will be seen.

23. You are the administrator for your company network. You have an Azure Active Directory (Azure AD) tenant that contains several Windows 10 devices. When new Windows 10 devices are joined to the network, the users are prompted to set up a four-digit pin number. You need to ensure that the users are prompted to set up a six-digit pin when they join. What should you do?

A. Configure the Authentication methods from the Azure Active Directory admin center.

B. Configure automatic mobile device management (MDM) enrollment from the Azure Active Directory admin center. Then, from the Device Management admin center, configure the Windows Hello for Business enrollment options.

C. Configure automatic mobile device management (MDM) enrollment from the Azure Active Directory admin center. Then, from the Device Management admin center, create and assign a device restrictions profile.

D. You cannot use a six-digit pin—you must use the four-digit pin only.

24. You are the administrator for your company network. You and a colleague are discussing Azure Active Directory (Azure AD) and a way in which data is automatically encrypted prior to leaving the user's Windows 10 device by using Azure Rights Management (Azure RMS). This data also stays encrypted in the cloud. What is this called?

A. Folder Redirection

B. Enterprise State Roaming

C. Folder Redirection in Microsoft OneDrive

D. Home folders

25. You are the administrator for your company network. A user often works with a large number of files. The user tells you that the bigger the files get, the longer it takes to access them. You think that the issue is related to the files being spread out over the disk. What utility can you use to store the files sequentially on the disk?

A. Disk Administrator

B. Disk Cleanup

C. Disk Defragmenter

D. Disk Manager

26. You are the administrator for your company network. You are installing a new hard drive onto a computer that dual-boots between Windows 10 and Windows 7. You will be storing large and sensitive files on this drive. You will need to access these files from either operating system. What file system should you use when formatting the new disk?

A. CDFS

B. FAT16

C. FAT32

D. NTFS

27. You are the administrator for your company network. You have 100 Windows 10 Professional devices that are joined to Azure AD and enrolled in Microsoft Intune. You need to upgrade the computers to Windows 10 Enterprise. What should you configure in Intune to upgrade the computers?

A. A device cleanup rule

B. A device compliance policy

C. A device configuration profile

D. A device enrollment policy

28. You are the administrator for your company network. You have several hundred Windows 10 computers that are joined to Microsoft Azure Active Directory (AD) and enrolled in Microsoft Intune. You have been tasked with enabling self-service password reset on the sign-in screen. In Microsoft Intune, what settings should you configure?

A. You should configure Conditional Access.

B. You should configure Device Configuration.

C. You should configure Device Compliance.

D. You should configure Device Enrollment.

29. You are the administrator for your company network. You have 200 Windows 10 computers that are joined to Microsoft Azure Active Directory (Azure AD) and enrolled in Microsoft Intune. You redirect Windows Known Folders to Microsoft OneDrive for Business. What folder will be included in the redirection?

A. The Documents folder

B. The Downloads folder

    C. The Music folder

    D. The Saved Games folder

30. You are the administrator for your company network. Your network contains an Active Directory domain. The functional level of the forest and the domain is Windows Server 2012 R2. The domain contains 500 Windows 10 computers. All of the corporate computers are managed using Microsoft System Center 2012 R2 Configuration Manager. What should you do first if you want to enable co-management?

    A. Deploy the Microsoft Intune client.

    B. Raise the domain functional level.

    C. Raise the forest functional level.

    D. Upgrade Configuration Manager to Current Branch.

31. You are the administrator for your company network. Your company uses Microsoft Intune. You have more than 500 Android and iOS devices enrolled in the Intune tenant. You are planning on deploying new Intune policies. Different policies will apply depending on which version of Android or iOS is installed on the device. What should you configure first if you need to ensure that the policies can target the devices depending on their version?

    A. The corporate device identifiers in Intune

    B. The device categories in Intune

    C. The device settings in Microsoft Azure Active Directory (Azure AD)

    D. The groups that have dynamic membership rules in Microsoft Azure Active Directory (Azure AD)

32. You are the administrator for your company network. You have 500 Windows 10 computers that are joined to Microsoft Azure Active Directory (Azure AD) and enrolled in Microsoft Intune. You are planning to distribute certificates to the computers by using Simple Certificate Enrollment Protocol (SCEP). The servers are shown here:

Name	Configuration
Server1	Domain Controller
Server2	Root Certification Authority (CA)
Server3	Subordinate Certification Authority (CA)
Server4	Network Device Enrollment Service (NDES)

NDES issues the certificates from the subordinate CA. You are configuring a device profile. The settings are as follows:

Name: Computer1

Platform: Windows 10 and later

Profile Type: SCEP Certificate

You are finishing the configuration. The SCEP certificate is currently configured with the following:

Certificate Type: User

Subject Name Format: Common name including email

Certificate Validity Period: Years 1

Key Storage Provider (KSP): Enroll to Trusted Platform Module (TPM) KSP if present, otherwise Software KSP

Key Usage: 2 selected

Key Size (Bits): 2048

Hash Algorithm: SHA-2

Root Certificate: <Select a Certificate>

What server should you select for the SCEP profile?

A. Server1

B. Server2

C. Server3

D. Server4

33. You are the administrator for your company network. The company wants to set up a way to integrate its onsite Active Directory with its Azure Active Directory (Azure AD). What tool can you use to implement this task?

A. Azure AD Connect

B. Azure AD Replication

C. Active Directory Replicator

D. Site-to-Site VPN Gateway Connectors

34. You are the administrator for your company network. Your organization has 100 devices that run Windows 10 Pro. The devices are all joined to Azure Active Directory (Azure AD) and enrolled in Microsoft Intune. You need to upgrade the computers to Windows 10 Enterprise. What should you configure in Intune?

A. A device cleanup rule

B. A device configuration profile

C. A device compliance policy

D. A device enrollment policy

35. You are the administrator for your company network. Your company is planning on deploying Windows 10 tablets to several conference rooms. These tablets will be managed by using Microsoft Intune. The tablets have an application named App1 that many users will utilize. You need to configure the tablets so that any user can use the application without having to sign in. Users must not be able to use other applications on the tablets. What device configuration profile type should you utilize?

A. Device restrictions profile type

B. Endpoint protection profile type

   C. Identity protection profile type

   D. Kiosk profile type

36. You are the administrator for your company network. You and a colleague are discussing systems that are normally designed to be in one location where many people can use them. This is usually the same device, and that device will run only a limited number of applications. What is this called?

   A. Computer stalls

   B. Kiosks

   C. Rotundas

   D. Stand-alone computers

37. You are the administrator for your company network. You have a few hundred Windows 10 computers that are joined to Microsoft Azure Active Directory (Azure AD) and enrolled in Microsoft Intune. You want to redirect Windows known folders to Microsoft OneDrive for Business. What folder should you include?

   A. The Documents folder

   B. The Downloads folder

   C. The Music folder

   D. The Saved Games folder

38. You are the administrator for your company network. Your company allows users to use their personal devices to access corporate data. A user has a personal tablet that runs Windows 10. The tablet is enrolled in Microsoft Intune. This user leaves the company. What will be deleted from the tablet if you perform a selective wipe of the tablet?

   A. All of the apps that are installed from the Microsoft Store for Business will be removed.

   B. All of the files located in `%ProgramData%\Package Cache` will be removed.

   C. All of the files located in `%userprofile\AppData\Roaming` will be removed.

   D. All of the user profiles will be removed.

39. You are the administrator for your company network. You and a colleague are discussing a Windows 10 ability that allows you to manage Windows 10 devices concurrently by using both Configuration Manager and Microsoft Intune. What is this configuration method called?

   A. Coexistence

   B. Cohabitation

   C. Co-management

   D. Co-occurrence

40. You are the administrator for your company network. You and a colleague are discussing Configuration Manager. While using Configuration Manager, an administrator can view a dashboard with information regarding co-management. The dashboard helps an administrator review machines that are co-managed in the environment. What workspace do you need to access in order to review the machines that are co-managed?

A. Administration

B. Assets and Compliance

C. Monitoring

D. Software Library

41. You are the administrator for your company network. You and a colleague are discussing the Configuration Manager Monitoring workspace. Which section of the dashboard are you reviewing if you are looking at a bar chart with the number of devices that have been transitioned to Microsoft Intune for the available workloads?

A. Client OS distribution

B. Co-managed devices

C. Enrollment errors

D. Workload transition

42. You are the administrator for your company network. You and a colleague are discussing the Known Folder Move Group Policy object (GPO). One of the settings under this GPO forces users to keep their known folders directed to OneDrive. What setting is being discussed?

A. Prevent Users From Moving Their Windows Known Folders To OneDrive

B. Prevent Users From Redirecting Their Windows Known Folders To Their PC

C. Prompt Users To Move Windows Known Folders To OneDrive

D. Silently Move Windows Known Folders To OneDrive

43. You are the administrator for your company network. You and a colleague are discussing a set of rules put onto devices that allow them access to resources within your organization by using Intune. What are these sets of rules known as?

A. Accordance policies

B. Compliance policies

C. Device rules

D. System compliance policies

44. You are the administrator for your company network. You and a colleague are discussing a feature used by Azure Active Directory (Azure AD) to bring together signals, to make decisions, and to enforce organizational policies. What is this tool called?

A. Conditional access

B. Device access

C. Microsoft Cloud App Security (MCAS)

D. Microsoft Empowerment

45. You are the administrator for your company network. You and a colleague are discussing how to run PowerShell scripts on Windows 10 devices using Intune. What is the name of the tool available in Intune that allows you to run PowerShell scripts on your devices?

A. PowerShell Extension

B. Intune Management Extension

C. Intune Script Maker

D. Intune Windows PowerShell Extension

46. You are the administrator for your company network. You and a colleague are discussing creating a device profile in Microsoft Intune. One of the profile options allows you to check the status of your profiles for successes or failures, and it also allows you to view logs on your profiles. What profile option is being discussed?

A. By platform

B. Monitor

C. Overview

D. Policy

47. You are the administrator for your company network. You need to ensure that when managers join Azure Active Directory (Azure AD), their computers are enrolled automatically into mobile device management (MDM). What tool should you use to do this?

A. The Configuration Manager console

B. The Group Policy Management Editor

C. The Azure portal

D. The Microsoft Intune portal

48. You are the administrator for your company network. You need to ensure that when managers join Azure Active Directory (Azure AD), their computers are enrolled automatically into mobile device management (MDM). What settings should you configure?

A. The Add Workstations to Domain settings

B. The Device configuration settings

C. The Device enrollment settings

D. The Mobility (MDM and MAM) settings

49. You are the administrator for your company network. You have the following Windows 10 computers:

Name	Configuration
Computer1	Active Directory Domain Joined
Computer2	Microsoft Azure Active Directory (Azure AD) Joined
Computer3	Hybrid Microsoft Azure Active Directory (Azure AD) Joined

Computer2 and Computer3 are enrolled in Microsoft Intune. In a Group Policy object (GPO) linked to the domain, you enable the `Computer Configuration/ Administrative Templates/Windows Components/Search/Allow Cortana` setting. In an Intune device configuration profile, you configure the following:

- `Device/Vendor/MSFT/Policy/Config/ControlPolicyConflict/ MDMWinsOverGP` to a value of 1

- `Experience/AllowCortana` to a value of 0

Which of the following statements is true?

A. Computer1 can use Cortana for search.

B. Computer2 can use Cortana for search.

C. Computer3 can use Cortana for search.

D. None of the computers can use Cortana for search.

50. You are the administrator for your company network. You and a colleague are discussing a tool used to evaluate existing GroupPolicies to figure out whether a candidate is suitable for migration into Microsoft Intune. What is this tool called?

A. Intune Migration Tool (IMT)

B. Migration Analysis Tool (MAT)

C. Migration Assistant Tool (MAT)

D. MDM Migration Analysis Tool (MMAT)

51. You are the administrator for your company network. You and a colleague are discussing the use of the MDM Migration Analysis Tool (MMAT). Once the tool is run on the device, the tool will generate a report. What file extension will the report have?

A. .docx

B. .exe

C. .xls

D. .xml

52. You are the administrator for your company network. You and a colleague are discussing a configuration model that allows Configuration Manager and Intune to balance the workloads to make sure that there are no conflicts. What is this configuration known as?

A. Coexistence

B. Cohabitation

C. Co-management

D. Co-occurrence

53. You are the administrator for your company network. You and a colleague are discussing Azure Active Directory (Azure AD) and the flow process of the procedure. When a client device requests access to corporate resources such as information contained in a controlled application, what does Azure AD check for first?

A. It will first check whether any conditional access policies are in place with Intune.

B. It will first check whether any device compliance policies are in place with Intune.

C. It will first check whether any conditional access policies are in place with Active Directory.

D. It will first check whether any device compliance policies are in place with Active Directory.

54. You are the administrator for your company network. You and a colleague are discussing several of the conditional access policy conditions. One of these conditions is used to apply or exclude devices that are hybrid Azure AD joined or marked as compliant in Intune. What condition is being discussed?

A. Client Apps

B. Device Platforms

C. Device State

D. Locations

55. You are the administrator for your company network. You and a colleague are discussing co-management and the two main paths that are used to reach co-management. What are the paths? (Choose two.)

A. Cloud connect with co-management

B. Existing Configuration Manager clients

C. Third-party MDM coexistence

D. New Internet-based devices

56. You are the administrator for your company network. You and a colleague are discussing conditional access policy access controls. There are a number of access controls available. If you want to require multifactor authentication (Azure Multi-Factor Authentication), what setting should you choose?

A. Device State

B. Session

C. Grant – Block Access

D. Grant – Grant Access

57. You are the administrator for your company network. You and a colleague are discussing conditional access policies and specifically configuring the Session section. The Session setting that you are discussing uses a reverse proxy architecture, and it is uniquely integrated with Azure AD conditional access. Azure AD conditional access allows you to implement access controls on your apps based upon certain conditions. What setting is being discussed?

A. App Enforced Restrictions

B. Conditional Access App Control

C. Persistent Browser Session

D. Sign-In Frequency

58. You are the administrator for your company network. You and a colleague are discussing a tool that allows you to connect your local Active Directory Domain Services (AD DS) environment to your Azure Active Directory (Azure AD). What is the name of this tool?

A. Azure Connection Tool

B. Azure AD Connect

C. Azure AD Connect Health

D. Forefront Identity Manager

59. You are the administrator for your company network. You and a colleague are discussing conditional access policies and how to set one up. One section of the conditional access policy controls how a policy is enforced. What section is being discussed?

A. Access Controls

B. Admission Control

C. Assignments

D. Tasks

60. You are the administrator for your company network. You and a colleague are discussing conditional access policies and how to set one up. One section of the conditional access policy controls the who, what, and where of the conditional access policy. What section is being discussed?

A. Access Controls

B. Admission Control

C. Assignments

D. Tasks

61. You are the administrator for your company network. You and a colleague are discussing device profiles. You are discussing a profile type that will allow you to run devices as a dedicated device. What is this profile type called?

A. Administrative Templates

B. Device Restrictions

C. Kiosk

D. Windows Information Protection

62. You are the administrator for your company network. You and a colleague are discussing the ability of Windows 10 Azure Active Directory (Azure AD) users to roam their profile data between multiple devices, allowing the user and app settings to sync between the devices regardless of where the user is located. What is this called?

A. Azure Readiness Roaming

B. Enterprise State Roaming

    C. Mandatory User Profile

    D. Roaming User Profile

63. You are the administrator for your company network. You and a colleague are discussing implementing a transition to co-management. You are planning to deploy a phased approach that will allow you to roll out features and functionality slowly to an increasing number of devices over a certain period of time. What rollout group would you be in if the rollout incorporates the devices, findings, and feedback from the initial pilot group and this is applied to a larger number of devices and users?

    A. Exclusion group

    B. Extended pilot group

    C. Pilot group

    D. Production group

64. You are the administrator for your company network. You and a colleague are discussing conditional access policies. You know that you can assign conditional access policies under Assignments to several object types, except which one of the following?

    A. Access controls

    B. Cloud Apps or Actions

    C. Conditions

    D. Users and Groups

65. You are the administrator for your company network. You and a colleague are discussing Administrative Templates. The templates come with two file extensions. What are the file extensions used by Administrative Templates? (Choose two.)

    A. .adml

    B. .admx

    C. .docx

    D. .xls

66. You are the administrator for your company network. You and a colleague are discussing user profiles. You know that a user profile contains an `ntuser.dat` file. When a user signs onto a Windows machine, the system loads the file into the registry and maps it to a specific registry subtree. What registry subtree is the `ntuser.dat` file mapped to?

    A. The `HKEY_USERS\.DEFAULT` registry subtree

    B. The `HKEY_CURRENT_USER` registry subtree

    C. The `HKEY_CURRENT_CONFIG` registry subtree

    D. The `HKEY_LOCAL_MACHINE\Security` registry subtree

67. You are the administrator for your company network. You and a colleague are discussing using PowerShell scripts on Windows 10 devices using Intune. When you choose to run a PowerShell script using Intune, three script settings are available. One of these settings has a default that will run the script in the system context. What setting is being discussed?

    A. Enforce Script Signature Check

    B. Run Script In 64-Bit PowerShell Host

C. Run Script In 32-Bit PowerShell Host

D. Run This Script Using The Logged-On Credentials

68. You are the administrator for your company network. You and a colleague are discussing using PowerShell scripts on Windows 10 devices using Intune. When you choose to run a PowerShell script using Intune, three script settings are available. One of these settings has a default setting that there isn't a requirement for the script to be signed. What setting is being discussed?

A. Enforce Script Signature Check

B. Run Script In 64-Bit PowerShell Host

C. Run Script In 32-Bit PowerShell Host

D. Run This Script Using The Logged-On Credentials

69. You are the administrator for your company network. You and a colleague are discussing the different user profiles available. A user makes changes to their desktop settings and then logs off. When the user signs back in, they notice that the desktop settings they made are not there. What user profile is being utilized that will not keep the changes the user makes to the desktop?

A. Local user profiles

B. Mandatory user profiles

C. Roaming user profiles

D. Super-mandatory user profiles

70. You are the administrator for your company network. You and a colleague are discussing a tool that allows an organization to automate the detection and remediation of identity-based risks. What is this tool called?

A. Azure AD User Security

B. Azure AD Identity Protection

C. Azure AD Security add-on

D. Azure Identity Protection

71. You are the administrator for your company network. You and a colleague are discussing a way to upload PowerShell scripts into Intune so that they can be run on Windows 10 devices. What is the name of the tool that helps upload the scripts to Intune?

A. Enterprise Mobility Management

B. Microsoft Intune Administration Extension

C. Microsoft Intune Management Extension

D. Mobil Application Management

72. You are the administrator for your company network. You and a colleague are discussing the different user profiles available. A user makes changes to their desktop settings and then logs off. When the user signs back in using another computer, they are able to see the changes they made to the desktop settings. What user profile is being utilized?

A. Local user profiles

B. Mandatory user profiles

    C. Roaming user profiles

    D. Super-mandatory user profiles

73. You are the administrator for your company network. You and a colleague are discussing creating Intune policies. There is a setting that you can assign and filter policies to specific groups. What is the name of this item that you can add to a profile?

    A. Device groups

    B. Intune licenses

    C. Roles

    D. Scope tags

74. You are the administrator for your company network. You support Windows 10 Enterprise computers that are members of an Active Directory domain. Recently, several user accounts have been configured with super-mandatory user profiles. A user informs you that all their personal data is lost after a computer restart. What should you do if you need to configure the user's computer to prevent possible user data loss in the future?

    A. You should add the `.dat` extension to the user profile name.

    B. You should configure Folder Redirection by using the domain group policy.

    C. You should configure the user's Documents library to include folders from network shares.

    D. You should remove the `.man` extension from the user profile name.

75. You are the administrator for your company network. You and a colleague are discussing common issues and troubleshooting when using Intune policies and profiles. Which statement is true when two profile settings are applied to the same device?

    A. When two profile settings are applied to the same device, the most restrictive value will be applied.

    B. When two profile settings are applied to the same device, the least restrictive value will be applied.

    C. When two profile settings are applied to the same device, both values will be applied.

    D. When two profile settings are applied to the same device, neither value will be applied.

76. You are the administrator for your company network. You have several Windows 10 Enterprise desktop computers that are members of an Active Directory domain. The standard domain user accounts are configured with mandatory user profiles. What should you do if you have several users who have been transferred into a different department and you need to modify their profiles?

    A. Change the extension of the `ntuser.man` file in the user profile directory to `ntuser.dat`.

    B. Configure the user's document library to include folders from network shares.

    C. Remove the `.man` extension from the user profile name.

    D. Use Group Policy to configure Folder Redirection.

77. You are the administrator for your company network. You and colleague are discussing compliance policy and configuration policy interactions. Which of the following statements is not true regarding how the policies will interact?

A. Compliance policy settings will take priority over configuration profile settings.

B. Configuration profile settings will take priority over compliance policy settings.

C. If you have a compliance policy and it includes the same settings that are found in another compliance policy, then the most restrictive setting will be applied.

D. If you have a configuration policy setting that clashes with the setting in another configuration policy, then the issue will be displayed in Intune, and the administrator will need to resolve the issue manually.

78. You are the administrator for your company network. You and a colleague are discussing ways to minimize user profile sizes. One way that you can minimize user profile size is to limit the space that is available to the user on a volume or a shared folder. What is the method that you can use to apply limits to the space that a user can use?

A. You can apply quotas.

B. You can configure the sync settings.

C. You can limit the user profile size using Group Policy.

D. You can redirect the profile folders.

79. You are the administrator for your company network. You and a colleague are discussing default storage space for OneDrive users. Most subscription plans allot for a certain amount of space. What is the default storage space for most subscription plans?

A. 1 TB

B. 2 TB

C. 5 TB

D. 10 TB

80. You are the administrator for your company network. You and a colleague are discussing troubleshooting Intune policies. What should you do first if you have a policy that is not being applied to a certain device or a PowerShell script that is set to be run but is not being started by Intune?

A. You should first perform a restart of the device by holding down the Alt key and then selecting Restart from the Start menu.

B. You should first completely log off and log back into the device.

C. You should first perform a full reboot of the device by holding down the Shift key and then selecting Shutdown from the Start menu.

D. You should first perform a full reboot of the device by holding down the Ctrl key and then selecting Shutdown from the Start menu.

81. You are the administrator for your company network. You and a colleague are discussing a tool that allows you to troubleshoot conditional access. This tool allows you to validate that a configuration setting is successful. What is the name of the tool being discussed?

A. Condition Checker

B. Condition Manager

C. What Else tool

D. What If tool

82. You are the administrator for your company network. You and a colleague are discussing ways to minimize user profile sizes. One way that you can minimize user profile size is to forward specific folders, such as a Documents folder, to a location outside the user profile. These can be stored on a shared location on a file server or sent to OneDrive for Business. What is this method that is being discussed?

A. You can apply quotas.

B. You can configure the sync settings.

C. You can limit the user profile size using Group Policy.

D. You can redirect the profile folders.

83. You are the administrator for your company network. You and a colleague are discussing Folder Redirection. There are several requirements that must be met to set up Folder Redirection. To administer Folder Redirection, you must be a member of certain security groups except which one of the following?

A. The Domain Administrators group

B. The Enterprise Administrators group

C. The Group Policy Creator Owners group

D. The Schema Administrators group

84. You are the administrator for your company network. You and a colleague are discussing enabling device Sync settings. You'd like to sync the background, system color, system sounds, screen saver, slideshow wallpaper, and taskbar settings. What setting should you set in sync?

A. Ease of Access

B. Language Preference

C. Passwords

D. Theme

85. You are the administrator for your company network. You and a colleague are discussing the benefits of using OneDrive for Business. One of the features offered by OneDrive is the ability to allow users to view, search for, and interact with files stored in OneDrive from within File Explorer without downloading them all to their device. What is being discussed?

A. eDiscovery

B. Known Folder Move

    C. OneDrive Files On-Demand

    D. OneDrive Files Restore

86. You are the administrator for your company network. You and a colleague are discussing roles and permissions. You are using Azure Active Directory (Azure AD), and you want to assign permissions to users for maintaining conditional access. What role should you assign to the users if you'd like them to be able to view, create, modify, and delete conditional access policies?

    A. The Application Administrator role

    B. The Compliance Administrator role

    C. The Conditional Access Administrator role

    D. The Conditional Admission Administrator role

87. You are the administrator for your company network. You and a colleague are discussing enabling device Sync settings. You'd like to sync the on-screen keyboard, sticky keys, filter keys, and toggle keys. What setting should you set?

    A. Ease of Access

    B. Language Preference

    C. Passwords

    D. Theme

88. You are the administrator for your company network. You deploy a new computer. You have a file named `MyData.docx`, which is stored on Microsoft OneDrive. From File Explorer, you try to open the file but discover that the file is corrupt. What should you do if you need to access a previous version of the document?

    A. Use Backup and Restore (Windows 7)

    B. Use File History

    C. Use OneDrive online

    D. Use Recycle Bin

89. You are the administrator for your company network. Your company has a shared OneDrive for Business location with video files that are used by staff for self-paced training. When users attend training, they synchronize files from the OneDrive for Business location to their computers. A user is removed from the company and in anger deletes all of the files that were on the local machine, thus causing all of the files on the OneDrive for Business and synchronized files for all users to be deleted. This user also clears the Recycle Bin on the local machine. What should you do to restore the training video files?

    A. You should restore the files by using the `Clear-RecycleBin` Windows PowerShell cmdlet.

    B. You should restore the files from another computer's Recycle Bin.

    C. You should restore the files from OneDrive for Business's Recycle Bin.

    D. You should restore the files from the second-stage OneDrive for Business Recycle Bin.

90. You are the administrator for your company network. You and a colleague are discussing which law requires that healthcare-related organizations must be in compliance with certain security standards. What is this law called?

A. Federal Information Processing Standard (FIPS) Publication 140-2 (FIPS PUB 140-2)

B. Gramm-Leach-Bliley Act of 1999 (GLBA)

C. Health Insurance Portability and Accountability Act of 1996 (HIPPA)

D. Sarbanes-Oxley Act of 2002 (SARBOX)

91. You are the administrator for your company network. You and a colleague are discussing the benefits of using OneDrive for Business. One of the features offered by OneDrive is the ability to redirect a user's personal folders and important files automatically to their OneDrive for Business account and the files are stored in the cloud. This feature gives users the ability to access their files while using different devices and applications. What feature is being discussed?

A. eDiscovery

B. Known Folder Move

C. OneDrive Files On-Demand

D. OneDrive Files Restore

92. You are the administrator for your company network. You and a colleague are discussing OneDrive Known Folder Move using Group Policy. You know that there are some requirements that must be met when configuring OneDrive Known Folder Move. All of the following are requirements, except which one?

A. On client devices, OneDrive sync build 18.111.0603.0004 or later must be installed.

B. Any existing Windows Folder Redirection Group Policy settings used within the domain need to be removed.

C. Move users' OneNote notebooks out of their known folders because known folders, which include OneNote notebooks, won't be moved.

D. There is no need to move users' OneNote notebooks out of their known folders because known folders are automatically moved with OneDrive Known Folder Move.

93. You are the administrator for your company network. You and a colleague are discussing the GPO settings that can be used to refine the configuration of OneDrive Known Folder Move (KFM). One of the settings will post a pop-up notification allowing the users to move their Documents, Pictures, and Desktop folders to OneDrive. What is the name of the setting being discussed?

A. Prevent Users From Moving Their Windows Known Folders To OneDrive

B. Prevent Users From Redirecting Their Windows Known Folders To Their PC

C. Prompt Users To Move Windows Known Folders To OneDrive

D. Silently Move Windows Known Folders To OneDrive

94. You are the administrator for your company network. You and a colleague are discussing which law regulates how financial institutions handle their customers' personal information. What is this law called?

A. Federal Information Processing Standard (FIPS) Publication 140-2 (FIPS PUB 140-2)

B. Gramm-Leach-Bliley Act of 1999 (GLBA)

C. Health Insurance Portability and Accountability Act of 1996 (HIPPA)

D. Sarbanes-Oxley Act of 2002 (SARBOX)

95. You are the administrator for your company network. You and a colleague are discussing the GPO settings that can be used to refine the configuration of OneDrive Known Folder Move (KFM). One of the settings will move a user's Documents, Pictures, and Desktop folders to OneDrive. Typically, the user will not know that you have performed this function unless you choose to display a notification to the users that their folders have been redirected. What is the name of the setting being discussed?

A. Prevent Users From Moving Their Windows Known Folders To OneDrive

B. Prevent Users From Redirecting Their Windows Known Folders To Their PC

C. Prompt Users To Move Windows Known Folders To OneDrive

D. Silently Move Windows Known Folders To OneDrive

96. You are the administrator for your company network. Your network contains an Active Directory domain. What should you use if you need to create a Central Store for Group Policy Administrative Template files?

A. Dcgpofixdcgpofix.exe

B. File Explorer

C. Group Policy Management Console (GPMC)

D. Server Manager

97. You are the administrator for your company network. You and a colleague are discussing device compliance policies and noncompliant devices. There are several actions that you can configure for noncompliant devices. One of the configuration settings will allow the noncompliant device to be given access to resources as long as the device is made compliant within the specified period of time. What setting is being discussed?

A. Allow The Device Access

B. Mark Device Non-Compliant

C. Remotely Lock The Noncompliant Device Devices

D. Send Email To End User

98. You are the administrator for your company network. You have a Microsoft 365 subscription. You have a conditional access policy that requires multifactor authentication (MFA) for users in the Marketing group when the users sign in from a trusted location. The policy is configured as follows:

Name: Policy1

Users and groups: Specific users included

Cloud apps or actions: 1 app included

Conditions: 1 condition selected

Access controls - Grant: 1 control selected

Access controls - Session: 0 controls selected

Enable policy: On

You create a compliance policy, and now you need to make sure that the users are authenticated only if they are using a compliant device. What should you configure in the conditional access policy?

A. A cloud app

B. A condition

C. A grant control

D. A session control

99. You are the administrator for your company network. You have an Azure Active Directory (Azure AD) tenant that contains a user named User1. The user has the devices in the following table:

Name	Operating System	Version	Join Type	Mobile Device Management (MDM)
Device1	Windows	10.0.18362.0	Azure AD Registered	None
Device2	Windows	10.0.18362.30	Azure AD Registered	Microsoft
Device3	Windows	10.0.18362.0	Azure AD Joined	None
Device4	Windows	10.0.18362.30	Azure AD Joined	Microsoft

Enterprise State Roaming is configured for this user. The user signs onto Device4 and changes the desktop settings. Which devices will have the changed desktop settings?

A. Device1, Device2, Device3, and Device4

B. Device2, Device3, and Device4 only

C. Device2 and Device4 only

D. Device4 only

100. You are the administrator for your company network. Your network contains an Active Directory domain that syncs to Azure Active Directory (Azure AD). The domain contains the following users:

Name	Source	User Profile Path
User1	Windows Active Directory	\\ServerA.mysite.com\users\User1
User2	Azure Active Directory (Azure AD)	Not Applicable

Enterprise State Roaming is enabled for User2. You have the following devices:

Name	Operating System	Joined To
Computer1	Windows 10	Azure AD Tenant
Computer2	Windows 8.1	On-Premises Active Directory Domain
Computer3	Windows 10	Azure AD Tenant

Which of the following statements is true?

A. If User1 modifies the desktop icons on Computer1, the changes will be available when the user signs into Computer2.

B. If User1 modifies the desktop icons on Computer1, the changes will be available when the user signs into Computer3.

C. If User2 modifies the desktop icons on Computer1, the changes will be available when the user signs into Computer3.

D. If User2 modifies the desktop icons on Computer1, the changes will be available when the user signs intoComputer2.

101. You are the administrator for your company network. You and a colleague are discussing Enterprise State Roaming data retention and the Explicit Deletion settings. One of the settings will allow an Azure Active Directory (Azure AD) admin to file a ticket with Azure support to delete a specific user's data or settings data manually. What setting is being discussed?

A. Azure Support Deletion

B. Directory Deletion

C. On Request Deletion

D. User Deletion

102. You are the administrator for your company network. You and a colleague are discussing Enterprise State Roaming data retention. Data synced to the Microsoft cloud using Enterprise State Roaming is retained until it is manually deleted or until the data in question is determined to be no longer used. One of the settings will delete data that has not been accessed for one year (the retention period). What is this called?

A. Explicit deletion

B. Stale data deletion

    C. Deleted data recovery

    D. Out-of-date data deletion

103. You are the administrator for your company network. You and a colleague are discussing compliance policies. You are discussing built-in compliance policy settings that will report the time period that devices report the status for all received compliance policies. Devices that don't return a status within the time period are treated as noncompliant. What setting is being discussed?

    A. Compliance Status Validity Period (Days) setting

    B. Compliance Status Validity Period (Hours) setting

    C. Enhanced Jailbreak Detection setting

    D. Mark Devices With No Compliance Policy Assigned As setting

104. You are the administrator for your company network. You and a colleague are discussing compliance policy statuses. Which of the following statements is *false* in regard to having multiple compliance policies and devices having different compliance statues for two or more of the assigned compliance policies?

    A. When a device has multiple compliance policies, then the highest severity level of all the policies is assigned to that device.

    B. If a device has two policies applied and one is compliant and the other noncompliant, the resulting status for the device will be noncompliant.

    C. If a device has two policies applied and one is compliant and the other noncompliant, the resulting status for the device will be compliant.

    D. If a device has multiple compliance policies and the device has different compliance statuses for two or more of the assigned compliance policies, then a single compliance status is assigned.

105. You are the administrator for your company network. You and a colleague are discussing device policy refresh cycle times. If a device has been recently enrolled, the compliance, noncompliance, and configuration check-ins run more often. What is the estimated policy refresh cycle time for Windows 10 computers enrolled as devices?

    A. Every 15 minutes for 6 hours, and then every 6 hours

    B. Every 3 minutes for 15 hours, and then every 2 hours

    C. Every 3 minutes for 15 minutes, then every 15 minutes for 2 hours, and then around every 8 hours

    D. Every 5 minutes for 15 minutes, then every 15 minutes for 2 hours, and then every 8 hours

106. You are the administrator for your company network. You and a colleague are discussing device identity management in Azure Active Directory (Azure AD). How should you manage device identity management?

    A. Use the Azure portal.

    B. Use the Configuration Manager console.

   C. Use the Group Policy Management Editor.

   D. Use the Microsoft Intune portal.

107. You are the administrator for your company network. You and a colleague are discussing the use of mandatory profiles. Which of the following statements is *false* regarding mandatory profiles?

   A. Only members of the Administrators group can manage mandatory profiles.

   B. Mandatory profiles must be named `WinUser.man`.

   C. Group Policy objects (GPOs) can be used with mandatory profiles to specify what folders should be loaded with the mandatory profiles.

   D. Mandatory profiles can only be used with roaming profiles.

108. You are the administrator for your company network. You currently have a large number of Windows 10 Enterprise computers. These computers are managed using Group Policy objects (GPOs) and Microsoft Endpoint Configuration Manager. You purchase Microsoft 365 licensing and want to utilize the mobile device management (MDM) functionality. Most users will work from the corporate office, while approximately 20 users will work remotely. What tool in Microsoft 365 can be used to implement co-management?

   A. A Group Policy object (GPO)

   B. Microsoft Deployment Toolkit (MDT)

   C. Microsoft Intune

   D. Microsoft System Center Configuration Manager

109. You are the administrator for your company network. You currently have a large number of Windows 10 Enterprise computers. These computers are managed using Group Policy objects (GPOs) and Microsoft Endpoint Configuration Manager. You purchase Microsoft 365 licensing and want to utilize the mobile device management (MDM) functionality. Most users will work from the corporate office, while approximately 20 users will work remotely. What tool can you deploy on the managed devices to evaluate and migrate policies to MDM?

   A. The Intune Migration Tool (IMT)

   B. The Migration Analysis Tool (MAT)

   C. The Migration Assistant Tool (MAT)

   D. The MDM Migration Analysis Tool (MMAT)

110. You are the administrator for your company network. You currently have a large number of Windows 10 Enterprise computers. These computers are managed using Group Policy objects (GPOs) and Microsoft Endpoint Configuration Manager. You purchase Microsoft 365 licensing and want to utilize the mobile device management (MDM) functionality. Most users will work from the corporate office, while approximately 20 users will work remotely. You want to synchronize the on-premises Active Directory domain users to Azure Active Directory (Azure AD). What tool should you use to sync the users to the cloud?

   A. Azure AD Connect

   B. Azure AD Replication

   C. Active Directory Replicator

   D. Site-to-Site VPN Gateway Connectors

111. You are the administrator for your company network. You currently have a large number of Windows 10 Enterprise computers. These computers are managed using Group Policy objects (GPOs) and Microsoft Endpoint Configuration Manager. You purchase Microsoft 365 licensing and want to utilize the mobile device management (MDM) functionality. Most users will work from the corporate office, while approximately 20 users will work remotely. You want to implement co-management for all the devices. You want to recommend a strategy on how the organization should roll out co-management. What should you recommend be done first?

   A. An exclusion group

   B. An extended pilot group

   C. A production group

   D. A rollout group

112. You are the administrator for your company network. Your company has a large number of remote employees that work from their home offices. You are currently using a virtual private network (VPN) that allows these remote employees to access the corporate network, and these workers also access a web-based line-of-business (LOB) application. You purchase Microsoft 365 licensing, and you plan on utilizing mobile device management (MDM). You will be phasing out the VPN connection. You want to ensure that when employees access the LOB, it is done securely. You are going to implement a conditional access policy. What type of condition should you include?

   A. A device platform conditional access policy

   B. A dual-factor authentication conditional access policy

   C. A multifactor authentication conditional access policy

   D. A preconfigured multifactor authentication template

113. You are the administrator for your company network. Your company has a large number of remote employees who work from their home offices. You are currently using a virtual private network (VPN) that allows these remote employees to access the corporate network, and these workers also access a web-based line-of-business (LOB) application. You purchase Microsoft 365 licensing, and you plan on utilizing mobile device management (MDM). You will be phasing out the VPN connection. You are going to implement a conditional access policy. What type of condition can be used to replace VPN connections and strengthen authentication to the LOB application?

   A. A client app conditional access policy

   B. A device platform conditional access policy

   C. A location conditional access policy

   D. A sign-in risk conditional access policy

114. You are the administrator for your company network. Your company has a large number of remote employees who work from their home offices. You are currently using a virtual private network (VPN) that allows these remote employees to access the corporate network, and these workers also access a web-based line-of-business (LOB) application. You purchase Microsoft 365 licensing, and you plan on utilizing mobile device management (MDM). You will be phasing out the VPN connection. You are going to implement a conditional access policy. You want the location to be marked as a trusted location. To implement this solution, what information is needed from the employees?

A. The country of their home networks

B. The default gateway addresses of their home networks

C. The IP addresses of their home networks

D. The region of their home networks

115. You are the administrator for your company network. Your company has a large number of remote employees who work from their home offices. You are currently using a virtual private network (VPN) that allows these remote employees to access the corporate network, and these workers also access a web-based line-of-business (LOB) application. You purchase Microsoft 365 licensing, and you plan on utilizing mobile device management (MDM). You will be phasing out the VPN connection. You are going to implement a conditional access policy for the remote employees. What should you suggest be done prior to deploying the policy?

A. A conditional access assessment proposal

B. A conditional access test plan

C. Implement the conditional access policy as is

D. Put the conditional access policy on all of the remote machines

Chapter

7

Manage and Protect Devices

THE MD-101 EXAM TOPICS COVERED IN THIS CHAPTER INCLUDE:

✓ **Domain 7: Manage and Protect Devices**

- 7.1: Manage Microsoft Defender
    - Implement and manage Microsoft Defender Application Guard
    - Implement and manage Microsoft Defender Credential Guard
    - Implement and manage Microsoft Defender Exploit Guard
    - Implement Microsoft Defender Advanced Threat Protection
    - Integrate Microsoft Defender Application Control
    - Manage Microsoft Defender Antivirus
- 7.2: Manage Intune device enrollment and inventory
    - Configure enrollment settings
    - Configure Intune automatic enrollment
    - Enable device enrollment
    - Enroll non-Windows devices
    - Enroll Windows devices
    - Generate custom device inventory reports' Review device inventory
- 7.3: Monitor devices
    - Monitor device health (e.g., log analytics, Desktop Analytics, or other cloud-based tools, etc.)
    - Monitor device security

1. You are the administrator for your company network. You have several hundred Windows 10 computers that are joined to an Azure Active Directory (Azure AD) and enrolled in Intune. You want to enable self-service password reset (SSPR) on the sign-in screen. From the Microsoft Intune blade, what setting should you configure?

    A. Conditional access

    B. Device compliance

    C. Device configuration

    D. Device enrollment

2. You are the administrator for your company network. Your company has an Azure Active Directory (Azure AD) tenant. All users are licensed for Microsoft Intune. What should you configure first if you need to make sure that users enroll their iOS device in Intune?

    A. An Automated Device Enrollment (ADE), formerly known as a Device Enrollment Program (DEP), token

    B. An Intune device configuration profile

    C. A Device Enrollment Manager (DEM) account

    D. An Apple MDM push certificate

3. You are the administrator for your company network. You and a colleague are discussing software that runs as a service (SaaS). All of the supporting infrastructure runs in Azure and is handled by Microsoft. What is the name of this program that was created to perform analytics, diagnostics, and monitoring?

    A. Azure Monitor

    B. Event Viewer

    C. Network Monitor

    D. Performance Monitor

4. You are the administrator for your company network. You have about 1,000 Windows 10 computers that are members of an Active Directory domain. You create a workspace in Microsoft Azure Log Analytics. You plan on capturing the event logs from the computer to Azure. What Azure service should you use?

    A. Azure Cosmos Database

    B. Azure Storage account

    C. Azure SQL Database

    D. Log Analytics

5. You are the administrator for your company network. You have about 1,000 Windows 10 computers that are members of an Active Directory domain. You create a workspace in Microsoft Azure Log Analytics. You plan on capturing the event logs from the computer to Azure. What action should you perform on the computers?

    A. Register to Azure Active Directory (Azure AD).

    B. Create a collector-initiated subscription.

C. Enroll in Microsoft Intune.

D. Install the Microsoft Monitoring Agent.

6. You are the administrator for your company network. You use the Antimalware Assessment solution in Microsoft Azure Log Analytics. From the Protection Status dashboard, you discover the following computers:

Name	Issue
Computer1	No real-time protection
Computer2	Not reporting

You confirm that both computers are connected to the network and running. What is a possible cause of the issue on Computer1?

A. The Microsoft Monitoring Agent (MMA) is uninstalled.

B. The Microsoft Windows Malicious Software Removal Tool is installed.

C. Microsoft Defender is disabled.

D. Microsoft Defender Application Guard is misconfigured.

7. You are the administrator for your company network. You and a colleague are discussing a tool that works with Microsoft Edge to isolate untrusted websites, thus protecting the organizational network and data while users are working on the Internet. What is this tool called?

A. Microsoft Defender Application Guard

B. Microsoft Defender Credential Guard

C. Microsoft Defender Exploit Guard

D. Microsoft Defender Firewall with Advanced Security

8. You are the administrator for your company network. Your company has an Azure Active Directory (Azure AD) tenant. You use Microsoft Intune to manage your iOS, Android, and Windows 10 devices. You want to purchase 1,000 new iOS devices, and each will be assigned to a specific user. You need to ensure that the iOS devices are automatically enrolled in Intune the first time that the assigned user signs on. What actions should you perform? (Choose three.)

A. Add an Apple Automated Device Enrollment (ADE) token.

B. Create a device compliance policy.

C. Create an Apple enrollment profile.

D. Create a Device Enrollment Manager (DEM) account.

E. Assign an enrollment profile.

9. You are the administrator for your company network. You have a Microsoft Azure Log Analytics workplace that collects all of the event logs from the corporate computers. You have a Windows 10 computer named ComputerA. You need to view the events collected from this computer. In Log Analytics, what query should you run?

   A. `Event | where Computer = = "ComputerA"`

   B. `Event | where SourceSystem = = "ComputerA"`

   C. `ETWEvent | where Computer = = "ComputerA"`

   D. `ETWEvent | where SourceSystem = = "ComputerA"`

10. You are the administrator for your company network. Your company has a Microsoft Azure Active Directory (Azure AD) tenant, and all user computers run Windows 10. The computers are joined to Azure AD and are managed using Microsoft Intune. What should you create in Intune if you want to make sure that you can centrally monitor the computers using Desktop Analytics?

    A. A conditional access policy

    B. A device compliance policy

    C. A device configuration profile

    D. An update policy

11. You are the administrator for your company network. You and a colleague are discussing a tool that is virtualization-based security to help isolate critical files so that only system software that is privileged can access those critical files. What is this tool called?

    A. Microsoft Defender Application Control

    B. Microsoft Defender Credential Guard

    C. Microsoft Defender Exploit Guard

    D. Microsoft Defender Firewall with Advanced Security

12. You are the administrator for your company network. You and a colleague are discussing enabling Microsoft Defender Credential Guard by using Intune. When enabling Microsoft Defender Credential Guard using Intune, what profile type should you use?

    A. The Endpoint Protection profile type

    B. The Administrative Templates profile type

    C. The Identity Protection (Windows) profile type

    D. The Device Restrictions profile type

13. You are the administrator for your company network. You and a colleague are discussing the different Intune profile types that you can create. These profiles are used to allow or prevent some features on the devices. One of the profile types includes hundreds of settings that can be configured for Microsoft Edge, Internet Explorer, OneDrive, Remote Desktop, Word, Excel, and more. What profile type is being discussed?

    A. Administrative templates

    B. Certificates

C. Custom profiles

D. Device restrictions

14. You are the administrator for your company network. Your company has an Active Directory domain and a cloud-based Azure Active Directory (Azure AD). You want to protect your systems from common malware attacks that use executable files and scripts. What should you use to accomplish this?

A. Microsoft Defender Application Control

B. Microsoft Defender Credential Guard

C. Microsoft Defender Exploit Guard

D. Microsoft Defender Firewall with Advanced Security

15. You are the administrator for your company network. Some of your duties require that you to perform the following tasks:

- Collect data from local or remote Windows 10 computers on the network. Collect data either from a single computer or from multiple computers concurrently.

- View data as it is being collected in real time or historically from collected data.

What Windows 10 application should you use?

A. Computer Monitor

B. Event Viewer

C. Performance Monitor

D. Reliability Monitor

16. You are the administrator for your company network. Your company uses Microsoft Intune to manage devices. You want to make sure that only Android devices that use the Android Enterprise work profile can enroll in Intune. What configurations should you perform in the device enrollment restrictions? (Choose two.)

A. Set the Android Enterprise work profile to Allow From Platform Settings.

B. Set Android Personally Owned to Block From Configure Platforms.

C. Set Android Personally Owned to Allow From Configure Platforms.

D. Set Android to Block From Platform Settings.

17. You are the administrator for your company network. You have an Azure Active Directory (Azure AD) tenant that contains Windows 10 devices that are enrolled in Microsoft Intune. You create an Azure Log Analytics workspace and add the Device Health solution to the workspace. You want to create a custom device configuration profile that will enroll the Windows 10 devices in Device Health. What OMA-URI should you add to the profile?

A. ./Vendor/MSFT/DMClient/Provider/MS DM Server/Push

B. ./Vendor/MSFT/DMClient/Provider/MS DM Server/CommercialID

C. ./Vendor/MSFT/DMClient/Provider/MS DM Server/ ManagementServerAddressList

D. ./Vendor/MSFT/DMClient/Provider/MS DM Server/Push/ChannelURI

C. Device compliance

D. Device enrollment

E. On-premises access

25. You are the administrator for your company network. You have a Microsoft Azure subscription that contains an Azure Log Analytics workspace. You deploy a new Windows 10 computer that is part of a workgroup. What should you do on this new computer if you want to make sure that you can use Log Analytics to query events?

   A. You should configure the CommercialID.

   B. You should create an event subscription.

   C. You should install the Microsoft Monitoring Agent.

   D. You should join Azure Active Directory (Azure AD).

26. You are the administrator for your company network. You use Microsoft Defender Advanced Threat Protection (Microsoft Defender ATP) to protect your Windows 10 computers. What tool should you use if you want to evaluate the differences between the configuration of Microsoft Defender ATP and the Microsoft-recommended configuration baseline?

   A. Microsoft Secure Score

   B. Windows Analytics

   C. Microsoft Defender ATP Power BI app

   D. Microsoft Defender Security Center

27. You are the administrator for your company network. You have a shared computer that runs Windows 10. Unfortunately, this computer is infected with a virus. You determine that a malicious TTF font was used to compromise the computer. What should you use if you need to prevent this type of threat from affecting computers in the future?

   A. Microsoft Defender Application Guard

   B. Microsoft Defender Credential Guard

   C. Microsoft Defender Exploit Guard

   D. Microsoft Defender System Guard

28. You are the administrator for your company network. You want to enable Microsoft Defender Credential Guard on computers that are running Windows 10. What should you install on these computers?

   A. Containers

   B. A guarded host

   C. Hyper-V

   D. Microsoft Defender Application Guard

29. You are the administrator for your company network. What tool can you use if you want to use a Microsoft Azure monitoring tool to monitor devices and change settings?

   A. Azure Performance Center

   B. Intune Performance Center

   C. Microsoft Azure IoT Central

   D. Performance Monitor

30. You are the administrator for your company network. Your computers are running Windows 10. You want to collect performance data for a specified period of several weeks. In the data collected, you want the CPU utilization, disk utilization, and memory utilization included. What should you do to accomplish this?

   A. Create a custom performance set.

   B. Create a session data collector set.

   C. Create a Trace event.

   D. Create a user-defined data collector set.

31. You are the administrator for your company network. You have several hundred computers that run Windows 10 that are joined to Microsoft Azure Active Directory (Azure AD) and enrolled in Microsoft Intune. What should you use if you want to choose which websites are defined as trusted sites?

   A. Microsoft Defender Antivirus

   B. Microsoft Defender Application Guard

   C. Microsoft Defender Credential Guard

   D. Microsoft Defender Exploit Guard

32. You are the administrator for your company network. You have several hundred Windows 10 computers that are joined to Microsoft Azure Active Directory (Azure AD) and enrolled in Microsoft Intune. You want to configure an Intune device configuration profile to meet the following requirements:

   ▪ Preventing Microsoft 365 applications from launching child processes

   ▪ Blocking users from transferring files over FTP

What settings should you configure in endpoint protection? (Choose two.)

   A. Microsoft Defender Application Guard

   B. Microsoft Defender Exploit Guard

   C. Microsoft Defender Firewall

   D. Microsoft Defender Security Center

   E. Windows Encryption

33. You are the administrator for your company network. You have about 100 Windows 10 devices that are joined to Microsoft Azure Active Directory (Azure AD). What should you do if you want to prevent users from joining their home computer to Azure AD?

   A. Modify the Device Enrollment Manages settings from the Device Enrollment blade in the Intune admin center.

   B. Modify the Device settings from the Devices blade in the Azure Active Directory admin center.

    C. Modify the Enrollment Restriction settings from the Device Enrollment blade in the Intune admin center.

    D. Modify the Microsoft Intune Enrollment settings from the Mobility (MDM and MAM) blade in the Azure Active Directory admin center.

34. You are the administrator for your company network. You and a colleague are discussing the different Intune profile types that you can create. These profiles are used to allow or prevent some features on the devices. One of the profile types lets an administrator assign device settings that aren't built into Intune. What profile type is being discussed?

    A. Administrative templates

    B. Certificates

    C. Custom profiles

    D. Device restrictions

35. You are the administrator for your company network. You and a colleague are discussing the Microsoft Defender Application Guard. You know that there are a few hardware requirements that must be met to be able to utilize this feature. What is the minimum amount of RAM that Microsoft recommends to utilize Microsoft Defender Application Guard?

    A. 2 GB

    B. 4 GB

    C. 8 GB

    D. 12 GB

36. You are the administrator for your company network. All of your computers run Windows 10. You want to ensure that critical files are isolated so that only system software with privileges can access those files. What should you implement?

    A. Microsoft Defender Application Control

    B. Microsoft Defender Antivirus

    C. Microsoft Defender Credential Guard

    D. Microsoft Defender Exploit Guard

37. You are the administrator for your company network. You want to set up inbound and outbound rules on your Windows 10 machines. What should you use to accomplish this?

    A. Microsoft Defender Application Control

    B. Microsoft Defender Credential Guard

    C. Microsoft Defender Exploit Guard

    D. Microsoft Defender Firewall with Advanced Security

38. You are the administrator for your company network. You are attempting to set up your Microsoft Defender Firewall to allow DNS inbound and outbound rules. Which protocol and port number would you configure?

    A. TCP port 20

    B. TCP port 25

   C. UDP port 53

   D. TCP port 80

39. You are the administrator for your company network. You have about 100 Windows 10 computers that are joined to Microsoft Azure Active Directory (Azure AD) and enrolled in Microsoft Intune. You want to configure the following device restrictions:

- Block users from browsing to suspicious websites.

- Scan all scripts that are loaded into Microsoft Edge.

What settings should you configure in Device Restrictions? (Choose two.)

   A. Microsoft Edge Browser

   B. Network Proxy

   C. Reporting and Telemetry

   D. Microsoft Defender Antivirus

   E. Microsoft Defender SmartScreen

40. You are the administrator for your company network. Your company has employees in the Sales department who are allowed to bring their own personal Windows 10 devices to the office. The Sales staff members are allowed to install corporate software and use their personal devices to retrieve their emails using a management infrastructure agent. You receive a frantic call that one member of the Sales staff has had their laptop stolen. You want to make sure that the corporate data and emails cannot be accessed. What should you do to ensure that the corporate information and emails aren't stolen? (Choose two.)

   A. Perform a wipe on the user's laptop.

   B. Prevent the computer from connecting to the corporate wireless network.

   C. Remove the computer from the management infrastructure.

   D. Reset the user's password.

41. You are the administrator for your company network. You are attempting to set up your Microsoft Defender Firewall to allow FTP inbound and outbound rules. Which protocol and port numbers would you configure?

   A. TCP port 20 and TCP port 21

   B. TCP port 25 and UDP port 53

   C. UDP port 53 and TCP port 80

   D. TCP port 80 and TCP port 443

42. You are the administrator for your company network. You want to stop an application from running by using Task Manager. What tab should you use to stop an application from running?

   A. The Details tab

   B. The Options tab

   C. The Performance tab

   D. The Users tab

43. You are the administrator for your company network. You are running Windows 10 machines. You want to use Event Viewer to review event logs for Critical and Error events only. What should you do if you need to see all of these events from the logs?

A. Use the Administrative Events view.

B. Create a custom view and choose Administrative Events.

C. Create a custom view and select Critical, Error, and Verbose for all logs.

D. Perform a search on the system log for all of the required events.

44. You are the administrator for your company network. You and a colleague are discussing the output modes for Performance Monitor. You view the output mode, as shown in the following graphic:

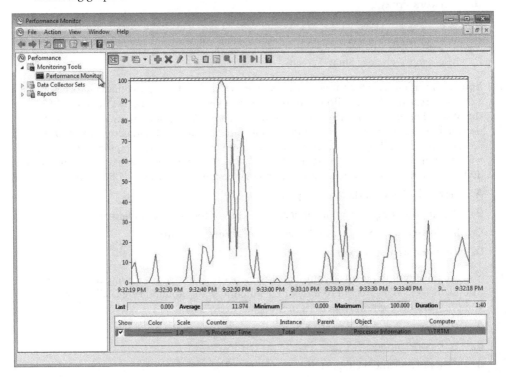

What output mode are you observing?

A. Grid view

B. Histogram Bar view

C. Line view

D. Report view

45. You are the administrator for your company network. Several users indicate that a certain app is taking too long to load. You use Performance Monitor to create a baseline report for one of the computers. You monitor the processor, the disk subsystem, and the network subsystem. You notice that the disk subsystem has a high load of activity. What other subsystem should you monitor before knowing if there is a bottleneck?

A. The Application counters

B. The Memory counters

C. The Network counters

D. The Processor counters

46. You are the administrator for your company network. You and a colleague are discussing the Microsoft Defender Application Guard. You know that there are a few hardware requirements that must be met to utilize this feature. What is the minimum amount of hard disk space that Microsoft recommends to utilize Microsoft Defender Application Guard?

A. 5 GB of free space

B. 10 GB of free space

C. 15 GB of free space

D. 20 GB of free space

47. You are the administrator for your company network. You and a colleague are discussing the ways to enable Microsoft Defender Credential Guard. Microsoft Defender Credential Guard can be enabled by using Group Policy, the registry, or the Hypervisor-Protected Code Integrity (HVCI) and the Microsoft Defender Credential Guard hardware readiness tool. You decide that you'd like to enable it using Group Policy. What setting in Group Policy should you enable?

A. Deploy Microsoft Defender Application Control

B. Install Microsoft Defender Application Control

C. Turn On Virtualization Based Security

D. Turn Off Virtualization Based Security

48. You are the administrator for your company network. You and a colleague are discussing a tool that was available for Windows 10 versions prior to 2004 that allows an administrator to perform a clean installation and update of Windows while maintaining the personal data and keeping most Windows settings intact. This tool also removes most of the apps, including Microsoft 365, third-party antivirus software, and desktop apps that came pre-installed on a device. What is this tool called?

A. Fresh Start

B. Refresh Inventory

C. Renewed Star

D. Restart Computer

49. You are the administrator for your company network. You and a colleague are discussing Windows Security. You'd like to view the health report of your devices. Using Windows Security, what section do you select to view the health report?

A. Account Protection

B. Device Performance & Health

C. Device Security

D. Virus & Threat Protection

50. You are the administrator for your company network. You and a colleague are discussing the primary management features of Configuration Manager. One primary feature allows you to give users in your network access to data and applications from remote locations. This feature includes Wi-Fi, VPN, email, and certificate profiles. What management feature is being discussed?

A. App Management

B. Company Resource Access

C. Device Security and Configuration

D. Endpoint Protection

51. You are the administrator for your company network. You and a colleague are discussing Microsoft Defender Exploit Guard components. One of the components extends Microsoft Defender SmartScreen protection in Microsoft Edge to other applications to prevent access to Internet domains that may host phishing scams, exploits, and other malicious content. What is being discussed?

A. Attack surface reduction rules

B. Controlled folder access

C. Exploit protection

D. Network protection

52. You are the administrator for your company network. You and a colleague are discussing different threat protection tools. One of these tools helps administrators protect users when they attempt to visit websites that have previously been reported as phishing or malware websites, or if a user tries to download a potentially malicious file. What is this tool called?

A. Microsoft Defender Application Control

B. Microsoft Defender Credential Guard

C. Microsoft Defender Exploit Guard

D. Microsoft Defender SmartScreen

53. You are the administrator for your company network. You and a colleague are discussing mobile device management (MDM) device enrollment. You know that the enrollment process varies depending upon the device platform. You are planning on purchasing a few new Apple iOS 9.0 and macOS 10.9 devices. How should you enroll these new devices?

A. Acquire an Apple Push Notification service certificate.

B. From the Intune portal, install the Microsoft Intune software client.

C. On each device, download the Microsoft Intune Company Portal app from the Google Play store.

D. You don't need to do anything further—enrollment will be automatic.

54. You are the administrator for your company network. You and a colleague are discussing Apple mobile device management (MDM) push certificates. How long is an Apple push certificate valid?

A. One year.

B. Two years.

C. Three years.

D. It does not expire.

55. You are the administrator for your company network. You and a colleague are discussing Microsoft Defender Advanced Threat Protection (Microsoft Defender ATP) and its built-in features and capabilities. Once this capability is put in place, it will detect, investigate, and respond to advanced threats. What is the name of this Microsoft Defender ATP capability?

A. Attack Surface Reduction

B. Endpoint Detection and Response

C. Next Generation Protection

D. Threat & Vulnerability Management

56. You are the administrator for your company network. You and a colleague are discussing device enrollment. When a device is enrolled in Intune, it is supplied with a mobile device management (MDM) certificate that is used to communicate with the Intune service. You know that there are several ways to enroll a device depending upon the device's ownership, device type, and management requirements. One of these methods includes personally owned phones, tablets, and computers. The users install and run the Company Portal app to enroll the devices. What is this method known as?

A. Apple Automated Device Enrollment (ADE)

B. Bring your own device (BYOD)

C. Corporate-owned device (COD)

D. Device Enrollment Manager (DEM)

57. You are the administrator for your company network. You and a colleague are discussing Microsoft Defender Antivirus. You know that there are a number of scan options available with Microsoft Defender Antivirus. You want to perform a scan that will scan all of the files on a hard disk and that scans all of the running programs for spyware, malware, and viruses. What scan option is being discussed?

A. A custom scan

B. A full scan

C. A quick scan

D. A Microsoft Defender offline scan

58. You are the administrator for your company network. You and a colleague are discussing how you'd like to enroll a large number of devices into the network using Intune. You know that there is a special user account that is used to enroll and manage multiple corporate-owned devices. What is the name of this user account?

   A. Device Enrollment Manager

   B. Global Administrator

   C. Intune Administrator

   D. Intune Enrollment Manager

59. You are the administrator for your company network. You have a Windows 10 computer that has an app running. You want to collect data regarding the processor utilization that the app is using. You decide to use Performance Monitor. What performance object should you monitor to see the processor utilization?

   A. The Process performance object

   B. The Processor Routine object

   C. The Process Information performance object

   D. The Processor performance object

60. You are the administrator for your company network. You and a colleague are discussing a way to allow users to enroll themselves into Intune. What should you configure to allow them to enroll their own devices?

   A. Automatic enrollment

   B. Automatic device enrollment

   C. Self-enrollment

   D. Self-device enrollment

61. You are the administrator for your company network. You and a colleague are discussing Microsoft Defender Exploit Guard components. One of the components helps protect against ransomware and malware by stopping changes to files in protected folders if the app attempting to make changes is malevolent or exhibits malicious behavior. What is being discussed?

   A. Attack surface reduction rules

   B. Controlled folder access

   C. Exploit protection

   D. Network protection

62. You are the administrator for your company network. You and a colleague are discussing the different ways in which a user can self-enroll their Windows devices. One of these methods allows users to enroll their personally owned devices by choosing to connect a Work and School account from Settings of the device. This method will register the device with Azure Active Directory (Azure AD) and will enroll the device in Intune. What method is being discussed?

   A. Autopilot

   B. Azure Active Directory (Azure AD) join

C. Bring your own device (BYOD)

D. MDM-only enrollment

63. You are the administrator for your company network. You are getting ready to migrate your network to Windows 10. You want to perform the following tasks:

   ▪ Collect data from local or remote Windows 10 computers on the network. You can collect data from a single computer or multiple computers at the same time.

   ▪ View the data as it is being collected in real time, or historically.

   What Windows 10 application will allow you to perform the required tasks?

   A. Computer Monitor

   B. Event Viewer

   C. Performance Monitor

   D. Windows Monitor

64. You are the administrator for your company network. You and a colleague are discussing Windows Security. One section of Windows Security covers the Microsoft Defender SmartScreen settings and Exploit protection mitigations. What section is being discussed?

   A. Account Protection

   B. App & Browser Control

   C. Device Security

   D. Virus & Threat Protection

65. You are the administrator for your company network. Your company wants to use Azure Active Directory (Azure AD) and Microsoft Intune. You have been checking into this because users have been using multiple devices on the network. When users get added to Intune and get licensed, how many devices by default can each user add?

   A. 5 devices.

   B. 10 devices.

   C. 15 devices.

   D. None. Device administrators are the only ones who can add devices to Intune.

66. You are the administrator for your company network. You and a colleague are discussing the different ways in which a user can self-enroll their Windows devices. One of these methods allows a device to join a device with Azure Active Directory (Azure AD), and it enables users to sign in to Windows with their Azure AD credentials. If Auto Enrollment is enabled, the device will be automatically enrolled in Intune and marked as a corporate-owned device. What method is being discussed?

   A. Active Directory join

   B. Autopilot

   C. Azure Active Directory (Azure AD) join

   D. Bring your own device (BYOD)

67. You are the administrator for your company network. You and a colleague are discussing Windows Security and Exploit Protection. Which section of Windows Security covers Exploit Protection mitigations?

   A. Account Protection

   B. App & Browser Control

   C. Device Security

   D. Virus & Threat Protection

68. You are the administrator for your company network. You and a colleague are discussing a way to create an inventory of applications that are currently running within your company. There is a service that works in conjunction with Configuration Manager that allows you to create an inventory of applications. What is this service called?

   A. Delivery Optimization

   B. Desktop Analytics

   C. Upgrade Readiness

   D. Windows Analytics

69. You are the administrator for your company network. You and a colleague are discussing enrolling Android devices using Intune. Where should the Android devices go to install the Intune Company Portal app?

   A. Amazon Appstore

   B. App Store for Android

   C. Google Play

   D. Mobile Store

70. You are the administrator for your company network. You and a colleague are discussing the retirement of Windows Analytics. However, one component has been continued through the Azure portal. What is the name of this feature?

   A. Device Health

   B. Device Strength

   C. Update Compliance

   D. Upgrade Readiness

71. You are the administrator for your company network. You and a colleague are discussing using log queries to help you fully leverage the value of the data collected in Azure Monitor Logs. There is a tool in the Azure portal that is used for writing log queries. What is the name of this tool?

   A. Azure Log Creator

   B. Azure Monitor Log Maker

   C. Log Analytics

   D. Log Query Analyzer

72. You are the administrator for your company network. You and a colleague are discussing the use of reports in Intune. You'd like to review a report that will show detailed information regarding the managed devices. This report can be used for planning hardware purchases and to get an idea of user hardware needs. What type of report is being discussed?

A. Computer Inventory Reports

B. Detected Software Reports

C. License Installation Reports

D. Update Report

73. You are the administrator for your company network. You and a colleague are discussing a Microsoft utility that allows you to collect information in a log and analyze the data in real time. What is this utility called?

A. Disk Cleanup

B. Event Viewer

C. Performance Monitor

D. Resource Monitor

74. You are the administrator for your company network. You and a colleague are discussing Intune reports. Reports allows you to monitor the health and activity of endpoints across your corporate network. Report types are organized into four different focus areas. What type of report provides a wider summary of the overall view, such as the device management state?

A. Historical

B. Operational

C. Organizational

D. Specialist

75. You are the administrator for your company network. You and a colleague are discussing Microsoft Defender Exploit Guard components. One of the components consists of rules that help prevent attack vectors that are applied by scripts, email, and Office-based malware. What is being discussed?

A. Attack surface reduction rules

B. Controlled folder access

C. Exploit protection

D. Network protection

76. You are the administrator for your company network. You and a colleague are discussing reports and how to customize the view to meet your needs. You want to generate a custom device inventory report to show the Device Name, Managed By, and OS Version information. What should you modify to see the needed information?

A. Columns

B. Export

   C. Filter

   D. Refresh

77. You are the administrator for your company network. You and a colleague are discussing a service that will recognize compatibility issues and receive mitigation suggestions based upon cloud-enabled data insights. What is this service called?

   A. Configuration Associate

   B. Desktop Analytics

   C. Windows Analytics

   D. Windows Services Manager

78. You are the administrator for your company network. You and a colleague are discussing the use of PowerShell to configure Exploit Protection. There are two PowerShell cmdlets that can be used to configure Exploit Protection. What are they? (Choose two.)

   A. `Get-ExploitMigration`

   B. `Get-ProcessMitigation`

   C. `Set-ExploitMigration`

   D. `Set-ProcessMitigation`

79. You are the administrator for your company network. You and a colleague are discussing the use of reports in Intune. You'd like to review a report that allows you to compare installed software with your current license agreement coverage. What type of report is being discussed?

   A. Computer Inventory Reports

   B. Detected Software Reports

   C. License Installation Reports

   D. Update Report

80. You are the administrator for your company network. You and a colleague are discussing how to customize attack surface reduction rules using PowerShell. What is the associated GUID if you want to block executable content from email clients and webmail?

   A. BE9BA2D9-53EA-4CDC-84E5-9B1EEEE46550

   B. D4F940AB-401B-4EFC-AADC-AD5F3C50688A

   C. 3B576869-A4EC-4529-8536-B80A7769E899

   D. 75668C1F-73B5-4CF0-BB93-3ECF5CB7CC84

81. You are the administrator for your company network. You and a colleague are discussing reports and how to customize the view to meet your needs. You want to generate a custom device inventory report that will only show certain requirements that have been selected and to display only the requested devices. What should you modify to see the needed information?

   A. Columns

   B. Export

C. Filter

D. Refresh

82. You are the administrator for your company network. You and a colleague are discussing the benefits of using Desktop Analytics. One of the benefits allows using collected market data along with data from your environment, the service will predict probable issues and then suggest possible mitigations. What benefit of Desktop Analytics is being discussed?

    A. Configuration Manager integration

    B. Device and software inventory

    C. Issue identification

    D. Pilot identification

83. You are the administrator for your company network. You and a colleague are discussing enabling network protection by using Intune. What do you need to enable?

    A. Attack Surface Reduction

    B. Controlled Folder Access

    C. Exploit Protection

    D. Network Filtering

84. You are the administrator for your company network. You and a colleague are discussing Intune reports. Reports allows you to monitor the health and activity of endpoints across your corporate network. Report types are organized into four different focus areas. What type of report provides timely, targeted data that helps an administrator focus and take action?

    A. Historical

    B. Operational

    C. Organizational

    D. Specialist

85. You are the administrator for your company network. You and a colleague are discussing Microsoft Defender Antivirus. You know that there are a number of scan options available with Microsoft Defender Antivirus. You want to perform a scan that will scan the most likely areas on a hard disk where spyware, malware, and viruses are commonly known to infect. What scan option is being discussed?

    A. A custom scan

    B. A full scan

    C. A quick scan

    D. A Microsoft Defender offline scan

86. You are the administrator for your company network. You and a colleague are discussing Microsoft Defender Exploit Guard components. One of the components uses Microsoft Defender Antivirus or, if installed, a third-party antivirus software to help exploit techniques used against corporate apps. What is being discussed?

    A. Attack surface reduction rules

    B. Controlled folder access

C. Exploit protection

D. Network protection

87. You are the administrator for your company network. You and a colleague are discussing Microsoft Defender Application Guard. You know that you can configure the mode used by Microsoft Defender Application Guard. What mode allows users to manage their own device settings?

A. Enterprise mode

B. Readiness mode

C. Stand-alone mode

D. User mode

88. You are the administrator for your company network. You and a colleague are discussing setting up network protection by using PowerShell. What command should you use to set up network protection?

A. `Get-MpPreference`

B. `Remove-MpPreference`

C. `Set-MpPreference`

D. `Update-MpPreference`

89. You are the administrator for your company network. You and a colleague are discussing device enrollment. When a device is enrolled in Intune, it is supplied with a mobile device management (MDM) certificate that is used to communicate with the Intune service. You know that there are several ways to enroll a device, depending upon the device's ownership, device type, and management requirements. One of these methods includes phones, tablets, and computers that are owned by the corporation and are given to the users. What is this method known as?

A. Apple Automated Device Enrollment (ADE)

B. Business-owned device (BOD)

C. Corporate-owned device (COD)

D. Device Enrollment Manager (DEM)

90. You are the administrator for your company network. You and a colleague are discussing Microsoft Defender Advanced Threat Protection (Microsoft Defender ATP) and its built-in features and capabilities. This capability helps assess the security state of a corporate network, identifies unprotected systems, and takes recommended actions to improve the overall corporate security. What is the name of this Microsoft Defender ATP capability?

A. Attack Surface Reduction

B. Configuration Score

C. Next Generation Protection

D. Threat & Vulnerability Management

91. You are the administrator for your company network. You and a colleague are discussing reports and how to customize the view to meet your needs. You want to generate and save a custom device inventory report that will show only certain requirements that have been selected. You filter the report to meet your needs. Where should you go next if you want to save the report?

A. Columns

B. Export

C. Filter

D. Refresh

92. You are the administrator for your company network. You and a colleague are discussing the Microsoft Defender Application Guard. You know that it is turned off by default, and you want to install it using Control Panel. Where in Control Panel do you install it?

A. Ease of Access

B. Network and Internet

C. Programs and Features

D. System and Security

93. You are the administrator for your company network. You and a colleague are discussing device enrollment and the enrollment configuration options that are available on the Intune Navigation Pane under Device Enrollment. One of the configuration options allows you to access a number of settings that include automatic enrollment, Windows Hello for Business, CNAME validation, enrollment status, and so on. What configuration option is being discussed?

A. Apple Enrollment

B. Android Enrollment

C. Device Categories

D. Windows Enrollment

94. You are the administrator for your company network. You and a colleague are discussing the best way to monitor performance. What is it called when you monitor performance over a given period of time?

A. A baseline

B. A computer precedent

C. An event criterion

D. A paradigm

95. You are the administrator for your company network. You and a colleague are discussing the Microsoft Defender Application Guard. You are currently using Microsoft Edge to surf the Internet. You want to open a New Application Guard window. You are using Microsoft Defender Application Guard in stand-alone mode. What do you need to do to open a new secure window?

A. From the menu, select Open With Internet Explorer.

B. Click the ellipsis button (. . .) on the upper-right side of the screen.

    C. From the menu, select Private Browsing.

    D. Open a new tab.

96. You are the administrator for your company network. You and a colleague are discussing a record of events that generates a change in Intune. These include actions such as create, update (edit), delete, assign, and remote actions that create audit events that can be reviewed. What is this called?

    A. Audit logs

    B. Audited events

    C. Data paging

    D. Device reports

97. You are the administrator for your company network. You and a colleague are discussing Microsoft Defender Advanced Threat Protection (Microsoft Defender ATP) and the ability of using the Microsoft Defender Security Center portal to manage the Microsoft Defender ATP settings. What is the URL of how to access the Microsoft Defender Security Center portal?

    A. `https://account.microsoft.com/devices`

    B. `https://devicemanagement.microsoft.com`

    C. `https://securitycenter.microsoft.com`

    D. `https://securitycenter.windows.com`

98. You are the administrator for your company network. You and a colleague are discussing device enrollment and the enrollment configuration options that are available on the Intune Navigation Pane under Device Enrollment. One of the configuration options can help with managing devices using Microsoft Intune and Azure Active Directory. What configuration option is being discussed?

    A. Apple Enrollment

    B. Android Enrollment

    C. Device Categories

    D. Windows Enrollment

99. You are the administrator for your company network. You and a colleague are discussing a tool that was created to perform analytics, diagnostics, and monitoring. What is the name of this tool?

    A. Azure Monitor

    B. Azure Observer

    C. Log Analytics

    D. Log Analyzer

100. You are the administrator for your company network. You and a colleague are discussing a tool that allows companies to control what drivers and applications are permitted to run on their Windows 10 clients. It does this by blocking any unsigned apps and scripts. What is this tool called?

A. Microsoft Defender Application Control

B. Microsoft Defender Credential Guard

C. Microsoft Defender Exploit Guard

D. Microsoft Defender Firewall with Advanced Security

101. You are the administrator for your company network. You and a colleague are discussing an ability that will allow users to see how the enrollment process works, how to access corporate resources, and the use of the Company Portal app. The users must accept these items prior to using the Company Portal app to enroll and access their work. What is this called?

A. Expressions and circumstances

B. Device categories

C. Terms and conditions

D. Windows enrollment

102. You are the administrator for your company network. You and a colleague are discussing Microsoft Defender Application Guard. You know that you can configure the mode used by Microsoft Defender Application Guard. What mode allows administrators to manage users' device settings?

A. Enterprise mode

B. Readiness mode

C. Stand-alone mode

D. User mode

103. You are the administrator for your company network. You and a colleague are discussing Azure Monitor. The data that is collected by Azure Monitor fits into one of two fundamental types. What are these types? (Choose two.)

A. Logs

B. Records

C. Measurement

D. Metrics

104. You are the administrator for your company network. You and a colleague are discussing how to set a device limit restriction to prevent users from enrolling a large number of devices. What should you do to set device limit restrictions?

A. Modify the Device Enrollment Manages settings from the Device ➤ Enrollment blade in the Intune admin center.

B. Modify the Device settings from the Devices blade in the Azure Active Directory admin center.

Chapter

8

Manage Apps and Data

THE MD-101 EXAM TOPICS COVERED IN THIS CHAPTER INCLUDE:

✓ **Domain 8: Manage Apps and Data**

- 8.1: Deploy and update applications

  - Assign apps to groups

  - Deploy apps by using Intune

  - Deploy apps by using Microsoft Store for Business

  - Deploy O365 ProPlus

  - Enable sideloading of apps into images

  - Gather Office readiness data

  - Configure and implement kiosk (assigned access) or public devices

- 8.2: Implement Mobile Application Management (MAM)

  - Implement MAM policies

  - Manage MAM policies

  - Plan MAM

  - Configure Windows Information Protection

  - Implement Azure Information Protection templates

  - Securing data by using Intune

1. You are the administrator for your company network. Your company has a main office and six branch offices. The branch offices use a WAN link when connecting to the main office. All offices have a local Internet connection and a Hyper-V host cluster. The company has a Microsoft System Center Configuration Manager (SCCM) deployment. The main office is the primary site, and each branch has a distribution point. All computers that run Windows 10 are managed by using both Configuration Manager and Microsoft Intune. You are planning on deploying the latest build of Microsoft 365 Apps for Enterprise to all of the computers. What should be included in the deployment plan if you want to minimize the amount of network traffic on the company's Internet links?

    A. Configure app assignments for Microsoft 365 Apps for Enterprise from Intune. Copy the Microsoft 365 Apps for Enterprise distribution files to a Microsoft Deployment Toolkit (MDT) deployment share in each office.

    B. Configure app assignments for Microsoft 365 Apps for Enterprise from Intune. Copy the Microsoft 365 Apps for Enterprise distribution files to a Configuration Manager distribution point in each office.

    C. Create an application deployment from Configuration Manager. Copy the Microsoft 365 Apps for Enterprise distribution files to a Configuration Manager cloud distribution point.

    D. Create an application deployment from Configuration Manager. Copy the Microsoft 365 Apps for Enterprise distribution files to a Configuration Manager distribution point in each office.

2. You are the administrator for your company network. Your company has a computer that runs Windows 10 Professional. You develop a Universal Windows Platform (UWP) app named App1. The app is signed with a certificate from a trusted certification authority (CA). You want to sideload the app to the Windows 10 Pro computer. What should you do to enable sideloading?

    A. In the Settings app, configure the Apps & Features settings.

    B. In the Settings app, configure the For Developers settings.

    C. Run the `Enable-WindowsOptionalFeature` PowerShell cmdlet.

    D. Run the `Set-WindowsEdition` PowerShell cmdlet.

3. You are the administrator for your company network. Your company has a computer that runs Windows 10 Professional. You develop a Universal Windows Platform (UWP) app named App1. The app is signed with a certificate from a trusted certification authority (CA). You want to sideload the app to the Windows 10 Pro computer. What should you do to sideload the company app?

    A. Double-click `App1.appx` in File Explorer.

    B. Run the `Add-AppxPackage` PowerShell cmdlet.

    C. Run the `Install-Package` PowerShell cmdlet.

    D. Use the Add A Package option in the Settings app.

4. You are the administrator for your company network. Your company has decided to allow employees to bring in their own devices. You use Microsoft Azure Active Directory (Azure AD) and Intune for all applications and network authentication. You want to make sure that if the employees are using iPads, as well as Windows 10 devices, they will have full access. What should you do to ensure that all of the iOS devices can get access?

A. Configure an Intune Service Connector for Exchange.

B. Create a Device Enrollment Manager account.

C. From the Apple App Store, add an Employee Portal app.

D. Import an Apple Push Notification service (APNs) certificate.

5. You are the administrator for your company network. You have a Microsoft 365 subscription. Users have iOS devices that are not enrolled in Microsoft 365 Device Management. You create an app protection policy for the Microsoft Outlook app. The policy is configured as follows:

Name: Policy1

Platform: iOS

Target to all app types: No

App types: Apps on unmanaged devices

Apps: 1 app selected

Settings ➢ Data Protection: Default settings configured

Settings ➢ Access Requirements: Default settings configured

Settings ➢ Conditional Branch: Default settings configured

Settings ➢ Scope (Tags): 0 scope(s) selected

You want to configure the policy to meet the following requirements:

- Prevent users from using the Outlook app if the operating system version is less than 12.0.0.

- Require users to use an alphanumeric passcode to access the Outlook app.

What should you configure in an app protection policy to prevent the users from using Outlook if the operating system version is less than 12.0.0?

A. You should configure access requirements.

B. You should configure conditional launch.

C. You should configure data protection.

D. You should configure a scope.

6. You are the administrator for your company network. You have a Microsoft 365 subscription. Users have iOS devices that are not enrolled in Microsoft 365 Device Management. You create an app protection policy for the Microsoft Outlook app. The policy is configured as follows:

Name: Policy1

Platform: iOS

Target to all app types: No

App types: Apps on unmanaged devices

Apps: 1 app selected

Settings ➤ Data Protection: Default settings configured

Settings ➤ Access Requirements: Default settings configured

Settings ➤ Conditional Branch: Default settings configured

Settings ➤ Scope (Tags): 0 scope(s) selected

You want to configure the policy to meet the following requirements:

- Prevent users from using the Outlook app if the operating system version is less than 12.0.0.

- Require users to use an alphanumeric passcode to access the Outlook app.

What should you configure in an app protection policy to require the users to use an alphanumeric passcode to access the Outlook app?

A. You should configure access requirements.

B. You should configure conditional launch.

C. You should configure data protection.

D. You should configure a scope.

7. You are the administrator for your company network. Your company has a Microsoft Intune subscription. All of your client computers are running Windows 10 Enterprise. Your users are complaining that they are getting prompted to restart their systems after mandatory updates. You want to stop the prompts from appearing on the Windows 10 systems. What Intune policy template should you use?

A. You should create a Custom Windows 10 Policy.

B. You should use the Microsoft Intune Agent Settings.

C. You should use the Microsoft Intune Security Settings.

D. You should use the Windows Intune Policy Configuration.

8. You are the administrator for your company network. You and a colleague are discussing the different Windows PowerShell commands that can be run. What PowerShell command allows an administrator to create a new application in Azure?

A. `Create-AzureApplication`

B. `Get-AzureADApplication`

C. `New-AzureApplication`

D. `New-AzureADApplication`

9. You are the administrator for your company network. Your company plans to deploy tablets to all of your conference rooms. The tablets run Windows 10, are managed using Microsoft Intune, and have a corporate application installed. You want to configure the tablets so that any user can use the app without having to sign in. The users must be prevented from using other applications on the tablets. What device configuration profile type should you use?

   A. The Device restrictions profile type

   B. The Endpoint protection profile type

   C. The Identity protection profile type

   D. The Kiosk profile type.

10. You are the administrator for your company network. Your network contains an Active Directory domain that is synced to Microsoft Azure Active Directory (Azure AD). All computers are joined to the domain and are registered to Azure AD. The network contains a Microsoft System Center Configuration Manager (SCCM) deployment that is configured for co-management with Microsoft Intune. The Finance department computers are managed using Configuration Manager. All of the computers in the Marketing department are managed by using Intune. You install several new computers for the users in the Marketing department using the Microsoft Deployment Toolkit (MDT). You purchase an application that uses an MSI package. You want to install the new app onto the Finance and Marketing computers. How should you deploy the application to the Finance department?

   A. Add an application registration from Azure AD.

   B. Add an application from Configuration Manager.

   C. Add a line-of-business app from Intune.

   D. Add an app to the private store from Microsoft Store for Business.

11. You are the administrator for your company network. Your network contains an Active Directory domain that is synced to Microsoft Azure Active Directory (Azure AD). All computers are joined to the domain and registered to Azure AD. The network contains a Microsoft System Center Configuration Manager (SCCM) deployment that is configured for co-management with Microsoft Intune. The Finance department computers are managed using Configuration Manager. All of the computers in the Marketing department are managed by using Intune. You install several new computers for the users in the Marketing department using the Microsoft Deployment Toolkit (MDT). You purchase an application that uses an MSI package. You want to install the new app onto the Finance and Marketing computers. How should you deploy the application to the Marketing department?

   A. Add an application registration from Azure AD.

   B. Add an application from Configuration Manager.

   C. Add a line-of-business app from Intune.

   D. Add an app to the private store from Microsoft Store for Business.

12. You are the administrator for your company network. Your users use both tablets and mobile phones to access the corporate network. The tablets do not have cellular service, but the phones have Internet access. How should you allow the tablets to connect to the mobile phones for Internet access?

    A. Configure the broadband connection as a metered network.

    B. Enable tablet metering in the tablets' settings.

    C. Enable tablet tethering.

    D. Turn on cellular tethering.

13. You are the administrator for your company network. Your company has a Microsoft 365 subscription. All of your users in the Finance department have personal devices that run iOS or Android. All of the devices are enrolled in Microsoft Intune. The Finance department adds several new users every month. The company develops a mobile application for the users in the Finance department. What should you do after you have added the application to Intune so that only the Finance department users can download the app?

    A. You should add the application to a Microsoft Deployment Toolkit (MDT) deployment share.

    B. You should assign the app to users and groups.

    C. You should add the application to Microsoft Store for Business.

    D. You should add the application to the vendor stores for iOS and Android applications.

14. You are the administrator for your company network. Your company uses Microsoft Intune to manage Windows 10, Android, and iOS devices. Several employees purchase new iPads and Android devices. You want to inform the employees about how to enroll their device in Intune. How should you instruct the users to enroll their Android devices?

    A. Instruct them to go to `https://myapps.microsoft.com`.

    B. Instruct them to go to `https://portal.manage.microsoft.com`.

    C. Instruct them to go to the Intune Company Portal app.

    D. Instruct them to go to the Settings app.

15. You are the administrator for your company network. Your company uses Microsoft Intune to manage Windows 10, Android, and iOS devices. Several employees purchase new iPads and Android devices. You want to inform the employees about how to enroll their device in Intune. How should you instruct the users to enroll their iPad devices?

    A. Instruct them to go to `https://myapps.microsoft.com`.

    B. Instruct them to go to `https://portal.manage.microsoft.com`.

    C. Instruct them to go to the Intune Company Portal app.

    D. Instruct them to go to the Settings app.

16. You are the administrator for your company network. You and a colleague are discussing the different Windows PowerShell commands that can be run. What PowerShell command allows an administrator to update an application?

    A. `Add-AzureADApplication`

    B. `Add-AzureADApplicationSetting`

    C. `Set-AzureADApplication`

    D. `Set-AzureADApplicationSetting`

17. You are the administrator for your company network. Your company has purchased an application where all of the employees need to have access to the application. You have decided that you want to install the application for all of the employees by using the Microsoft Store. How should you perform this task?

    A. BranchCache

    B. Image Installation

    C. Sideloading

    D. WS Installations

18. You are the administrator for your company network. Your company implements Microsoft Azure Active Directory (Azure AD), Microsoft 365, Microsoft Intune, and Azure Information Protection. The company's security policy indicates the following:

- Personal devices do not need to be enrolled in Intune.

- Users must authenticate by using a PIN before they can access corporate email data.

- Users can use their personal iOS and Android devices to access corporate cloud services.

- Users must be prevented from copying corporate email data to a cloud storage service other than Microsoft OneDrive for Business.

What should you create if you want to configure a solution to meet the corporate security policies?

    A. You should add an app protection policy from the Intune admin center.

    B. You should add a data loss prevention (DLP) policy from the Security & Compliance admin center.

    C. You should add a device configuration profile from the Intune admin center.

    D. You should add a supervision policy from the Security & Compliance admin center.

19. You are the administrator for your company network. You have a Microsoft Azure Active Directory (Azure AD) tenant. All Windows 10 devices are enrolled in Microsoft Intune. You configure the following settings in Windows Information Protection (WIP):

Protected apps: App1

Exempt apps: App2

Windows Information Protection mode: Silent

App1, App2, and App3 use the same file format. In App1, you create a file named File1. You want to identify which apps can open File1. From which app(s) can you open File1?

    A. App1 only

    B. App1 and App2 only

C.   App1 and App 3 only

D.   App1, App2, and App3

20. You are the administrator for your company network. You and a colleague are discussing setting up groups in Intune. When creating groups, you can assign a membership type. Which membership type is being used when administrators create dynamic group rules to add and remove devices automatically?

   A.   Assigned

   B.   Dynamic Device

   C.   Dynamic User

   D.   Un-Assigned

21. You are the administrator for your company network. Your company has Windows 10 computers, and you use Microsoft Intune to manage the computers. You have an app protection policy for Microsoft Edge. You assign the policy to a group. On a computer named Computer1, you open Microsoft Edge. On Computer1, you want to verify whether Microsoft Edge is protected by the app protection policy. In Task Manager, which column should you add?

   A.   The Data Execution Prevention column

   B.   The Enterprise Context column

   C.   The Operating System context column

   D.   The UAC Virtualization column

22. You are the administrator for your company network. Your company uses Microsoft Intune and has a Microsoft Store for Business account. You want to ensure that you can deploy Microsoft Store for Business apps using Intune. You perform the following:

   - You add a management tool from Microsoft Store for Business.

   - You assign apps to people from Microsoft Store for Business.

   What is the next step to deploy the app?

   A.   Create an app configuration policy from Intune.

   B.   Enable Microsoft Store for Business from Intune.

   C.   Sync Microsoft Store for Business from Intune.

   D.   There are no further steps required.

23. You are the administrator for your company network. You and a colleague are discussing the different Windows PowerShell commands that can be run. What PowerShell command allows an administrator to remove the password credentials from an application?

   A.   `Delete-AzureApplicationPasswordCredential`

   B.   `Delete-AzureADApplicationPasswordCredential`

   C.   `Remove-AzureApplicationPasswordCredential`

   D.   `Remove-AzureADApplicationPasswordCredential`

24. You are the administrator for your company network. Your network contains an Active Directory domain that is synced to Microsoft Azure Active Directory (Azure AD). The domain contains computers that run Windows 10, which are enrolled in Microsoft Intune and Desktop Analytics. Your company protects documents by using Windows Information Protection (WIP). What should you use if you want to identify nonapproved apps that attempt to open corporate documents?

A. The App Protection status report in Intune

B. The Device Health solution in Desktop Analytics

C. Intune Data Warehouse

D. Microsoft Cloud App Security

25. You are the administrator for your company network. Your employees use both desktops and tablets to access the network. The tablet users use a 4G mobile broadband Wi-Fi connection. What should you do if you need to see how much data the users are using on the Wi-Fi connection?

A. Configure the broadband connection as a metered network.

B. Enable Performance Monitor.

C. Enable tablet metering in the tablets' settings.

D. Turn on network resource monitoring.

26. You are the administrator for your company network. Your company has an Active Directory domain and a cloud-based Azure Active Directory. The two are synchronized by using the Azure Active Directory Synchronization Tool. The company also uses System Center Configuration Manager (SCCM). What should you do if you want to use Configuration Manager to manage devices registered with Intune? (Choose two.)

A. Using Configuration Manager, configure the Microsoft Intune Connector role.

B. Using Configuration Manager, create the Microsoft Intune subscription.

C. Using Microsoft Intune, create a new Device Enrollment Manager account.

D. Using Microsoft Intune, configure an Active Directory connector.

27. You are the administrator for your company network. You and a colleague are discussing how to assign an application by using Intune. In the process of assigning the app to a group, you have the option to pick an assignment type. One of these assignment types will assign the app to groups of users who can install the app from the Company Portal app or website. What assignment type was selected?

A. Available For Enrolled Devices

B. Available With Or Without Enrollment

C. Required

D. Uninstall

28. You are the administrator for your company network. You and a colleague are discussing how Intune supports a wide variety of application types and deployment scenarios. One of supported Windows 10 device app types includes modern apps, such as Universal Windows Platform (UWP) apps and Windows App Packages (AppX), as well as Win 32 apps, such as Microsoft Installer package files (MSI). You must manually upload and deploy updates of this app type. What app type is being discussed?

   A. Line-of-business (LOB) apps

   B. Microsoft Store for Business apps

   C. Microsoft Storefront for Business apps

   D. Place-of-business (POB) app

29. You are the administrator for your company network. You and a colleague are discussing how to assign a group to an app that was just added to Intune. You sign into Intune and select Apps and then All Apps, and then you choose the app that you want the group assigned to. What do you do next?

   A. Click Assignments to add the group.

   B. Click Device Install Status to add the group.

   C. Click Overview to add the group.

   D. Click Properties to add the group.

30. You are the administrator for your company network. You and a colleague are discussing Intune mobile application management. Mobile application management supports two configurations. One of these configurations allows you to manage apps only using MAM and app protection policies on devices that are enrolled with Intune mobile device management (MDM). What is this configuration known as?

   A. Intune MAM + MOM

   B. Intune MDM + MAM

   C. MAM without device enrollment

   D. MAM with device enrollment

31. You are the administrator for your company network. You and a colleague are discussing the name change for Office 365 ProPlus. What is the new name?

   A. Microsoft 365 Apps Advantage

   B. Microsoft 365 Apps for Enterprise

   C. Microsoft 365 Apps Initiative

   D. Microsoft 365 Apps for Readiness

32. You are the administrator for your company network. You and a colleague are discussing deploying, configuring, and managing apps in Microsoft Intune. From the Client Apps section under the Manage heading, which option is used to configure policies that help to protect against data leakage from deployed apps?

   A. App Protection Policies

   B. App Configuration Policies

   C. App Selective Wipe

   D. iOS App Provisioning Profiles

33. You are the administrator for your company network. You and a colleague are discussing Intune and the suite of Intune management features that allows an administrator to publish, push, configure, secure, monitor, and update mobile apps for users. What is the name of this suite of Intune management features?

   A. Mobile application management (MAM)

   B. Mobile method management (MMM)

   C. Portable application management (PAM)

   D. Transportable application management (TAM)

34. You are the administrator for your company network. You and a colleague are discussing deploying, configuring, and managing apps in Microsoft Intune. From the Client Apps section under the Monitor heading, which option allows you to view the app-related activity for all Intune administrators?

   A. App Licenses

   B. Audit Logs

   C. App Protection Status

   D. Discovered Apps

35. You are the administrator for your company network. You and a colleague are discussing deploying, configuring, and managing apps in the Intune ➢ Client Apps node. Under which heading would you find Discovered Apps, which displays information regarding apps that are assigned by Intune or installed on devices?

   A. Manage

   B. Monitor

   C. Setup

   D. System

36. You are the administrator for your company network. You and a colleague are discussing how Intune supports a wide variety of application types and deployment scenarios. One of the supported Windows 10 device app types includes modern apps that have been purchased. These purchased apps are then synced to Microsoft Intune for management. What app type is being discussed?

   A. Line-of-business (LOB) apps

   B. Microsoft Store for Business apps

   C. Microsoft Storefront for Business apps

   D. Place-of-business (POB) app

37. You are the administrator for your company network. You and a colleague are discussing a Windows 10 built-in feature that allows you to maintain and monitor company data and that helps protect against possible data leakage without interfering with the users' experience. What is this feature called?

A. Enterprise Data Protection (EDP)

B. Azure Rights Management Data Protection (ARMDP)

C. Microsoft Data Protection (MDP)

D. Windows Information Protection (WIP)

38. You are the administrator for your company network. You and a colleague are discussing using Microsoft Intune to create and deploy a Windows Information Protection (WIP) policy. What must you configure before you can configure a WIP policy in Intune?

A. An MDP provider in Azure AD.

B. A provider in Microsoft Active Directory.

C. An MDM or MAM provider in Azure AD.

D. There are no special requirements prior to creating a WIP policy in Intune.

39. You are the administrator for your company network. You and a colleague are discussing Intune mobile application management. Mobile application management supports two configurations. One of these configurations allows you to manage apps that are managed by Intune but are on devices enrolled with third-party Enterprise Mobility Management (EMM) providers. What is this configuration known as?

A. Intune MAM + MOM

B. Intune MDM + MAM

C. MAM without device enrollment

D. MAM with device enrollment

40. You are the administrator for your company network. You and a colleague are discussing the installation of apps on devices. You can install an app on a Windows 10 device in one of two ways. One of the ways is when the managed app is installed on the device for the user when the user signs into the device. What type of installation is this called?

A. Device Context

B. Device Environment

C. User Context

D. User Environment

41. You are the administrator for your company network. You and a colleague are discussing the creation of a Windows Information Protection (WIP) policy in Intune. To which of the following nodes do you navigate in order to create a WIP policy?

A. Client Apps ➢ App Configuration Policies

B. Client Apps ➢ App Protection Policies

C. Device Enrollment ➤ App Selective Wipe

D. Device Enrollment ➤ iOS App Provisioning Profiles

42. You are the administrator for your company network. You and a colleague are discussing mobile application management (MAM). MAM manages only the apps on a user's personal device. Which one of the following statements is not true in regard to MAM?

A. MAM supports many devices per user.

B. MAM has added Access settings for Windows Hello for Business.

C. MAM can selectively wipe corporate data from a user's personal device.

D. MAM requires an Azure Active Directory (Azure AD) Premium license.

43. You are the administrator for your company network. You and a colleague are discussing the Intune dashboard. What section under the Apps workload should you go to if you want to view the tenant name, the mobile device management (MDM) authority, the tenant location, the account status, the app installation status, and the app protection policy status?

A. The All Apps section

B. The Monitor section

C. The Outline section

D. The Overview section

44. You are the administrator for your company network. You and a colleague are discussing Windows Information Protection (WIP). You are discussing the WIP management modes. Which mode looks for inappropriate data sharing and will warn users if they are about to do something that is considered potentially unsafe?

A. Allows Overrides

B. Block

C. Off

D. Silent

45. You are the administrator for your company network. You and a colleague have just created a Windows Information Protection (WIP) policy and now are going to deploy it to your corporate enrolled devices. In the Client Apps section, what do you click to deploy the WIP policy?

A. App Protection Policies

B. App Configuration Policies

C. App Selective Wipe

D. iOS App Provisioning Profiles

46. You are the administrator for your company network. You and a colleague are discussing an application that will be added to all corporate-managed devices. This app was written by your Development team in-house. What is this type of app called?

A. It is known as an Android enterprise app.

B. It is known as a line-of-business (LOB) app.

    C. It is known as a Microsoft Store app.

    D. It is known as a Windows app.

47. You are the administrator for your company network. You and a colleague are discussing signing up for the Microsoft Store for Business. What must you have first before you can sign up for an account?

    A. You need to make sure that you are an Administrator for your company.

    B. You need to make sure that you are a Global Administrator for your company.

    C. You need to make sure that you are a Groups Admin for your company.

    D. You need to make sure that you are a Service Admin for your company.

48. You are the administrator for your company network. You and a colleague are discussing the Windows Information Protection (WIP) policy and how WIP classifies apps into two categories. One of these categories can differentiate between corporate and personal data, properly determining which apps to protect, depending upon your policies. What WIP category is being discussed?

    A. Educated apps

    B. Enlightened apps

    C. Uneducated apps

    D. Unenlightened apps

49. You are the administrator for your company network. You and a colleague are discussing Microsoft Store for Business. You know that the main administrator for the Microsoft Store is the Global Administrator, but what other role offered through the Microsoft Store allows the performance of all tasks?

    A. Billing Account Owner

    B. Billing Account Contributor

    C. Billing Account Reader

    D. Purchaser

50. You are the administrator for your company network. You and a colleague are discussing a feature in Microsoft Store for Business that allows a company to set up a tab that corporate users can view and download apps. What is this feature called?

    A. Exclusive Store

    B. Personal Collection

    C. Private Store

    D. Reserved Collection

51. You are the administrator for your company network. You and a colleague are discussing the licensing models used by the Microsoft Store for Business. Microsoft Store for Business supports two options to license apps. One of these methods is the default licensing model, and it requires that users and devices connect to the Microsoft Store to obtain an app and its license. What is this licensing model called?

    A. Connected Licensing

    B. Offline Licensing

C. Online Licensing

D. Unconnected Licensing

52. You are the administrator for your company network. You and a colleague are discussing deploying, configuring, and managing apps in Microsoft Intune. From the Client Apps section under the Manage heading, which option allows you to remove corporate data from a device's apps?

A. App Protection Policies

B. App Configuration Policies

C. App Selective Wipe

D. iOS App Provisioning Profiles

53. You are the administrator for your company network. You and a colleague are setting up the Private Store in Microsoft Store for Business. You want to change the name of the Private Store tab. Which section should you go to in order to change the tab name?

A. Settings ➤ Devices

B. Settings ➤ Distribute

C. Settings ➤ Notifications

D. Settings ➤ Shop

54. You are the administrator for your company network. You are setting up your Microsoft Store for Business, and the company has decided that they want to allow the users with the Purchasers and Basic Purchasers roles the ability to purchase apps and services without entering a credit card each time. You go out to the Account Information page and enter the corporate credit card number, but what else must you make sure is done prior to them being able to purchase apps and services?

A. Enable the Allow Users To Shop setting.

B. Disable the Allow Users To Shop setting.

C. Enable the Permit Users To Spree setting.

D. Disable the Permit Users To Spree setting.

55. You are the administrator for your company network. You and a colleague are discussing app protection policies (APPs). You know that APPs can be applied to apps running on devices that may or may not be managed using Intune. APP data protection is organized into three different configuration levels. Which level ensures that apps are protected with a PIN, encrypted, and can perform selective wipe operations?

A. Enterprise basic data protection

B. Enterprise enhanced data protection

C. Enterprise high data protection

D. Enterprise improved data protection

56. You are the administrator for your company network. You and a colleague are discussing how to add an app to your Private Store. In the Manage section, what do you click next?

  A. Apps & Programs

  B. Apps & Software

  C. License Types

  D. Program Types

57. You are the administrator for your company network. You and a colleague are setting up sideloading using the Settings app. Once you're on the For Developers page under the Use Developer Features, what should you select next?

  A. Developers Mode

  B. Enable Device Portal

  C. Microsoft Store Apps

  D. Sideload Apps

58. You are the administrator for your company network. You and a colleague are setting up sideloading using the Group Policy object (GPOs). You open the Group Policy object editor. Where should you navigate to in order to enable sideloading?

  A. `Local Computer Policy\Computer Configuration\Administrative Templates\Windows Components\App Package Deployment`

  B. `Local Computer Policy\Computer Configuration\Administrative Templates\Windows Components\Application Compatibility`

  C. `Local Computer Policy\User Configuration\Administrative Templates\Windows Components\App Package Deployment`

  D. `Local Computer Policy\Computer Configuration\Windows Settings\ Windows Components\App Package Deployment`

59. You are the administrator for your company network. You and a colleague are discussing deploying, configuring, and managing apps in Microsoft Intune. From the Client Apps section under the Setup heading, which option enables an administrator to view and apply code-signing certificates that can be used to distribute line-of-business (LOB) apps to managed Windows devices?

  A. App Categories

  B. Managed Google Play

  C. Windows Enterprise Certificate

  D. Windows Symantec Certificate

60. You are the administrator for your company network. You and a colleague want to sideload an application to more than one computer using a Windows image. You want to service the app package (`.appx` or `.appxbundle`) for an offline image. What tool should you use to perform this task?

  A. Deployment Image Servicing and Management (DISM)

  B. Distributed File System (DFS)

C. System Preparation Tool (Sysprep)

D. Windows System Image Manager (Windows SIM)

61. You are the administrator for your company network. You and a colleague want to create a provisioning package on a Windows 10 device. The device that we want to provision is a bring your own device (BYOD) type of device. What tool can you utilize to help create a provisioning package?

A. Use the Control Panel to go to the Settings app.

B. Use the Local Group Policy Editor (`gpedit.msc`).

C. Use the System Configuration Utility (`msconfig.exe`).

D. Use the Windows Configuration Designer (WCD).

62. You are the administrator for your company network. You and a colleague are discussing Intune and app protection policy advantages. One of these advantages is that an administrator has the ability to manage and protect the company's data from within the application that the user is using. What is the name of this suite that allows an administrator to manage and protect company data from within the app that the user is using?

A. Mobile application management (MAM)

B. Mobile method management (MMM)

C. Portable application management (PAM)

D. Transportable application management (TAM)

63. You are the administrator for your company network. You have a workgroup computer that runs Windows 10 and has the following users:

- User1 is a member of Group1.

- User2 is a member of Group2.

- User3 is a member of Group3.

- User4 is a member of Group2.

Group1 is a member of Group3. You are creating a file named `kiosk.xml` that specifies a lockdown profile for a multi-app kiosk. `kiosk.xml` contains the following section:

```
<Configs>
 <Config>
  <UserGroup Type="LocalGroup" Name="Group3"/>
  <DefaultProfile Id="{9A2A490F-10F6-4764-974A-43B19E722C23}"/>
 </Config>
</Configs>
```

You apply the `.xml` file to your Windows 10 computer. Which one of the following statements is true?

A. The lockdown profile applies to User1.

B. The lockdown profile applies to User2.

  C. The lockdown profile applies to User3.

  D. The lockdown profile applies to User4.

64. You are the administrator for your company network. You and a colleague are discussing setting up a device in the lobby that will run a corporate line-of-business (LOB) app. What is this device known as if it will only serve the function of running this corporate app?

  A. Computer stall

  B. Kiosk

  C. Rotunda

  D. Standalone computer

65. You are the administrator for your company network. You and a colleague are discussing the planning phases of transitioning to Microsoft 365 Apps for Enterprise. To assist you with the planning phase, Microsoft has created a tool to help with the assessment effort. This tool provides a basic solution for application compatibility and readiness assessment. What is this tool called?

  A. Configuration Manager

  B. Office Deployment Assistant

  C. Office Telemetry Dashboard

  D. Readiness Toolkit for Office add-ins and VBA

66. You are the administrator for your company network. You and a colleague are discussing mobile application management (MAM). Which one of the following statements regarding apps that are managed using Intune is not true?

  A. You can add and assign mobile apps to user groups and devices, including users and devices in specific groups.

  B. You can configure apps to start and run with specific settings enabled and update existing apps that are already on a device.

  C. You can perform a selective wipe by removing only corporate data from apps.

  D. You can view reports on which apps are used but are not able to track their usage.

67. You are the administrator for your company network. You download the Readiness Toolkit for Office add-ins and VBA, and you now would like to run a report. The report will be run using the built-in Readiness Report Creator. You want to select what information will be used to create the report. Microsoft provides several options. One of these options will only scan for Office documents that are in the user's list of most recently used files. What report option type was chosen?

  A. Add-in Data From Office Telemetry Dashboard

  B. Most Recently Used Office Documents And Installed Add-ins On This Computer

  C. Office Documents In A Local Folder Or Network Share

  D. Previous Readiness Results Saved Together In A Local Folder Or Network Share

68. You are the administrator for your company network. You and a colleague are discussing the Intune dashboard. What section under the Apps workload should you go to if you want to display an entire list of available apps?

  A. The All Apps section

  B. The Monitor section

  C. The Outline section

  D. The Overview section

69. You are the administrator for your company network. You and a colleague are configuring the mobile application management (MAM) provider. During the setup process, you want to make sure that all users can be enrolled in MAM. What setting should you configure?

  A. MAM Compliance URL

  B. MAM Discovery URL

  C. MAM Terms Of Use URL

  D. MAM User Scope

70. You are the administrator for your company network. You are using the Readiness Report Creator to create a readiness report. This report is generated in what file format?

  A. An Access .mdb file

  B. An Excel .xls file

  C. A OneNote .one file

  D. A Word .docx file

71. You are the administrator for your company network. You and a colleague are discussing Windows Information Protection (WIP). You are discussing the WIP management modes. Which mode will log any inappropriate data sharing without blocking anything?

  A. Allows Overrides

  B. Block

  C. Off

  D. Silent

72. You are the administrator for your company network. You typically use Microsoft Edge to browse the Internet. However, you are trying to open a website that you use frequently, and the site will not function properly. You see that the website uses ActiveX controls and will not open properly using Edge. What tool can you download from Microsoft that will allow you to enter the URL and specify the appropriate compatibility mode or specific browser?

  A. Internet Explorer Enterprise Mode

  B. Microsoft Edge Enterprise Mode

  C. Website Compatibility Checker

  D. Website Extension Tool

73. You are the administrator for your company network. You and a colleague are discussing deploying, configuring, and managing apps in Microsoft Intune. From the Client Apps section under the Setup heading, which option allows you to change the Intune Company Portal app?

    A. App Categories

    B. Branding And Customization

    C. Windows Enterprise Certificate

    D. Windows Symantec Certificate

74. You are the administrator for your company network. You and a colleague are discussing Intune device types. You know that there are several device types. Which device type are devices where Intune MDM management has not been detected, including devices managed by third-party MDM vendors?

    A. Android Device Administrator

    B. Android Enterprise

    C. Intune Managed Devices

    D. Unmanaged

75. You are the administrator for your company network. You and a colleague are discussing the managing phase of transitioning to Microsoft 365 Apps for Enterprise. To assist with this phase, Microsoft has created a tool to help if you want specific usage and health information. This tool gathers an inventory through usage, so you need to collect the inventory over a period of time, such as at least 30 days. What is this tool called?

    A. Configuration Manager

    B. Office Deployment Assistant

    C. Office Telemetry Dashboard

    D. Readiness Toolkit for Office add-ins and VBA

76. You are the administrator for your company network. You and a colleague are discussing app protection policies (APPs). You know that APPs can be applied to apps running on devices that may or may not be managed using Intune. APP data protection is organized into three different configuration levels. Which level introduces advanced data protection mechanisms, enhanced PIN configuration, and APP Mobile Threat Defense?

    A. Enterprise basic data protection

    B. Enterprise enhanced data protection

    C. Enterprise high data protection

    D. Enterprise improved data protection

77. You are the administrator for your company network. You and a colleague are discussing Intune device types. You know that there are several device types. Which device type are Intune-managed devices using the Android Device Administration API?

    A. Android Device Administrator

    B. Android Enterprise

    C. Intune Managed Devices

    D. Unmanaged

78. You are the administrator for your company network. You and a colleague are discussing the installation of apps on devices. You can install an app on a Windows 10 device in one of two ways. One of the ways is when the managed app is installed directly to the device by Intune. What type of installation is this called?

    A. Device Context

    B. Device Environment

    C. User Context

    D. User Environment

79. You are the administrator for your company network. You and a colleague are discussing the Windows Information Protection (WIP) policy and how WIP classifies apps into two categories. One of these categories considers all data as corporate and encrypts everything. What WIP category is being discussed?

    A. Educated apps

    B. Enlightened apps

    C. Uneducated apps

    D. Unenlightened apps

80. You are the administrator for your company network. You and a colleague are discussing some troubleshooting issues with Intune. You have an Office app policy that is not applying. The app protection policies are not applying to any support Office App for any user. What should you do to correct the issue?

    A. Confirm that the user is licensed for Intune, and the Office apps are targeted by a deployed app protection policy.

    B. Ensure that you are using User Affinity with Apple Device Enrollment Program (DEP). User Affinity is required for any app that requires user authentication under DEP.

    C. If a user is newly targeted by an app protection policy, it can take up to 24 hours for that user to show up in reports as a targeted user.

    D. If applicable, the user can log out of the app and log back in to force sync with the service.

81. You are the administrator for your company network. You and a colleague are discussing deploying, configuring, and managing apps in Microsoft Intune. From the Client Apps section under the Monitor heading, which option displays information about the standing of the app protection policy?

    A. App Licenses

    B. Audit Logs

    C. App Protection Status

    D. Discovered Apps

82. You are the administrator for your company network. You purchased several new apps and their licenses from the Microsoft Store, and you list the apps in your corporate Private Store. You want to inform the users on how to install the applications. What should the users use to install the new apps?

A. They should use a web browser and a Microsoft Azure Active Directory (Azure AD) account.

B. They should use a web browser and a Microsoft account.

C. They should use the Microsoft Store app and a Microsoft account.

D. They should use the Microsoft Store app and a Microsoft Azure Active Directory (Azure AD) account.

83. You are the administrator for your company network. You downloaded the Readiness Toolkit for Office add-ins and VBA, and now you would like to run a report. The report will be run using the built-in Readiness Report Creator. You want to select what information will be used to create the report. Microsoft provides several options. One of these options will allow you to create a consolidated report composed of individual readiness results from multiple stand-alone computers. What report option type was chosen?

A. Add-in Data From Office Telemetry Dashboard

B. Most Recently Used Office Documents And Installed Add-ins On This Computer

C. Office Documents In A Local Folder Or Network Share

D. Previous Readiness Results Saved Together In A Local Folder Or Network Share

84. You are the administrator for your company network. Your network contains an Active Directory domain that is synced to Microsoft Azure Active Directory (Azure AD). You also have a Microsoft 365 subscription. You plan on creating a conditional access policy for Microsoft Exchange Online. What setting should you configure if you want the policy to prevent access to Exchange Online, unless the user is connecting from a device that is hybrid Azure AD–joined?

A. The Device Platforms settings

B. The Device State settings

C. The Locations settings

D. The Sign-In Risk settings

85. You are the administrator for your company network. You and a colleague are discussing Azure Information Protection, which helps classify, label, and protect documents and email. Because this is an Azure service, what technology is used to allow you to define rules and conditions?

A. Active Directory Rights Management Services (AD RMS)

B. Azure Active Directory Rights Management (AADRM)

C. Azure Rights Management (Azure RMS)

D. Windows Azure Active Directory Rights Management

86. You are the administrator for your company network. You and a colleague are discussing the licensing models used by the Microsoft Store for Business. Microsoft Store for Business supports two options to license apps. One of these methods allows corporations to cache apps and their licenses to deploy within their network. What is this licensing model called?

A. Connected Licensing

B. Offline Licensing

C. Online Licensing

D. Unconnected Licensing

87. You are the administrator for your company network. You and a colleague are discussing the different ways to monitor app information assignments by using Microsoft Intune. One of the ways is by using the App Overview pane and viewing the device status list. What section is being reviewed?

A. Device And User Status Graphs

B. Device Install Status

C. Essentials

D. User Install Status

88. You are the administrator for your company network. You and a colleague are discussing Microsoft Store for Business. You know that the main administrator for the Microsoft Store is the Global Administrator, but what other role offered through the Microsoft Store can only view the account information?

A. Billing Account Owner

B. Billing Account Contributor

C. Billing Account Reader

D. Purchaser

89. You are the administrator for your company network. You and a colleague are discussing Intune device types. You know that there are several device types. Which device type is managed by Intune MDM?

A. Android Device Administrator

B. Android Enterprise

C. Intune Managed Devices

D. Unmanaged

90. You are the administrator for your company network. You and a colleague are discussing some troubleshooting issues with Intune. If user accounts are missing from app protection policy reports and the Admin console reports do not show the user accounts to an app protection policy that has just been recently deployed, what should you do to correct the issue?

A. Confirm that the user is licensed for Intune, and the Office apps are targeted by a deployed app protection policy.

B. Ensure that you are using User Affinity with Apple Device Enrollment Program (DEP). User Affinity is required for any app that requires user authentication under DEP.

    C. If a user is newly targeted by an app protection policy, it can take up to 24 hours for that user to show up in reports as a targeted user.

    D. If applicable, the user can log out of the app and log back in to force sync with service.

91. You are the administrator for your company network. You and a colleague are discussing the different ways to monitor app information assignments by using Microsoft Intune. One of the ways to do this is by using the App Overview pane, which shows the username, the installation type, and any failures. What section is being reviewed?

    A. Device And User Status Graphs

    B. Device Install Status

    C. Essentials

    D. User Install Status

92. You are the administrator for your company network. You and a colleague are discussing app protection policies (APPs). You know that APPs can be applied to apps running on devices that may or may not be managed using Intune. APP data protection is organized into three different configuration levels. Which level introduces APP data leakage prevention mechanisms and minimum OS requirements?

    A. Enterprise basic data protection

    B. Enterprise enhanced data protection

    C. Enterprise high data protection

    D. Enterprise improved data protection

93. You are the administrator for your company network. You and a colleague are discussing ways to protect company data by using data loss prevention (DLP) policies. What is the name of a tool that allows you to use a public cloud service to help set up automated workflows between your favorite apps and services to synchronize, get notifications, collect data, and more?

    A. Automated Flows

    B. Authority Control

    C. Command Power

    D. Power Automate

94. You are the administrator for your company network. You and a colleague are discussing managing data loss prevention policies (DLPs). To create a DLP policy, you must have which one of the following?

    A. Permissions to at least one environment

    B. Permissions to at least two environments

    C. Manage DLP administrative rights permissions

    D. Monitor DLP administrative rights permissions

95. You are the administrator for your company network. Your company has a Microsoft Intune subscription. You set up three separate Intune Security groups called Group1, Group2, and Group3. Group1 is a parent group to Group3. Group3 has about 80 users in the group. You then realize that you need to make Group2 the parent to Group3. What is the first thing that you should do to make Group2 the parent to Group3?

A. Delete Group3 and then re-create it under Group2.

B. Edit the security properties of Group1.

C. Edit the security properties of Group2.

D. Remove all 80 users from Group3.

96. You are the administrator for your company network. You and a colleague are discussing setting up groups in Intune. When creating groups, you can assign a membership type. Which membership type is when administrators manually assign users or devices to a group and manually remove users or devices?

A. Assigned

B. Dynamic Device

C. Dynamic User

D. Un-Assigned

97. You are the administrator for your company network. You and a colleague are discussing setting up groups in Intune. When creating groups, you can assign a membership type. Which membership type is when administrators create membership rules to add and remove members automatically?

A. Assigned

B. Dynamic Device

C. Dynamic User

D. Un-Assigned

98. You are the administrator for your company network. You and a colleague are discussing how Windows Information Protection (WIP) works and the benefits that it provides. Which one of the following is not a benefit of using WIP?

A. WIP helps control network and data access and data sharing for apps that are not enterprise aware.

B. WIP helps to maintain the ownership and control of your corporate data.

C. WIP helps to stop enterprise data leaks on corporate-owned devices, but it cannot prevent data leakages on personally owned devices that can't be locked down.

D. WIP reduces user frustration due to the restrictive data management policies on corporate-owned devices.

99. You are the administrator for your company network. You and a colleague are discussing sideloading applications. You can sideload line-of-business (LOB) Windows apps to a Windows 10 user by using PowerShell. What PowerShell command should you run to sideload a LOB application?

A. Add-AppxPackage

B. Get-AppxLog

C. Get-AppxPackage

D. Add-AppxLog

100. You are the administrator for your company network. You and a colleague are discussing Azure Information Protection templates. You know that the protection settings for Azure are saved into templates. You'd like to use PowerShell to create a protection template for Azure Information Protection with the specified name, description, and policy and set the status of the template either to archived or to published. Which cmdlet should you run?

A. Add-AipServiceTemplate

B. Export-AipServiceTemplate

C. Get-AipServiceTemplate

D. Import-AipServiceTemplate

Chapter
9

Practice Exam 1: MD-100

1. You and an assistant are discussing the process of performing a clean installation of Windows 10. If you are performing a clean installation to the same partition as an existing Windows installation, the contents of the original Windows directory will be retained in which directory?

   A. `C:\Windows`

   B. `C:\Windows.old`

   C. `C:\Windows\old`

   D. `C:\WindowsOS`

2. You are planning on deploying 100 new Windows 10 computers. Each computer will be configured the same way. You want to create a reference image that will then be applied to the remaining images. Which of the following utilities should you use?

   A. `wdsutil.exe`

   B. `setup.exe`

   C. Windows SIM

   D. `dism.exe`

3. You currently have a computer that is still running Windows XP Professional. You are planning on installing Windows 10. Which of the following installation options should you choose?

   A. A clean installation to Windows 10

   B. A promotion to Windows 10

   C. A renovation to Windows 10

   D. An upgrade to Windows 10

4. You are planning on upgrading a computer to Windows 10, 32-bit. You need to determine whether you have enough RAM on this machine. What is the minimum memory requirement for a 32-bit version of Windows 10?

   A. 1 GB

   B. 2 GB

   C. 4 GB

   D. 5 GB

5. You have asked a colleague to perform some tasks on a user's computer that will modify some Registry settings. However, you do not want this colleague to open the Registry directly. What utility can this colleague use to perform the tasks?

   A. Control Panel

   B. Microsoft Management Console (MMC)

   C. Sync Center

   D. Windows to Go

6. You have recently installed Windows 10 on a new computer, and you want to see whether there are any updates available. What is one way to check for available updates?

   A. Click the Check For Updates button.

   B. Click the Does My Computer Need To Be Updated button.

   C. Click the Restore Hidden Updates button.

   D. Click the View Update History button.

7. You have a training department in your company that requires that the same software be installed from scratch each week on their training computers. You decide to use a tool called Image Capture Wizard to deploy the disk images. Which Windows 10 utility can you use along with Image Capture Wizard to create these images for the training computers?

   A. Answer Manager

   B. Setup Manager

   C. System Preparation Tool (Sysprep)

   D. User Account Control (UAC)

8. You and an assistant are discussing how to configure Windows Update. Where should you go to configure Windows Update?

   A. Personalization

   B. Restore Hidden Updates

   C. Settings

   D. View Update History

9. You are planning on using the `wdsutil.exe` command-line utility to configure your Windows Deployment Services (WDS) server. What switch would you use if you wanted to initialize the configuration of the WDS?

   A. `/copy-image`

   B. `/enable`

   C. `/initialize-server`

   D. `/modify-server`

10. You have an employee who has just transferred from Spain. Even though this employee speaks perfect English, they have asked if you can configure their work computer to be in Spanish. Where do you go to configure this request?

   A. Accounts

   B. Personalization

   C. System

   D. Time & Language

11. A user has reached out to you and tells you that she would like to use her favorite picture for a password. Where do you set this up on the user's computer?

A. Windows Hello

B. Password

C. Sign-in Options

D. Your Info

12. You and an assistant are discussing the differences between the various Internet browsers that are available for Windows 10. One of the browsers available provides users with a new way to find pages and to read and write on the web. Plus, they can get assistance from Cortana when needed. What is the name of the Internet browser that you are discussing?

A. Chrome

B. Edge

C. Firefox

D. Internet Explorer

13. Some employees want to change the wallpaper picture on their computers. What setting should you direct them to so that they can change their wallpaper?

A. Background

B. Colors

C. Theme

D. Wallpaper

14. You have decided to take advantage of the security provided by shared permissions. Which of the following settings is the default shared permission for Administrators?

A. Change

B. Full Control

C. Read

D. Write

15. You have a user who is a member of the Marketing, R & D, and HR groups. There is a folder called MySharedInfo on the server. The current permissions of the folder are as follows:

Group/User	NTFS Permission
Marketing	Read
Sales	Modify
R & D	Modify
HR	Deny
Admin	Full Control

What is this user's effective NTFS permission?

A. Deny

B. Full Control

C. Modify

D. Read

16. You are using the `diskpart.exe` command-line utility. You want to use the switch that will allow you to make a partition on a disk, a volume on one or more disks, or a virtual hard disk (VHD). What switch command do you use to perform this?

A. `/assign`

B. `/create`

C. `/convert`

D. `/reduce`

17. A user wants to use a picture to log into the system. Windows 10 provides the ability to use a picture for logon along with gestures. How many gestures do you add to a photo for logon?

A. One

B. Two

C. Three

D. Four

18. You and an assistant are discussing using BitLocker. You know that there is a requirement for the number of partitions that are needed. What is the minimum number of partitions that are needed to use BitLocker?

A. One

B. Two

C. Three

D. Four

19. You and an assistant are discussing the benefits of the NTFS file system. You are thinking about setting up disk quotas. By default, Windows 10 supports disk quota restrictions, but at what level?

A. The drive level

B. The folder level

C. The partition level

D. The volume level

20. You and an assistant are discussing Shared folder permissions. Which of the following is true regarding Shared folder permissions? (Choose all that apply.)

   A. Shared folder permissions apply to files.

   B. Shared folder permissions apply to folders.

   C. Shared folder permissions apply locally to the data.

   D. Shared folder permissions apply remotely to the data.

21. You and an assistant are discussing the `convert` command. What does the command `convert e: /fs:ntfs` do?

   A. It will convert the E: drive from FAT to NTFS.

   B. It will convert the E: drive from NTFS to FAT.

   C. It will format the E: drive to FAT.

   D. It will scan the E: drive for errors.

22. You have a computer that runs Windows 10 and is used by several users. The computer is joined to an Active Directory domain. All of the users are members of the Administrators group. Each user has an Active Directory account. You have a confidential Microsoft Word document. You want to ensure that you are the only user who can open this confidential document. What should you configure?

   A. The account policies

   B. The Encrypting File System (EFS) settings

   C. The NTFS permissions

   D. The Share permissions

23. You want to set up Home Folders for a user. You open the user's Properties dialog box by accessing the Local Users and Groups utility, opening the user's folder, and then double-clicking the user account. What tab should you go to in order to set up the Home Folder?

   A. The General tab

   B. The Member Of tab

   C. The Home Folder tab

   D. The Profile tab

24. You have a computer that runs Windows 10. You have been tasked with configuring Windows Hello. You want to configure the PIN complexity rules for this computer. Which policy setting should you modify?

   A. Biometric

   B. Credential User Interface

   C. Smart Cards

   D. Windows Hello for Business

25. Your network contains an Active Directory domain that includes a group named GroupA. All of the computers in this domain are running Windows 10. Every computer has a folder named C:\Documents that has the default NTFS permissions assigned. You add a folder named Masters to the C:\Documents directory on all of the computers. New corporate policy states that all domain users must be able to open the files within the Masters folder, but that only the members of GroupA can edit the files within the Masters folder. You need to configure the NTFS permissions to meet the requirements for the new company policy. How should you configure the NTFS settings on the Masters folder in regard to the permissions for GroupA?

    A. Assign Allow Modify permission.

    B. Assign Allow Read & Execute permission.

    C. Assign Deny Modify permission.

    D. Assign Deny Read & Execute permission.

26. You are attempting to set up Microsoft Defender Firewall to allow Domain Name System (DNS) inbound and outbound rules. What protocol and port number should you configure?

    A. TCP port 20

    B. TCP port 25

    C. UDP port 53

    D. TCP port 80

27. You have a Windows 10 machine that needs to be able to communicate with all of the computers on an internal network. The company decides to add 15 new segments to its IPv6 network. How should you configure the IPv6 address so that the server can communicate with all of the segments?

    A. fd00::2b0:e0ff:dee9:4143/8

    B. fe80::2b0:e0ff:dee9:4143/32

    C. ff80::2b0:e0ff:dee9:4143/64

    D. fe80::2b0:e0ff:dee9:4143/64

28. You and an assistant are discussing Remote Desktop Connection (RDC). What tab in the RDC options is used to configure remote audio settings, keyboard settings, and local device and resource access on the remote computer?

    A. The General tab

    B. The Display tab

    C. The Local Resources tab

    D. The Advanced tab

29. You are speaking to a co-worker regarding the use of Classless Inter-Domain Routing (CIDR). Which of the following subnet masks are represented with the CIDR of /29?

    A. 255.255.255.224

    B. 255.255.255.240

    C. 255.255.255.248

    D. 255.255.255.254

30. You and a co-worker are discussing the use of network IDs. Because the network ID bits must always be chosen in a contiguous manner from the high-order bits, a shorthand way of expressing a subnet mask is to denote the number of bits that define the network ID as a network prefix using the network prefix notation: /<# of bits>. What is the network prefix for Class B?

A. /8

B. /16

C. /24

D. /64

31. A user has come to you explaining the she cannot access website on her computer. You run the ping command and examine the results, shown here:

```
IPv4 Address. . . . . . : 168.254.254.1
Subnet Mask . . . . . . : 255.255.255.0
Default Gateway . . . . : 168.254.254.255
DNS Servers . . . . . . : 127.0.0.1
```

What is misconfigured and is the reason why the user cannot access the Internet?

A. The default gateway

B. The DNS server

C. The IP address

D. The subnet mask

32. You are troubleshooting a network connectivity problem. A command is run, and the following results appear:

```
Request timed out.
Request timed out.
Request timed out.
Request timed out.
Packets: Sent = 4, Received = 0, Lost = 4 (100% loss),
```

Which of the following commands has generated the results you are viewing?

A. ipconfig

B. nbtstat

C. netstat

D. ping

33. A user contacts you to let you know that they cannot connect to the Internet. You examine the `ipconfig` results, as shown here:

```
IPv4 Address. . . . . . . .: 10.254.254.1
Subnet Mask . . . . . . . : 255.255.255.0
Default Gateway . . . . . .: 10.254.254.255
```

What is most likely the cause of the issue given the `ipconfig` results?

   A. The subnet mask is incorrect.

   B. The IP address is incorrect.

   C. The default gateway is incorrect.

   D. The subnet mask and the IP address are incorrect.

34. You have several Windows 10 computers and laptops that have been connected to a wireless network. To make the wireless local area network (WLAN) more secure, which of the following tasks prohibits additional client access to the wireless access point (WAP)?

   A. Disable SSID broadcasting.

   B. Disable WPA2.

   C. Enable channel bonding.

   D. Enable the frame aggregation.

35. You want to view a list of all of the MAC addresses to which a computer has connected in the past. What command should you use to view this list?

   A. `arp -a`

   B. `arp -s`

   C. `netstat -a`

   D. `ping 127.0.0.1`

36. You and an assistant are discussing the steps on how to connect a Windows 10 machine to a domain. What must be set up first in order to connect a computer to a network?

   A. A firewall

   B. A network access point (NAP)

   C. A network interface card (NIC)

   D. A router

37. Your company uses Windows 10 Enterprise client computers. Using Remote Desktop, users report that they are currently unable to connect to the office from their home computers. You need to make sure that the users can remotely connect from their home offices. What setting should you configure on the home computers so that the users won't be able to access other corporate network resources from their home computers?

   A. The DirectAccess connection

   B. The Remote Desktop Gateway IP address

   C. The Remote Desktop local resources

   D. The Virtual Private Network connection

38. Your users use Windows tablets to access the network. The company tablets use a broadband Wi-Fi connection. You want to watch how much data the users are using on the broadband Wi-Fi connection. What should you do?

A. Configure the broadband connection as a metered network.

B. Enable Performance Monitor.

C. Enable tablet metering in the tablet's settings.

D. Turn on network resource monitoring.

39. You and an assistant are discussing ways to back up and restore a system. What utility allows you to back up and restore the operating system, volumes, files, folders, and applications by using the command prompt?

A. ntbackup.exe

B. setup.exe

C. sysprep.exe

D. wbadmin.exe

40. You and an assistant are discussing Microsoft's subscription-based storage system called OneDrive. OneDrive allows users to use up to a certain amount of cloud storage for free without a subscription. How much cloud storage is provided for free with OneDrive?

A. 3 GB

B. 5 GB

C. 8 GB

D. 10 GB

41. You and an assistant are discussing the wide range of Windows 10 recovery techniques that Microsoft provides. One of these techniques can be used if a computer will not boot into Safe Mode, and it can be used to replace corrupted system files. What is this recovery technique called?

A. Backup and Restore

B. Safe Mode

C. Startup Repair Tool

D. System Restore

42. You and an assistant are discussing the different ways to access the Control Panel. What command should you run if you want to access the Control Panel by using Windows PowerShell?

A. Get-ControlPanel

B. Get-ControlPanelItem

C. Get-EventLog

D. Get-MyInformation

43. You have performed a System Restore on a Windows 10 machine. However, there was an issue with the restore point, and now the computer will not boot. What should you do to try to resolve the issue?

    A. Manually delete all of the files that changed.

    B. Restart the computer.

    C. There is nothing that can be done—it's too late.

    D. Undo the System Restore.

44. You and an assistant are discussing System Protection and restore points. By default, how often does Windows 10 automatically create restore points?

    A. Daily

    B. Once every 3 days

    C. Once every 7 days

    D. Once every 30 days

45. You and an assistant are discussing the Windows 10 Security and Maintenance screen. If the Security and Maintenance section discovers an issue that requires immediate attention, what does the icon display?

    A. A green box

    B. An orange flashing triangle

    C. A red circle with a white X

    D. A yellow triangle with a black exclamation point

46. You and an assistant are discussing how Microsoft processes updates and when they become available to the public. Updates are typically released on a certain day of the week. When updates are released, what is this day of the week referred to?

    A. Maintenance Mondays

    B. Patch Tuesdays

    C. Update Wednesdays

    D. Fixed Fridays

47. During the boot process, you want to see what is being loaded. Using the Advanced Boot Options menu, you have enabled boot logging. Where will this log file be stored?

    A. \Windows\Bootlog.txt

    B. \Windows\Logging.txt

    C. \Windows\Ntbtlog.txt

    D. \Windows\Startup.txt

48. You and an assistant are discussing offline OneDrive files and folders statuses. You open File Explorer and see an icon showing two blue arrows forming a circle. What does this symbol represent?

A. It is in sync with the online version.

B. It is syncing.

C. It is out of sync.

D. This icon is not used with OneDrive.

49. You have a large number of Windows 10 computers. All of the computers in the network are joined to Microsoft Azure Active Directory (Azure AD). All of the computers are configured differently in terms of update settings. Some of the computers are configured for manual updates. You want to configure Windows Update for these machines. You must meet the following requirements:

▪ The computers must be managed from a central location.

▪ You must minimize traffic across the Internet.

▪ You must keep costs to a minimum.

How should you manage the traffic if you are setting up Windows Update?

A. Use BranchCache.

B. Use Client Peer Cache.

C. Use Delivery Optimization.

D. Use Peer Cache.

50. A few users have indicated that a certain application is taking too long to load. You create a baseline report for one of the computers using Performance Monitor. You monitor the processor, the disk subsystem, and the network subsystem. You notice that the disk subsystem has a high load of activity. What other subsystem should you also monitor before you will know for sure if there is a disk subsystem bottleneck?

A. The Application counters

B. The Memory counters

C. The Network counters

D. The Processor counters

Chapter

10

Practice Exam 2: MD-101

1. You and a colleague are discussing the use of intricate Windows Hello personal identification numbers (PINs). You understand that a PIN may require or block certain special characters, uppercase and lowercase characters, and digits. What is the maximum length that a PIN can have?

    A. Up to 8 characters

    B. Up to 32 characters

    C. Up to 69 characters

    D. Up to 127 characters

2. You have a Windows 10 computer, and you want to configure Windows Hello on it. You want to set a PIN complexity rule for this computer. What policy setting should you modify?

    A. Biometrics

    B. Credential User Interface

    C. Smart Cards

    D. Windows Hello for Business

3. You and a colleague are discussing Azure Multi-Factor Authentication (Azure MFA) and the different methods that can be enabled. One of these methods uses a risk policy to enforce two-step verification for signing into all cloud applications. What method is being discussed?

    A. Azure AD Identity Protection

    B. Changing the device state

    C. Changing the user state

    D. Conditional access policy

4. You and a colleague are discussing multi-factor authentication. Your colleague asks you for an example of multi-factor authentication. What do you tell her?

    A. That multi-factor authentication is using biometric fingerprints and voice recognition to verify the user's identity

    B. That multi-factor authentication is using smart cards and PINs to verify the user's identity

    C. That multi-factor authentication is using retina scans and voice recognition to verify the user's identity

    D. That multi-factor authentication is using usernames, PINs, and employee ID numbers to verify the user's identity

5. You and a colleague are discussing Windows Update for Business and how it can be configured by using Group Policy object (GPO) settings. There are several important GPO settings for Windows Update for Business. One of these settings allows you to specify when to receive quality updates or to defer receiving quality updates. What Windows Update for Business group policy is being discussed?

    A. Manage Preview Updates setting

    B. Manage Windows Diagnostics

    C. Select When Preview Builds And Feature Updates Are Received setting

    D. Select When Quality Updates Are Received setting

6. You and a colleague are discussing configuring Delivery Optimization settings using Group Policy download mode. Which download mode is being discussed if it is described as an HTTP downloading and peering in the same private group on a local LAN?

    A. Group

    B. HTTP Only

    C. Internet

    D. Simple

7. You and a colleague are discussing using the User State Migration Tool (USMT) to migrate user profiles. Several migration types are available. One such migration type is used when the source and destination computers for the upgrade are the same machine. What is this type of migration called?

    A. An in-place migration

    B. An inline migration

    C. A side-by-side migration

    D. A wipe-and-load migration

8. You and a colleague are discussing files that can be used with the User State Migration Tool (USMT). What file extension is used with the migration files?

    A. `.csv`

    B. `.docx`

    C. `.txt`

    D. `.xml`

9. You and a colleague are discussing Upgrade Readiness. You have just learned that Microsoft has recently retired Windows Analytics and that Upgrade Readiness was part of this service. You want to switch to the newer product called Desktop Analytics. What should you do?

    A. Demote the Upgrade Readiness connection.

    B. Promote the Upgrade Readiness connection.

    C. Remove the Upgrade Readiness connection.

    D. Upgrade the Upgrade Readiness connection.

10. You and a colleague are discussing ways in which to deploy a provisioning package. Several methods are available, but you want to use PowerShell. Which PowerShell cmdlet allows you to apply a provisioning package?

    A. `Add-ProvisioningPackage`

    B. `Export-ProvisioningPackage`

    C. `Get-ProvisioningPackage`

    D. `Import-ProvisioningPackage`

11. You and a colleague are discussing the User State Migration Tool (USMT). The USMT can be used to automate migration. Which of the following statements is *not* true regarding the USMT?

    A. You can migrate the access control lists (ACL) information for specified files and folders.

    B. You can migrate folders from the Public profiles.

    C. You can migrate local and domain-based user accounts and folders from each user profile.

    D. You can migrate passwords.

12. You are planning on installing Windows 10 on a computer that has a 1 GHz CPU, 2 GB RAM, and a 15 GB hard drive. Which version of Windows 10 can you install?

    A. The 32-bit version of Windows 10 Enterprise

    B. The 64-bit version of Windows 10 Enterprise

    C. The 64-bit version of Windows 10 Home

    D. The 64-bit version of Windows 10 Professional

13. You have a department that needs the same software installed from scratch on their training computers each week. You decide that you'd want to use Deployment Image Servicing and Management (DISM) to capture the images. What Windows 10 utility can you use along with DISM to create the images?

    A. Answer Manager

    B. Setup Manager

    C. System Preparation Tool (sysprep)

    D. Universal Authentication Factor (UAF)

14. You want to update an Azure Active Directory (Azure AD) application policy for a user's applications. What PowerShell command can you use to accomplish this task?

    A. `Add-AzureADPolicy`

    B. `Add-AzureADApplicationPolicy`

    C. `Create-AzurePolicy`

    D. `Set-AzureADPolicy`

15. You and a colleague are discussing conditional access policy conditions. One of these conditions is used to apply or exclude devices that are hybrid Azure AD joined or marked as compliant in Intune. What condition is being discussed?

A. Client Apps

B. Device Platforms

C. Device State

D. Locations

16. You have several hundred Windows 10 computers that are joined to Microsoft Azure Active Directory (Azure AD) and enrolled in Microsoft Intune. What folder should you include if you want to redirect Windows known folders to Microsoft OneDrive for Business?

A. The Desktop folder

B. The Downloads folder

C. The Music folder

D. The Saved Games folder

17. You currently have a large number of Windows 10 Enterprise computers. These computers are managed using Group Policy objects (GPOs) and Microsoft Endpoint Configuration Manager. You purchase Microsoft 365 licensing and want to utilize the mobile device management (MDM) functionality. Most users will work from the corporate office while a small group will work remotely. You want to implement co-management for all the devices. What should you recommend be done first if you want to recommend a strategy on how the company should roll out co-management?

A. Suggest an exclusion group.

B. Suggest an extended pilot group.

C. Suggest a production group.

D. Suggest a rollout group.

18. You have several Windows 10 computers that are joined to Microsoft Azure Active Directory (Azure AD). You have a Microsoft 365 subscription. You are planning to replace these computers with new computers that also run Windows 10. The new computers will be joined to Azure AD. What should you do if you need to ensure that the desktop background, Favorites, and browsing history are available on the new computers?

A. Configure Enterprise State Roaming.

B. Configure Folder Redirection.

C. Configure system settings.

D. Configure roaming user profiles.

19. You and a colleague are discussing device identity management in Azure Active Directory (Azure AD). How should you manage device identity management?

A. Use the Azure portal.

B. Use the Configuration Manager console.

C. Use the Group Policy Management Editor.

D. Use the Microsoft Intune portal.

20. Your network contains an Active Directory domain. What should you use if you need to create a Central Store for Group Policy administrative template files?

    A. dcgpofixdcgpofix.exe

    B. File Explorer

    C. Group Policy Management Console (GPMC)

    D. Server Manager

21. You and a colleague are discussing a law that regulates how financial institutions handle their customers' personal information. What is this law called?

    A. Federal Information Processing Standard (FIPS) Publication 140-2 (FIPS PUB 140-2)

    B. Gramm-Leach-Bliley Act of 1999 (GLBA)

    C. Health Insurance Portability and Accountability Act of 1996 (HIPPA)

    D. Sarbanes-Oxley Act of 2002 (SARBOX)

22. You and a colleague are discussing enabling device Sync settings. You'd like to sync the on-screen keyboard, sticky keys, filter keys, and toggle keys. What setting should you set in sync?

    A. Ease of Access

    B. Language Preference

    C. Passwords

    D. Theme

23. You and a colleague are discussing ways to minimize user profile sizes. One way to minimize user profile size is to forward specific folders, such as a Documents folder, to a location outside of the user profile. These can be stored in a shared location on a file server or sent to OneDrive for Business. What is this method that is being discussed?

    A. Applying quotas

    B. Configuring sync settings

    C. Limiting the user profile size using Group Policy

    D. Redirecting the profile folders

24. You support Windows 10 Enterprise computers that are members of an Active Directory domain. Recently, several user accounts have been configured with super-mandatory user profiles. A user informs you that all of their personal data is lost after the computer restarts. What should you do if you need to configure the user's computer to prevent possible user data loss in the future?

    A. Add the .dat extension to the user profile name.

    B. Configure Folder Redirection by using the domain group policy.

    C. Configure the user's documents library to include folders from network shares.

    D. Remove the .man extension from the user profile name.

25. You and a colleague are discussing creating Intune policies. There is a setting that you can assign and filter policies to specific groups. What is the name of this item that you can add to a profile?

A. Device groups

B. Intune licenses

C. Roles

D. Scope tags

26. You and a colleague are discussing user profiles. You know that a user profile contains an ntuser.dat file. When a user signs onto a Windows machine, the system loads the file into the registry and maps it to a specific registry subtree. To what registry subtree is the ntuser.dat file mapped?

A. HKEY_USERS\.DEFAULT

B. HKEY_CURRENT_USER

C. HKEY_CURRENT_CONFIG

D. HKEY_LOCAL_MACHINE\Security

27. You and a colleague are discussing a tool that allows you to connect your local Active Directory Domain Services (AD DS) environment to your Azure Active Directory (Azure AD). What is the name of this tool?

A. Azure Connection Tool

B. Azure AD Connect

C. Azure AD Connect Health

D. Forefront Identity Manager

28. You and a colleague are discussing the steps to set up Desktop Analytics. What is the name of the process that you must complete first to be able to sign into Desktop Analytics and to configure your subscription?

A. Initial Onboarding

B. Initial Setup Process

C. Primary Onboarding

D. Primary Setup Process

29. You and a colleague are discussing how Windows Security monitors devices and provides a health report. You want to look at this report. Where does this report appear?

A. Account Protection

B. Device Performance & Health

C. Device Security

D. Virus & Threat Protection

30. You and a colleague are discussing Microsoft Defender Application Guard. You know that you can configure this mode used by Microsoft Defender Application Guard. What mode allows administrators to manage the users' device settings?

    A. Enterprise mode

    B. Readiness mode

    C. Stand-alone mode

    D. User mode

31. You and a colleague are discussing a tool that allows companies to control what drivers and applications are allowed to run on their Windows 10 clients. It does this by blocking any unsigned apps and scripts. What is this tool called?

    A. Microsoft Defender Application Control

    B. Microsoft Defender Credential Guard

    C. Microsoft Defender Exploit Guard

    D. Microsoft Defender Firewall with Advanced Security

32. You and a colleague are discussing device enrollment and the enrollment configuration options that are available on the Intune Navigation pane under Device Enrollment. One of the configuration options can help with managing devices using Microsoft Intune and Azure Active Directory. What configuration option is being discussed?

    A. Apple enrollment

    B. Android enrollment

    C. Device categories

    D. Windows enrollment

33. You and a colleague are discussing the best way to monitor system performance. What is it called when you monitor performance over a given period of time?

    A. A baseline

    B. IA computer precedent

    C. An event criterion

    D. A paradigm

34. You and a colleague are discussing the Microsoft Defender Application Guard. You know that it is turned off by default, and you want to install it using Control Panel. Where in Control Panel do you install it?

    A. Ease of Access

    B. Network and Internet

    C. Programs and Features

    D. System and Security

35. You and a colleague are discussing device enrollment. When a device is enrolled in Intune, it is supplied with a mobile device management (MDM) certificate that is used to communicate with the Intune service. You know that there are several ways to enroll a device, depending upon the device's ownership, device type, and management requirements. One of these methods includes phones, tablets, and computers that are owned by the corporation and are given to the users. What is this method known as?

A. Apple Automated Device Enrollment (ADE)

B. Business-owned device (DOD)

C. Corporate-owned device (COD)

D. Device Enrollment Manager (DEM)

36. You and a colleague are discussing Microsoft Defender Antivirus. You know that there are a number of scan options available with Microsoft Defender Antivirus. You want to perform a scan that will scan the most likely areas on a hard drive where spyware, malware, and viruses are commonly known to infect. What scan option is being discussed?

A. A custom scan

B. A full scan

C. A quick scan

D. A Microsoft Defender offline scan

37. You and a colleague are discussing a Microsoft utility that allows you to collect information in a log and analyze the data in real time. What is this utility called?

A. Disk Cleanup

B. Event Viewer

C. Performance Monitor

D. Resource Monitor

38. You and a colleague are discussing using log queries to help you leverage completely the value of the data collected in Azure Monitor Logs. There is a tool in the Azure portal that is used for writing log queries. What is this tool called?

A. Azure Log Creator

B. Azure Monitor Log Maker

C. Log Analytics

D. Log Query Analyzer

39. Your company wants to use Azure Active Directory (Azure AD) and Microsoft Intune. You have been checking into this because users have been using multiple devices on the network. When users get added to Intune and get licensed, how many devices by default can each user add?

A. 5 devices.

B. 10 devices.

C. 15 devices.

D. None. Device administrators are the only people who can add devices to Intune.

40. You and a colleague are discussing a way to allow users to enroll themselves in Intune. What should you configure to allow them to enroll their own devices?

A. Automatic Enrollment

B. Automatic Device Enrollment

C. Self-Enrollment

D. Self-Device Enrollment

41. You and a colleague are discussing sideloading applications. You can sideload line-of-business (LOB) Windows apps to a Windows 10 user by using PowerShell. What PowerShell command should you use to sideload LOB applications?

A. `Add-AppxPackage`

B. `Get-AppxLog`

C. `Get-AppxPackage`

D. `Add-AppxLog`

42. You and a colleague are discussing setting up groups in Intune. When creating groups, you can assign a membership type. Which membership type is when administrators create membership rules to add and remove members automatically?

A. Assigned

B. Dynamic Device

C. Dynamic User

D. Un-Assigned

43. You and a colleague are discussing app protection policies (APPs). You know that APPs can be applied to apps running on devices that may or may not be managed using Intune. APP data protection is organized into three different configuration levels. Which level introduces APP data leakage prevention mechanisms and minimum OS requirements?

A. Enterprise basic data protection

B. Enterprise enhanced data protection

C. Enterprise high data protection

D. Enterprise improved data protection

44. You and a colleague are discussing Microsoft Store for Business. You know that the main administrator for the Microsoft Store is the Global Administrator, but what other role offered through the Microsoft Store can only view the account information?

A. Billing Account Owner

B. Billing Account Contributor

C. Billing Account Reader

D. Purchaser

45. Your network contains an Active Directory domain that is synced to Microsoft Azure Active Directory (Azure AD). You also have a Microsoft 365 subscription. You plan on creating a conditional access policy for Microsoft Exchange Online. What setting should you configure if you want the policy to prevent access to Exchange Online unless the user is connecting from a device that is hybrid Azure AD joined?

A. Device Platforms settings

B. Device State settings

C. Locations settings

D. Sign-In Risk settings

46. You and a colleague are discussing Windows Information Protection (WIP) policy and how WIP classifies apps into two categories. One of these categories considers all data as corporate and encrypts everything. What WIP category is being discussed?

A. Educated apps

B. Enlightened apps

C. Uneducated apps

D. Unenlightened apps

47. You usually use Microsoft Edge to browse the Internet. However, you are trying to open a website that you use frequently, and the site will not function properly. You see that the website uses ActiveX controls and will not open properly using Edge. What tool can you download from Microsoft that will allow you to enter the URL and specify the appropriate compatibility mode or specific browser?

A. Internet Explorer Enterprise mode

B. Microsoft Edge Enterprise mode

C. Website Compatibility Checker

D. Website Extension Tool

48. You and a colleague are discussing Windows Information Protection (WIP). You are discussing the WIP management modes. Which mode will log any inappropriate data sharing without blocking anything?

A. Allows Overrides

B. Block

C. Off

D. Silent

49. You and a colleague are discussing the Intune dashboard. What section under the Apps workload should you go to if you want to display an entire list of available apps?

A. All Apps section

B. Monitor section

C. Outline section

D. Overview section

50. You and a colleague want to create a provisioning package on a Windows 10 device. This device that you want to provision is a bring your own device (BYOD) type of device. What tool can you utilize to help create a provision package?

    A. Settings app

    B. Local Group Policy Editor (gpedit.msc)

    C. System Configuration Utility (msconfig.exe)

    D. Windows Configuration Designer (WCD)

Appendix

Answers and Explanations

Chapter 1: Deploy Windows

1. **A, B.** Use the User State Migration Tool (USMT) to simplify user state migration during deployment of Windows operating systems. USMT captures user accounts, user files, operating system settings, and application settings, and then it migrates them to a new Windows installation. The two commands that USMT uses are `loadstate.exe` and `scanstate.exe`.

2. **A.** A tool for managing shared printers in Windows 10 is the Print Management Console. It allows users to update and manage printer drivers, control printer driver installation, create new printer filters, view the extended features of the printers, and more. The Print Management Console has a utility called Migrate Printers. This allows an administrator to migrate the print server queues from one machine to another.

3. **A.** Using Device Manager to disable a hardware device is a useful tool if you'd like to ignore the piece of hardware. When you disable a driver, the driver is still installed on the Windows 10 system, but it is not active. Administrators like to use the disable feature so that they can re-enable the device again at a later time. To disable devices using Device Manager, perform the following:

   1. Click the Start button, type **device manager** in the search box, and then click Device Manager in the menu.

   2. Expand the category that has the device that you'd like to disable.

   3. Right-click the device and select the Disable Device option.

   4. Click Yes to confirm. The device is now disabled and is no longer available to be used.

4. **C.** Windows 10 in S mode is a version of Windows 10 that is designed for security and performance while providing a Windows experience with which users are familiar. To increase security, it requires Microsoft Edge for safe browsing, and it only allows apps from the Microsoft Store. Azure AD Domain join is available for Windows 10 Pro in S mode and Windows 10 Enterprise in S mode. It's not available in Windows 10 Home in S mode.

5. **C.** Windows PowerShell is a Windows command-line shell designed for system administrators. It includes an interactive prompt and a scripting environment that can be used individually or in conjunction with other scripts. It allows you to run multiple configurations by using scripts. Windows PowerShell uses cmdlets (pronounced "command-lets"), which are lightweight commands used in the Windows PowerShell environment.

6. **A.** Within Device Manager in all versions of Windows is the Roll Back Driver feature. It is used to uninstall the current driver for a hardware device and then automatically install the previously installed driver. The Roll Back Driver option is the easiest way to roll back to a known good driver.

7. **D.** The `setup.exe` command-line setup utility is used to initiate the installation process. By using the /unattend switch with the `setup.exe` command, it allows an administrator to use an answer file for the Windows setup. The syntax is /unattend:<answer_file>.

8. D. Boot Configuration Data Editor (`bcdedit.exe`) is used to change the Boot Configuration Data (BCD) Store, which controls how the operating system loads. Use `bcdedit.exe` in Windows to change the `/default` boot entry. The `/default` switch specifies the default entry that the boot manager selects when the timeout expires. Change the default boot entry to ensure that the operating system configuration you prefer is loaded automatically.

9. B. Configuring the Lock Screen and Screen Timeout settings allows you to select a screen-saver that will start after the system has been idle for a specified period of time. Windows 10 allows you to customize the look of the Lock screen by using the Windows Spotlight service. You can use a single image, or you can use a collection of images. If you want to see a specific image, you can customize the Lock screen to display a single image by following these steps:

   1. Open Settings ➤ Personalization and click Lock Screen.

   2. Use the Background drop-down menu and select the Picture option.

   3. Click the Browse button to locate the desired image.

   To set the screen timeout in the Lock screen, follow these steps:

   1. Open Settings ➤ Personalization and click Lock Screen.

   2. Click the Screen Timeout Settings option.

   3. Use the Screen drop-down menu to specify the time wanted.

   To return to your active session, press Ctrl+Alt+Delete and enter the password for your user account to resume.

10. B. The Start section allows you to configure what you will see on the Start Menu and which folders will appear. To modify the Start Menu, go to Settings ➤ Personalization ➤ Start and you will see these configuration options:

   - Show more tiles on Start
   - Show app list in Start menu
   - Show recently added apps
   - Show most used apps
   - Show suggestions occasionally in Start
   - Use Start full screen
   - Show recently opened items in Jump Lists on Start or the taskbar
   - Choose which folders appear on Start

11. A. In Windows 10, sleep mode is the preferred power-saving mode. Sleep mode puts a computer into a low-power state and turns off the display when it's not being used. It does not shut down the computer. When you "wake up" from sleep mode, it resumes where you left off. Sleep mode is a mixture of both standby mode and hibernation mode. When in sleep mode, data is saved to the hard disk.

12. B. The easiest way to restore an accidentally deleted file is to restore it from the Recycle Bin. The Recycle Bin is a special folder that holds the files and folders that have been deleted. You can restore or permanently delete a file from the Recycle Bin by opening the Recycle Bin, right-clicking that file, and selecting the appropriate action from the context menu.

13. C. The User State Migration Tool (USMT) captures user accounts, user files, the operating system settings, and application settings and then migrates them to a new Windows installation. USMT has two tools that migrate settings and data: `scanstate` and `loadstate`. The `scanstate` tool collects the information from the source computer, and `loadstate` applies that information to the destination computer. The next step is to run `loadstate.exe` and specify the `C:\Users` subfolder.

14. D. Windows Deployment Services (WDS) enables the deployment of the Windows operating system. WDS can be used to set up new clients with network-based installations without requiring an administrator to go to each and every computer or to install directly from CD or DVD media. In this scenario, you'd want to install the WDS MMC snap-in tool. It is used to manage the server. This MMC provides an easy way to manage images, computers, and server settings. An administrator can perform almost all tasks using this snap-in.

15. B. Deployment Image Servicing and Management (DISM) is a command-line utility that can be used to mount and service Windows images prior to deployment. You can use DISM image management commands to mount and obtain information regarding Windows image (.wim) files or virtual hard disks (VHDs). Use DISM servicing commands to see what drivers, packages, and other files and settings are included in a Windows image. Using the `/get-drivers` parameter displays the basic information about driver packages in the online or offline image.

16. A, B. The Registry is a database used by the operating system to store configuration information. You can edit the Registry in Windows 10 by using `regedit` or `regedt32`. Always use caution when editing the Registry because any misconfigurations may cause the computer to fail to boot.

17. C. Backgrounds are images that you set as your wallpaper. To configure the Windows desktop and how it looks, simply right-click an area of open space on the desktop and choose Personalize from the context menu.

18. B. Use Windows Update Delivery Optimization to help get Windows updates and Microsoft Store apps more quickly and reliably. Windows Update Delivery Optimization (WUDO) is a Windows 10 tool that is designed to reduce bandwidth by having computers obtain updates from other users on the network that have already downloaded the content, thus reducing the amount of traffic generated.

19. A. Deployment Image Servicing and Management (DISM) is a command-line utility that works along with `sysprep.exe` to create and manage Windows 10 image files for deployment. DISM is included with Windows 10, and it is installed to `%WINDIR%\system32\dism.exe`. DISM provides additional functionality when used with Windows 10 and Windows Server. DISM can do the following:

   - Add, remove, and enumerate drivers
   - Add, remove, and enumerate packages

- Apply changes to an `unattend.xml` answer file

- Capture Windows images

- Configure international settings

- Copy and move Windows images

- Enable or disable Windows features

- Install Windows images

- Prepare a Windows PE image

- Upgrade a Windows image to a different edition

- Use Package Manager scripts

- Work with all platforms (32-bit, 64-bit, and so on)

20. D. The Recovery tab allows an administrator to define the actions that can happen upon a service failure. This tab also provides support for resetting failure counters and how long to wait before taking the action. The Recovery tab allows an administrator to configure the service to attempt a restart or a reboot.

21. A. Deployment Image Servicing and Management (DISM) is a command-line tool that is used to create and manage Windows 10 image (`.wim`) files. You can use DISM image management commands to mount and obtain information regarding Windows image (`.wim`) files or virtual hard disks (VHDs).

22. C. Run sysprep.exe to prepare a Windows installation to be captured. The `sysprep .exe /generalize` command removes system-specific information from the Windows installation so that it can be reused on different computers. The /oobe switch restarts the computer in out-of-box experience (OOBE) mode, and the `/unattend:<answerfile>` switch applies the settings that are in the answer file to Windows during an unattended installation.

23. A. Run sysprep.exe to prepare a Windows installation to be captured. The `sysprep .exe /generalize` command removes system-specific information from the Windows installation so that it can be reused on different computers. There are many options that can be used in conjunction with the sysprep.exe command. To see a complete list, type **sysprep.exe /?** at a command-line prompt.

24. C. To activate the computers in the testing environment, you need to use Key Management Service (KMS). KMS is an activation service that allows organizations to activate systems within their own network, removing the need for individual computers to connect directly to Microsoft for activation. The KMS server will activate the client computers.

25. B. Instruct the user to go to the Control Panel to configure the keyboard and mouse settings. Use the Control Panel to change the settings for Windows. The Control Panel allows a user to change a variety of computer hardware and software features. Some settings that can be modified with the Control Panel include the mouse, display, sound, network, and keyboard.

26. A. Instruct the user to use the Battery Meter on the laptop to view the percentage of battery life available and to confirm that the laptop is set to hibernate. So, to check the status of the battery, select the battery icon in the taskbar. It is located on the bottom-right part of the taskbar, next to the date and time.

27. B. The Narrator app is an accessibility feature included on a Windows 10 computer that will read aloud any text that is on the screen as well as announcing notifications when they appear.

28. D. To perform synchronization of files between the laptop and their network folder, you must first upgrade the laptop to Windows 10 Enterprise. Windows 10 Home Edition does not support synchronization; therefore, you must first upgrade the laptop to a version that supports it.

29. D. Windows System Image Manager (SIM) is used to create unattended answer files using a GUI-based interface that allows you to set up and configure some common options within an answer file. Some advantages of using Windows SIM to create answer files is that you can easily create and edit answer files, which reduces syntax errors. It also simplifies the process of adding user-specific or computer-specific configuration information.

30. C. The Boot Configuration Data (BCD) store contains boot information parameters. To edit the boot options in the BCD store, use the bcdedit utility. This can be launched only from a command prompt. Configuring the bcdedit utility will allow you to configure the boot order.

31. C, D. You cannot distribute offline-licensed apps directly from Microsoft Store to the computers without Internet access. To distribute the app to the machines without Internet, you will need to use Deployment Image Servicing and Management (DISM) to deploy an AppX package and create a provisioning package using Windows Imaging and Configuration Designer (ICD).

32. C. To display basic license and activation information about the current system, run the slmgr.vbs script with the /dli parameter. This command lets you know the edition of Windows currently running, a part of the product key, and if the system is activated. By default, the /dli parameter displays the license information for the installed active Windows edition.

33. A. Users can use the Credential Manager to store credentials, such as usernames and passwords. These usernames and passwords get stored in vaults so that a user can easily log onto computers or websites. There are two sections in the Credential Manager: Web Credentials and Windows Credentials. On Windows 10, Credential Manager is the feature that stores sign-in information for websites (using Microsoft Edge), applications, and networks (such as mapped drivers or shared folders). You can add credentials by clicking the link next to each of the two credential sections. Credential Manager allows you to view, edit, and delete saved credentials. One way to get to the Credential Manager is to go to Control Panel ➤ User Accounts ➤ Credential Manager. Select Web Credentials or Windows Credentials to access the credentials that you want to manage. To edit an existing credential, click the appropriate tab (either Windows Credentials or Web Credentials), select the account, and click the Edit button.

34. A. Utilize the driverquery.exe command to view the installed devices and drivers. Driverquery is command-line tool. Driverquery provides a detailed list of all the device drivers installed on a computer. This enables an administrator to display a list of installed device drivers and their properties. If used without parameters, Driverquery will run on the local machine. The syntax for using Driverquery is as follows: `driverquery.exe [/s <system> [/u [<domain>\]<username> [/p <password>]]] [/fo {table | list | csv}] [/nh] [/v | /si]`.

35. B. Sysprep is a utility that comes on all Windows operating systems. By default, the Sysprep utility can be found on Windows Server and Windows 10 operating systems in the `C:\Windows\system32\sysprep` directory. The `/generalize` switch allows Sysprep to remove all system-specific data from the image. If you are running the GUI version of Sysprep, this is a checkbox option. `/generalize` prepares the Windows installation to be imaged. The security ID (SID) will be reset, any system restore points will be cleared, and event logs will be deleted. The next time that the computer starts, the specialize configuration pass runs, a new SID is created, and the clock for Windows activation resets.

36. B. You should use the Microsoft Application Compatibility Toolkit (ACT) to determine the compatibility of applications that are current with Windows 10. ACT determines which applications are installed, identifies applications that may be affected by Windows updates, and identifies any potential compatibility problems with User Account Control (UAC) and Internet Explorer. Reports can then be exported for more detailed analysis.

37. C. Windows 10 comes with the User State Migration Tool (USMT) utility. It is used by administrators to migrate users from one computer to another using a command-line utility. The USMT consists of two executable files: `scanstate.exe` and `loadstate.exe`. The `scanstate.exe` command collects information from the source computer, and the `loadstate.exe` command applies that information to the destination computer. So, the first step to migrate is to run the `scanstate.exe` command on the Windows 7 computers.

38. B. Cortana is Microsoft's digital assistant whose task is to help you get things done. Cortana is a powerful search and help utility. If your system has a microphone, you can ask Cortana questions, and it will help find an answer for you. If you don't have a microphone, just type in your question, and Cortana will try to help find an answer. To get started with Cortana, select the Cortana icon in the taskbar or type a command in the search bar. You can also activate the "Hey Cortana" mode.

39. A. An administrator can configure a system to hibernate through using Power Options or by choosing Start and then clicking the arrow and selecting Hibernate from the drop-down menu. This option will appear only if hibernation has been enabled. So, an administrator can minimize the power usage by configuring Hibernation mode. Hibernation means that anything stored in memory is written to the hard disk. This ensures that when the computer shuts down, there will be no data loss of the information stored in memory. When the computer is taken out of hibernation, it will return to its previous state by loading the hibernation reserved area of the hard disk back into memory.

40. B, C. An administrator can configure and manage power settings by using a command-line tool called `powercfg.exe`. This tool allows an administrator to control power settings and configure computers to default to either hibernate or standby mode. By default, the `powercfg.exe` tool is installed with Windows 10. `powercfg.exe` uses a few switches that provide functionality. The syntax for using `powercfg` is as follows: powercfg /option [arguments] [/?]. So, for this question, the /X modifies a setting value in the current power scheme. /export exports a power scheme, represented by a specified globally unique identifier (GUID), to a specified file. /import imports a power scheme from the specified file, and /S makes a power scheme active on the system. For a complete list of switches, go to this page:

docs.microsoft.com/en-us/windows-hardware/design/device-experiences/powercfg-command-line-options

So, for this question, you are using powercfg /X on one of the IT computers to modify the power scheme. After configuring the desired settings, the power scheme settings will be exported to a file by using powercfg /export. Then the administrator will import the power scheme from the file on each of the remaining computers using powercfg /import. Once imported, the powercfg /S command is run to activate the power scheme.

41. B. The Microsoft Store allows an administrator to download and purchase applications. The Microsoft Store contains thousands of Windows 10 business and personal applications. One advantage for corporations is that they can create their own applications and load them into the Microsoft Store for users to download (called *sideloading*). Sideloading, in Windows 10, is the process of installing applications on a computer that hasn't gone through the certification process to appear in the Store and to run on a Windows device. As of Windows Insider Build 18956, sideloading is enabled by default. Now you can deploy a signed package onto a device without a special configuration. In Windows 10, an administrator can unlock a device for sideloading by using an enterprise policy or by using Settings. So, for this question, you will use Settings to turn on sideloading for unmanaged devices. Follow these steps:

1. Open Settings.

2. Click Update & Security ➤ For Developers.

3. On Use Developer Features, select Sideload Apps.

42. C. The /oobe option restarts the computer into Windows Welcome mode. Windows Welcome enables end users to customize their Windows operating system, create user accounts, name their computer, and perform other tasks. OOBE allows users to enter their account information, a select language, accept the Microsoft Terms of Service, and set up networking.

43. B. A private network is for trusted networks, such as a home or work network. When a network is set to private, the computer is discoverable to other devices on the network, and the computer can be used for file and printer sharing. A public network is used for networks that you can connect to when you're out and about, such as a Wi-Fi network at a coffee shop. The computer will be hidden from other devices on the network and cannot be used for file and printer sharing. One way to check to see whether a machine is on a private or public network is by going into Settings ➤ Network And Internet ➤ (and in this case, since we are using Wi-Fi) ➤ Wi-Fi.

44. A. An administrator can configure and manage power settings by using a command-line tool called powercfg.exe. This tool allows an administrator to control power settings and configure computers to default to either hibernate or standby mode. By default, the

powercfg.exe tool is installed with Windows 10. You can generate a battery report by running the powercfg /batteryreport command. The report will be saved under C:\Windows\System32 as battery-report. The report will provide details about the battery including the name, manufacturer, serial number, chemistry, and cycle count. You can also view a usage report over a period of time.

45. C. To configure KMS in Windows 10, follow these steps:

1. Open an elevated command prompt.

2. Enter one of the following commands:

- To install a KMS key, enter **slmgr.vbs /ipk <KmsKey>**.

- To activate online, enter **slmgr.vbs /ato**.

- To activate by using the telephone, enter **slui.exe 4**.

The /ato command causes the operating system to attempt activation by using whichever key has been installed in the operating system. The syntax is as follows: slmgr.vbs [<computername> [<user> <password>]] [<options>].

46. A, D. Microsoft offers both a 32-bit version and a 64-bit version of Windows 10. Windows 7 can be upgraded to both Windows 10 Enterprise and Windows 10 Professional. This question states that you are looking at performing an in-place upgrade, so you can only upgrade to the same bit architecture. So, since you are currently using 32-bit, you can only upgrade to the 32-bit version of either Windows 10 Enterprise or Windows 10 Professional.

47. C. You can verify KMS volume activation from the KMS host server or from the client computer. On a client computer or the KMS host, open an elevated Command Prompt window, type **slmgr.vbs <computername> /dlv**, and then press the Enter key. The /dlv command displays the detailed licensing information. The slmgr.vbs syntax is as follows: slmgr.vbs [<computername>] [<options>].

48. D. A driver is a piece of software that tells a component how to run on a certain operating system. The drivers need to be signed since they obtain access to the kernel. By default, if a driver is not signed by Microsoft, then it is not allowed to be installed on your computer. Usually, when you are installing an unsigned driver, you will receive a pop-up window informing you that Windows cannot verify the publisher of the driver software. However, you can still install an unsigned driver. There are multiple ways to do this, but one way is to use the Advanced Boot Menu. This temporarily allows you to disable driver signature enforcement. To use the Advanced Boot Menu to load an unsigned driver, follow these steps:

1. Click the Start button, choose the Power button, press Shift, and click Restart.

2. After Windows enters the Windows Recovery Environment (WinRE), go to Troubleshoot ➤ Advanced Options ➤ Startup Settings ➤ Restart.

3. To install a driver without a digital signature, press F7 to choose the Disable Driver Signature Enforcement option.

4. The system will boot to Windows, and then you can install any driver that is not signed. After installation, you can restart Windows to let the option get enabled automatically.

49. C. Cortana's Notebook is a central location where Cortana keeps items that she has learned from the user, such as their interests and favorite places. You can access Cortana's Notebook as follows:

1. Open Cortana.

2. Click the menu button (a set of three of horizontal lines in the top-left corner).

3. Click the Notebook button.

The Cortana News features allow you to fine-tune the type of news that Cortana offers when a user clicks inside the Search window on the taskbar.

50. B. With Miracast, Windows 10 allows you to project a Windows 10 laptop or mobile device to a projector or television. Miracast allows you to connect to an external device through the use of your mobile Wireless Display (WiDi) adapter.

51. C. With the release of Windows 10, Microsoft brought back the Start Menu. This was the menu that users were used to with Windows 7. Many people missed this feature, so Microsoft brought it back. The Windows 10 Start Menu combines the best of both Windows 7 and Windows 8. The Start Menu gives you a menu that we were familiar with in Windows 7, as well as the Live Tiles that users liked in Windows 8. However, Microsoft is in the process of unveiling a new Start Menu. It appears that with the new Windows 10 Start menu, Live Tiles will be replaced with static icons that use Microsoft's new Fluent Design style.

52. A, C. Microsoft Mobility Center (`mblctr.exe`) is an application that comes bundled with certain versions of Windows 10. It is present by default on mobile devices such as laptops and tablets. It allows changing brightness, volume, power plans, screen orientation, display projection, Sync Center settings, and presentation settings of devices. The Microsoft Mobility Center is available on Windows 10 Professional and Windows 10 Enterprise.

53. A. Microsoft offers both a 32-bit version and a 64-bit version of Windows 10. To install Windows 10 successfully, the system must meet or exceed certain minimum hardware requirements:

- CPU (processor): 1 GHz or faster processor or system-on-a-chip (SoC)
- Memory (RAM): 1 GB for 32-bit or 2 GB for 64-bit
- Hard disk: 16 GB for 32-bit OS or 20 GB for 64-bit OS
- Video adapter: DirectX 9 or later with WDDM 1.0 driver
- Optional drive: DVD-R/W drive
- Network device: Compatible network interface card

In this question, since we only have an 18 GB hard drive, this does not meet the requirement to install the 64-bit versions. Hence, given the options, we can only install the 32-bit version of Windows 10 Enterprise.

54. B. The Compatibility Administrator tool helps to resolve potential application compatibility issues before deploying a new version of Windows. The Compatibility Administrator tool provides the following:

- Compatibility fixes, compatibility modes, and AppHelp messages that can be used to resolve specific compatibility issues

- Tools for creating customized compatibility fixes, compatibility modes, AppHelp messages, and compatibility databases

- A query tool that can be used to search for installed compatibility fixes on local computers

55. A. An upgrade to Windows 10 can be performed only if the following conditions are true:

- The machine is running Windows 7 or Windows 8.

- You want to keep the existing applications and preferences.

- You want to preserve any local users and groups that have been created.

In this question, the existing machine is currently running Windows 2000. Since you cannot upgrade from this version of Windows, you must perform a clean installation.

56. A, C, D. The three phases of performing a clean install of Windows 10 are as follows:

- *Collecting Information*: During this phase, Windows 10 gathers the necessary information to complete the installation. Windows 10 gathers the local time, location, keyboard, license agreement, installation type, and installation disk partition information.

- *Installing Windows*: This phase is where the Windows 10 files are copied to the hard disk and the installation is completed.

- *Setting Up Windows*: In this phase, the username, the computer name, and the password are set up; the product key is entered; the security settings are configured; and the date and time are reviewed. Once this is finished, the installation is done.

57. B. When Windows 10 is installed, the Setup program generates several different log files. An administrator can review these logs to check for any installation issues. Two log files that are useful when troubleshooting installation issues are as follows:

- The action log is stored as `C:\Windows\setupact.log`. This log includes all of the actions that were executed during the setup process and a description of each action. These actions are listed in chronological order.

- The error log is stored as `C:\Windows\setuperr.log`. This log includes any errors that occurred during the installation. Each error gives a description and an indication of the severity of the error.

58. A, B, C, D. If an administrator needs to install Windows 10 on multiple computers, they can install the operating system on each computer manually. However, it would make the task much easier if the administrator chose a tool that would automate the installation. Windows 10 comes with several utilities that can be used for deploying and automating the Windows 10 installation. Some of these automation tools include the following:

- Microsoft Deployment Toolkit (MDT)

- System Preparation Tool (Sysprep), which is used to create images or clones

- Unattended installation, or unattended setup, which uses `setup.exe`

- Windows Assessment and Deployment Kit (ADK) for Windows 10

- Windows Automated Installation Kit (AIK)

- Windows Deployment Services (WDS) server

59. C. An administrator can use `bcdedit` to change the default boot entry. You can change the default boot entry to ensure that the operating system configuration that you prefer is loaded automatically. Using the `/timeout` parameter, specifies the amount of time used before the system boots to the default operating system. If you'd like to see all of the different `bcdedit` commands, just enter **`bcdedit /?`** at the command prompt.

60. C. Unattended installations allow an administrator to create customized installations that are environment specific. Custom installations can support custom hardware and software installations. Unattended installations utilize an answer file called `autounattend.xml` to provide configuration information during the installation process. The answer file allows questions to be answered without user interaction.

61. D. The steps for preparing the WDS server are as follows:

1. Make sure that the server meets the requirements for running WDS.

2. Install WDS.

3. Configure and start WDS.

4. Configure the WDS server to respond to client computers (if this was not configured when WDS was installed).

For WDS to work, the server on which you will install WDS must meet the requirements for WDS and be able to access the required network services.

62. A, B, C, D. There are many advantages to using unattended installations for automating Windows 10.

- It saves time and money since users do not have to respond to each installation query.

- It can be configured to provide automated query responses while selectively allowing users to provide specified input during installations.

- It can be used to install clean copies of Windows 10 or upgrade an existing operating system to Windows 10 (if allowed).

- It can be expanded to include installation instructions for applications, language support, service packs, and device drivers.

- The physical media for Windows 10 does not need to be distributed to all computers on which it will be installed.

Option E states that "the physical media must be distributed." The actual advantage is that it *does not need* to be distributed to all computers.

63. C. The Windows Deployment Services (WDS) server must meet several requirements. One is that at least one partition on the server must be formatted as New Technology File System (NTFS). The network environment must be configured with a Dynamic Host Configuration Protocol (DHCP) server, a Domain Name System (DNS) server, NTFS volumes, and Active Directory to connect to the WDS server. No other client software is required to connect to the WDS server.

64. B. The System Preparation Tool, or Sysprep (`sysprep.exe`), is used to prepare a computer for disk imaging. Sysprep is a free utility that comes on all Windows operating systems. By default, the Sysprep utility can be found on Windows Server and Windows 10 operating systems in the `C:\Windows\system32\sysprep` directory. The `/reboot` option stops and restarts the computer system.

65. D. The System Preparation Tool, or Sysprep (`sysprep.exe`), is used to prepare a computer for disk imaging. Sysprep is a free utility that comes on all Windows operating systems. By default, the Sysprep utility can be found on Windows Server and Windows 10 operating systems in the `C:\Windows\System32\Sysprep` directory.

66. B. One component to which you need to pay attention when using the Windows Deployment Services is the Preboot Execution Environment (PXE) network devices. PXE boot devices are network interface cards (NICs) that can talk to a network without the need for an operating system. As far as creating an image, there is no such tool called `imgcrt.exe`. Microsoft recommends that you use DISM for image creation and management.

67. C. Deployment Image Servicing and Management (DISM) is a command-line utility that allows you to manipulate a Windows image. When DISM was first released, it was used mainly for maintaining and managing Windows images. However, now DISM has become even more powerful, including capturing images and deploying images. The `/Get-ImageInfo` parameter displays information about the images that are contained in .wim, .ffu, .vhd, or .vhdx files.

68. C. You can restart the Windows activation clock using images. The Windows activation clock starts to decrease as soon as Windows starts for the first time. You can restart the Windows activation clock only three times using Sysprep.

69. B, C, D, E, F. The Windows 10 desktop is the interface that appears when a user logs into the operating system. The default Windows 10 desktop includes the wallpaper, Start Menu, tiles, icons, and the Recycle Bin. The Windows 10 Start Menu, located at the bottom left of the desktop by default, includes the default All Apps section. Users can configure their desktop to meet their needs and to work more proficiently.

70. A. The Windows Ease of Access tools are tools that are installed on a Windows 10 machine to help individuals who have difficulty seeing the screen. The Ease of Access tools can be accessed from Start ➤ All Apps ➤ Ease of Access and include a magnifier, a narrator, an on-screen keyboard, and Windows Speech Recognition. Ease of Access options can help make it easier to do the following:

- Use a computer without a display by using Narrator. Narrator allows you to hear audio descriptions for the items that are on the screen, such as text and buttons.

- See what's on the screen by making the content on the screen bigger by using the Magnifier or by using the high-contrast mode.

- Use the keyboard by turning on Sticky Keys, Toggle Keys, or Filter Keys, or by using the On-Screen Keyboard.

- Use the mouse by changing the pointer size or by turning on Mouse Keys that allow a user to use the keypad to move the mouse.

71. A. The Background setting allows a user to pick their desktop background. The background wallpaper can be either a picture or an HTML document. Setting up a desktop background can be as simple as picking a solid color and placing a favorite picture on top of it. To configure the Windows desktop and how it looks, right-click the desktop and select Personalize. When you choose to personalize the desktop, there are several different settings that can be configured. These include Background, Colors, Lock Screen, Themes, Fonts, Start, and Taskbar.

72. B. By default, Windows 10's Lock screen times out and switches off your monitor after one minute. The Lock screen allows you to select a screensaver that will start after the system has been idle for a specified amount of time. When the idle time has been reached and the screensaver is activated, the system will be locked, and you must enter the password of the user who is currently logged in to unlock the computer. To configure the Windows desktop and how it looks, right-click the desktop and select Personalize. When you choose to personalize the desktop, there are several different settings that can be configured. These include Background, Colors, Lock Screen, Themes, Fonts, Start, and Taskbar.

73. B. The `New-Service` cmdlet creates a new entry for a Windows service in the registry and in the service database. `New-Service` allows an administrator to create a new service. The cmdlet syntax is as follows:

```
New-Service
[-Name] <String>
[-BinaryPathName] <String>
[-DisplayName <String>]
[-Description <String>]
[-StartupType <ServiceStartMode>]
[-Credential <PSCredential>]
[-DependsOn <String[]>]
[-WhatIf]
```

```
[-Confirm]
[<CommonParameters>]
```

74. B. Offline Files allows network files to be available to users when a network connection to the server is unavailable or slow. The Offline Files feature is enabled by default on Windows 10. This feature is turned off by default on Windows Server operating systems. The best method is to use the Sync Center in Control Panel. To access the Sync Center, click Start ➤ Windows System ➤ Control Panel ➤ Sync Center. The first set to configure offline files is by clicking on the Manage Offline Files link.

75. B. Microsoft Edge gives users a new way to find pages and read and write on the web plus get help from Cortana. Microsoft Edge is the default browser for all Windows 10 devices. It is built to be compatible with the modern web. Edge brings Microsoft's digital assistant, Cortana, to the desktop. Using Cortana with Edge allows you to pull up pictures, explanations, and search results easily on any word or link while browsing just by right-clicking and selecting Ask Cortana.

76. C. You can sign onto a computer by using a picture password. You can select a picture and three gestures that will be used to create a customized password. Once you have chosen a picture, you will draw with the mouse, with the touchpad, or on a touchscreen to create a combination of circles, straight lines, and taps. The size, position, and direction of the drawn gestures become part of the picture password. To access a picture password, go to Sign-in Options by selecting Start ➤ Settings ➤ Accounts ➤ Sign-in Options. On the Sign-in Options page, the following sign-in methods are available:

- Windows Hello Face
- Windows Hello Fingerprint
- Windows Hello PIN
- Security key
- Password
- Picture Password

Click Picture Password, click Add, and follow the prompts.

77. D. Windows System Image Manager (SIM) is the tool that is used to create unattended Windows Setup answer files. It is a GUI that is used to create and manage answer files. Answer files are .xml files that are used in Windows Setup, Sysprep, Deployment Image Servicing and Management (DISM), and other deployment tools to configure and customize the default Windows installation. For this question, you will need to configure formatting and partitioning information in the Windows PE component of the answer file. The Windows PE sets specific configuration settings as well as several Windows Setup settings, such as partitioning and formatting the hard disk, selecting an image, and applying a product key.

78. D. An administrator can add an input language, set a display language, or install a language pack in Settings ➤ Time & Language. This allows you to change the language being used on Windows 10, applications, and websites. Adding an input language lets you set a language-preference order for websites and apps, as well as change the keyboard language. To change the system language on Windows 10, close any running app, and then follow these steps:

1. Open Settings ➤ Time & Language ➤ Language.
2. In the Preferred Languages section, click the Add A Preferred Language button.
3. Search for the language you want.
4. Select the language package from the result, and click the Next button.
5. Check the Set As My Display Language option.
6. Check the Install Language Pack option.
7. Check or clear the additional language features, as needed.
8. Click the Install button, then click Yes, and then click the Sign Out Now button.
9. Sign back into the Windows 10 account.

After these steps are completed, the language will change across the entire Windows 10 experience. The new changes will appear in the sign-in screen, the Settings app, File Explorer, the desktop, applications, your browser, and any websites you visit.

79. C. Windows Deployment Services (WDS) is a suite of components that allows an administrator to remotely install Windows 10 on client computers. You can configure WDS on a computer by using the Windows Deployment Services Configuration Wizard or by using the `wdsutil` command-line utility. The `/initialize-server` switch initializes the configuration of the WDS server.

80. D. Windows Deployment Services (WDS) is a suite of components that allows an administrator to remotely install Windows 10 on client computers. The answer for this question is option D—this is not a true statement. To be true, the statement should say: "The physical media does *not* need to be distributed to all computers that will be installed." Here is a list of some other advantages of using WDS:

- It can create reference images using the Image Capture Wizard.
- It can deploy multiple images for mixed environments.
- It can install a driver package to the server and configure the drivers to be deployed to client computers at the same time that the image is installed.
- It can remotely install Windows operating systems through the network, thus reducing the difficulty and associated costs.
- It can standardize the installations throughout a group or organization.
- It can use Windows setups including Windows Preinstallation Environment (Windows PE), .wim files, and image-based setups.
- End-user installation deployment can be controlled through the Group Policy utility.

- The physical media does *not* need to be distributed to all computers that will be installed.

- It uses multicasting to allow for the transmitting and image data to communicate with each other.

81. A. Once you have installed the Windows 10 operating system, the next thing that you will want to do is to load all updates and patches. These can be downloaded from Microsoft's website by using Windows Update. Windows Update is a utility that connects to the Microsoft website or to a local update server, called a Windows Server Update Services (WSUS) server, to ensure that the Windows 10 operating system (along with other Microsoft products) has the most up-to-date versions.

82. C. Windows Update allows you to check for new updates and to change settings. To configure Windows Update, do the following:

1. Select Start ➤ Settings ➤ Update And Security.

2. Configure the options that you want to use for Windows Update by clicking the Advanced Options link. You can access the following options from Windows Update:

- Give me updates for other Microsoft products

- Choose when updates are installed

- Pause updates

- Delivery Optimization

- Privacy settings

83. C. Once the reference computer is set up and installed, you can use the System Preparation Tool (Sysprep) to prepare the computer to be used with disk imaging. Image Capture Wizard is a utility that can be used to create a disk image after it is prepared using Sysprep. The image can then be transported to the destination computer(s).

84. C. Security updates are those that need to be installed to fix a security issue or concern. These security issues may be used by an attacker to break into either a device or software. An update is sometimes referred to as a *patch*, which is a set of modifications to a computer program or its supporting data intended to update, fix, or improve the component. This includes fixing security vulnerabilities and/or other bugs.

85. D. Windows System Image Manager (SIM) is used to create unattended answer files using a GUI-based interface that allows you to set up and configure some common options within an answer file. Some advantages of using Windows SIM to create answer files is that you can easily create and edit answer files, which reduces syntax errors. It also simplifies the process of adding user-specific or computer-specific configuration information. Answer files are used to automate the installation so that no user interaction is needed.

86. C. A service pack is a collection all current hotfixes and updates. Usually, service packs also contain additional fixes for known issues that are found since the release of the product. Service packs can also contain design changes or features that were requested by customers.

87. A. Windows 10 regularly checks for new updates automatically. However, if you want to check for new updates, then simply click the Check For Updates button on the Windows Update page to force Windows 10 to check for updates instantly. To check for updates, go to Settings ➢ Update And Security ➢ Windows Update and click the Check For Updates button. When you click this button, Windows Update will retrieve a list of all the available updates. You can then click View Available Updates to see what updates are available. Updates are marked as Important, Recommended, or Optional.

88. A. Windows To Go is a feature for users of Windows 10 Enterprise and Windows 10 Education that enables users to boot a full version of Windows from an external USB drive. It gives an administrator or user the ability to provision Windows 10 onto an external USB drive. Then use the Windows To Go workspace on the USB drive to load a complete and managed Windows 10 system image onto a managed or unmanaged Windows 10 host computer to boot and run the Windows 10 operating system. In this case, the error message received indicates that the bootable media was not created properly, and you will need to reapply the Windows To Go image onto the USB memory drive.

89. B. Microsoft normally releases its product updates on Tuesdays. Thus, this day was given the nickname Patch Tuesdays. However, before an update gets released to the public, it has already been tested. Only after Microsoft tests the updates are they released to the public. With Windows 10, Microsoft has introduced new methods of service updates. Microsoft's new servicing options are referred to as Semi-Annual Channel, Long-Term Servicing Channel (LTSC), and Windows Insider.

90. A. The Registry is a database used by the operating system to store configuration information. You can edit the Registry in Windows 10 by using `regedit` or `regedt32`. Always use caution when editing the Registry because any misconfigurations may cause the computer to fail to boot. You can just use the Control Panel if you don't want to open the Registry directly but you still want to perform some Registry changes. The Control Panel is a set of GUI utilities that allow you to configure Registry settings without the need to use a Registry Editor. The Control Panel consists of many tools. Some of these tools include the following (this is not a complete list):

- Administrative Tools
- BitLocker Drive Encryption
- Color Management
- Credential Manager
- Date and Time
- Default Programs
- Device Manager
- Devices and Printers
- Ease of Access Center
- File Explorer Options
- File History
- Fonts

- Indexing Options
- Internet Options
- Network and Sharing Center
- Power Options
- Programs and Features

91. B, C. There are several log files created during each phase of the upgrade. These log files are important when you need to troubleshoot upgrade issues. By default, the folders that contain the log files are hidden on the upgrade target computer. To view the log files, configure Windows File Explorer to view hidden items. The most useful log is `setupact.log`. The `setupact.log` file contains information about setup actions made, and the `setuperr.log` file contains information about setup errors during the installation.

92. D. Windows 10 system requirements are as follows:

- Processor: 1 gigahertz (GHz) or faster processor
- RAM: 1 gigabyte (GB) for 32-bit or 2 GB for 64-bit
- Hard disk space: 16 GB for 32-bit OS or 20 GB for 64-bit OS
- Graphics card: DirectX 9 or later with WDDM 1.0 driver
- Display: 800 x 600

This question asks the minimum memory for a 32-bit installation, which is one gigabyte (GB). Since the answer options are in megabytes, the answer is 1 gigabyte, which is the same as 1,024 megabytes.

93. A. The Windows Compatible Products List is a list of certified devices and systems that have been verified to work with Windows 10. When selecting hardware, you should always check the Windows Compatible Products List for compatibility.

94. A. If you are moving from Windows Vista, Windows XP, or earlier editions of Windows to Windows 10, then you must perform a clean install. If any of the following conditions exist, then you must perform a clean install:

- There currently is no operating system installed on the machine.
- You currently have an operating system installed that does not support an in-place upgrade to Windows 10. These earlier versions include DOS, Windows 9x, Windows NT, Windows ME, Windows 2000 Pro, Windows Vista, and Windows XP.
- You want to install from scratch without keeping any of the existing preferences.
- You want to be able to dual boot between Windows 10 and a previous operating system.

95. B. When performing a clean install to the same partition as an existing version of Windows, then the contents of the existing Users (or Documents And Settings), Program Files, and Windows directories will be placed in a directory called `C:\Windows.old`. This old operating system will no longer be available.

16. D. You will want to grant the new assistant the user right Restore Files And Directories. The Restore Files And Directories user right allows the new admin assistant to restore files and directories regardless of file and directory permissions. This setting allows users to bypass permissions when restoring files.

17. A. You will want to configure an Account Lockout Policy. This policy is used to specify options that will prevent a user from attempting multiple failed logon attempts. If the Account Lockout Threshold value is surpassed, the account will be locked. The account can be reset based on a specified amount of time or through administrator involvement. An Account Lockout Policy is a useful method of slowing down online password-guessing attacks.

18. C. Windows 10 has a feature called BitLocker Drive Encryption (BitLocker). It encrypts the drive so that if it's ever removed or stolen, the data cannot be accessed. To configure BitLocker, you must either use a Local Group Policy or use the BitLocker icon in Control Panel. BitLocker encrypts the entire system drive. New files added to this drive are encrypted automatically, and files moved from this drive to another drive or computers are decrypted automatically.

19. D. 64-bit versions of Windows 10 include a driver signature enforcement feature, meaning that they'll only load drivers that have been signed by Microsoft. `bcdedit.exe` is a command-line tool for managing Boot Configuration Data (BCD). These files provide a store that is used to describe boot applications and boot application settings. Given the choices, the `bcdedit.exe` utility will perform the task of installing the unsigned driver. This can also be performed by using the Advanced Boot Options.

20. A. Password policies ensure that security requirements are enforced on a computer. Password policies are set on a per-computer basis so that they cannot be configured for specific users. The Enforce Password History policy allows the system to keep track of an employee's password history for up to 24 passwords. This prevents them from reusing the same passwords.

21. A. A connection security rule forces two computers to authenticate before they can establish a connection and to secure the information that is transmitted between them. Windows Firewall with Advanced Security uses IPsec to enforce these rules. Connection security rules are used to configure how and when authentication occurs. These rules do not specifically allow connections; that's the role of the inbound and outbound rules. You can configure the following connection security rules:

- *Authentication Exemption*: Specifies which computers are exempt from authentication requirements
- *Custom*: Customized rules
- *Isolation*: Restricts a connection based on the authentication criteria
- *Server-to-Server*: Authenticates connections between computers
- *Tunnel*: Authenticates connections between gateway computers

22. C. On Windows 10 computers and devices, the Microsoft Store app offers various apps, games, music, movies and TV, and books that a user can browse through. These can be either purchased or obtained for free to download and install to the user's Microsoft account. To disable users from being able to access the Microsoft Store app, follow these steps:

1. Launch Group Policy Management Console (GPMC).

2. Navigate to Computer Configuration ➤ Administrative Templates ➤ Windows Components ➤ Store.

3. Locate the Disable All Apps From The Windows Store policy and double-click to open it. Select the radio button next to Enabled and then click the OK button to enable the policy. This will disable any application installed from the Microsoft Store and will not allow them to run.

23. D. One way to help secure Windows 10 is by using smart cards. Smart cards are plastic cards (about the size of a credit card) that can be used in combination with other methods of authentication. The process of using a smart card along with another authentication method is known as *two-factor authentication* or *multifactor authentication*. Authentication is the method of using user credentials to log on to either the local Windows 10 machine or the domain.

24. A. Windows Event Forwarding (WEF) reads any operational or administrative event log on a device in your network and forwards the chosen events to a Windows Event Collector (WEC) server. You should add the account of the computer to the Event Log Readers group, which has access to read the event log on the local computer. There are no default members of the Event Log Readers local group.

25. A. Every time a user logs onto a Windows 10 computer, the system checks to see whether they have a local user profile in the Users folder. The first time a user logs on, they receive a default user profile. A folder that matches the user's logon name is created for the user in the Users folder. The user profile folder that is created holds a file called NTuser.dat as well as subfolders that contain directory links to the user's desktop items. A mandatory profile is stored in a file named NTuser.man. To create a mandatory profile, just change the user's profile extension from .dat to .man. In this question, you are changing from a mandatory profile, so you need to change the extension back to .dat.

26. A, E. Power Options allow a user to maximize their Windows 10 machine's performance and to conserve energy. A Power Management policy setting may be configured independently for when the computer is plugged in or running on battery power. The Group Policy settings for Power Management can be found at Computer Management/ Policies/Administrative Templates/System/Power Management/Sleep Settings. The sleep settings are used to specify sleep and hibernation timeouts and behaviors. Once the GPO for Power Management has been created, you need to link it to the OU that contains the laptop computers.

27. C. BitLocker encrypts the entire system drive. New files added to this drive are automatically encrypted, and files moved from this drive to another drive or computers are decrypted automatically. However, BitLocker To Go allows you to put BitLocker on removable media such as external hard disks or USB drives. A user can save a copy of the BitLocker recovery key to a file, save it to a USB flash drive, or print a hard copy. The BitLocker recovery password is important. Do not lose it or you may not be able to unlock the drive.

28. B. The gpresult command displays the resulting set of policies that are applied on the computer and the specified user during the logon process. Windows 10 includes the Group Policy Result Tool, also known as the Resultant Set of Policy (RSoP) to determine what policies are actually be applied. This tool can be accessed using the gpresult command-line utility.

29. A. In this question, it states that you want to create and modify the shares remotely on the computers. In that case, because shares are being created remotely, the group to which you would add the user would be the Administrators group. The Power Users group can manage shares locally, but to connect to perform these tasks remotely, you need to be an administrator.

30. A. Windows Defender Firewall helps prevent unauthorized users from accessing Windows 10 machines from the Internet or the local network. Windows Defender Firewall does not allow unsolicited traffic, which is traffic that was not sent in response to a request, to pass through the firewall. By default, if you have a firewall enabled in Windows, ping requests are blocked. The ping command works by sending special packets known as Internet Control Message Protocol (ICMP) Echo Requests to a target device and then waiting for that device to send back an ICMP Echo Reply packet. Typically, you will want to create a rule for IPv4 addressing and another for IPv6. However, the options given in this question do not provide for IPv4. To configure the Windows firewall to allow pings, follow these steps:

1. Search for Windows Defender Firewall and click to open it.

2. Click Advanced Settings on the left.

3. From the left pane of the resulting window, click Inbound Rules.

4. In the right pane, find the rules titled File And Printer Sharing (Echo Request – ICMPv6-In).

5. Right-click each rule and choose Enable Rule.

6. Follow the same steps to create a rule for File And Printer Sharing (Echo Request – ICMPv4-In).

31. A. The New-LocalUser cmdlet creates a local user account. This cmdlet creates a local user account or a local user account that is connected to a Microsoft account. The –Name parameter specifies the username for the user account. The –NoPassword parameter indicates that the user account does not have a password. The Add-LocalGroupMember cmdlet adds users or groups to a local security group. All of the rights and permissions that are assigned to a group are assigned to all members of that group. The –Member parameter specifies an array of users or groups that this cmdlet adds to a security group.

32. B. There are two ways in which programs can be restricted in Windows 10. The first is through the Group Policy, and the second is through the Registry. Applications can be kept from running through a Group Policy. To remove these restrictions, follow these steps:

1. Open Local Group Policy Editor by clicking Start and typing **gpedit.msc**.

2. Expand User Configuration ➤ Administrative Templates ➤ System.

3. On the right side, locate a setting called Don't Run Specified Windows Applications. Double-click that setting and change it to Not Configured.

33. B. NTFS permissions control access to NTFS files and folders. Depending on group memberships, NTFS permissions are cumulative. The user obtains the highest level of security from all of the different groups to which they belong. The Modify permission allows the following rights:

- Create new files and write data to the files.

- Create new folders and append data to the files.

- Change a file's or folder's attributes.

- Delete files.

- List the contents of a folder and read the data in a folder's files.

- See a file's or folder's attributes.

- Navigate folders and execute files in the folders.

If the Modify permission is selected, the Read & Execute, List Folder Contents, Read, and Write permissions will be checked by default and can't be unchecked.

34. D. To use Remote Desktop Services to log on to a remote device successfully, the user or group must be a member of the Remote Desktop Users or Administrators group and be granted the Allow Log On Through Remote Desktop Services right. The Allow Log On Through Remote Desktop Services user right determines which users or groups can access the logon screen of a remote device through a Remote Desktop Services connection.

35. D. The Suspend-BitLocker cmdlet suspends BitLocker encryption, which allows users to access encrypted data on a volume that uses BitLocker Drive Encryption. This cmdlet makes the encryption key available in the clear. While suspended, BitLocker does not validate system integrity at startup. For firmware upgrades or system updates, you can suspend BitLocker protection. You can also specify the number of times that a computer restarts before the BitLocker suspension ends by using the RebootCount parameter. If the RebootCount parameter is not specified, the cmdlet uses a value of 1, and then BitLocker protection resumes after the next restart.

36. B. Folder Redirection enables users and administrators to redirect the path of a known folder to a new location, manually or by using Group Policy. Folder Redirection has to be configured using a server-based Group Policy object (GPO) and not a Local Group Policy object (LGPO). The new location can be a folder on the local computer or a directory on a file share.

37. D. Filename extensions for known files are hidden by default. To see the file extensions, you must uncheck the box Hide Extensions For Known File Types. The Windows 10 Folder Options dialog box allows for the configuration of properties associated with files and folders, such as what you see when you access folders and how Windows searches through files and folders. One way to open the Folder Options dialog box is to right-click Start ➤ File Explorer and then select View and then Options. The Folder Options dialog box has three tabs: General, View, and Search. The View tab is used to configure what users see when they open files and folders. Disabling Hide Extensions For Known File Types will allow all filename extensions to be displayed.

38. B. You should implement Windows Defender Firewall, which helps prevent unauthorized users or hackers from accessing your Windows 10 machines from the Internet or the local network. Windows Defender Firewall is included with Windows 10. Windows Defender Firewall does not allow uninvited traffic, which is traffic that was not sent in response to a request, to pass through the firewall.

39. B, D. Password policies ensure that security requirements are enforced on computers. It is important to know that password policies are set on a per-computer basis; they cannot be configured for specific users. Passwords that meet the Password Must Meet Complexity Requirements Passwords policy must be six characters or longer and cannot contain the user's account name or any part of the user's full name. Also, passwords must contain three of the following four character types:

- English uppercase characters (A through Z)

- English lowercase characters (a through z)

- Decimal digits (0 through 9)

- Symbols (such as !, @, #, $, and %)

In this case, the password 1587365Ab meets the complexity requirements because it is at least six characters long and contains an uppercase letter, a lowercase letter, and numbers. The password ABCde! also meets the complexity requirements because it is at least six characters long and contains an uppercase letter, lowercase letters, and a symbol. The other two password options do not meet complexity requirements as they contain characters that are not allowed.

40. C. The easiest way to handle this transition is simply to rename the old employee's account to the new hire's name. It is important to remember that rights and permissions are associated with a user's security identifier (SID) number and not a username. When you rename the old employee's account to the new hire's account, the new hire will automatically obtain all of the rights and permissions to any resource that the old employee had. Because every user account obtains a unique SID number, it is a good practice to disable an account rather than delete accounts for users who leave the company or have an extended absence.

41. C. You can apply audit policies to individual files and folders on a computer by setting the permission type to record successful access attempts or failed access attempts to the security log. Right-click the file or folder to be audited, click Properties, and then click the Security tab, click Advanced, and then select the Auditing tab. The Audit Object Access policy handles auditing access to all objects outside AD. If this policy is defined, you can specify whether to audit successes, audit failures, or not audit the event type at all.

42. B, C, D. BitLocker Drive Encryption (BitLocker) is a data protection feature available in the following Windows 10 editions: Education, Enterprise, and Professional. Only the operating system drive (usually C:) or internal hard drives can be encrypted with BitLocker. Files on other types of drives must be encrypted using BitLocker To Go. BitLocker To Go allows you to put BitLocker on removable media such as external hard disks or USB drives.

43. A. Windows Update is a utility that connects to the Microsoft website or to a local update server called a Windows Server Update Services (WSUS) server to ensure that the Windows 10 operating system (along with other Microsoft products) has the most current version of Microsoft operating system files or software. To allow this home user to change Windows Update manually, it must be configured in a Local Group Policy object (LGPO).

44. C. You should utilize the Microsoft BitLocker Administration and Monitoring (MBAM). It provides a simplified administrative interface that can be used to manage BitLocker Drive Encryption. It allows an administrator to use enterprise-based tools for managing and maintaining BitLocker and BitLocker To Go.

45. A, C. File History allows users to save copies of their files so that they can get them back in the event of a file being damaged or lost. A user can restore personal files, select drives, exclude folders, and even set advanced settings on the File History settings. File History takes regular backups of the data and saves them to a separate disk volume or external drive. By default, when File History is enabled, it backs up all of the system libraries and custom libraries. File History only backs up copies of files that are in the Documents, Music, Pictures, Videos, and Desktop folders and the OneDrive files available offline on your computer. If you have files or folders in another location on your computer that you'd like to be backed up, move them into one of the existing libraries or create a new library. If the originals are lost, corrupted, or deleted, you can restore all of them.

46. D. When a custom console is created for the Microsoft Management Console (MMC), the .msc filename extension is applied by default. The MSC file extension is a snap-in control file associated with MMC. Files attached with this extension are also known as Microsoft Saved Console Files. MMC allows users to customize the console or modules to hold snap-ins. They are used to configure and monitor Windows computer systems.

47. A, D. To create a group, you must be logged on as a member of the Administrators group. The Administrators group has full permissions to manage users and groups. Guidelines for creating groups include the following:

- The group name must be unique to the computer and different from all other group names and usernames that exist on that computer.

- The group name should be descriptive.

- Group names can be up to 256 characters. It is best to use alphanumeric characters for ease of administration. The backslash (\) character is not allowed. However, spaces can be included.

48. A. The Print Management MMC snap-in is available in the Administrative Tools folder. Administrators can use the Print Management tools to install, manage, and import/export print server settings, and view all of the printers and print servers within the organization's network. Administrators can also use Print Management to install printers and to monitor print queues remotely. If an administrator wants to use the command-line utility for Print Management, they can use printbrm.exe to manage printers and print servers. When using the printbrm.exe command, you must be in a command prompt with administrative privileges.

49. A. A roaming profile is stored on a network server and allows a user to access their user profile no matter what computer they are logging in to. Roaming profiles provide a constant desktop for users who move around, regardless of which computer they access. Only members of the Administrators group can manage mandatory profiles. Mandatory profiles can be created for a single user or a group of users.

50. A, B, C. Parental controls can help keep children safe when they use computers. You can restrict the programs that can be run and which websites they can visit. You can limit how much time is spent daily on the computer, as well as get detailed reports on the children's activity. With Windows 10, the children will need to have their own Microsoft accounts to log into. This allows you to apply the parental control settings across all of the Windows devices on the network.

51. C. FAT32 is an updated version of File Allocation Table (FAT). A main advantage of FAT32 is that it supports smaller cluster sizes. However, the situation in this question cannot be done. Windows 10 data compression is only supported on NTFS partitions. If this file is moved to a FAT32 partition, then it will be stored as uncompressed.

52. C. Windows 10 comes with the Printer Migration tool that allows users to export and import installed printers. The Migrate Printers utility within the Print Management tool is used to allow an administrator to migrate the print server queues from one computer to another while also transferring the settings.

53. B, C. To enable a volume on Windows 10 with BitLocker, it must include a Trusted Platform Module (TPM) chip. The TPM is a chip on the computer's motherboard that generates encryption keys, keeping part of the key to itself. When using BitLocker encryption or device encryption on a computer with a TPM, part of the key is stored in the TPM. This ensures that a hacker cannot simply remove the drive from the computer to access the file somewhere else. In this question, Computer1 does not have a TPM, so it cannot use BitLocker.

54. C. On a Windows 10 machine, Device Manager allows an administrator to configure the different devices. This utility allows you to configure such devices as disk drives, display adapters, DVD/CD-ROM drives, monitors, and network adapters. Device Manager ensures that all devices are working properly. While using Device Manager, you can do the following:

- Disable, enable, and uninstall devices.
- For each device, determine which device driver is installed.
- Install new devices.
- Manage and update device drivers.
- Troubleshoot device problems.
- Use driver rollback to return to a previous version of a driver.
- View a list of all hardware installed on your computer.

55. B. Windows 10 has a utility called `sigverif.exe` that scans a computer and verifies that all of the drivers are properly signed. `sigverif.exe` allows users to verify whether their drivers on their machines are digitally signed or not.

56. D. To disable previous versions from the `D:\` volume, use the System Protection settings from the computer system properties. System Protection is a Windows 10 feature that creates a backup and saves configuration information of a computer's system files and settings. System Protection saves multiple previous versions of saved configurations instead of overwriting them. Manage System Protection from the System Protection tab of the System Properties dialog box. The System Protection dialog box allows you to enable or disable system protection for the drive. When you enable protection, you can opt for previous versions of files or previous versions of files and system settings. To delete previous versions, from the System Protection dialog box for the selected disk, click the Delete button.

57. A, B. File History allows users to save copies of their files so that they can get them back in the event of a file being damaged or lost. A user can restore personal files, select drives, exclude folders, and even set advanced settings on the File History settings. In this case, two of the folders will not work with File History protection since they are formatted with FAT32. To use File History, the folders will need to be reformatted with NTFS.

58. D. There are three types of share permissions:

- *Full Control*: Enables users to read, change, and edit permissions, and take ownership of files

- *Change*: Allows users to change data within a file or to delete files and folders within a share

- *Read*: Allows a user to view and execute files in the shared folder

When both NTFS and share permissions are applied to a folder, the system will look at the effective rights for NTFS and share permissions and then applies the most restrictive of the cumulative permissions. If a resource has been shared and you access it from the local computer where the resource resides, then you will be governed only by the NTFS permissions.

59. D. Virtual smart cards use a cryptographic key technology that is stored on the actual Windows 10 computer. That computer must have a Trusted Platform Module (TPM) installed on the motherboard. Virtual smart card technology from Microsoft uses two-factor authentication. Virtual smart cards imitate the functionality of physical smart cards, but they use the TPM chip, rather than requiring the use of a separate physical smart card and reader.

60. D. A super-mandatory profile is a mandatory user profile with an additional layer of security. Super-mandatory user profiles are similar to regular mandatory profiles, with the exception that users who have super-mandatory profiles are unable to log on if the server that stores the mandatory profile is unavailable. Users with normal mandatory profiles can log on with the locally cached copy of the mandatory profile. The process for creating super-mandatory profiles is similar to that for creating mandatory profiles. User profiles become super-mandatory when the folder name of the profile path ends in .man. Folder Redirection enables users and administrators to redirect the path of a known folder to a new location, manually or by using Group Policy. The new location can be a folder on the local computer or a directory on a file share. Users interact with files in the redirected folder as if it still existed on the local drive.

61. B. NTFS permissions are cumulative, depending upon group membership. The user will get the highest level of security from all of the different groups to which they belong. However, if a user has been given deny permission through a user or group membership, then the deny permission always overrides the allowed permissions. When accessing a file locally, combine the NTFS permissions granted. The least restrictive permission is the permission that gets applied. In this question, the NTFS permission is the least restrictive of Read/Execute and Modify. So, Modify will be the effective NTFS permission. When accessing a folder or file across the network, combine the effective NTFS permissions; in this case, Modify is the effective Share permissions granted. Shared permissions are additive if you belong to multiple groups. Add up all of the permissions of the groups and get the highest permission. In this question, the Shared permissions are Read and Full Control. So, Full Control will be the Shared effective permission. Thus, now you have Modify and Full Control as your effective permissions. Nonetheless, since you need to apply the most restrictive permission when coming across the network, your effective permission will be Modify. When applying conflicting NTFS and Share permissions, the most restrictive permissions win. Remember that NTSF and Share permissions are both applied only when a user is accessing a shared resource over a network. Only NTFS permissions apply to a user accessing a resource locally.

62. A, E. The Admin group needs to have Full Control on both the NTFS permissions and the Shared permissions to perform their job duties. To be able to assign other users permissions, you must have Full Control permission.

63. A. AppLocker restricts unauthorized software and also enables greater security hardware requirements. Use AppLocker to configure a Denied list and an Accepted list for applications. Applications that are configured on the Denied list will not run on the system, and applications on the Accepted list will operate properly. Using AppLocker, you can do the following:

- Assign a rule to a security group or an individual user.
- Create exceptions to rules.
- Define rules based on file attributes, such as the digital signature, the publisher, product name, file name, and file version.
- Import and export rules.
- Simplify creating and managing AppLocker rules by using AppLocker PowerShell cmdlets.
- Use audit-only mode to deploy the policy to understand the impact prior to enforcing it.

64. B. File History allows users to save copies of their files so that they can get them back in the event of a file being damaged or lost. A user can restore personal files, select drives, exclude folders, and even set advanced settings on the File History settings. File History takes regular backups of the data and saves them to a separate disk volume or external drive. When File History is enabled, it backs up all the system libraries and custom libraries by default. In this question, you have used the Shift+Delete. Doing so will permanently delete the file or folder from the system. It will not go to the Recycle Bin.

65. B. A DLL is a library that contains code and data that can be used by more than one program at the same time. Some of the advantages when a program uses a DLL are as follows:

- It uses fewer resources.

- It promotes modular architecture.

- It eases deployment and installation.

66. A. By default, the name Administrator is given to a user account that is a member of the Administrators group. However, in Windows 10, this user account is disabled by default. To increase computer security, you may want to leave this account disabled and assign other users to the Administrators group. This way, a hacker will be unable to log on to the computer by using the Administrator user account.

67. B. User Account Control (UAC) helps prevent malware from damaging a computer. With UAC, applications and tasks are run in the security context of a nonadministrator account, unless the administrator specifically authorizes administrator-level access to the system. UAC can block the automatic installation of unauthorized applications and prevent accidental changes to system settings. You can set UAC to one of four levels of the slider that include the following:

- *Always notify me*: This is the highest UAC level, which requests validation for all applications, all software, and any changes to Windows settings.

- *Notify me only when applications try to make changes*: This is the default UAC level. It requests validation for new applications, but not Windows settings. This option will dim the desktop.

- *Notify me only when applications try to make changes (do not dim my desktop)*: This is the same as the default UAC level but does not dim the desktop when the validation prompt appears.

- *Never notify me*: The lowest UAC level—no notifications for any system changes will be received.

To access the User Accounts, go to Start ➤ Windows System ➤ Control Panel ➤ User Accounts.

68. C. When a new user account is created, a security identifier (SID) is created automatically for the user account. The username is a property of the SID. Windows 10 uses the SID as the user object so that you can rename a user while still keeping all the user's properties. All security settings get linked with the SID and not the user account. Because every user account receives a unique SID number, it is good practice to disable an account rather than delete it.

69. A, C, D. Windows 10 includes quotas that allow you to manage and control how much space users can use to prevent a single user from filling up the entire hard drive. Disk quotas give administrators the ability to limit how much storage space a user can have on a hard drive. You can set up disk quotas based on volume or by users. Here are some guidelines regarding quotas:

- They scan the volume every hour to update the storage usage for each user.

- They are configured per volume, not per computer.

- They are available only on volumes formatted using NTFS.

- They can be set per individual user or everyone, but you cannot set limits on groups of users.

- Users who have files already on the drive will have their quota initially disabled, while newly added users will start their quotas as normal.

Follow these steps if you'd like to enable quotas:

1. To start, right-click the partition or drive where you want to create the disk quota and select Properties.

2. In the Properties window, go to the Quota tab and click the button Show Quota Settings.

3. Check the Enable Quota Management option.

4. Check the Deny Disk Space To Users Exceeding Quota Limit option.

5. Select the Limit Disk Space To option and set the amount of space you want and specify the size.

6. Set the amount of space before a warning is triggered to the user and specify the size.

7. Click Apply and click OK.

8. Restart your computer.

70. B. Device Guard is a mixture of enterprise-related hardware and software security features that, when organized together, will lock a device down so that it can only run trusted applications. If the application is not trusted, then the application cannot run. It will lock a device so that it can only run trusted applications that are defined in your code integrity policies. The advantage to Device Guard is that it works on two levels: the kernel mode code integrity (KMCI) and the user mode code integrity (UMCI). Since Device Guard works at both levels, it protects against hardware- and software-based threats. There are several ways to manage Device Guard. You can manage it by using Group Policies, the Microsoft System Center Configuration Manager (SCCM), Windows PowerShell, and Microsoft Intune.

71. C. There are several ways to manage Device Guard. You can manage it by using Group Policies, the Microsoft System Center Configuration Manager (SCCM), Windows PowerShell, and Microsoft Intune. You can use Windows PowerShell to create and service code integrity policies. The `New-CIPolicy` command allows an administrator to create a Code Integrity policy as an XML file.

72. C. For users with the Windows 10 operating system, Microsoft Windows Defender Exploit Guard (EG) is an anti-malware software that provides intrusion protection. Exploit Guard is available as a part of Windows Defender Security Center and can protect machines against multiple different attack types. It helps protect systems from common malware hacks that use executable files and scripts that attack applications such as Microsoft 365. Windows Defender Exploit Guard also searches for suspicious scripts or behavior that is not normal on a Windows 10 computer.

73. A. Windows Defender Firewall helps secure Windows devices by filtering what network traffic is permitted to enter or exit the device. This tool is built as a snap-in on the Microsoft Management Console (MMC), and its executable file is named `wf.msc`. To configure Windows Defender Firewall to allow File Transfer Protocol (FTP) traffic, you will need to set up ports 20 and 21. Port 25 is for the Simple Mail Transfer Protocol (SMTP), and port 53 is for the Domain Name System (DNS). Port 80 is for the Hypertext Transfer Protocol (HTTP), and port 443 is for Hypertext Transfer Protocol Secure (HTTPS). Here are the steps for opening a port using the Windows Defender Firewall:

1. Open Windows Defender Security Center.

2. Click Firewall & Network Protection.

3. Click the Advanced Settings link.

4. Select Inbound Rules from the left pane.

5. Under Actions, from the right pane, click the New Rule option.

6. Select the Port option and then click the Next button.

7. Select the appropriate protocol depending on the application.

8. In the Specific Local Ports field, type the port number and then click the Next button.

9. Select the Allow The Connection option and then click the Next button.

10. Select the network type to which the new rule should apply (usually, this is left with the default selections) and then click the Next button.

11. Type a descriptive name for the rule and then click the Finish button.

74. D. Dynamic disks and basic disks are two types of hard drive configurations. A basic disk is the storage model that uses partition tables such as those found in MS-DOS and Windows to manage the partitions on the hard disk. A dynamic disk does not contain partition tables or logical drives; instead, the hard drive is divided into dynamic volumes. Dynamic disks are supported by all Windows operating systems above Windows Server 2000. Windows 10 supports simple volumes, extended volumes, spanned volumes, mirrored volumes, and striped volumes.

75. C. If you notice that a hard drive that you have been using for a long time is having its performance slowing down, you may need to run the Disk Defragmenter, so you will need to run a "defrag" on that drive. The Disk Defragmenter is a utility that is used to rearrange files so that they are stored sequentially across the disk. This improves access to those files. Optimizing the drives can help the computer run smoother and boot up faster. You can defragment disks through the command-line utility Defrag or by performing the following:

1. Select the search bar on the taskbar and enter **defrag**.

2. Select Defragment And Optimize Drives.

3. In Optimize Drives window that opens, select the disk drive to be optimized.

4. Click the Optimize button.

76. B. Windows Defender Firewall helps secure Windows devices by filtering what network traffic is permitted to enter or exit the device. This tool is built as a snap-in on the Microsoft Management Console (MMC), and its executable file is named wf.msc. To configure Windows Defender Firewall to allow Simple Mail Transfer Protocol (SMTP) inbound and outbound traffic, you would set up port 25. Ports 20 and 21 are for File Transfer Protocol (FTP) data, port 53 is for the Domain Name System (DNS), port 80 is for the Hypertext Transfer Protocol (HTTP), and port 443 is for Hypertext Transfer Protocol Secure (HTTPS).

77. B. Windows Defender Application Control (WDAC) was introduced with Windows 10 and lets a company control what drivers and applications are allowed to run on their Windows 10 clients. Administrators can use WDAC to ensure that only applications that have been company approved can run on the Windows 10 computers. WDAC is best utilized when:

- You are adopting application control for security reasons.

- Your application control policy can be applied to all users on the managed computers.

- All the devices are running Windows 10.

78. D. The Windows Defender Firewall with Advanced Security is a tool that provides detailed control over the rules that are applied by the Windows Defender Firewall. Windows Defender Firewall with Advanced Security allows you to set up inbound and outbound rules by using Windows Defender Firewall. Inbound and outbound rules consist of preconfigured rules that can be enabled or disabled. Inbound rules monitor inbound traffic, and outbound rules monitor outbound traffic.

79. C. To configure your Windows Firewall to allow Domain Name System (DNS) inbound and outbound traffic, you would set up port 53. Ports 20 and 21 are for the File Transfer Protocol (FTP) data, port 25 is for the Simple Mail Transfer Protocol (SMTP), port 80 is for the Hypertext Transfer Protocol (HTTP), and port 443 is for Hypertext Transfer Protocol Secure (HTTPS). Windows Defender Firewall helps secure Windows devices by filtering what network traffic is permitted to enter or exit the device.

80. C. BitLocker is an encryption feature that is available in Windows 10 Professional and Enterprise editions that requires a Trusted Platform Module (TPM) on the system. However, when the system does not have a TPM, you can enable the Require Additional Authentication At Startup setting. Using this policy enables the setting Allow BitLocker Without A Compatible TPM. To use BitLocker on a drive without TPM, run the gpedit.msc command (opening the Local Group Policy Editor). Then navigate to Computer Configuration ➢ Administrative Templates ➢ Windows Components ➢ Bit Locker Drive Encryption ➢ Operating System Drives under Local Computer Policy. Double-click the Require Additional Authentication At Startup setting. Now enable the feature and check the Allow BitLocker Without A Compatible TPM checkbox.

81. E. By assigning User1 Modify NTFS permissions, you are providing this user with just enough permissions to perform their job. You could also assign Sales or Finance the Modify permission, but then everyone in those groups would be able to delete, change, and do more than they all need. Also, User1 does not need Full Control to change or delete files.

82. B. Typically, the directory structure is organized in a hierarchical manner, meaning that there will be subfolders within a folder. By default, in Windows 10 the parent folder's permissions get applied to any files or subfolders within that folder as well as any newly created files or folders. These permissions are called *inherited permissions*. You can assign how permissions are inherited in subfolders and files by clicking the Advanced button on the Security tab of a folder's Properties dialog box. To edit these options, click the Disable Inheritance button. You can edit the following:

- Convert Inherited Permissions Into Explicit Permissions On This Object
- Remove All Inherited Permissions From This Object

So, by disabling inheritance and removing the permissions, this will meet the requirements set out in the new company policy.

83. B. The Read & Execute permission allows the following:

- Listing the contents of a folder and reading the data in a folder's files
- Navigating folders and executing files in the folders
- Seeing the attributes of a file or folder

If the Read & Execute permission is selected, the List Folder Contents and Read permissions will be checked by default and cannot be unchecked.

So, by assigning the Allow Read & Execute permission, this will meet the requirements set out in the new company policy.

84. A. The Modify permission allows the following:

- Changing the attributes of a file or folder
- Creating new files and writing data to the files
- Creating new folders and changing data to the files
- Deleting files
- Listing the contents of a folder and reading the data in a folder's files
- Navigating folders and executing files in the folders
- Seeing the attributes of a file or folder

If the Modify permission is selected, the Read & Execute, List Folder Contents, Read, and Write permissions will be checked by default and cannot be unchecked. So, by assigning the Allow Modify permission, this will meet the requirements set out in the new company policy.

85. A. To enable Windows Defender Firewall with Advanced Security and configure its default behavior, use the Windows Defender Firewall with Advanced Security node in the Group Policy Management console. To enable Windows Defender Firewall and to configure the behavior, you must be a member of the Domain Administrators group or have delegated permissions to modify the GPOs. To enable this, perform the following:

1. Open the Group Policy Management Console to Windows Defender Firewall with Advanced Security.

2. In the details pane, in the Overview section, click Windows Defender Firewall Properties.

3. For each network location type (Domain, Private, and Public), perform the following steps:

  a. Click the tab that corresponds to the network location type.

  b. Change Firewall State to On (Recommended).

  c. Change Inbound Connections to Block (Default).

  d. Change Outbound Connections to Allow (Default).

86. B. When you are creating a console file to be used by another user, it is best to prevent that user from modifying the console file. This can be done from the File menu, clicking Options, and then modifying the console mode. You can choose from four console modes as follows:

- *Author Mode*: Users have access to all MMC functionality and can add or remove snap-ins, create new windows, and navigate the entire console tree.

- *User Mode-full access*: Users have access to all window management functionality of the MMC and full access to the context tree. They cannot add or remove snap-ins or change console file options. The Save command is not available.

- *User Mode-limited access, multiple window*: Users cannot open new windows, and users do not have access to areas of the console tree that were not visible when the console file was not saved. Multiple child windows are allowed, but the user cannot close them.

- *User Mode-limited access, single window*: All restrictions in place for multiple-window limited-access user mode apply, except that there is only a single window.

In the Console Mode box, check the mode that best suits your administrative and security requirements. To restrict users from making changes to the custom console, click to select the Do Not Save Changes To This Console checkbox and then click OK. To save the new MMC console, click Save As on the Console menu and enter a name. The console is saved as a file that can be distributed to anyone who needs to configure a computer using this tool.

87. A. By default, File History is turned off. To turn File History on, go to the Start menu and click Settings. Then select Update & Security and choose Backup. File History allows users to save copies of their files so that they can get them back in the event of a file being lost or damaged. You can restore personal files and selected drives, exclude folders, and set advanced settings. The easiest way to restore missing files is to browse to the folder where the files were located in File Explorer and then click the History button on the Home tab of the ribbon.

88. A. Windows 10 Storage Spaces is a technology that protects data from drive failures. Storage Spaces is another way to give your Windows 10 users data redundancy. It is similar to Redundant Array of Inexpensive Disks (RAID), except that it is implemented in software. Windows 10 administrators have the ability to group hard drives together into storage pools. To implement Windows 10 Storage Spaces, combine three or more drives into a single logical pool. Format this drive using New Technology File System (NTFS) or the Resilient File System (ReFS) file system and store multiple copies of your data on these drives to protect it from data failures. In this question, you already have a storage pool created and are looking to add another disk to it. The command to be used is the Add-PhysicalDisk cmdlet. The Add-PhysicalDisk cmdlet lets you add a physical disk to the existing storage pool.

89. A, B, C. File History takes snapshots of your files and stores them. File History builds a library of past versions of your documents that you can recover. By default, File History will be set to back up important folders in your user account's home folder, including the Desktop, Documents, Downloads, Music, Pictures, and Videos folders. If you used Backup and Restore to back up files or create system image backups in Previous Versions of Windows, then your old backups are still available in Windows 10. To access this, go to the Control Panel ➢ System And Security ➢ Backup And Restore (Windows 7). The other option to ensure that your Previous Versions settings are working is by going to Settings ➢ Update & Security ➢ Backup. Once File History is enabled, you can right-click a file in File Explorer and then select Restore Previous Versions.

90. D. Windows Hello is a biometrics system integrated into Windows. Windows Hello is a Microsoft account that can be used to authenticate to a domain, a cloud-based domain, or a computer. To do this, you need to link your Microsoft account to your Windows 10 system. When you set up Windows Hello on a device, you can set up the system to use Windows Hello or a personal identification number (PIN). To configure the Windows Hello options, click the Start button and select Settings ➢ Accounts. Windows Hello for Business is a newer credential in Windows 10. It helps increase security when accessing corporate resources. Windows Hello for Business replaces passwords with strong two-factor authentication on computers and mobile devices. This authentication consists of a new type of user credential that is tied to a device and uses a biometric or PIN.

91. A, C. Creator Owner is the account that creates or takes ownership of an object. An object includes files, folders, printer, and print jobs. Members of the Creator Owner group have special permissions to resources. By assigning Full Control to the Creator Owner, you have all rights to the object. If you choose Full Control permission, then all permissions will be checked by default and cannot be unchecked. Any user with Full Control access can manage the security of a folder. By assigning Modify permissions to the CompanyNetworkUsers group, this allows the users to view and modify files and file properties, including adding files to or deleting files from a directory. If you select the Modify permission, then the Read & Execute, List Folder Contents, Read, and Write permissions will be checked by default and cannot be unchecked.

92. D. In Windows, a user who has ownership of a file or folder has the sole rights to change permissions on that object. That user is always allowed to access the file or folder, even if there are contradictory permissions in place. When you create a file or folder, the user account that creates the item is automatically granted ownership. There may be times when you need to take ownership of a file or folder. Here is how to take ownership of files and folders:

1. Open File Explorer.

2. Browse and find the file or folder to which you want to have full access.

3. Right-click the file or folder and then select Properties.

4. Click the Security tab to access the NTFS permissions.

5. Click the Advanced button.

6. On the Advanced Security Settings page, click the Change link in the Owner's field and then click the Advanced button.

7. On the Select User Or Group page, click the Find Now button.

8. From the search result, select your user account and click OK.

9. On the Select User Or Group page, click OK and then click Apply.

10. Click OK several times to finish.

It should be noted that if you are taking ownership of a folder, you check the Replace Ownership On The Subcontainers And Object option in the Advanced Security Settings page. This will allow you also to take ownership of all the subfolders inside the folder.

93. B. Controlled folder access helps protect valuable data from malicious apps and threats, such as ransomware. It is part of Windows Defender Exploit Guard. Controlled folder access is included with Windows 10 and Windows Server 2019. Controlled folder access protects files, folders, and memory areas on your device from unauthorized changes by unfriendly applications. You can enable controlled folder access by using any of these methods:

- Group Policy

- Microsoft Endpoint Configuration Manager

- Microsoft Intune

- Mobile Device Management (MDM)

- PowerShell

- Windows Security application

94. C. If you add a new hard disk drive to a computer and it doesn't show up in File Explorer, you may have to add a drive letter or initialize it before using it. You can only initialize a hard disk drive that has not yet been formatted. Initializing a hard disk drive erases everything on it and prepares it for use by Windows. Then you will be able to format it and store files on it. You can also use PowerShell by using the `Initialize-Disk` cmdlet. To initialize new disks using Disk Management, follow these steps:

1. Open Disk Management with administrator permissions.

2. In Disk Management, right-click the disk to initialize and then click Initialize Disk. If the disk is listed as Offline, first right-click it and select Online.

3. In the Initialize Disk dialog box, make sure that the correct disk is selected and then click OK to accept the default partition style. The disk status briefly changes to Initializing and then to the Online status.

4. Select and hold (or right-click) the unallocated space on the drive and then select New Simple Volume.

5. Select Next, specify the size of the volume, and then click Next again. (The default value is the size of the whole drive.)

6. Specify the drive letter to be assigned to the volume and then click Next.

7. Specify the file system to be used, typically NTFS, click Next, and then click Finish.

95. D. The Profile tab of the user's Properties dialog box allows you to customize the user's environment. You can specify the following:

- Home Folder

- Logon script

- User profile path

Users normally store their personal files and information in a private folder called a Home Folder. One reason that you would assign your users Home Folders on a server is because the servers are typically the only machines that get backed up. If the Home Folder that you are specifying does not exist, Windows 10 will try to create the folder for you. You can also use the variable %username% in place of a specific user's name. This variable will automatically change to the name of the user you are currently working on.

96. B. Permissions are cumulative among themselves. This means you will obtain the highest level of permissions. But when the two permissions meet, the most restrictive set of permissions will apply. In this question, the NTFS side (local permission) would be Modify, and the Shared permission (remote permission) would be Full Control. But when the two permissions meet, the most restrictive will apply, and the user's effective permission will be Modify.

97. B. The Encrypting File System (EFS) is a component of the NTFS file system. It enables transparent encryption and decryption of files by using cryptographic algorithms. Any individual or program that doesn't have the appropriate cryptographic key cannot read the encrypted data. EFS allows a user or administrator to secure files or folders by using encryption. The encryption uses the user's security identifier (SID) number to secure the file or folder. To implement encryption, open the Advanced Attributes dialog box for a folder and check the Encrypt Contents To Secure Data box.

98. D. You can use Windows PowerShell to enable data deduplication by using the Enable-DedupVolume cmdlet. Data deduplication is disabled by default. Data deduplication is not supported for certain volumes, such as any volume that is not an NTFS or ReFS file system or any volume that is smaller than 2 GB. Here's an example: Enable-DedupVolume -Volume "D:","E:","F:".

99. B, C. When selecting a file system for Windows 10, you can select from FAT32 or NTFS. You usually choose a file system based upon the features that you want to utilize. If you have a FAT32 partition and plan to update it to NTFS, you can use the Convert utility. It is recommended that you use the NTFS file system with Windows 10 since the NTFS file system offers features such as local security, file compression, and file encryption. You should utilize the FAT32 file system if you are planning on setting up a computer to dual boot with a version of Windows that does not support NTFS because FAT32 is backward compatible with other operating systems. Windows 10 also supports exFAT.

100. A. If you want to convert an existing partition from FAT or FAT32 to NTFS, you must use the `convert` command-line utility and insert the drive letter where d is in the command. The syntax is as follows: `convert [drive:]/fs:ntfs`.

101. B, D. Permissions are cumulative among themselves. This means you will obtain the highest level of permissions. But when the two permissions meet, the most restrictive set of permissions will apply. Shared folder permissions apply only across the network (remotely) and can only be placed on folders. NTFS permissions can apply locally and remotely and can be placed on files or folders.

102. E. There are many advantages to using NTFS. These include compression, encryption, quotas, and security. NTFS provides the highest level of service and features for Windows 10 computers. NTFS partitions can be up to 16 TB with 4 KB clusters or 256 TB with 64 KB clusters. NTFS offers complete folder-level and file-level security.

103. D. To restrict the amount of disk space used by users on the network, system administrators can establish disk quotas. By default, Windows 10 supports disk quota restrictions at the volume level. This allows you to restrict the amount of storage space that a specific user can use on a single disk volume. You can set up disk quotas based on volume or on users.

104. C. Administrators can use the remote storage features supported by NTFS to offload rarely used data automatically to a backup system or other device. These files still remain available to users. If a user requests an archived file, Windows 10 can automatically restore the file from a remote storage device and make it available. NTFS provides many disk management features, such as compression and encryption capabilities, as well as data-recovery features.

105. B. BitLocker requires that you have a hard disk with at least two NTFS partitions. One partition will be utilized as the system partition that will be encrypted, and the other partition will be the active partition that is used to start the computer. This partition will remain unencrypted.

106. C. A spanned volume is a simple volume that spans multiple disks. You can create a spanned volume from free space that exists on a minimum of 2 to a maximum of 32 physical drives. When the spanned volume is initially created in Windows 10, it can be formatted with either FAT32 or NTFS. If you extend a volume that already contains data, then the partition must be formatted with NTFS.

107. A. Permissions are cumulative among themselves. This means you will obtain the highest level of permissions. But when the two permissions meet, the most restrictive set of permissions will apply. In this question, the NTFS side (local permission) will be Full Control, and the Shared permission (remote permission) will be Deny. But when the two permissions meet, the most restrictive will apply, and the user's effective permission will be Deny.

108. D. When installed into a workgroup environment, Windows 10 has four built-in accounts that are created automatically at the time the operating system is installed. The Initial User account uses the name of the registered user. By default, the Initial User account is a member of the Administrators group.

109. D. Since you are creating a two-way mirror, it requires at least two disks. This will write two copies of your data on the drives, which can protect your data from a single driver failure. This question states that you want to minimize data loss, so you will need to utilize drive C: and drive D: since both of these drives do not have any data on them.

110. C. Windows 10 gives you the ability to set up a logon with a picture. If you want to use a picture for authentication, you first choose a picture, and then you add three gestures onto the picture. These gestures can be straight lines, circles, squares, or anything you want. Then when you log on to the system, you just re-create the gestures on the picture, and the system will log you in.

111. C. Secure Channel is another part of the authentication and encryption communications between a client and a server. It is also called the Schannel. It is a set of security protocols. It uses these four protocols on the Windows platforms:

- Transport Layer Security (TLS 1.1)

- Transport Layer Security (TLS 1.2)

- Secure Sockets Layer (SSL 3.0)

- Secure Sockets Layer (SSL 2.0)

To create the Schannel connection, the clients and servers are both required to obtain Schannel credentials and create a security session. Once the client and server connection is obtained, the security credentials become available. If a connection is lost for any reason, the client and server can automatically renegotiate the connection and finish all communications.

112. C. Mount points are used to surpass the limitation of 26 drive letters and to join two volumes into a folder on a separate physical disk drive. A mount point allows you to configure a volume to be accessed from a folder on another existing disk. It can be assigned to a drive instead of using a drive letter, and it can be used on basic or dynamic volumes that are formatted with NTFS. To assign a mount point folder path to a drive using the Windows interface, do the following:

1. In Disk Manager, right-click the partition or volume where you want to assign the mount point folder path.

2. Click Change Drive Letter And Paths and then click Add.

3. Click Mount in the empty NTFS folder.

4. Enter the path to an empty folder on an NTFS volume or click Browse to locate it. You can also assign a mount point folder path by using the `diskpart` command-line utility.

113. B. Using the `Diskpart` command helps you to manage a computer's drives (disks, partitions, volumes, or virtual hard disks). Using the `/create` switch creates a partition on a disk, a volume on one or more disks, or a virtual hard disk (VHD). The syntax is as follows:

- `create partition`

- `create volume`

- `create vdisk`

To create a partition, make sure you are using unallocated disk space. So, to create a partition, use `diskpart /create partition primary size=<partitionsize>`. You will see a message that states that `Diskpart` succeeded in creating the specified partition.

114. C. NTFS permissions control access to NTFS files and folders. However, the user who owns an object has control over the object. The owner or administrator can configure access by allowing or denying NTFS permissions to users and groups. NTFS permissions are cumulative, depending upon group memberships. The user receives the highest level of security from all of the different groups to which they belong. However, if a user has been denied access through user or group membership, then those deny permissions override the allowed permissions. The default security permission for Users is Read on new folders or shares. Read allows a user to view and execute files in the shared folder. Read is also the default permission on shared folders for the Everyone group.

115. A. Permissions are additive among themselves. This means you get the highest level of permissions. But when the two permissions meet, the most restrictive set of permissions applies. In this question, the NTFS side would be Full Control (this would be the local permission), and the Shared permission is Read. Therefore, the shared folder permission for Sales will need to be changed to Change so that the user can make their required changes to the document.

116. B. Permissions are additive among themselves. This means you get the highest level of permissions among the group membership. In this question, the user is a member of three different groups, which consist of Read, Modify, and Full Control. Since the permissions are additive and the user will get the highest level of permission, the user's effective permission will be Full Control.

117. A. Permissions are additive among themselves. This means you get the highest level of permissions among the group membership. In this question, the user is a member of three different groups, which consist of Read, Modify, and Deny. Since the permissions are additive and the user will get the highest level of permission, the user's effective permission will be Deny. Because the user has been denied access through the HR membership, the deny permissions override the allowed permissions.

118. B. The default shared permission for Administrators is Full Control. The shared permissions from lowest to highest are Read, Change, Full Control, and Deny. Share permissions can only be applied to folders.

119. D. Disk quotas give administrators the ability to limit how much storage space a user can have on a hard drive. You can set up disk quotas based on volume or on users. Quota templates are predefined ways to set up quotas. The templates allow you to set up disk quotas without the need to create a disk quota from scratch.

120. A. Print Management allows administrators to have a single application where they can monitor and manage their printers. The Print Management MMC snap-in is available through the Administrative Tools folder. Administrators can use this tool to install, manage, and import/export print server settings, as well as see all of the printers and print servers throughout the organization. Administrators can also use Print Management to remotely install printers and to monitor print queues.

121. C. Smart cards are plastic cards (about the size of a credit card) that can be used in combination with other methods of authentication. These cards can have a chip built into them that has the user's assigned rights and permissions. Many smart cards have the ability to have ID information printed directly onto it.

122. B, C, D. BitLocker Drive Encryption is a data protection feature available in Windows 10 Education, Enterprise, and Professional editions. It is also available on Windows 7 and Windows 8 corporate editions. However, it is not available in any Home editions. Only the operating system drive (usually C:) or internal hard drives can be encrypted with BitLocker.

123. B. Network Unlock allows an administrator to manage desktops and servers that are configured to use BitLocker. The Network Unlock allows you to configure BitLocker to unlock an encrypted hard drive automatically during a system reboot when that hard drive is connected to the trusted company network.

124. D. The NTFS file system offers the highest level of service and features for Windows 10 computers. NTFS partitions can be up to 16 TB with 4 KB clusters or 256 TB with 64 KB clusters. This file system offers comprehensive folder-level and file-level security. This allows you to set an additional level of security for users who access the files and folders locally or through the network. Only NTFS supports both file encryption and file compression. Both Windows 7 and Windows 10 can access NTFS partitions, so file access will not be an issue.

125. A. Windows 10 comes with a feature called BitLocker Drive Encryption. BitLocker encrypts the drive so that if it's removed or stolen, the data can't be accessed. Any new files added to this drive are encrypted automatically. To configure BitLocker, you must either use a Local Group Policy or use the BitLocker icon in Control Panel. However, this question states that it doesn't want the files to be copied or moved to a USB drive. If the files are moved from one drive to another drive, the files will become decrypted automatically. It doesn't prevent the files from being copied.

Chapter 3: Configure Connectivity

1. A. A default gateway allows devices on one subnet to communicate with devices on another subnet. The default gateway is the router's IP address. This question states that you can access computers on one network but not on the remote network. This is an indicator that the issue is with the IP address of the default gateway.

2. C, D. The `ipconfig` command displays your IP configuration. Using the `/release` switch will release an IPv4 address that has been assigned through DHCP. By using the `/renew`, this will renew your IPv4 address using DHCP.

3. D. You first need to ensure that your Windows systems can accept remote PowerShell commands by enabling remote PowerShell commands. To accomplish this, you must be an administrator and run the `Enable-PSRemoting` cmdlet. Then, once PowerShell is enabled, you can enter a PowerShell session and run the script for the Sales department computers. The Enable-PSRemoting cmdlet configures computers to receive PowerShell remote commands on the Windows 10 system.

4.   C. IP addresses are divided into classes, called Class A, Class B, and Class C. Class D and Class E exist as well, but they are not used by end users. Each of the address classes has a different default subnet mask. You can identify the class of an IP address by looking at the first octet, in this case 192.

Class A: Uses a default subnet mask of 255.0.0.0 and has 1–126 as the first octet

Class B: Uses a default subnet mask of 255.255.0.0 and has 128–191 as the first octet

Class C: Uses a default subnet mask of 255.255.255.0 and has 192–223 as the first octet

Because the IP address in the question starts with a 192, that makes it a Class C address.

5.   A. The Let Windows Manage This Connection option determines whether a Windows 10 device will automatically connect to the cellular data network whenever it's available. You will need to clear the checkbox if you want to connect manually every time you want to use the cellular data connection. If you want Windows to manage the connection for you, then select this option. When selected, the device will connect to the cellular data automatically (if not already connected to another network). To set this setting, select Start ➢ Settings ➢ Network & Internet ➢ Cellular ➢ Let Windows Manage This Connection.

6.   A, B. For this question, there are 650 employees. The addresses that can handle these hosts would be a Class A or a Class B address. The 10.0.0.0/8 address is a Class A address, and the 172.16.0.0/16 is a Class B address. The Class C addresses can handle only 254 users. The IPv4 class assignments are as follows:

Network Class	Address Range of First Octet	Number of Unique Networks Available	Number of Unique Hosts per Network
Class A	1–126	126	16,777,214
Class B	128–191	16,384	65,534
Class C	192–223	2,097,152	254

7.   A, D. First, you need to set up your computer so that it allows remote connections. To set up remote connections on the device to which you want to connect, select Start ➢ Settings ➢ System ➢ Remote Desktop and turn on Enable Remote Desktop. Then you can use Remote Desktop to connect to the computer you set up. On the local computer, while in the search box on the taskbar, type **Remote Desktop Connection** and then select Remote Desktop Connection. In Remote Desktop Connection, type the name of the computer you want to connect to and then select Connect.

To restrict who can access the computer, choose to allow access only with Network Level Authentication (NLA). When this option is enabled, users have to authenticate themselves to the network before they can connect to your computer. By allowing only connections from computers running Remote Desktop with NLA, it is a more secure method of authentication that can help protect computers from hackers and malicious software.

8. C. On Windows 10, if a device has more than one network adapter, such as an Ethernet and a Wi-Fi connection, then each interface will automatically receive a priority value based on its network metric. This defines the primary connection that the device will use to send and receive networking traffic. This can be done by using Control Panel ➢ Settings ➢ Network & Internet or by using Windows PowerShell. You can configure the interface metric by using the Windows PowerShell command `Set-NetIPInterface`. When network traffic routes are chosen and the `InterfaceMetric` parameter is configured, the overall metric that is used to determine the interface preference is the sum of the route metric and the interface metric.

9. D. You should set up a workgroup, also called a *peer-to-peer network*. All computers on a workgroup are equal. All of the peer-to-peer computers, also referred to as *nodes*, concurrently act as both clients and servers. Peer-to-peer networks are typically any combination of Microsoft Windows machines connected by a centralized device such as a router, switch, or hub. You should use this network configuration for smaller environments with 10 users or less. This enables smaller companies to share resources without needing expensive equipment, server software, or an internal IT department.

10. C. Computers can communicate only by using a series of numbers. The Domain Name System (DNS) is basically like the phonebook of the Internet. Web browsers use Internet Protocol (IP) addresses, and DNS translates those domain names into IP addresses so that the browsers can load the web pages. The `ipconfig` command displays a computer's IP address configuration. Using `ipconfig` with the `/registerdns` switch will automatically register the Windows 10 machine with the DNS server. The registration includes the Windows 10 machine name and the IP address.

11. B. A virtual private network (VPN) connection allows the ability to access another computer and network resources remotely in a secure fashion. By default, all Windows VPN connections use force tunneling where all Internet-bound traffic is redirected or "forced" back to the on-premises location. This happens when the Use Default Gateway On Remote Network option is selected. To allow the user to be able to connect to the virtual machine when connected to the VPN, this option needs to be unchecked. To modify this option, follow these steps:

1. Navigate to Control Panel ➢ Network And Sharing Center ➢ Change Adapter Settings.

2. Right-click the VPN connection and then choose Properties.

3. Select the Networking tab.

4. Select Internet Protocol Version 4 (TCP/IPv4) and click Properties.

5. Click Advanced.

6. Deselect the Use Default Gateway On Remote Network box.

7. Click OK to apply the changes to the interface.

12. A. A virtual private network (VPN) client is an end device, user, or software that is trying to establish a secure connection between the user and a VPN server. The client is part of the VPN infrastructure, and it is the end recipient of VPN services. A VPN allows you to create secure connections to another network using the Internet. The General tab has a field where you would enter the VPN server address or hostname.

13. A. Azure is Microsoft's subscription-based Active Directory service. It is a cloud-based Active Directory subscription. This is a great option if the company doesn't want to worry about managing and maintaining a server room. Azure is also ideal for accessing Active Directory from anywhere.

14. B. A Dynamic Host Configuration Protocol (DHCP) server runs the DHCP service, which will assign TCP/IP information to a computer automatically. Every computer uses three settings to operate properly with the Internet and an intranet. It needs a TCP/IP address, a subnet mask, and a default gateway. To create a static DHCP reservation, you will need to obtain the MAC address. The MAC address is a unique identifier assigned to a network interface controller (NIC) to be used as a network address in communications within a network segment. To find this information, use the ipconfig /all command to view the default configurations including IPv4 and IPv6. The ipconfig command displays your IP configuration. The /all switch will show information about the IP configuration, including the computer's physical address (MAC), the DNS server being used, and if DHCP is being used.

15. C. Classless Inter-Domain Routing (CIDR) is an IP addressing structure that improves the distribution of IP addresses. CIDR is the number of ON bits. So, a subnet mask of 255.255.224.0 equals a CIDR of /19. The CIDR representation is the number of bits turned on in the subnet mask. 255.255.224.0 is actually 11111111.11111111.11100000 .00000000 (1s are ON bits, and 0s are OFF), which equals 19 bits turned ON, or /19.

16. D. Classless Inter-Domain Routing (CIDR) is an IP addressing structure that improves the distribution of IP addresses. CIDR is the number of ON bits. So, a subnet mask of 255.255.255.224 equals a CIDR of /27. The CIDR representation is the number of bits turned on in the subnet mask. 255.255.255.224 is actually 11111111.11111111.11111111 .11100000 (1s are ON bits, and 0s are OFF), which equals 27 bits turned ON, or /27.

17. C. The subnet mask is used to specify which part of the IPv4 address defines the network value and which part defines the unique host value. The subnet mask is used to break down the ranges of a network. For this question, you should use the subnet mask of 255.255.255.0. The IP network address 192.168.10.0 is a Class C address. Class C addresses, by default, use the 255.255.255.0 subnet mask. The network portion of the address is 192.168.10, and the host portion of the address can be 1 to 254.

18. D. By default, only administrators can connect through PowerShell remoting. If you want to enable PowerShell remoting for a single nonadministrator, you need to add the user account to the local Remote Management Users group. To enable PowerShell remoting on a single machine, you can log on to the computer locally or through the Remote Desktop and then execute Enable-PSRemoting at a PowerShell prompt with administrator rights.

19. C. Remote Desktop is a Windows 10 tool that allows an administrator to take control of a remote computer's keyboard, video, and mouse. This tool does not require another user to be available on the remote computer. To enable Remote Desktop, do the following:

1. Open the System tool by right-clicking Start ➤ Windows System ➤ Control Panel ➤ System.

2. On the left side, click the Remote Settings link.

3. In the Remote Desktop section, click the radio button Allows Connections From Computers Running Any Version Of Remote Desktop (Less Secure).

4. Click OK.

5. Close the System Properties screen.

20. D. The Media Sensing feature is used on Windows-based computers that use TCP/IP to detect whether the network media is in a link state. Ethernet network adapters and hubs usually have a link light that shows the connection status. When a Windows machine detects a down state, it will remove the bound protocols from the adapter until it is detected as up again. There are times when you may not want the network adapter to detect the link state. If that's the case, you need to run the `Set-NetIPv6Protocol` command. The `Set-NetIPv6Protocol` cmdlet modifies the global IPv6 protocol configuration for a computer. If you do not specify parameters with the cmdlet, it will set the default values for the IPv6 protocol configuration. Running the `Set-NetIPv6Protocol` cmdlet with the `-DhcpMediaSense` parameter will specify a value for the Media Sense. The acceptable values for this parameter are `Enabled` and `Disabled`. The default value is `Enabled`.

21. B. A Domain Name System (DNS) server has the DNS service running on it. DNS is a name-resolution service that resolves a hostname to a TCP/IP address (called *forward lookup*). DNS can also resolve a TCP/IP address to a name (called *reverse lookup*). If you can connect to a machine by using its TCP/IP address but not the name, then DNS is the issue.

22. D. Network Discovery is a setting that determines whether a Windows 10 system can locate other computers and devices on the network and whether other computers on the network can see your computer. To enable or disable Network Discovery, complete the following steps:

1. Select Start ➤ Windows System ➤ Control Panel.

2. Choose Network And Sharing Center and then Change Advanced Sharing Settings.

3. Click Turn On/Turn Off Network Discovery and then click the Save Changes button.

23. C. Windows PowerShell is one way to remotely configure and maintain Windows 10. You need to make sure that your Windows systems can accept remote PowerShell commands. If this feature is not already enabled on a system, you can enable this feature by running the `Enable-PSRemoting` cmdlet. To enable remote PowerShell commands, you must be an administrator to run this cmdlet. After PowerShell is enabled, you can then enter a PowerShell session on the Windows 10 system to run the `Invoke-Command`.

24. C. A Domain Name System (DNS) server has the DNS service running on it. DNS is a name-resolution service that resolves a hostname to a TCP/IP address (called *forward lookup*). DNS can also resolve a TCP/IP address to a name (called *reverse lookup*). The `ipconfig` command displays your IP configuration. Using `ipconfig` with the `/flushdns` switch will purge the DNS resolver cache on the machine.

25. D. If you use a number of services with different accounts, the Settings app will allow you to add them to make accessing apps faster and easier. By adding the account to Settings ➢ Accounts ➢ Email & App Accounts, the user credentials will be saved, so you don't have to enter a username and password every time you try to access a resource. When adding accounts for other apps, Windows 10 uses this information to sign you in to services automatically instead of having to re-enter the same account information every time. To register additional accounts, follow these steps:

1. Open Settings ➢ Accounts ➢ Email & App Account.

2. Click the Add An Account button to register a new account.

3. Select an account type.

4. Continue with the on-screen instructions to add the new account.

5. Once completed, the account information will be available whenever you connect to the resource.

26. C. View Available Networks (VAN) is a default Windows 10 feature that, when a user is using a wireless network adapter, the user can choose the wireless network that they want to connect to by using the wireless network adapter properties. It is a flyout menu that has a list of quick actions when a user right-clicks one of the listed Wi-Fi networks. The options include Connect, Disconnect, View Properties, and Forget Network.

27. A. Classless Inter-Domain Routing (CIDR) is an IP addressing structure that improves the distribution of IP addresses. To determine the subnet mask, you need to count the 1s that are ON. The CIDR /27 tells you that 27 1s are turned ON in the subnet mask. 1s are ON bits, and 0s are OFF bits. /27 equals 27 bits turned ON, or /27. Twenty-seven 1s ON equals 11111111.11111111.11111111.11100000, which is equivalent to 255.255.255.224.

28. B, C. IP addresses are divided into classes, called Class A, Class B, and Class C. Class D and Class E exist as well, but they are not used by end users. Each of the address classes has a different default subnet mask. You can identify the class of an IP address by looking at the first octet.

- Class A IP addresses range from 1–126 as the first octet.

- Class B IP addresses range from 128–191 as the first octet.

- Class C IP addresses range from 192–223 as the first octet.

Since both 131.107.10.150 and 189.10.14.1 fall within the range of 128–191 in the first octet, that makes them Class B addresses.

29. B. Resource Monitor is a tool that shows real-time information about the usage of hardware and software resources. The program uses tabs to separate data. The five tabs of the program are Overview, CPU, Memory, Disk, and Network. There are many ways to open Resource Monitor. Some of the ways include the following:

- Use the Windows+R key sequence to open the run box; then type **resmon.exe** and press Enter.

- Use Windows+R to open the run box; then type **perfmon.exe /res** and press Enter.

- On Windows 10, select Start ➤ All Apps ➤ Windows Administrative Tools ➤ Resource Monitor.

30. D. In Windows 10, there are multiple ways to connect to a Wi-Fi network. Some of the ways include using the taskbar, Settings app, Control Panel, and command prompt. To connect to a Wi-Fi network using the Settings app, go to Settings ➤ Network & Internet ➤ Wi-Fi. This will show you the wireless networks that a computer can connect to.

31. A. The Connect From Anywhere settings are used when you want to manage remote access to computers on a network using the Remote Desktop Gateway. When you connect to a computer using a Remote Desktop client, you have created a peer-to-peer connection. The Connect From Anywhere option can be found in the Advanced tab of the Remote Desktop Connections window.

32. C. When you connect to a Wi-Fi network on Windows 10, it saves a list of the networks to which you connect along with their passphrases and other settings. If you want to stop a computer from connecting automatically to a network, you will need to make Windows forget about the Wi-Fi network. Windows 10 offers several different ways to do this, but given the options provided, you can do this from the command prompt with these steps:

  1. Open the Start menu.

  2. Search for *command prompt*.

  3. Right-click the Command Prompt shortcut.

  4. Select Run As Administrator.

  The syntax to forget a Wi-Fi network is `netsh wlan delete profile name="PROFILE NAME"`.

33. D. A Windows computer will automatically connect to any known existing wireless connection by default. Once you connect to a network and provide the credentials, Windows will connect automatically to that network when it detects it. The connection information is stored in a network profile. Windows 10 offers several different ways to do this. To disable automatic connections in Windows 10, do the following:

  1. At the bottom-right corner, select the Action Center icon and choose All Settings.

  2. Select Network & Internet.

  3. On the left side, select Wi-Fi.

  4. Select Change Adapter Options in the right panel under Related Settings to open the Network Connections dialog.

5. Double-click (or right-click and select Properties) on the Wi-Fi connection to open the Wi-Fi Status dialog.

6. On the General tab, select Wireless Properties to open the Wireless Network Properties dialog.

7. On the Connection tab, uncheck the Connect Automatically When This Network Is In Range option.

34. A, C. By default, Windows Firewall blocks Network Discovery, but you can enable it. Network Discovery is a setting that determines whether your Windows 10 system can locate other computers and devices on the network and whether other computers on the network can see your computer. To enable or disable Network Discovery, you need to complete the following steps:

1. Select Start ➤ Windows System ➤ Control Panel.

2. Choose Network And Sharing Center and then Change Advanced Sharing Settings.

3. Click Turn On/Turn Off Network Discovery and then click the Save Changes button. When you change the Wired1 connection to Public, all of the networks will be in the Public profile. Enabling Network Discovery for the Public profile will allow the computers to see other computers on each network. To prevent Network Discovery on the HotSpot1 network, select No, and don't turn on sharing or connect to devices for that network. This will disable Network Discovery for the computer's connection to the HotSpot1 network.

35. B. The solution is to deploy Remote Desktop Gateway in the office. Remote users can then connect to their computers on the office network by using Remote Desktop client on their home computers configured with the IP address of the Remote Desktop Gateway. Remote Desktop Gateway (RD Gateway) is a role service that enables authorized remote users to connect to resources on an internal company or private network from any Internet-connected device that can run the Remote Desktop Connection (RDC) client. Virtual private network connections would enable remote access to the office network, but this solution would not prevent users from accessing other corporate network resources. Remote Desktop local resources determine which local resources (printers, drives, and so forth) are available in a Remote Desktop connection. However, this solution makes no provision for actually connecting to the office network. DirectAccess connections would enable remote access to the office network, but this solution would not prevent users from accessing other corporate network resources.

36. D. Remote Server Administration Tools (RSAT) enables administrators to manage roles and features remotely in Windows Server from a computer that is running Windows 10. RSAT cannot be installed on computers that are running Home or Standard editions of Windows. You can install RSAT only on Professional and Enterprise editions of the Windows client operating system. RSAT includes Server Manager, Microsoft Management Console (mmc) snap-ins, consoles, Windows PowerShell cmdlets and providers, and some command-line tools for managing roles and features that run on Windows Server.

37. B. The loopback address allows an administrator to treat the local machine as if it were a remote machine. The loopback address sends outgoing signals back to the same computer for testing. In a TCP/IP network, the loopback IP address for IPv4 is 127.0.0.1, and pinging this address will return a reply unless there is a firewall preventing it. 127.0.0.1 is the diagnostic loopback address.

38. A. The loopback address allows an administrator to treat the local machine as if it were a remote machine. The loopback address sends outgoing signals back to the same computer for testing. In a TCP/IP network, the loopback IP address for IPv6 is `::1` (or `0:0:0:0:0:0:0:0001`), and pinging this address will return a reply unless there is a firewall preventing it. `::1` (or `0:0:0:0:0:0:0:0001`) is the diagnostic loopback address.

39. A. In this case, User1 is attempting to access a share only while using Computer1. The user is not remoting into the computer to gain access to the share. Since this user has been granted Full Control to the share, they will not be prompted for credentials.

40. B. In this case, User1 is attempting to remote into Computer2 while using Computer1. Since the user is remoting into the other machine, the user will be prompted for their credentials and able to log in as User1 since an account was created for the user on Computer2.

41. B. Using the `ipconfig` command displays all of current TCP/IP network configuration values and refreshes Dynamic Host Configuration Protocol (DHCP) and Domain Name System (DNS) settings. Used without parameters, it will display the Internet Protocol version 4 (IPv4) and IPv6 addresses, subnet mask, and default gateway for all adapters. In this case, notice that the DNS server has an IP address that is not in the same network as the rest of the IP addresses. It starts with a 131.107.10 network versus a 192.168.0 network. So, the issue is that the primary DNS server is wrong.

42. C. A Private network is used for networks that are trusted, such as a corporate network or a home network. When a network is set to Private, the computer is discoverable to other devices on the network, and the computer can be used for file and printer sharing. A Public network is used for networks to connect to when out and about, such as a Wi-Fi network at a coffee shop. The computer will be hidden from other devices on the network and cannot be used for file and printer sharing. After you connect to a network for the first time, an administrator can change it from Public or Private at any time. In this case, the current network profile is configured as Public and cannot be used for WinRM. You must change the network profile to Private.

43. A. If you want to configure the laptop to connect to the RD Session Host server, then you need to configure the Connect From Anywhere settings. The Connect From Anywhere settings are used when you want to manage remote access to computers on a network using the Remote Desktop Gateway (RD Gateway). When you connect to a computer using a Remote Desktop client, you have created a peer-to-peer connection. The Connect From Anywhere option can be found in the Advanced tab of the Remote Desktop Connections window.

44. B. Remote Desktop is a tool that allows you to take control of a remote computer's keyboard, video, and mouse. This tool does not require that someone work together with you on the remote computer. Remote Desktop is used to access remote machines' applications and troubleshoot. By using Remote Desktop, you can connect to your corporate computer. To do so, you need to enable Remote Desktop on the desktop computer. You can then run the Remote Desktop Client on the tablet to connect to the office computer. You can connect to a computer that is running Windows from another computer running Windows that is connected to the same network or through the Internet by using Remote Desktop Connection.

45. C. By using Remote Desktop, you can connect to your corporate computer. To do so, you need to enable Remote Desktop on the desktop computer. You can then run the Remote Desktop Client on the tablet to connect to the office computer. You can connect to a computer that is running Windows from another computer running Windows that is connected to the same network or through the Internet by using Remote Desktop Connection.

46. C. Quick Assist is a tool for inviting help by using instant messages, email, or a file. To use Quick Assist, both computers must have Quick Assist capabilities, and the feature needs to be enabled. Both computers must have network connectivity. It is used for diagnosing problems that are difficult to explain or reproduce and for helping a new user to perform a complex set of actions.

47. B. Easy Connect is integrated into Windows 10 and Remote Assistance and is a method for obtaining remote assistance. To utilize this feature, both users—the novice and the helper—need to have Easy Connect available. This requires peer-to-peer networking features. Easy Connect uses Peer Name Resolution Protocol (PNRP) to set up a direct peer-to-peer transfer using a central machine on the Internet to establish the connection. PNRP uses IPv6 and Teredo tunneling to register a machine as globally unique. To start using Easy Connect, the user will select Invite Someone You Trust To Help You. If a user selects Easy Connect, they'll obtain a password. This password will need to be provided to the other person so that they can use it to connect to the computer. This password is valid only for connecting to a computer while the window is open, and it changes every time the Windows Remote Assistance is restarted. In April 2020, Microsoft implemented a newer tool called Quick Assist.

48. C. When connecting to a remote Windows host using the Microsoft RDP client, you can save your login credentials in order not to have to enter them each time. You just need to select the Remember Me option in the RDP connection windows. This is done on the General tab. You can select the target remote computer and username and then save the user credentials. The connection settings will be saved to a file. To save your user credentials, follow these steps:

1. Launch Remote Desktop Connection.

2. Click Show Options to extend the option list.

3. Type in your username, check the option Allow Me To Save Credentials, and click the Save As button to save this setting to an RDP file. Then click Connect.

4. When prompted by the Windows Security pop-up, which will ask for your password, enter your credentials and select the checkbox Remember My Credentials.

5. Click OK.

49. C. The first thing that will need to be done is to create a session configuration file. This is done by using the `New-PSSessionConfigurationFile` cmdlet. This cmdlet creates a file of settings that define a session configuration and the environment of sessions. The syntax is `New-PSSessionConfigurationFile -Path .\Defaults.pssc`. The session configuration file that `New-PSSessionConfigurationFile` creates is a text file that contains a hash table of the session configuration properties and values.

50. A. VPN Reconnect uses the Internet Key Exchange v2 (IKEv2) tunneling protocol. VPN Reconnect can be used in combination with DirectAccess. IKEv2 is a VPN encryption protocol that handles request and response actions. VPN Reconnect is automatically built into the IKEv2 protocol.

51. C. A Dynamic Host Configuration Protocol (DHCP) server runs the DHCP service, which assigns the TCP/IP information to computers automatically. All computers need three items to operate with the Internet and an intranet. They need a TCP/IP address, a subnet mask, and a default gateway (router address). DHCP can assign any TCP/IP configuration information, including the address of a DNS server, WINS server, time servers, and so forth. Stateful means that DHCP is going to give IPv6 clients all of their TCP/IP information such as their IP address, the default gateway, and all DHCP options.

52. D. The Remote Access server role is a logical grouping of Remote Access Service (RAS), Routing, and Web Application Proxy (WAP). These are the role services of the Remote Access Server role. When the Remote Access Server role is installed using the Add Roles and Features Wizard or Windows PowerShell, you are able to install one or more of these three role services. Secure Socket Tunneling Protocol Secure Socket Tunneling Protocol (SSTP) works by allowing encapsulated Point-to-Point Protocol (PPP) packets to be transmitted over an HTTPS connection. Because of this, firewalls or Network Address Translation (NAT) devices allow SSTP VPN connections to be more easily established. For securing a VPN connection, SSTP is the best option.

53. A. A Domain Name System (DNS) resolver cache is a temporary database that holds records of all recent visits to websites and other Internet domains. The Internet uses DNS to keep an index of all public websites and their IP addresses. When a user visits a website by using its name, the web browser initiates a request, and the request converts the name to an IP address. Running the `ipconfig` command with the `/flushdns` switch will purge the DNS resolver cache on the machine.

54. C. A VPN connection provides a secure connection to a company's network and the Internet. Before a user can connect to a VPN, they must first have a VPN profile on the computer. A user can either create a VPN profile on their own or set up a work account to obtain the VPN profile from an organization. To create a VPN profile, do the following:

1. Select the Start button and then select Settings ➤ Network & Internet ➤ VPN ➤ Add A VPN connection.

2. In Add A VPN connection, perform the following:

- For the VPN provider, choose Windows (Built-In).

- In the Connection Name box, enter a recognizable name.

- In the Server Name Or Address box, enter the address for the VPN server.

- For the VPN type, choose the type of VPN connection to be created.
- For Type Of Sign-In Info, choose the type of sign-in info (or credentials) to use. This could be a username and password, one-time password, certificate, or smart card if connecting to a corporate VPN. Enter the username and password in the respective boxes (optional).

3. Select Save.

To edit the VPN connection information or to specify additional settings, choose the VPN connection and then select the Advanced options.

55. C. By default, Remote Desktop Connection (RDC) automatically chooses the right experience setting depending upon the network connection between the server and client computers. Using the Experience tab in RDC allows an administrator to establish a number of settings, such as disabling wallpaper, bitmap cache, showing contents of windows while dragging, menu and windows animation, and font smoothing. The administrator can also use the Experience tab to select the connection speed to influence network bandwidth performance.

56. B. A virtual private network (VPN) sits between the internal network and the Internet, accepting connections from clients in the outside world. A VPN is a way to establish a connection between a client machine (VPN client) and server machine (VPN server). It provides the ability to connect (called *tunneling*) to a server through the use of the Internet or a dial-up connection, typically with the intention of accessing resources that are available on the network where the VPN server is connected. The VPN server acts as a bridge for the external user connecting from the Internet or other external connection points to the internal network. In a nutshell, a VPN allows you to connect to a private network from a public network.

57. A. The General tab of the Properties dialog box allows an administrator to specify whether an RRAS server is a router, a Remote Access server, or both. The first step in converting an existing RRAS server to handle VPN traffic is to make sure that the IPv4 Remote Access Server or IPv6 Remote Access Server checkbox is selected on this tab.

58. B. 127.0.0.1 is a special IP address that is reserved for the loopback address and can be used with the ping command to test the local computer. The loopback address allows an administrator to treat the local machine as if it were a remote machine. The loopback address sends outgoing signals back to the same computer for testing. Pinging this address will return a reply unless there is a firewall preventing it.

59. C. Remote Desktop allows you to connect to a computer and take over the session. Remote Assistance requires that a user invite you to the connection. Remote Desktop is a Windows 10 tool that allows you to take control of a remote computer's keyboard, video, and mouse. This tool does not require someone to be available to collaborate with you on the remote computer. While the remote computer is being accessed locally, it remains locked, and any actions that are performed remotely will not be visible to the monitor that is attached to the remote computer. Remote Desktop uses Remote Desktop Protocol (RDP) to provide the data between a host and a client machine. Windows 10 Remote Desktop features include the following:

- Bidirectional audio support.

- Direct 2D and Direct 3D 10.1 application support.

- Multimedia and Media Foundation support.

- RDP Core performance enhancements.

- Remote FX has a few end-user enhancements for RDP. These enhancements allow for an enhanced desktop environment on a corporate network.

- True multimonitor support.

60. A. Using the `ipconfig /all` command-line utility will show the verbose information about a computer's IP configuration, including the computer's physical address, the DNS server being used, and if DHCP is being used. Every computer uses three settings to operate properly with the Internet and an intranet. It needs a TCP/IP address, a subnet mask, and a default gateway.

61. A. If the TCP/IP address on a computer starts with 169.254.x.x and you are not connecting to a DHCP server, this indicates that the Windows 10 machine is using APIPA. Automatic Private IP Addressing (APIPA) is used to assign private IP addresses automatically for home or small business networks that contain a single subnet, have no DHCP server, and are not using static IP addressing. If APIPA is being used, then clients will be able to communicate only with other clients on the same subnet that are also using APIPA. APIPA uses a reserved Class B network address space. The address is the 169.254.0.0 network, where the range of 169.254.0.1–169.254.255.254 is available.

62. C. For the 240 subnet mask, the ranges go by 16. Because this is a Class C subnet mask, the ranges would be 16–31, 32–47, 48–63, 64–79, 80–95, 96–111, 112–127, 128-143, 144–159, 160–175, 176–191, 192–207, 208–223, and 224–239. You must remember that in a Class C address, not all numbers are usable. You need to subtract the first number, which is the network ID, and the last number, which is the broadcast.

63. B. A virtual private network (VPN) is a way to establish a connection between a client computer (VPN client) and server computer (VPN server). A VPN allows you to connect (called *tunneling*) to a server through the use of the Internet, usually with the intention of accessing network resources. The VPN server acts as a bridge for the external user connecting from the Internet to the internal network. So, a VPN allows you to connect to a private network from a public network. Sometimes the simplest solutions are overlooked. The first thing you will want to check is to make sure that the clients can connect to the ISP.

64. B. A subnet mask is a number that defines the range of IP addresses that are available in a network. A single subnet mask limits the number of valid IP addresses for a specific network. A subnet mask hides (or masks) the network part of a system's IP address and leaves only the host part as the machine identifier. It uses the same format as an IPv4 address; four octets of one to three numbers, separated by periods. Each section of the subnet mask can contain a number from 0 to 255. A subnet mask of 255.255.224.0 uses subnet ranges of 32.

Subnet Mask	Number Ranges
225	1
254	2
252	4
248	8
240	16
224	32
192	62
128	128

65. D. Windows 10 has a feature called *transparent caching* that helps to reduce the time needed for retrieving shared files and folders. It reduces the time required to access files. With Windows 10 transparent caching, computers can cache remote files, reducing the number of times a computer retrieves the same data. When a user opens a file for the first time, Windows 10 accesses the file and then stores the file in the cache of the local disk. Then, from that point on, the user reads the same cached file instead of reading it from the remote computer. To ensure that the file is accurate, the Windows 10 client always contacts the remote computer to ensure the cached copy is up-to-date.

66. A. One advantage of Windows 10 and mobility is broadband tethering. Windows 10 broadband tethering allows at least 10 devices to connect to an Internet connection and use the Internet for their access. As long as the devices have broadband-enabled capabilities, they can connect to a computer and use the Internet. When broadband tethering is set up, you can set up a connection name and password for the other users to allow them to connect to a system.

67. A, D. Microsoft uses two networking models: domain-based networks and workgroup networks. HomeGroup networks were removed from Windows 10 (version 1803). Even though it was removed, you still have the ability to share files and printers using features that are built into Windows 10. Workgroup networks are called *peer-to-peer*. A domain-based network uses Microsoft's Active Directory, which is a single distributed database that contains all of the objects in your network. A domain is a logical grouping of objects into a distributed database. These objects include user accounts, group accounts, and published objects (folders and printers).

68. D. Shortcut trusts are trusts that are set up between two domains in the same forest. Shortcut trusts are one-way or two-way transitive trusts that can be used when administrators need to optimize the authentication process. A one-way trust is a unidirectional authentication path that is created between two domains, meaning that in a one-way trust between SiteA and SiteB, users in SiteA can access resources in SiteB, but users in SiteB cannot access resources in SiteA. In a two-way trust, all domain trusts in a Windows forest are two-way, transitive trusts. When a new child domain is created, a two-way, transitive trust is created automatically between the new child and the parent. In a two-way trust, SiteA trusts SiteB, and SiteB trusts SiteA.

69. B. You create Wi-Fi profiles by using Configuration Manager. Configuration Manager is used to deploy wireless network settings to users within an organization. You make it easier for your users to connect to the Wi-Fi by deploying these settings. For example, you have a Wi-Fi network that you'd like enabled on all the Windows laptops, so you create a Wi-Fi profile that contains all of the settings needed to connect to the wireless network. Then the profile will be deployed to all of the users who have Windows laptops. The laptop users will see the network in the list of wireless networks and can then connect to the network. To create a Wi-Fi profile, follow these steps:

1. In the Configuration Manager console, go to the Assets And Compliance workspace, expand Compliance Settings, expand Company Resource Access, and select the Wi-Fi Profiles node.

2. On the Home tab, in the Create group, choose Create Wi-Fi Profile.

3. On the General page of the Create Wi-Fi Profile Wizard, specify information such as name, description, and so forth.

4. On the Wi-Fi Profile page of the wizard, specify information such as network name and SSID.

5. On the Security Configuration page, specify information such as the security type, encryption type, encryption, and so on.

6. On the Advanced Settings page of the wizard, specify additional settings for the Wi-Fi profile.

7. On the Proxy Settings page, if the wireless network uses a proxy server, select the option Configure Proxy Settings For This Wi-Fi Profile. Then provide the configuration information for the proxy.

8. On the Supported Platforms page, select the OS versions where this Wi-Fi profile is applicable.

9. Complete the wizard.

70. A. Administrators have the ability to limit and monitor network usage by configuring the network as a metered network. Network metering allows network downloading to be watched or metered, and then administrators can charge individuals or departments for the network usage. A metered connection is an Internet connection that has a data limit associated with it. Cellular data connections are set as metered by default. By default, Wi-Fi and Ethernet networks are not metered. To set a Wi-Fi network connection as metered, use the following steps:

1. Select Start ➢ Settings ➢ Network & Internet ➢ Wi-Fi ➢ Manage Known Networks.

2. Select the Wi-Fi network, go to Properties, and turn on Set As Metered Connection.

71. B. You need to configure a subnet mask that can accommodate 1,600 clients. The way to figure this out is to use the formula $2^x - 2$ = Mask Number. So, 1,600 clients means it is $2^{11} - 2 = 2,048$. 2,048 is the first power number that is greater than 1,600. So, since it is 2^{11}, that means our subnet mask has 11 zeros. Thus, it looks like the following: 11111111. 11111111.11111000.00000000. This translates to 255.255.248.0.

72. C. Windows 10 Quick Assist allows an administrator to access a Windows 10 computer remotely. This feature gives the administrator full control over the computer. Quick Assist, like Remote Assistance, enables an administrator to receive or provide assistance over a remote connection. To get started, the helper needs to launch the Quick Assist app, obtain a six-digit code, and then share the code with the novice.

To provide assistance using Quick Assist, do the following:

1. Select Start ➤ Windows Accessories ➤ Quick Assist.

2. Select Assist Another Person and then send the six-digit code to that person.

3. Once they've entered the six-digit code, select either Take Full Control or View Screen.

4. Select Continue and wait for the person that you're helping to allow the connection.

To get assistance using Quick Assist, do the following:

1. Select Start ➤ Windows Accessories ➤ Quick Assist.

2. In the Code From Assistant box, enter the six-digit code you were given and select Share Screen.

3. Wait for the helper and then select Allow in the window that is displayed.

73. B. A Remote Desktop Gateway (RD Gateway) enables authorized remote users to connect to resources on an internal corporate or private network from anywhere using the Internet. You can create and manage your gateways using the Remote Desktop client. You will want to deploy Remote Desktop Gateway in the corporate office, and the remote users will then be able to connect to their work computers by using Remote Desktop client on their home computers. The home computers need to be configured with the IP address of the Remote Desktop Gateway.

74. B. The Enable-PSRemoting cmdlet configures a computer to receive Windows PowerShell remote commands. You must be an administrator to enable remote PowerShell commands. After PowerShell is enabled, you can then enter a PowerShell session on the Windows 10 system by using New-PSSession. To exit the PowerShell session when completed, run the Exit-PSSession cmdlet.

75. C. By using Remote Assistance, a user can allow another user to view their computer screen or allow another user to have access to their computer in order to move the mouse cursor on the screen and enter commands into their computer. To establish a Remote Assistance session using the command prompt, the novice should open the Windows Remote Assistance screen by entering **msra.exe**.

76. D. In this example, you have a router that is using a Class C IP address of 192.168.1.1. The first three octets are the network ID, so you are on the 192.168.1 network. Valid IP addresses must start with this network ID, so 192.168.0.1 and 192.168.100.1 are not correct as they are not on the same network. Both 192.168.1.1 and 192.168.1.100 are on the correct network; however, the IP address of 192.168.1.1 is already being used by our router. So, 192.168.1.100 is the only valid IP address that can be used for the network adapter.

77. C. Network Discovery is a setting that determines whether a Windows 10 computer can locate other computers and devices on the network and whether those other computers can see your computer. This feature is usually automatically turned on when connected to a private network. On Windows 10, to keep a device more secure, you can configure different network profiles depending on the network environment. To enable or disable Network Discovery, follow these steps:

1. Select Start ➤ Windows System ➤ Control Panel.

2. Choose Network And Sharing Center and then Change Advanced Sharing Settings.

3. Click Turn On/Turn Off Network Discovery and then click the Save Changes button.

78. C. Packet Internet Groper (ping) is a diagnostic tool that tests the connection between two nodes or devices across a network. It verifies whether a network data packet is able to be distributed to an address without errors. You can ping your own computer using the loopback address, also known as the *local loopback*. Every Windows computer gets this address automatically; it's 127.0.0.1. You can either enter **ping localhost** or enter **ping 127.0.0.1**.

79. C. Before you can connect a Windows 10 machine to the domain, you must set up the network interface card (NIC). The NIC is a hardware component that is used to connect computers or other devices to the network to allow the machine to communicate on the network. NICs are responsible for providing the physical connection that recognizes the physical address (MAC address) of the device.

80. B. A network adapter, also called a *network interface card* (NIC), is a hardware component that is used to connect computers or other devices to the network to allow the machine to communicate. NICs are responsible for providing the physical connection that recognizes the physical address (MAC address) of the device. The Details tab of the network adapter's properties dialog box lists the resource settings for a network adapter. Information found on the Details tab will vary depending upon the hardware device.

81. A. Every NIC card has a hardware address known as a Media Access Control (MAC) address associated with it. The MAC address is assigned to a network adapter when it's manufactured. The Address Resolution Protocol (ARP) is a communication protocol that is used to discover the link layer address, such as a MAC address. Using arp with the -a switch will display all of the MAC addresses of recently resolved IP addresses.

82. A. In networking, a bridge joins two networks together so that they can communicate with each other. A wireless bridge is used to connect a wireless network to an Ethernet network. The wireless standards supported for the wireless bridge are usually 802.11n, 802.11g, or 802.11a/b/g. You should make sure that the wireless bridge can support the wireless standard of your existing wireless network.

83. B, C. If a network adapter is not functioning properly, there are a number of things that could be causing the issue. It could be an issue with the hardware, the driver software, or the network protocols. If the network adapter has outdated drivers, make sure you have the most current drivers. Windows 10 can check for an updated driver using the Driver tab of the Properties dialog box for the adapter. You just need to click the Update Driver button. If the network adapter is not recognized by Windows, you can use Device Manager to see whether Windows 10 recognizes the adapter. If you don't see the adapter, then you can try to install it manually.

84. A. Windows 10 includes a feature called Hosted Network that allows you to turn a computer into a wireless hotspot. Whether you're connecting to the Internet using a wireless or wired adapter, Windows 10 allows you to share your Internet connection with other devices. Hosted Network is a feature that included the Network Shell (Netsh) command-line utility, which allows you to use the operating system to create a virtual wireless adapter.

85. A. Most routers and other wireless access points (APs) communicate their network name (SSID) automatically every few seconds. SSID broadcasting makes it so that wireless users can see and connect to the network. In this question, you want to make the WLAN more secure, so you should disable SSID broadcasting. When SSID broadcast is disabled, the wireless network cannot be automatically detected until the wireless network it is manually configured to connect.

86. D. Virtualization creates a virtual computing environment rather than a physical environment. Virtualization can include computer-generated versions of hardware, operating systems, storage devices, and more. Virtualization allows an administrator to partition a single physical computer or server into several virtual machines. Each virtual machine can then interact separately and run different operating systems or applications while sharing the resources of a single host machine. Windows 10 Professional and Enterprise come with Hyper-V and all the needed software to run a virtual machine inside Windows. Virtual machines allow you to run an operating system in an app window on a desktop that acts like a full, separate computer. The virtual machine runs as a process in a window on the current operating system.

87. A. IP addresses are divided into classes, called Class A, Class B, and Class C. Class D and Class E exist as well, but they are not used by end users. Each of the address classes has a different default subnet mask. You can identify the class by looking at the octets of the subnet mask.

- *Class A*: Uses the first octet and has a default subnet mask of 255.0.0.0
- *Class B*: Uses the first two octets and has a default subnet mask of 255.255.0.0
- *Class C*: Uses the first three octets and has a default subnet mask of 255.255.255.0

Because the subnet mask is using only the first octet, this is a Class A subnet mask.

88. D. IP addresses are divided into classes, called Class A, Class B, and Class C. Class D and Class E exist as well, but they are not used by end users. You can identify the class of an IP address by looking at the first octet.

- *Class A*: Uses a default subnet mask of 255.0.0.0 and has 1–126 as the first octet

- *Class B*: Uses a default subnet mask of 255.255.0.0 and has 128–191 as the first octet

- *Class C*: Uses a default subnet mask of 255.255.255.0 and has 192–223 as the first octet

For this question, you want to use a Class A IP address. Class A addresses range from 1–126. The only IP address that qualifies as a Class A address would be 10.0.0.0 since the first octet falls within the Class A range.

89. D. Remote Desktop is a tool in Windows 10 that allows you to take control of a remote computer's keyboard, video, and mouse. This tool does not require a user to be available to collaborate with you on the remote machine. While accessing the remote computer locally, it remains locked, and any actions that are conducted remotely will not be visible on the monitor that is attached to the remote machine.

90. B. PowerShell Remoting lets an administrator run PowerShell commands or access PowerShell sessions on remote Windows systems. To start an interactive session with a single remote computer, use the `Enter-PSSession` cmdlet. The syntax is `Enter-PSSession <remote computername>`. The command prompt changes to display the name of the remote computer. Any commands entered at the prompt will run on the remote computer, and the results will be displayed on the local computer. To end the interactive session, type **Exit-PSSession**.

91. D. IPv6 link-local and site-local addresses are called *scoped addresses* and use the `fe80::/10` prefix. If you look at the `ipconfig` command, you will see a link-local IPv6 address as `fe80::a425:ab9d:7da4:ccba`. The last 8 bytes (64 bits) are random. The link-local address is to be used on a network segment, and it will never be routed.

92. C. The `ipconfig` results are showing that this is a Class A address that is being used as a Class C network. On a Class C network, you *cannot* use the first or last numbers in the IP range (0 and 255). The first number of any range represents the network ID. The last number of any range represents the broadcast ID (255). So, having the default gateway set as .255 is not correct. The highest number on a Class C network that can be issued to a device is 254.

93. C. The `ipconfig` results are showing that this is a Class A address that is being used as a Class C network. So, the first three octets are currently on the 10.254.254.0 network. The IP address for the DNS server is showing as 10.255.254.1, so they are not on the same network. In this case, the second octet of the DNS server will need to be changed from 255 to 254, and then it will work correctly.

94. A. Internet Protocol Security (IPsec) is a secure network protocol suite that encrypts and authenticates data packets to provide secure encrypted communication between two computers over an Internet Protocol (IP) network. IPsec is used in virtual private networks (VPNs). Layer 2 Tunneling Protocol (L2TP) is a tunneling protocol that has no encryption included. L2TP uses IPsec to make L2TP secure.

95. D. Packet Internet Groper (ping) is a diagnostic tool that tests the connection between two nodes or devices across a network. It verifies whether a network data packet is able to be distributed to an address without errors. You can ping your own computer using the loopback address, also known as the *local loopback*. Every Windows computer gets this address automatically; it's 127.0.0.1. You can either type **ping localhost** or type **ping 127.0.0.1**. The loopback address is used as a way of testing the functionality of a network adapter. The results in this question have failed, and the packets are being lost.

96. B. Network prefixes are determined directly from the subnet mask of the network. A ClassxB subnet mask would be 255.255.0.0. To determine the network prefix on a Class B subnet, you would need to convert each octet of the subnet mask to a binary value. So, for Class B it would be 11111111.11111111.00000000.00000000. Count the consecutive 1s to determine the prefix. So, the answer would be /16.

97. A. First turn both numbers into their binary equivalents and line them up. Then perform the AND operation on each bit and write down the result.

10000001 00111000 10111101 00101001 IP Address
11111111 11111111 11110000 00000000 Subnet Mask
10000001 00111000 10110000 00000000 Network ID

The result of the bit-wise logical AND of the 32 bits of the IP address and the subnet mask is the network ID 129.56.176.0.

98. D. To calculate the network mask, you need to figure out which power number (2x) is greater than or equal to the number you need. Since you are looking for 1000, 210 = 1024. You then add the power (10) to the current network mask (53 + 10 = 63).

99. B. The Domain Name System (DNS) turns a hostname into an IP address so that you can connect to a machine by the machine name. If you can connect to a machine by using the TCP/IP address but not the name, then DNS is the issue. DNS is a name-resolution service that resolves a hostname to a TCP/IP address. DNS also has the ability to resolve a TCP/IP address to a name. In this question, the DNS server in the ping results is listed as 127.0.0.1. This is the loopback diagnostic address, and it cannot be used for IP configuring.

100. C. Network prefixes are determined directly from the subnet mask of the network. A Class C subnet mask would be 255.255.255.0. To determine the network prefix on a Class C subnet, you would need to convert each octet of the subnet mask to a binary value. So, for a Class C subnet, it would be 11111111.11111111.11111111.00000000. Count the consecutive 1s to determine the prefix. So, the answer would be /24.

101. D. Tracert is a diagnostic utility that determines the route to a destination by sending Internet Control Message Protocol (ICMP) echo packets to the destination. In these packets, tracert uses varying IP time-to-live (TTL) values. You can use tracert to find out where a packet has stopped on a network.

102. B. The CIDR /28 tells you that 28 1s are turned on in the subnet mask. Twenty-eight 1s equals 11111111.11111111.11111111.11110000. This would then equal 255.255.255.240.

103. C. Remote Desktop Connection (RDC) allows a local computer to connect to and control a remote computer over a network or the Internet. From the Local Resources tab, you can configure remote audio settings, keyboard settings, and local device and resource access. The options include Remote Audio, the Apply Windows Key Combinations drop-down list, and Local Devices And Resources.

104. C. A Class B address with a default subnet mask of 255.255.0.0 will support up to 65,534 hosts. To increase the number of networks that this network will support, you need to subnet the network by borrowing bits from the host portion of the address. The subnet mask 255.255.252.0 uses 6 bits from the host's area, and it will support 64 subnets, while leaving enough bits to support 1,022 hosts per subnet. The subnet mask 255.255.248.0 uses 5 bits from the hosts and will support 32 subnetworks, while leaving enough bits to support 2,046 hosts per subnet. 255.255.252.0 is the better answer because it leaves quite a bit of room for further growth in the number of networks while still leaving room for more than 1,000 hosts per subnet, which is a fairly large number of devices on one subnet. The subnet mask 255.255.254.0 uses 7 bits from the host's area and will support 126 networks, but it will leave only enough bits to support 500 hosts per subnet. The subnet mask 255.255.240.0 uses 4 bits from the hosts and will support only 16 subnetworks, even though it will leave enough bits to support more than 4,000 hosts per subnet.

105. A. When you look at an IPv6 address, the first sections tell you the IPv6 address space prefix. fd00:: /8 is the unique local unicast prefix, and this allows the server to communicate with all local machines within your intranet.

Chapter 4: Maintain Windows

1. A. Windows Update is a tool that connects to the Microsoft website or to a local update server called a Windows Server Update Services (WSUS) server. This will ensure that the Windows 10 operating system and other Microsoft products have the most up-to-date version running. By modifying the changes on the Local Group Policy, an administrator can manually configure the Windows Update settings. You can configure the Windows Update settings by creating a Group Policy Object (GPO).

2. B. The Windows 10 Advanced Boot Options are used to troubleshoot any errors that may prevent Windows 10 from booting successfully. To access the Windows 10 Advanced Boot Options, hold the Shift key down and click the Restart option from either the login screen or the Start menu.

3. A. On Windows 10, Performance Monitor is used to analyze data, such as hard drive, memory, processor, and network usage. Since you'd like to collect data about the processor utilization, you need to monitor the Process performance object. Performance Monitor is used for viewing real-time statistics. By default, only one counter is selected: the %Processor Time counter. There are several ways to open Performance Monitor.

- Open Start and search for *Performance Monitor.* Then click the result.

- Use the Windows key+R keyboard shortcut to open the Run command, type **perfmon**, and click OK.

- Use the Windows key+X keyboard shortcut to open the Power User menu, select Computer Management, and click Performance.

The Add Counters window of Performance Monitor shows the counters and options that are available for a process. The list on the left shows all of the available counters for a process that can be selected. The list on the right shows all of the instances of a process object that can be selected for monitoring.

4. D. There are several ways to repair system files on Windows 10. You can use the installation disc and choose Repair during the installation, or you can boot to the advanced options and select Repair Your Computer. The Last Known Good Configuration is not available in Windows 10. When you need to restore an image, you will use the System Image Recovery tool. To restore an image using this tool, perform the following steps:

1. Boot the computer using the Windows 10 media or using the recovery partition instructions provided by the manufacturer of the computer.

2. When the Install Windows dialog box appears, select the language, the time and currency format, and the keyboard or input method. Click Next to continue.

3. The Install Now button appears in the center of the screen. Click Repair Your Computer.

4. This opens the Windows Recovery Environment (WinRE). You can choose the Troubleshoot option and then choose Advanced Options.

5. The Advanced Options dialog box appears. Choose one of the following options:

   - System Restore
   - Startup Repair
   - Go Back To The Previous Version
   - Command Prompt
   - System Image Recovery
   - UEFI Firmware Settings (if applicable)

   Choose System Image Recovery to continue.

6. Select the user account that has administrative privileges and then enter the password for that user account.

7. The Re-image Your Computer wizard will appear and the Use The Latest Available System Image (Recommended) option will be selected by default. Click Next to continue.

8. If you want to select a different image, choose Select A System Image and then click Next and follow the prompts.

9. You will get a dialog box where you can choose additional restore options, such as installing drivers and formatting and repartitioning disks, as well as choosing if the system will automatically install updates and reboot. Click Next.

10. Review the selections and then click Finish to continue.

11. You will see a warning that all the data on the drive is to be replaced. Choose Yes to continue.

5. D. Safe Mode loads the minimum number of drivers and services needed to boot Windows 10. If a computer can be booted into Safe Mode, you can temporarily disable an application or processes, troubleshoot services, or uninstall software. When running a computer in Safe Mode on Windows 10, you are streamlining the Windows configuration as much as possible. By starting the computer in Safe Mode, it will load only the basic video drivers and will allow you to fix any video issues, including using the Driver Rollback utility.

6. A. Corrupted or misconfigured files, hard drive and upgrade issues, and corrupt sectors in the hard drive are some of the reasons for a BOOTMGR error. The `bootrec.exe` utility is a tool in the Windows Recovery Environment (Windows RE). By using the `bootrec /RebuildBcd` command, it will scan the computer for installations on the hard drive and allow you to select which to add to the BCD. Use the `bootrec.exe` tool to troubleshoot a "Bootmgr Is Missing" error. If rebuilding the BCD store doesn't fix the startup issue, export and delete the BCD store and then run this option again. By doing this, you make sure that the BCD store is completely rebuilt.

7. A. BranchCache reduces WAN link utilization and improves how an application responds for branch office users who need to access content from servers at a remote location. To reduce traffic over a WAN link, the computers at the branch office use a locally maintained cache of data. The cache can be distributed across client computers in a Distributed Cache mode, or it can be stored on a server in the branch, called Hosted Cache mode. In Hosted Cache mode, designated servers at specific locations act as a cache for files requested by clients. Then the hosted cache server provides the content rather than the client recovering files from the main office machines.

8. B. Windows 10 includes a full backup and restore application called Backup and Restore (Windows 7) that allows a user or an administrator to keep a backup copy of any of the Windows 10 component files and data files that are critical to the day-to-day operations. The Backup and Restore utility is used to safeguard your computer. The Backup and Restore (Windows 7) utility is used to restore personal files from backup media and to restore an image of your computer. Images allow you to back up and restore your entire Windows 10 machine.

9. B. You should use the Driver Rollback utility. If a driver is installed that causes issues on a computer, you can use this tool to return the driver to its previous version. To access the Driver Rollback utility, use Device Manager. Right-click the component that is causing issues and choose Properties. Then click the Driver tab and the Roll Back Driver button (Driver Rollback).

10. D. Because BitLocker is enabled on the computer, you need to unlock the encrypted drive by using the `manage-bde` with the `-unlock` parameter. `manage-bde` is used to turn BitLocker on or off. This command-line tool can be used in lieu of the BitLocker Drive Encryption Control Panel item. Using the `-unlock` parameter allows access to BitLocker-protected data with a recovery password or a recovery key.

11. A. The Windows 10 Backup and Restore utility enables you to create and restore backups. The Backup and Restore (Windows 7) utility is used to restore personal files from backup media and to restore a complete image of your computer. Backups protect data in the event of system failure by storing the data on another medium. If the original data is lost due to corruption, deletion, or media failure, you can restore the data by using a backup. If you want to back up and restore a Windows 10 machine, you will need to use the Windows 10 Backup and Restore Center.

12. B. Reliability Monitor is part of the Windows Reliability and Performance Monitor snap-in for Microsoft Management Console (MMC). One way to access the Reliability Monitor is to type **perfmon /rel** in the Start Search box and press Enter. The Reliability Monitor provides a system stability overview, and it allows an administrator to get details about events that may be affecting reliability. The Reliability Monitor shows information about application failures, Windows failures, miscellaneous failures, warnings, and information. It shows an administrator a certain period of time on a Windows 10 system, and an administrator can click any of the events during that specific period of time and see what information, warnings, or errors may have happened during that time period.

13. C. The Performance Monitor is a Windows 10 utility for monitoring computer performance in real time or from a log. It collects data from a local computer or remote Windows 10 machine. Data can be collected from a single computer or from multiple computers at the same time. It allows you to view data collected in real time or historically from collected data.

14. A. Windows Recovery Environment (WinRE) can repair common causes of operating systems that don't boot properly. WinRE is based on Windows Preinstallation Environment (Windows PE) and can be customized with additional drivers, languages, Windows PE Optional Components, and other troubleshooting and diagnostic tools. By default, WinRE is preloaded onto Windows 10 Home, Professional, Enterprise, and Education desktop edition installations. Users can access WinRE using the Boot Options menu. This menu can be launched from Windows in several ways.

- From the login screen, click Shutdown and then hold down the Shift key while selecting Restart.

- In Windows 10, select Start ➢ Settings ➢ Update & Security ➢ Recovery, and under Advanced Startup, click Restart now.

- Boot to recovery media.

15. B. Typically, if you delete a file or folder in OneDrive, you may be able to recover it by using the OneDrive Recycle Bin. However, this question states that the files were deleted two months ago. When you're signed into OneDrive with a Microsoft account, items in the Recycle Bin are automatically deleted after 30 days. So, in this case, to recover the deleted files, you will need to use the full backup from the external USB drive.

16. C, E. Administrators use event collection to get events from remote computers and store them in a local event log on the collector computer. You can subscribe to receive events on a local computer (the event collector) that are forwarded from remote computers (the event sources) by using a collector-initiated subscription. In a collector-initiated subscription, the subscription has to contain a list of all of the event sources. Before a collector computer can subscribe to events and a remote event source can forward events, both computers must be configured for event collection and forwarding. So, on the Windows 10 computers, you would want to add Computer1 to the Event Log Readers group, and also on the Windows 10 computers, you would want to enable Windows Remote Management (WinRM).

17. B. A metered connection is an Internet connection that has a data limit associated with it. Cellular data connections are set as metered by default. If enabled, Windows updates won't be installed. A metered connection is available on all Windows 10 editions. To set a Wi-Fi network connection as metered, follow these steps:

1. Select Start ➤ Settings ➤ Network & Internet ➤ Wi-Fi ➤ Manage Known Networks.

2. Select the Wi-Fi network, go to Properties, and turn on Set As Metered Connection.

18. C. Device Manager in Windows 10 allows you to see which devices are connected to a machine. Device Manager can be used to ensure that all devices are working correctly and to troubleshoot devices. Using Device Manager, an administrator can configure devices such as disk drives, display adapters, DVD/CD-ROM drives, monitors, and network adapters. To obtain the latest drivers for any hardware, you need to use the Upgrade Drivers button in Device Manager. After the upgrade button is selected, you can use either downloaded drivers or drivers from a DVD. To view devices using Device Manager, do the following:

1. Click Start ➤ Windows System ➤ Control Panel ➤ Device Manager.

2. Click the triangle next to Network Adapters (or double-click Network Adapters) to expand Network Adapters.

19. C. A system image is an exact copy of the Windows 10 drive. By default, system images include the drives that are needed for Windows to work properly. They include Windows and all of the system settings, programs, and files. In the event of a major hard disk or computer crash, system images can restore all of the contents of the crashed system and get the machine running again. An entire system can be restored using system images.

20. A. File History allows a user to save copies of their files so that in the event of a file being damaged or lost, it can be restored. In the File History settings, you can restore personal files, select particular drives, exclude folders, or set advanced settings. By default, File History is set to back up important folders in the user's home folder. These folders include Desktop, Documents, Downloads, Music, Pictures, and Videos. Placing your folder, D:\MyFolder, in the Documents folder will ensure that the folder is copied since it is in the Documents folder and is copied by default.

21. C. The Microsoft Windows Performance Monitor is a tool that administrators can use to examine how programs running on their computers affect the computer's performance. The tool can be used in real time and can also be used to collect information in a log to analyze the data at a later time. With Performance Monitor, you can set up counter logs and alerts. All performance statistics fall into three main categories that you can measure: performance objects, counters, and instances.

22. C. There are several methods used to uninstall an update. Updates can be removed using the command-line tool called Windows Update Standalone Installer, or wusa.exe. Using this command with the /uninstall switch will uninstall the specified package or KB number. The syntax is wusa /uninstall /kb:[id].

23. B. File History allows a user to save copies of their files so that in the event of a file being damaged or lost, it can be restored. In the File History settings, you can restore personal files, select particular drives, exclude folders, or set advanced settings. By default, File History is set to back up important folders in the user's home folder. These folders include Desktop, Documents, Downloads, Music, Pictures, and Videos folders. Placing your folder, C:\MyFolder, in the Documents folder will ensure that the folder is copied. When you click any folder and choose Properties, the last tab to the right is the Previous Versions tab. You can easily restore any folder by choosing one of these previous versions.

24. C. Driver rollback allows you to replace a newly installed driver with the previous driver. This can be done using driver rollback in the Device Manager utility. To get a stalled computer up and running as quickly as possible, you should first start with the Driver Rollback option. If a driver is installed that causes issues on a computer, use this tool to return the driver to its previous version. To access the Driver Rollback utility, use Device Manager. Right-click the component that is causing the issue and choose Properties. Then click the Driver tab and the Roll Back Driver button (Driver Rollback).

25. A, B, D. Performance Monitor is a Windows 10 utility for monitoring computer performance in real time or from a log. It collects data from a local computer or remote Windows 10 machine. Data can be collected from a single computer or multiple computers at the same time. It allows you to view data collected in real time or historically from collected data. Performance objects, counters, and instances may be displayed in each of three views: Graph View, Histogram View, and Report View.

26. A, D. Windows Update is a utility that connects to the Microsoft website or to a local update server called a Windows Server Update Services (WSUS) server to ensure that the Windows 10 operating systems and other Microsoft products are up-to-date. WSUS provides a single location for Windows updates within a company. When using WSUS to manage updates on Windows client devices, start by configuring the Configure Automatic Updates and Intranet Microsoft Update Service Location Group Policy settings for the environment. Using these settings forces the clients to contact the WSUS server so that it can manage them.

27. D. System Protection creates and saves information about drivers, programs, system files, and settings. Windows will create restore points automatically. If you need to disable previous versions on the D: volume, this needs to be done from the System Protection settings in the computer system properties. Perform the following to turn off System Protection:

1. Type Control Panel in the search box.

2. Navigate to Control Panel ➢ System ➢ System Protection.

3. Highlight the drive on which you want to turn System Protection off and click Configure.

    4. Select Turn Off System Protection.

    5. Click Apply and then OK.

28. C. The Windows Insider Program allows you to preview builds of Windows 10 and Windows Server 2019. It allows you to try new features and provide feedback directly to Microsoft. On the Windows 10 computer, go to Settings ➤ Update & Security ➤ Windows Insider Program. You will need to have administrator rights to the computer.

29. D. To generate a log file that contains detailed information regarding update failures, run the `Get-WindowsUpdateLog` cmdlet. This cmdlet merges and converts Windows Update `.etl` files into a single readable `WindowsUpdate.log` file. Windows Update Agent uses Event Tracing for Windows (ETW) to generate diagnostic logs.

30. B. In Windows 10, Windows Hello for Business replaces passwords with strong two-factor authentication on computers and mobile devices. This consists of a new type of user credential that is linked to the device and uses a biometric or PIN. As an administrator in an enterprise organization, you can create policies to manage Windows Hello for Business that are used on the Windows 10–based devices that connect to the network. In this question, you are connecting the new computer to an Azure AD, so the machine would need to be upgraded to Windows 10 Enterprise.

31. A. File History allows a user to save copies of their files so that in the event of a file being damaged or lost, it can be restored. In the File History settings, you can restore personal files, select particular drives, exclude folders, or set advanced settings. By default, File History is set to back up important folders in the user's home folder. These folders include Desktop, Documents, Downloads, Music, Pictures, and Videos. Adding your folder, `D:\ Photos`, to the Pictures folder will ensure that the folder is copied since it is in the Pictures folder and thus is copied by default.

32. A, B, C, D. The answer to this question is all of them. Restore points allow you to bring a system back to a previous point in time, and they should be created at all of the times listed. Restore points are snapshots of the Windows 10 system that can be used to revert to other snapshots. Restore points contain Registry and system information as it existed at a certain point in time. Restore points are created at the following times:

- Before installing applications or drivers
- Before significant system events
- Before System Restore is used to restore files in the event that the changes need to be undone
- Manually upon request
- Weekly

Restore points are created before most significant events, such as installing a new driver. They are also created automatically every seven days. To create a restore point manually, do the following:

    1. Select Start ➤ Windows System ➤ Control Panel ➤ System ➤ System Protection.

    2. Click the Create button on the bottom of the screen.

> **3.** At the System Protection dialog box, enter a description for the restore point. Click Create.
>
> **4.** A dialog box states that the restore point was created. Click Close.

33. B. Windows Update is a utility that connects to the Microsoft website or to a local update server called a Windows Server Update Services (WSUS) server to ensure that the Windows 10 operating system and Microsoft products have the most current versions of Microsoft operating system files or software. In Windows 10 Windows Update, there is the option Check Online For Updates From Microsoft Update. The option can be used when newer updates exist and the WSUS administrator hasn't approved them yet.

34. C. Restore points are snapshots of the Windows 10 system that can be used to revert to other snapshots. Restore points contain Registry and system information as it existed at a certain point in time. Restore points are created before most significant events, such as installing a new driver. Restore points are created automatically every seven days.

35. A. The Windows 10 Backup and Restore utility enables you to create and restore backups. Backups protect data in the event of a system failure by storing the data on another medium. To back up files, follow these steps:

> **1.** Select Start ➤ Windows System ➤ Control Panel ➤ Backup And Restore (Windows 7).
>
> **2.** Click the Back Up Now button.
>
> **3.** Select the location where you want to save the backup and then click Next.
>
> **4.** When the What Do You Want To Back Up? screen appears, click the Let Me Choose radio button and then click Next.
>
> **5.** Select the files to back up and click Next.
>
> **6.** At the Review Your Backup Settings screen, select how often you want a backup to be performed automatically.
>
> **7.** To start the backup, click the Save Settings And Run Backup button. Windows begins backing up files, and a progress bar indicates how the backup is progressing.
>
> **8.** When the backup is complete, click Close.

So, for this question, the answer is that the Back Up Now button allows you to start a backup and configure a Windows 10 backup.

36. D. One of the easiest ways to restore an accidentally deleted file or folder is to check the Recycle Bin. When you choose the Delete option in Windows, your files are automatically moved to the Recycle Bin. The Recycle Bin has a limited amount of storage, and it will temporarily keep the files there. To restore files from the Recycle Bin, perform the following:

> **1.** Open the Recycle Bin.
>
> **2.** When Recycle Bin opens, you'll see all deleted files. If the file is available, right-click it and choose Restore.

37. B. System Protection is a feature of Windows 10 that creates a backup and saves the configuration information of a computer's system files and settings. System Protection saves multiple previous versions of saved configurations rather than just overwriting them. These are called *restore points*. You manage System Protection and the restore points using the System Protection tab of the System Properties dialog box. You can also access this tab directly by entering **restore point** into the Windows 10 search box or by clicking the Recovery icon in Control Panel.

38. A. Windows To Go provides an administrator or user with the ability to provision Windows 10 onto an external USB drive. You can then use the USB drive (also called a Windows To Go workspace) to load a complete and managed Windows 10 system image onto a managed or unmanaged Windows 10 host computer to boot and run the Windows 10 operating system. In this case, the error message received indicates that the bootable media was not created properly, and you will need to reapply the Windows To Go image onto the USB memory drive.

39. C. Windows indexing services is a process of automatically scanning and storing files to create a database. You can disable the Windows indexing services temporarily by pausing it by clicking the paused option in indexing options. However, there is no resume button if you want to resume it. So, to resume indexing services, you need to either restart the computer or restart the Windows Search service. To restart the service, go to Control Panel ➢ Administrative Tools ➢ Services ➢ Windows Search ➢ Restart Service.

40. B. Windows 10 Performance Monitor is designed to allow users and system administrators to monitor performance statistics for various operating system parameters. You can collect, store, and analyze information about items such as CPU, memory, disk, and network resources. By collecting and analyzing performance values, this allows an administrator to identify potential issues. To access the Performance Monitor MMC, open Administrative Tools and then choose Performance Monitor. To receive alerts about events that you predefine, you will want to use Subscriptions. In the Subscription Properties dialog box, an administrator can define what type of events that they want notifications about and the notification method. The Subscriptions section is an advanced alerting service to help watch for events.

41. A, B. The Windows Event Viewer shows a log of application and system messages. It also includes errors, informational messages, and warnings. It is a handy tool for troubleshooting. The security event log records events that have been defined by the audit policies that have been set on each object. Security logging is off by default, but when enabled, this log records events related to security events, such as logon attempts and resource access. Only members of the Administrators group and the Event Log Readers can view the security log in Event Viewer. To view the security event log, follow these steps:

1. Open Event Viewer.

2. In the console tree, expand Windows Logs and then click Security. The results pane lists the individual security events.

3. For more detailed information regarding a specific event, in the results pane, click the event and read the information provided.

42. A, B, C, D, E. The Windows Event Viewer shows a log of application and system messages. It also includes errors, informational messages, and warnings. It is a handy tool for troubleshooting. The System event log records events related to programs installed on the system. All of the users listed in the question can view the system event log of a computer in Event Viewer. To view the system event log, follow these steps:

1. Open Event Viewer.

2. In the console tree, expand Windows Logs and then click System. The results pane lists individual system events.

3. For more detailed information regarding a specific event, in the results pane, click the event and read the information provided.

43. A. File History allows a user to save copies of their files so that in the event of a file being damaged or lost, it can be restored. In the File History settings, you can restore personal files, select particular drives, exclude folders, or set advanced settings. You can also add other folders and drives. File History is designed to be a quick and convenient way to back up folders. To add a new folder to use File History, do the following:

1. From the Start menu, open the Settings app from the Start menu and then navigate to Update & Security ➤ Backup.

2. Click the Add A Drive Option under Back Up Using File History.

3. Select a drive. The Automatically Back Up My Files option will appear and be turned on. Windows will automatically back up the files to the drive.

44. A. To allow the users to utilize the Event Viewer on Computer1 to view the event logs on Computer2 remotely, you need to modify the Windows Firewall settings on Computer2. You want to enable the Remote Event Log Management exception in the Windows Firewall Settings on the remote computer. To access the Event Log on a remote computer, enable the rules in the Windows Firewall With Advanced Security console by going to the Start button and selecting Windows System ➤ Control Panel ➤ System And Security ➤ Windows Defender Firewall. Click the Advanced Settings link on the left side and enable all of the rules in the Remote Event Log Management group.

45. C. Device Manager shows all the installed hardware on a machine. It also keeps information regarding storage, both removable and fixed, and communication devices such as network interface cards and wireless and Bluetooth devices. In this case, the fastest way to be able to access the network resources again is by returning the driver to the previous version by using the Roll Back Driver option. If a driver is installed that causes issues on a computer, use this tool to return the driver to its previous version. To access the Driver Rollback utility, use Device Manager. Right-click the component that is causing issues and choose Properties. Then click the Driver tab and the Roll Back Driver button (Driver Rollback).

46. B. Reliability Monitor is part of the Windows Reliability and Performance Monitor snap-in for Microsoft Management Console (MMC). One way to access the Reliability Monitor is to type **perfmon /rel** in the Start Search box and press Enter. This tool provides a system stability overview and allows an administrator to get details about events that may be affecting reliability. It shows information regarding application failures, Windows failures, miscellaneous failures, warnings, and information. It also shows an administrator a certain period of time on a Windows 10 system, and they can click any of the events during that specific period of time and see what information, warnings, or errors may have occurred during that time period.

47. A. Windows 10 Task Manager provides a quick overview of important system performance statistics without requiring any configuration. There are several ways to access Task Manager, including the following:

- Right-click the Windows Taskbar and then click Task Manager.
- Press Ctrl+Alt+Del and then select Task Manager.
- Press Ctrl+Shift+Esc.
- Type **Taskman** in the Windows search box.

All of the applications that are running on the Windows 10 machine will appear on the Details tab. Using this tab allows you to stop an application from running by right-clicking the application and then choosing Stop.

48. C. By default, Microsoft's OneDrive is built into Windows 10. OneDrive is a cloud-based storage subscription service designed so that users can store their documents and then, by using the Internet, access those documents from anywhere in the world. You cannot recover corrupted files directly from Windows 10. You can recover files and folders by clicking File Explorer and then choosing OneDrive from the left side. Files saved to OneDrive are available online at OneDrive.com and offline on your computer. This question states that the file located on the computer has become corrupt. The best way to recover this file is by using OneDrive online.

49. D. Using an elevated command prompt, administrators have the ability to configure and manage backups and restores using a utility called wbadmin. Wbadmin allows you to back up and restore your operating system, volumes, files, folders, and applications. You must be a member of the Administrators group to configure a regularly scheduled backup. To perform other tasks, you must be a member of either the Backup Operators group or the Administrators group or have been given the appropriate permissions.

50. B. By default, Microsoft's OneDrive is built into Windows 10. OneDrive is a cloud-based storage subscription service designed so that users can store their documents and then, by using the Internet, access those documents from anywhere in the world. You cannot recover corrupted files directly from Windows 10. You can recover files and folders by clicking File Explorer and then choosing OneDrive from the left side. Files saved to OneDrive are available online at OneDrive.com and offline on your computer. The best way to recover these deleted files is by restoring the files from the OneDrive for Business Recycle Bin. To restore deleted files in OneDrive for Business, perform the following:

1. Sign into your OneDrive for Business account.

2. Navigate to the Recycle Bin in the navigation pane.

3. Identify the files or folders to be restored, click the radio button, and click Restore. *Note*: The option Restore All Items is not available in OneDrive for Business.

51. D. Since this application won't uninstall, the best option is to take the computer back to an earlier point in time. This is called a *system restore point*. Restore points are created whenever you install a new app or driver, or they have been created manually. Restoring from a restore point will not affect your personal files, but it will remove apps, drivers, and updates installed after the restore point was made. To restore from a System Restore point, perform the following steps:

1. Open the Control Panel, and in the search box, type **recovery**.

2. Select Recovery ➢ Open System Restore.

3. In the Restore System Files And Settings box, select Next.

4. Select the restore point that you want to use from the list of results and then select Scan For Affected Programs.

5. You will see a list of items that will be deleted. If you are OK with the deletions, select Close ➢ Next ➢ Finish.

52. C. Windows 10 includes Microsoft OneDrive with the operating system. It is a cloud-based storage system where corporate users or home users can store their data on the cloud. Microsoft OneDrive allows users to use up to 5 GB of cloud storage for free without a subscription. A user can use File History to save copies of their files so that they can get them back in the event of a file being damaged or lost. A user can restore personal files, select drives, exclude folders, and even set advanced settings.

53. C. Event Viewer is a useful tool for monitoring network information. You can use the logs to view any information, warnings, or alerts related to the functionality of the network. You can access Event Viewer by selecting Windows Administrative Tools ➢ Event Viewer or by right-clicking the Start button and choosing Event Viewer. Event Viewer can display hundreds of events. In this case, you would want to create a custom view to achieve the goal. You would not be able to use the Administrative Events view, which is the default view, because it also includes all warnings. This question states that you want to see Critical and Error events only. Custom Views allow you to filter events to create your own customized look and to filter events by event level (critical, error, warning, and so forth), by logs, and by source. You also have the ability to view events occurring within a specific time frame. This allows you to look only at the events that you want to see.

54. D. The Task Manager allows you to see what applications are running on a Windows system. You can also use the Task Manager to stop applications from running on a system. There are several ways to open the Task Manager, including the following:

- Press Ctrl+Shift+Esc.

- Press Ctrl+Alt+Delete.

- Right-click the taskbar at the bottom of the desktop and choose Task Manager from the menu that appears.

- Right-click the Start Menu icon and choose Task Manager.

When open, Task Manager will show all of the programs that are currently running on the system. Click More Details (at the bottom-left corner). To see the startup items, click the Start-up tab. Items will be marked as Disabled or Enabled. If disabled, then it is not causing any issues with the startup. If you see an application that you do not want to be part of the startup process, you can disable it. To disable the app from starting at startup, right-click the unwanted app and then select the Disable option from the pop-up menu. Remember to reboot the machine for these changes to take effect.

55. D. Windows 10 Performance Monitor includes Data Collector Sets. Data Collector Sets work with performance logs. Data Collector Sets are groups of performance counters, event logs, and system information that can be used to collect multiple datasets on demand or over a period of time. They are used to collect data into a log so that the data can be reviewed. You can view the log files with Performance Monitor. Data Collector Sets are broken down into two categories.

- User-Defined Data Collector Sets are created and configured by an administrator. They are custom sets that contain counters, event logs, and trace information.

- System Data Collector Sets are automatically created and defined by the operating system, applications, and components.

56. B. Windows 10 Performance Monitor is designed to allow users and system administrators to monitor performance statistics for various operating system parameters. You can collect, store, and analyze information about items such as CPU, memory, disk, and network resources. By collecting and analyzing performance values, this allows an administrator to identify potential issues. You should also monitor the Memory counters. If a computer does not have enough memory, this can cause excessive paging, which can be observed as a disk subsystem bottleneck. You should look at a snapshot of current activity for a few important counters. This will allow you to find areas of possible bottlenecks and to monitor the load on the servers at a certain point in time.

57. A. An important aspect of monitoring performance is that it should be done over a period of time. This is called a *baseline*. Many performance problems can't be identified by just looking at performance at a quick glance. Instead, you need a baseline to analyze the performance. Then, when a problem occurs, you can compare the current performance to the baseline to see what the differences are. Since performance can also change gradually over time, it is highly recommended that you create a baseline regularly so that you can chart your performance measures and identify trends.

58. C. In this question, the connection property of a metered connection is set to On. This needs to be set to Off. A metered connection is an Internet connection that has a data limit associated with it. Cellular data connections are set as metered by default. If enabled, Windows updates won't be installed. Metered connections are available on all Windows 10 editions. To set a Wi-Fi network connection as metered, follow these steps:

1. Select Start ➤ Settings ➤ Network & Internet ➤ Wi-Fi ➤ Manage Known Networks.

2. Select the Wi-Fi network, go to Properties, and turn off Set As Metered Connection.

59. D. The Windows Event Viewer shows a log of application and system messages. It also includes errors, informational messages, and warnings. It is a handy tool for troubleshooting. You can access Event Viewer by selecting Start ➤ Windows Administrative Tools ➤ Event Viewer or by right-clicking the Start button and choosing Event Viewer. Event Viewer uses icons to depict issues; they are as follows:

Information: This event describes the successful operation of a task, such as an application. This event is shown as a white circle with a blue "i" in it.

Warning: This event is not necessarily significant but may indicate that there might be a possible future problem. This event is shown as a yellow triangle with a black "!" in it.

Error: This event indicates a significant problem such as loss of data or loss of functionality. This event is shown as a red circle with a white "!" in it.

60. B. Windows Update is a tool that connects to the Microsoft website or to a local update server called a Windows Server Update Services (WSUS) server. This will ensure that the Windows 10 operating system and other Microsoft products have the most up-to-date version. An advantage to using WSUS is that administrators can approve the updates prior to them being deployed onto the network. Another advantage is that the clients only need to download updates locally, without using Internet bandwidth. Microsoft offers WSUS for free.

61. C. Delivery Optimization is a peer-to-peer distribution method used in Windows 10. Users can obtain content from other devices on the local network that have already downloaded the updates or from peers over the Internet. Delivery Optimization can be used for Windows Update, Windows Update for Business, and Windows Server Update Services (WSUS). Delivery Optimization reduces the amount of network traffic to external Windows Update sources as well as the time it takes for users to obtain the updates.

62. D. Storage Spaces help protect data from drive failures and extends storage over time. Use Storage Spaces to group two or more drives together in a storage pool and then use capacity from that pool to create virtual drives called *storage spaces*. Storage Spaces store two copies of the data, so if one of the drives fails, there will still be a complete copy of the data. If you're running low on space, just add more drives to the storage pool. Mirror spaces are designed to increase performance and protect files from drive failure by keeping multiple copies. Two-way mirror spaces make two copies of the files and can withstand one drive failure, while a three-way mirror space can withstand two drive failures. In this question, you are creating a two-way storage space, so you will want to use Drive3 and Drive4 since they contain no data. When you're creating a storage pool, all of the data currently on the drives will be erased.

63. A. The Windows Event Viewer shows a log of application and system messages. It also includes errors, informational messages, and warnings. It is a handy tool for troubleshooting. You can access Event Viewer by selecting Start ➤ Windows Administrative Tools ➤ Event Viewer or by right-clicking the Start button and choosing Event Viewer. An Event Viewer task is created and modified by using Event Viewer.

64. A. The figure shown is an example of a Graph view output. The three options are Line view, Histogram Bar view, and Report view. The Graph view is the default display when you first access the Windows 10 Performance Monitor. The chart shows values by using a vertical axis and time using a horizontal axis. This view is beneficial if you want to display values over a period of time. Each point that is plotted on the graph is based on an average value calculated during the period for the measurement being made.

65. B. The graphic is an example of a Histogram Bar view output. The three options are Line view, Histogram Bar view, and Report view. The Histogram view shows performance statistics and information using a set of comparative bar charts. This view is beneficial if you want to see a snapshot of the latest value for a given counter. You can set the histogram to display an average measurement as well as minimum and maximum thresholds.

66. B. OneDrive is free online storage that comes with a Microsoft account. If you save files into OneDrive folders, you can access them from any computer, tablet, or phone. To access files in OneDrive, open File Explorer. Click a OneDrive folder (it will have a cloud icon), and you will be able to see the files within the folder. If you want to view a OneDrive folder or file online, right-click it and select View Online. If you see an icon showing two blue arrows forming a circle, then the file or folder is in the process of syncing.

67. A. OneDrive is free online storage that comes with a Microsoft account. If you save files into OneDrive folders, you can access them from any computer, tablet, or phone. To access files in OneDrive, open File Explorer. Click a OneDrive folder (it will have a cloud icon), and you will be able to see the files within the folder. If you want to view a OneDrive folder or file online, right-click it and select View Online. If you see an icon showing a green circle with a green check mark inside of it, then the file or folder is currently in sync with the online version.

68. C. OneDrive is free online storage that comes with a Microsoft account. If you save files into OneDrive folders, you can access them from any computer, tablet, or phone. To access files in OneDrive, open File Explorer. Click a OneDrive folder (it will have a cloud icon), and you will be able to see the files within the folder. If you want to view a OneDrive folder or file online, right-click it and select View Online. If you see an icon showing a red circle with a red X inside of it, then the file or folder is currently out of sync.

69. D. A service is a program, routine, or process that performs a specific function for the Windows 10 operating system. You can manage services using the Services window. There are several ways to access services. One way to access services is by using the Computer Management utility. Select Start ➤ Windows System ➤ Computer Management ➤ Services And Applications. You can also use Administrative Tools in Control Panel. The Recovery tab allows an administrator to determine what action will occur if a service fails to load. Actions include the following:

- Take No Action
- Restart The Service
- Run A Program
- Restart The Computer

70. A, B. The Windows 10 Advanced Boot Options is used to troubleshoot any errors that may prevent Windows 10 from booting successfully. To access the Windows 10 Advanced Boot Options, hold the Shift key down and choose the Restart option from either the login screen or the Start menu. The shutdown command is a command-prompt command that powers off, restarts, logs off, or hibernates a computer. If you have access over the network, the shutdown command can also remotely shut down or restart a computer. The /r switch will shut down and restart the local computer or the remote computer specified. The /o switch will end the current Windows session and open the Advanced Boot Options menu. This option must be used with /r.

71. C. Windows 10 comes with a full backup and restore application called Backup and Restore (Windows 7) that allows a user or an administrator to back up a copy of any of the Windows 10 component files and data files that are critical to day-to-day operations. Use the Backup and Restore (Windows 7) utility to restore personal files from the backup media and to restore a complete image of your computer.

72. A, B, D. File History allows a user to save copies of their files so that in the event of a file being damaged or lost, it can be restored. You can restore personal files, select particular drives, exclude folders, or set advanced settings. By default, File History is set to back up important folders in the user's home folder (Desktop, Documents, Downloads, Music, Pictures, and Videos). Placing your folder in the Documents folder will ensure that the file is copied. When you click any folder and choose Properties, the last tab to the right is the Previous Versions tab. You can easily restore any folder by choosing one of these previous versions. Windows 10 comes with a full backup and restore application called Backup and Restore (Windows 7). Use this utility to restore personal files from the backup media and to restore a complete image of your computer.

To add a new folder or drive using File History, follow these steps:

1. Select Start ➢ Settings ➢ Update & Security ➢ Backup.

2. Click the Add A Drive option under Back Up Using File History.

3. Select a drive. The Automatically Back Up My Files option will appear and be turned on. Windows will automatically back up the files to the drive.

73. B. File History allows a user to save copies of their files so that in the event of a file being damaged or lost, it can be restored. In the File History settings, you can restore personal files, select particular drives, exclude folders, or set advanced settings. By default, File History is set to back up important folders in the user's home folder. To add a new folder or drive using File History, follow these steps:

1. Select Start ➢ Settings ➢ Update & Security ➢ Backup.

2. Click the Add A Drive option under Back Up Using File History.

3. Select a drive. The Automatically Back Up My Files option will appear and be turned on. Windows will automatically back up the files to the drive.

74. C. Windows 10 includes a full backup and restore application called Backup and Restore (Windows 7) that allows a user or an administrator to keep a backup copy of any of the Windows 10 component files and data files that are critical to the day-to-day operations. The Backup and Restore utility is used to safeguard your computer. The Backup and Restore (Windows 7) utility is used to restore personal files from backup media and to restore an image of your computer. Images allows you to back up and restore your entire Windows 10 machine. Backups of the local drive will create ZIP files. Since the first backup was performed on Monday, then Tuesday, and then Wednesday prior Thursday at 23:00, there will be three backups.

75. D. Windows 10 includes a full backup and restore application called Backup and Restore (Windows 7) that allows a user or an administrator to keep a backup copy of any of the Windows 10 component files and data files that are critical to the day-to-day operations. The Backup and Restore utility is used to safeguard your computer. The Backup and Restore (Windows 7) utility is used to restore personal files from backup media and to restore an image of your computer. Images allows you to back up and restore your entire Windows 10 machine. Backups of the system images will create VHDX files. Since the first backup was performed on Monday, then Tuesday, and then Wednesday prior Thursday at 23:00, there will be three backups.

76. C. Boot logging creates a log file that tracks the loading of drivers and services. When you choose the Enable Boot Logging option from the Advanced Boot Options menu, Windows 10 loads normally, not in Safe Mode. This allows you to see all of the processes that take place during a normal boot sequence. This log file can be used to troubleshoot the boot process. When logging is enabled, the log file is written to \Windows\Ntbtlog.txt. This option won't fix any problems on a device, but it can be used to analyze what might be preventing a Windows 10 machine from loading property.

77. B. Safe Mode allows the system to boot up with only the minimum drivers for the system to operate. It loads the utter minimum of services and drivers needed. If you can boot the computer to Safe Mode and you think there may be a system conflict, you can temporarily disable an application or processes, troubleshoot services, or uninstall software. Safe Mode runs at a screen resolution of 800 × 600.

78. B. System protection is a feature of Windows 10 that creates a backup and saves the configuration information of a computer's system files and settings on a regular basis. It saves multiple previous versions of configurations rather than just overwriting them each time. To delete the previous versions in system protection, you have to run the Disk Cleanup utility and then run Shadow Copies. The Disk Cleanup utility removes temporary files, empties the Recycle Bin, and removes a variety of system files and other items that are no longer needed. To use the Disk Cleanup utility, select Start ➢ Windows System ➢ Control Panel ➢ Administrative Tools ➢ Disk Cleanup.

79. C. Windows 10 cannot back up encrypted files. To back up the encrypted files, you will need to copy them manually to an external hard drive or first decrypt the files prior to performing the backup.

80. B. The Startup Repair tool can be used if a computer will not boot into Safe Mode. The Startup Repair tool can be used to replace corrupted system files. This option will not help if there are hardware errors. If a computer won't boot because of missing or corrupted system files, use this tool to fix the issues. Startup Repair cannot be used to recover personal files that have become corrupted, damaged by viruses, or deleted. If the Startup Repair tool is unable to fix the issue, you may have to reinstall Windows 10, but this should be a last resort. This is why it's important to perform backups of your Windows 10 machines.

81. A. Windows Update Delivery Optimization (WUDO) is a peer-to-peer distribution method used in Windows 10. Users can obtain content from other devices on the local network that have already downloaded the updates or from peers over the Internet. Delivery Optimization can be used for Windows Update, Windows Update for Business, and Windows Server Update Services (WSUS). It reduces the amount of network traffic to external Windows Update sources as well as the time it takes for users to obtain the updates. Delivery Optimization was designed to reduce bandwidth by having computers obtain their updates from other users on the network that have already downloaded the content.

82. C. Windows Update allows you to check for new updates and change settings. To configure Windows Update, do the following:

   1. Select Start ➢ Settings ➢ Update & Security.

   2. Configure the options that you want to use for Windows Update by clicking the Advanced Options link. You can access the following options from Windows Update:

   - Give me updates for other Microsoft products
   - Choose when updates are installed
   - Pause updates
   - Delivery Optimization
   - Privacy settings

83. C. Security Updates are updates that need to be installed to fix a security issue or concern. These security issues may be used by an attacker to break into either a device or software. These are sometimes referred to as *patches*. A patch is a set of modifications to a computer program or its supporting data intended to update, fix, or improve the component. This includes fixing security vulnerabilities and/or other bugs.

84. C. With Windows Startup Settings, you can start Windows in different advanced trouble-shooting modes to help find and correct issues on a computer. To use the Windows Startup settings to select Enable Safe Mode With Command Prompt, perform the following steps:

   1. Select the Start button and then choose Settings ➢ Update & Security ➢ Recovery.

   2. Under Advanced Startup, select Restart Now.

   3. After the computer restarts to the Choose An Option screen, select Troubleshoot ➢ Advanced Options ➢ Startup Settings ➢ Restart.

   4. The computer restarts, and another Startup Settings screen opens showing a list of different startup options. Press 6 or the F6 key for Enable Safe Mode With Command Prompt.

85. A. Windows 10 automatically checks for new updates regularly, but if you want to check for new updates, then simply click the Check For Updates option on the Windows Update page to force Windows 10 to check for updates instantly. To check for updates, go to Settings ➢ Update & Security ➢ Windows Update and click the Check For Updates options. When you click this option, Windows Update will retrieve a list of all of the available updates. You can then click View Available Updates to see what updates are available. Updates are marked as Important, Recommended, or Optional.

86. B. Microsoft typically releases product updates on Tuesdays. So, this day was given the nickname of Patch Tuesdays. Updates are tested prior to being released to the public. With Windows 10, Microsoft has introduced new ways to service updates. Microsoft's new servicing options are referred to as Semi-Annual Channel, Long-Term Servicing Branch (LTSB), and Windows Insider.

87. B. Windows 10 Task Manager provides a quick overview of important system performance statistics without requiring any configuration. There are several ways to access Task Manager, including the following:

- Right-click the Windows Taskbar and then click Task Manager.

- Press Ctrl+Alt+Del and then select Task Manager.

- Press Ctrl+Shift+Esc.

- Type **Taskman** in the Windows search box.

The Services tab shows an administrator what services are currently running on the computer. From here, an administrator can stop a service from running by right-clicking the service and choosing Stop. The Open Services link launches the Services MMC.

88. A. The Disk Cleanup utility is used to remove temporary files, empty the Recycle Bin, and remove an assortment of system files and other items that are no longer needed. To use the Disk Cleanup utility, select Start ➢ Windows System ➢ Control Panel ➢ Administrative Tools ➢ Disk Cleanup. This utility removes a variety of unnecessary files from a computer. The unnecessary files include the following:

- Downloaded program files

- Temporary Internet files

- Offline web pages

- Recycle Bin files

- Setup log files

- Temporary files in the TEMP folder

- Windows error reporting files

89. D. The Windows 10 Security And Maintenance window is used as a troubleshooting tool. You should check here to see if you are having any issues with a Windows 10 machine. The Security And Maintenance screen can help keep you informed of any issues that may affect a computer's health. The screen is divided into Security and Maintenance sections. This was previously called the Action Center. To view the Maintenance section, do the following:

1. In the System window, select Security And Maintenance in the lower-left corner.

2. The Security And Maintenance window opens.

3. Select the Maintenance heading to see the Maintenance functions. They consist of the following:

- Check for solutions to problem reports

- Automatic Maintenance

- HomeGroup
- File History
- Drive status
- Device software

Another way to open the Security And Maintenance window is to type **Security And Maintenance** in the search box on the Windows taskbar.

90. C. The Windows 10 Security And Maintenance window is used as a troubleshooting tool. If it discovers an issue that requires immediate attention, you will see a red circle with a white X in it.

91. B. Disk Defragmenter is a utility that rearranges the pieces of discontiguous parts of files on a computer's hard drive so that the empty storage spaces adjacent to pieces can be used. By using Disk Defragmenter, it updates and optimizes the logical structure of a disk partition. Using defragmentation will move all parts of these files to adjoining sectors of the hard drive. This will speed up the computer and improve performance. Optimizing drives can help a computer run more smoothly and boot faster. There are a couple different ways to access the Disk Defragmenter. One way to optimize Window 10 is by doing the following:

1. Select the search bar on the taskbar and enter **defrag**.

2. Select Defragment And Optimize Drives.

3. Select the disk drive to be optimized.

4. Select the Optimize button.

This will analyze the disk's fragmentation level and start the defragmentation process. This can take several hours to finalize. While this is working, you should limit the work that is being done on the machine.

92. D. Disk Defragmenter is a utility that rearranges the pieces of discontiguous parts of files on a computer's hard disk so that the empty storage spaces adjacent to pieces can be used. If a Windows 10 computer becomes slow, it may be because the files on the hard drive have become fragmented. Windows 10 provides a built-in utility, Disk Defragmenter, to help defragment a Windows machine. By default, Windows 10 automatically defragments files regularly, once a week. However, there may be times when it doesn't run as expected and you need to optimize the drive manually.

93. A. The Windows Malicious Software Removal Tool (MSRT) helps remove malicious software. Microsoft normally releases the MSRT monthly as part of Windows Update or as a stand-alone tool. Use this utility to find and remove threats and to reverse any changes the threat may have made. The easiest way to download and run the MSRT is to turn on Automatic Updates. By turning on Automatic Updates, you are guaranteeing that you'll receive the tool automatically each month. This tool must be run with local administrator privileges.

94. A. Task Scheduler allows an administrator to automate tasks on Windows 10. It is a tool that allows an administrator to create and run tasks automatically. An administrator can start applications, run commands, and execute scripts at any given date or time. Tasks can also be triggered to run when a specified event happens. Task Scheduler works by keeping track of the time and events on a computer and then executes tasks when needed.

95. C. Within a few days of their release, the Semi-Annual Channel servicing option receives all upgrades and updates (patches) from Microsoft. There are currently two release channels for Windows 10:

- The Semi-Annual Channel
- The Long-Term Servicing Channel

There have been a number of name changes in regard to the Windows 10 Servicing options:

- Long-Term Servicing Channel (LTSC) was previously known as Long-Term Servicing Branch (LTSB).
- Semi-Annual Channel was previously known as Current Branch for Business (CBB).
- Semi-Annual Channel (Targeted) is no longer being used.

96. D. The Windows Malicious Software Removal Tool (MSRT) helps remove malicious software. Microsoft normally releases the MSRT monthly as part of Windows Update or as a stand-alone tool. Use this utility to find and remove threats and to reverse any changes the threat may have made. The easiest way to download and run the MSRT is to turn on Automatic Updates. By turning on Automatic Updates, you guarantee that you are receiving the tool automatically every month. Microsoft generally delivers MSRT with Windows Update the second Tuesday of the month.

97. A, C, D, E. The backup location can be all of the options listed, except you will not want to store a backup onto the same drive that is being backed up. It's basically defeating the purpose of a backup. If the hard drive fails, then all of the partitions fail too. Thus, the backup would be no good. The Windows 10 Backup and Restore utility allows an administrator to create and restore backups. Backups protect data in the event of system failure by storing the data on another medium, such as a hard drive, CD, DVD, or network location. If the original data is lost due to corruption, deletion, or media failure, then you can restore the data using the backup.

98. C. System Protection creates and saves information about drivers, programs, system files, and settings. Windows will create restore points automatically. System protection saves multiple previous versions of saved configurations rather than just overwriting them. This makes it possible to return to multiple configurations in your Windows 10 history, known as *restore points*. These restore points are created before most significant events, such as installing a new driver. Restore points are also created automatically every seven days. System protection is turned on by default in Windows 10 for any drive formatted with NTFS.

99. B. System protection creates and saves information about drivers, programs, system files, and settings. Windows will create restore points automatically. System protection saves multiple previous versions of saved configurations rather than just overwriting them. This makes it possible to return to multiple configurations in your Windows 10 history; these are known as *restore points*. These restore points should be created before most significant events, such as installing a new driver. Restore points are also created automatically every seven days. System Protection is turned on by default in Windows 10 for any drive formatted with NTFS.

100. B. Safe Mode allows the system to boot up with only the minimum drivers for the system to operate. It loads the utter minimum of services and drivers needed. If you can boot the computer to Safe Mode and you think there may be a system conflict, you can temporarily disable an application or processes, troubleshoot services, or uninstall software. The drivers that are loaded with Safe Mode include basic ones for the mouse, monitor, keyboard, hard drive, standard video driver, and default system services. In this question, though, you know that the computer is affected by a virus. You will want to avoid booting into Safe Mode with Networking. If booting into Safe Mode with Networking, you could potentially risk other computers on the network getting infected with the virus.

101. A. One way to protect a Windows 10 computer system is by creating and using system images. System images are exact duplicates of the Windows 10 drive. By default, system images include the drives that are needed for Windows to operate correctly. System images include Windows and all of the system settings, programs, and files. System images help in the event of a major hard drive or computer crash. They allow an administrator to restore all of the contents of the crashed system and get the system back up and running. To create a full backup of Windows 10 with the system image tool, follow these steps:

1. Open the Settings app and select Update & Security ➤ Backup.
2. Under the Looking For An Older Backup? section, click the Go To Backup And Restore (Windows 7) option.
3. On the left pane, click the Create A System Image option.
4. Under the Where Do You Want To Save The Backup? section, select the On A Hard Disk option.
5. Using the On A Hard Disk drop-down menu, select the storage location to save the full backup of Windows 10.
6. Click the Next button.
7. If applicable, select additional drives that you may want to include in the backup.
8. Click the Next button.
9. Click the Start Backup button and then click No and then click Close.

102. D. Restore points allow you to bring a system back to a previous point in time. Restore points are snapshots of the Windows 10 system that can be used to revert to another snapshot. Restore points contain Registry and system information as it was at a certain point in time. Restore points are automatically generated when you install a new app, driver, or Windows update, and they are generated when you manually create a restore point. Using a restore point will not affect the personal files in the %UserProfile% folder, but it can remove apps, drivers, and updates that were installed after a restore point was created. If a system restore doesn't provide the expected results, then you can undo the restore point to return the system to how it was before doing the system restore.

103. B. File History allows a user to save copies of their files so that in the event of a file being damaged or lost, it can be restored. In the File History settings, you can restore personal files, select particular drives, exclude folders, or set advanced settings. By default, File History is set to back up important folders in the user's home folder. These folders include Desktop, Documents, Downloads, Music, Pictures, and Videos.

104. D. Windows Recovery Environment (WinRE) is a recovery environment that can repair common causes of an unbootable operating system. WinRE will automatically boot after two failed attempts to boot the operating system. You can then perform a Safe Mode boot from the advanced boot options. By default, WinRE comes with Windows 10 for desktop editions (Home, Professional, Enterprise, and Education).

105. B. Restore points allow you to bring a system back to a previous point in time. They are snapshots of the Windows 10 system that can be used to revert to another snapshot. Restore points contain Registry and system information as it was at a certain point in time. Restore points are automatically generated when you install a new app, driver, or Windows update, and they are generated when you manually create a restore point. Using a restore point will not affect the personal files in the %UserProfile% folder, but it can remove apps, drivers, and updates that were installed after a restore point was created. If a system restore doesn't provide the expected results, then you can undo the restore point to return the system to how it was before doing the system restore.

106. D. Windows Recovery Environment (WinRE) is a recovery environment that can repair common causes of unbootable operating systems. WinRE is based on Windows Preinstallation Environment (Windows PE) and can be customized with additional drivers, languages, optional Windows PE components, and other troubleshooting and diagnostic tools. By default, WinRE is preloaded into the Windows 10 for desktop edition installations (Home, Professional, Enterprise, and Education).

107. B. Windows PowerShell is a task-based command-line utility designed especially for system administration. The powershell.exe command-line tool starts a Windows PowerShell session in a Command Prompt window. Windows 10 has several PowerShell configuration commands that can be used to help manage and configure a Windows 10 system. Using the Get-ComputerInfo command will return the computer's system information.

108. D. Windows 10 Task Manager provides a quick overview of important system performance statistics without requiring any configuration. There are several ways to access Task Manager, including the following:

- Right-click the Windows Taskbar and then click Task Manager.
- Press Ctrl+Alt+Del and then select Task Manager.
- Press Ctrl+Shift+Esc.
- Type **Taskman** in the Windows search box.

All of the applications that are running on the Windows 10 machine will appear on the Details tab. Using this tab allows you to stop an application from running by right-clicking the application and then choosing Stop.

109. B. Windows PowerShell is a task-based command-line utility designed especially for system administration. The powershell.exe command-line tool starts a Windows PowerShell session in a Command Prompt window. Windows 10 has a wide variety of PowerShell configuration commands that can be used to help manage and configure a Windows 10 system. By using the Get-ControlPanelItem command, this allows an administrator to find Control Panel items on a local computer by name, category, or description. The syntax for using this command is PS C:\> Get-ControlPanelItem -Name "<ITEM WANTED>" | Show-ControlPanelItem.

110. C. The Sync Center allows an administrator to configure synchronization between a Windows 10 machine and a network server. It is built into Windows 10, and it is a tool to meet all of your synchronization needs, including working with offline files. The Sync Center allows you to see when synchronization occurred, if it was successful, and if there are errors. You can use Sync Center to access shared files and folders on a network at any time, even when not connected to the network. Changes made offline will automatically be reflected on the server the next time you connect. To access the Sync Center in Control Panel, select Start ➢ Windows System ➢ Control Panel ➢ Sync Center.

111. C. Windows PowerShell is a task-based command-line utility designed especially for system administration. The powershell.exe command-line tool starts a Windows PowerShell session in a Command Prompt window. Windows 10 has a wide variety of PowerShell configuration commands that can be used to help manage and configure a Windows 10 system. The PS prefix is added to the command prompt to indicate that you are in a Windows PowerShell session.

112. B. A service is a program, routine, or process that performs a specific function for the Windows 10 operating system. You can manage services using the Services window. There are several ways to access services. One way to access the Computer Management utility is by selecting Start ➢ Windows System ➢ Computer Management ➢ Services And Applications. You can also use Administrative Tools in Control Panel. The General tab allows you to view and configure the following:

- The service display name

- A description of the service

- The path to the service executable

- The startup type, which can be automatic, manual, or disabled

- The current service status

- Start parameters that can be applied when the service is started

- Change the service state to Start, Stop, Pause, or Resume

113. C. The Windows Event Viewer shows a log of application and system messages. It also includes errors, informational messages, and warnings. It is a handy tool for troubleshooting. Event Viewer is a useful tool for monitoring network information. You can use the logs to view any information, warnings, or alerts related to the functionality of the network. You can access Event Viewer by selecting Windows Administrative Tools ➢ Event Viewer or by right-clicking the Start button and choosing Event Viewer. Event Viewer can display hundreds of events.

114. B. The Windows 10 advanced boot options can be used to troubleshoot errors that keep Windows 10 from successfully booting. To access the Windows 10 advanced boot options, hold down the Shift key and choose the Restart option (from either the login screen or the Start menu). System images are exact copies of the Windows 10 drive. By default, system images include the drives that are needed for Windows to function properly. System images include Windows and all of the system settings, programs, and files. This allows you to restore all of the contents of the crashed system and get the system back up and functioning.

115. C. The Windows 10 advanced boot options can be used to troubleshoot errors that keep Windows 10 from successfully booting. To access the Windows 10 advanced boot options, hold down the Shift key and choose the Restart option (from either the login screen or the Start menu). If a Windows 10 computer will not boot because of missing or corrupted system files, you can use the Startup Repair tool to fix the issue. Startup Repair cannot fix hardware failures or recover any personal files that have been corrupted, damaged by viruses, or deleted.

116. E. The Startup Repair tool can be used if a computer will not boot into Safe Mode. This tool can be used to replace corrupted system files. If there are hardware errors, then this option will not help. If a computer won't boot because of missing or corrupted system files, use this tool to fix the issues. Startup Repair cannot be used to recover personal files that have become corrupted, damaged by viruses, or deleted. If this tool is unable to fix the issue, you may have to reinstall Windows 10, but this should be a last resort. This is why it's important to perform backups of your Windows 10 machines.

117. B. By default, Microsoft's OneDrive is built into Windows 10 and is a cloud-based storage system where corporate or home users can store their data in the cloud. Microsoft OneDrive allows users to use up to 5 GB of cloud storage for free without a subscription. Users can obtain more cloud-based storage by purchasing a higher subscription. Users can store and then access those documents from anywhere in the world using Internet access.

118. C. By default, Microsoft's OneDrive is built into Windows 10 and is a cloud-based storage system where corporate or home users can store their data in the cloud. To set up a corporate or home user with Microsoft OneDrive, you must first have a Microsoft account. Once you have a Microsoft account, you then sign into the Microsoft OneDrive system.

119. F. System Restore is used to create known checkpoints of a system's configuration. In the event that a system becomes misconfigured, an administrator can restore the system configuration to an earlier version of the checkpoint. Restore points are snapshots of the Windows 10 system and can be used to revert to another snapshot.

120. D. Windows Update is a free service, provided by Microsoft, which is used to provide updates such as service packs and patches for the Windows operating system and other Microsoft software. Windows Update can also be used to update drivers for popular hardware devices. These updates are regularly released through Windows Update on the second Tuesday of every month. This day is called Patch Tuesday. Windows Update is a shortcut that allows you to receive updates and security patches for the Windows 10 operating system. Updates can be received either from Microsoft's website or by using a Windows Server Update Services (WSUS) server.

121. B. Enable Boot Logging creates a log file that tracks the loading of drivers and services. When you choose the Enable Boot Logging option (F2 or option 2) from the Advanced Boot Options menu, Windows 10 loads normally, not in Safe Mode. This allows you to see all of the processes that take place during a normal boot sequence. This log file can be used to troubleshoot the boot process. When logging is enabled, the log file is written to \Windows\Ntbtlog.txt. This option won't fix any issues on a device but can be used to analyze what might be preventing a Windows 10 machine from loading properly. The boot log file is cumulative. Every time you have to boot into Safe Mode, you are writing to this file.

122. C. Using the Launch Recovery Environment, open the Windows 10 Recovery Environment (WinRE). It is used to repair common causes of bootable operating system problems. By default, WinRE is preloaded into the Windows 10 for desktop editions (Home, Professional, Enterprise, and Education). Pressing the F10 function key from the Advanced Boot Options menu will boot the computer in the Launch Recovery Environment. This option allows your computer to boot normally. Selecting this option will return you to a menu screen that offers these three options:

- Continue Exit And Continue To Windows 10

- Troubleshoot Reset Your PC Or See Advanced Options

- Turn Off Your PC

123. D. wbadmin.exe allows an administrator to back up and restore an operating system, volumes, files, folders, and applications while using the command prompt. The wbadmin.exe command replaces the ntbackup.exe command that was released with previous versions of Windows. To run the wbadmin.exe command, you must start it from an elevated command prompt.

124. A. wbadmin.exe allows an administrator to back up and restore an operating system, volumes, files, folders, and applications while using the command prompt. Using the wbadmin enable backup command creates and enables a daily backup schedule or modifies an existing backup schedule. With no parameters specified, it displays the currently scheduled backup settings.

125. A. wbadmin.exe allows an administrator to back up and restore an operating system, volumes, files, folders, and applications while using the command prompt. Using the wbadmin start recovery runs a recovery operation based on the specified parameters. The syntax is as follows:

```
wbadmin start recovery
-version:<VersionIdentifier>
-items:{<VolumesToRecover> | <AppsToRecover> |
<FilesOrFoldersToRecover>}
-itemtype:{Volume | App | File}
[-backupTarget:{<VolumeHostingBackup> |
<NetworkShareHostingBackup>}]
[-machine:<BackupMachineName>]
[-recoveryTarget:{<TargetVolumeForRecovery> |
<TargetPathForRecovery>}]
[-recursive]
[-overwrite:{Overwrite | CreateCopy | Skip}]
[-notRestoreAcl]
[-skipBadClusterCheck]
[-noRollForward]
[-quiet]
```

Chapter 5: Deploy and Update Operating Systems

1. B. Windows Autopilot is a way to set up and preconfigure devices. You can use Windows Autopilot to reset, repurpose, and recover devices. Windows Autopilot user-driven mode is designed to enable Windows 10 devices to be converted from their initial state into a ready-to-use state without an administrator working on the device. The process is designed to be user friendly so that anyone can complete it. The user will do the following:

    - Unbox the device, plug it in, and turn it on.

    - Choose a language, locale, and keyboard.

    - Connect it to a wireless or wired network with Internet access.

    - Specify their e-mail address and password for their organization account.

    Once they have completed those steps, the rest of the process is automated, with the device being joined to the organization, enrolled in Intune or another Mobile Device Management (MDM) service, and be fully configured as defined by the company.

2. B. Windows Autopilot simplifies the enrollment process of adding devices in Intune. By using Microsoft Intune and Autopilot together, an administrator can give a device to an end user without having to build, maintain, and apply custom operating system images. When an administrator uses Intune to manage Autopilot devices, they can manage policies, profiles, apps, and more after they are enrolled.

3. A. To add a Windows Autopilot device, you will want to import a CSV file with the device's information. To add a device, follow these steps:

    1. In the Microsoft Endpoint Manager Admin Center, choose Devices ➤ Windows ➤ Windows Enrollment ➤ Devices (under Windows Autopilot Deployment Program ➤ Import).

    2. Under Add Windows Autopilot Devices, browse to a CSV file listing the devices to be added. The CSV file should list the serial numbers, Windows product IDs, hardware hashes, optional group tags, and optional assigned user.

    3. Choose Import to start importing the device information. This may take several minutes.

    4. After the import is complete, choose Devices ➤ Windows ➤ Windows Enrollment ➤ Devices (under Windows Autopilot Deployment Program ➤ Sync). A message will be displayed stating that the synchronization is in progress. This may take a few minutes to complete, depending on how many devices are being synchronized.

    5. Refresh the view to see the new devices.

4. C. You should use the Sysprep utility. Run `sysprep.exe` to prepare a Windows installation to be captured. The `sysprep.exe` `/generalize` command removes system-specific information from the Windows installation so that it can be reused on different computers. The `/oobe` switch restarts the computer in out-of-box experience (OOBE) mode, and `/unattend:<answerfile>` applies the settings that are in the answer file to Windows during an unattended installation.

5. B. For computers running Windows 7, Windows 8, or Windows 8.1, the recommended path to deploy Windows 10 is by using the Windows installation program, `setup.exe`, to perform the in-place upgrade. Using the in-place upgrade preserves all data, settings, applications, and drivers from the existing operating system version. The upgrade process cannot change from a 32-bit operating system to a 64-bit operating system, due to possible complications with installed applications and drivers. So, in this case, because only Computer2 and Computer4 are already using the 64-bit version, they are the only systems that can be upgraded to the Windows 10 64-bit version.

6. C. Windows Deployment Services (WDS) is a suite of components that allows an administrator to install Windows 10 remotely on client computers. The WDS server must be configured with the Preboot Execution Environment (PXE) boot files, the images to be deployed, and the answer file. A WDS server installs Windows 10 onto the client machines. You enable WDS servers to respond to client requests by using the Windows Deployment Services (WDS) Microsoft Management Console (MMC) snap-in. In the PXE Properties dialog box, enable the option Respond To Client Computers. You can configure WDS on a Windows Server computer by using the Windows Deployment Services MMC or by using the `wdsutil.exe` command-line utility.

7. B. By using an automatic deployment rule (ADR), you can configure automatic software update deployments. This method is used for deployments of software updates and for managing definition updates. An ADR allows you to set the criteria to automate the deployment process. ADRs can be used for Microsoft's Patch Tuesday updates. By setting this method, the actual installation deadline time is the displayed time plus a random amount of time up to two hours. The randomization reduces the possible impact of all the clients in the collection installing updates all at the same time. So, you would want to configure Automatic Maintenance Random Delay from the Maintenance Scheduler settings.

8. D. Intune stores only the update policy assignments, not the updates themselves. Devices access Windows Update directly for the updates. A Windows 10 update ring is a collection of settings that configures when Windows 10 updates get installed. Windows 10 update rings support scope tags. Administrators use scope tags with update rings to help filter and manage sets of configurations. You assign policies for Windows 10 update rings and Windows 10 feature updates to groups of devices. You can use both policy types in the same Intune environment to manage software updates for Windows 10 devices and to create an update strategy that meets your corporate needs. For the steps to create and assign update rings, go to the following Microsoft website:

docs.microsoft.com/en-us/mem/intune/protect/windows-update-for-
business-configure#create-and-assign-update-rings

9. B. Azure Active Directory (Azure AD) is Microsoft's cloud-based identity and access management service. It helps users sign in and access resources. Administrators can use the Windows PowerShell command `New-AzureADPolicy` to create a new Azure AD policy. The syntax is as follows:

```
New-AzureADPolicy -Definition <Array of Rules> -DisplayName <Name of
Policy> -IsTenantDefault
```

10. D. Using Microsoft Intune and Windows Autopilot, you can give devices to your end users without the need to build, maintain, and apply custom operating system images. When you use Intune to manage Autopilot devices, you can manage policies, profiles, applications, and more. For the steps on how to create and configure a Windows Autopilot deployment profile, go to the following Microsoft website:

docs.microsoft.com/en-us/mem/intune/enrollment/enrollment-autopilot#create-an-autopilot-deployment-profile

11. D. The Fresh Start device action removes any apps that are installed on a computer running Windows 10, version 1703 or later. In this question, only Computer2 and Computer3 are running Windows 10, so these are the only machines that can use the Fresh Start action. Fresh Start helps remove pre-installed (OEM) apps that are typically installed with a new computer.

12. E. By using the Retire or Wipe action, you can remove devices from Intune that are not needed, being repurposed, or missing. Using the Wipe action restores a device to its factory default settings. The user data is kept if you select the Retain Enrollment State And User Account checkbox. Otherwise, all data, apps, and settings will be removed. In this question, you can wipe all the operating systems listed. To wipe a device, perform the following actions:

1. Sign in to the Microsoft Endpoint Manager Admin Center.

2. Select Devices ➤ All Devices.

3. Select the name of the device to be wiped.

4. In the pane that shows the device name, select Wipe.

5. For Windows 10 version 1709 or later, you also have the Wipe Device, But Keep Enrollment State And Associated User Account option.

6. The Wipe Device And Continue To Wipe Even If Device Loses Power option makes sure that the wipe action can't be bypassed by turning the device off. This option will keep trying to reset the device until it succeeds.

7. Select Yes to confirm the wipe.

13. A, B. The Group Policy settings determine whether users are allowed, and prompted, to enroll for Windows Hello for Business. It can be configured for computers or users. If you configure the Group Policy for computers, then all users who sign in to those computers will be allowed and prompted to enroll. If configured for users, then only those users will be allowed and prompted to enroll. By default, Windows Hello for Business enables users to enroll and use biometrics, such as using a fingerprint, iris, or facial recognition to sign in to Windows rather than providing just a personal identification number (PIN) to sign in. When Windows Hello is set up, you are prompted to create a PIN first, which allows a user to sign in using a PIN instead of biometrics.

14. D. Whenever an issue occurs when using Windows Autopilot, you will see a generated error code. When a problem occurs during setup, some error codes will be displayed on the device. When using Windows Autopilot Reset, it requires that the Windows Recovery Environment (WinRE) be correctly configured and enabled on the device. If it is not enabled or configured, this message will be displayed: `Error code: ERROR_NOT_SUPPORTED (0x80070032)`. To make sure that WinRE is enabled, use the `REAgentC.exe` tool to run this command: `reagentc /enable`. Error `0x80070032` will appear when Windows Autopilot Reset is used to prepare an existing device to become business ready and you need to confirm that the WinRE is correctly configured and enabled on the device.

15. A, B. Secure Boot is a feature of Windows 10 that provides the ability to boot an operating system securely. Secure Boot validates all the drivers and operating system components before they are loaded. If you are going to implement Secure Boot, then you need to make sure that the system firmware is set up as Unified Extensible Firmware Interface (UEFI) and not BIOS. You also need to make sure that the disks are converted from Master Boot Record (MBR) disks to a GUID Partition Table (GPT) disk. Secure Boot prevents rootkits from loading when you start your device.

16. B. The `setupconfig.ini` file is a configuration file that is used to pass a set of flags or parameters to Windows `setup.exe`. Use this file as an alternative to passing parameters to Windows Setup on a command line. This ability is available in Windows 10 version 1511 and later. Administrators can use the `setupconfig.ini` file to add parameters to Windows Setup from Windows Update and Windows Server Update Services.

17. B. Windows Autopilot is a way to set up and preconfigure devices. You can use Windows Autopilot to reset, repurpose, and recover devices. Autopilot Reset removes all of the files, apps, and settings on a device (including the user profile), but it retains the connection to Azure AD, Intune, or third-party Mobile Device Management (MDM). Autopilot Reset will retain the following:

- The region/language and keyboard
- Any applied provisioning packages
- Wi-Fi connections

Autopilot Reset is the best option when reusing a device within your network. So, the Wi-Fi connection and passphrase will be retained by using Autopilot Reset.

18. B. Windows Autopilot is a way to set up and preconfigure devices. You can use Windows Autopilot to reset, repurpose, and recover devices. Autopilot Reset removes all of the files, apps, and settings on a device (including the user profile), but it retains the connection to Azure AD, Intune, or a third-party Mobile Device Management (MDM). Autopilot Reset will retain the following:

- The region/language and keyboard
- Any applied provisioning packages
- Wi-Fi connections

Autopilot Reset is the best option when reusing a device within your network. So, the app will be removed by using Autopilot Reset.

19. A. Windows Autopilot is a way to set up and preconfigure devices. You can use Windows Autopilot to reset, repurpose, and recover devices. Autopilot Reset removes all of the files, apps, and settings on a device (including the user profile), but it retains the connection to Azure AD, Intune, or a third-party Mobile Device Management (MDM). Autopilot Reset will retain the following:

- The region/language and keyboard

- Any applied provisioning packages

- Wi-Fi connections

Autopilot Reset is the best option when reusing a device within your network. So, the VPN connection will be removed.

20. B. A task sequence identifies a list of tasks that are required to install the OS after the PXE-enabled device boots. In this question, you want to make sure that the computers are configured with the correct product keys. This is done by configuring an MDT task sequence. For the steps on how to create a task sequence with Configuration Manager and MDT, go to the following Microsoft website:

docs.microsoft.com/en-us/windows/deployment/deploy-windows-cm/create-a-task-sequence-with-configuration-manager-and-mdt

21. A. BitLocker provides protection when used with a Trusted Platform Module (TPM) version 1.2 or later. The TPM is a hardware component installed by computer manufacturers. It works in conjunction with BitLocker to help shield user data, and it ensures that a computer has not been interfered with while offline. To use BitLocker, the device must be installed with Windows 10 Professional, Windows 10 Enterprise, or Windows 10 Education.

22. B. Deployment scenarios are assigned to one of three categories. The three categories are as follows:

Modern: Using Modern deployment methods is recommended by Microsoft unless there is a specific need to use a different procedure. Modern deployment scenarios include Windows Autopilot and In-Place Upgrades.

Dynamic: Using Dynamic deployment methods enables you to configure applications and settings for specific use cases. Dynamic deployment scenarios include Subscription Activation, Azure Active Directory Join (Azure AD) with Automatic Mobile Device Management (MDM), and Provisioning Packages.

Traditional: Traditional deployment methods use existing tools to deploy operating system images. Traditional deployment scenarios include Bare-Metal, Refresh, and Replace.

In this question, since you are discussing Subscription Activation, this falls into the Dynamic deployment category.

23. C, D. To meet your corporate requirements, you will want to configure the following:

- User Experience Settings ➤ Automatic Update Behavior ➤ Notify Download
- User Experience Settings ➤ Delivery Optimization Download Mode ➤ Not Configured

User experience settings control the user capability for device restart and reminders. The Notify Download option will notify the user before downloading the update. Then, the user can choose to download and install updates at that time. With Intune, Delivery Optimization settings are used to reduce bandwidth consumption when those devices are downloading applications and updates. Configure Delivery Optimization as part of a device's configuration profile. The Delivery Optimization Download Mode option should be set to Not Configured since delivery optimization is no longer configured as part of a Windows 10 update ring. Delivery optimization is now set through device configuration. Previous configurations are still part of the console. You remove the previous configurations by editing them to be Not Configured. For steps on how to remove Delivery Optimization from Windows 10 update rings, check out the following Microsoft website:

docs.microsoft.com/en-us/mem/intune/configuration/
delivery-optimization-windows#remove-delivery-optimization-from-
windows-10-update-rings

24. B. Device profiles allow an administrator to add and configure settings and then push those settings to devices within the corporate environment. With Intune, use Delivery Optimization settings for Windows 10 devices to reduce bandwidth consumption when those devices download applications and updates. You configure Delivery Optimization as part of a device configuration profile.

25. B. The shutdown command is a command-prompt command that powers off, restarts, logs off, or hibernates a computer. If you have access over the network, the shutdown command can also remotely shut down or restart a computer. To force an Autopilot profile to be downloaded, you should reboot the device during OOBE to allow the device to retrieve the profile. Press Shift+F10 to open a command prompt at the start of the OOBE and then enter shutdown /r /t 0 to restart the device immediately or enter shutdown /s /t 0 to shut down immediately. In this case, you want to enter into the shutdown process to restart the device immediately, so you use the shutdown /s /t 0 command. This command is used to shut down the local computer immediately. The /s switch will shut down the local machine. The /t switch is the time, in seconds, between the execution of the shutdown command and the actual shutdown or restart.

26. C, D. These settings are added to a device configuration profile in Intune and then assigned or deployed to the Windows 10 devices. Since you are looking at adding a custom image as the wallpaper and sign-in screen, you need to configure the Locked Screen Experience settings and the Personalization settings. The Lock Screen is the experience that you will see prior to signing in. The Lock Screen can be a single image or a collection of images. To change the wallpaper on a computer, you will configure the Personalization settings and then click Background. The background page allows you to preview the wallpaper picture and allows you to select several photos or customize it.

27. C, D. By default, Windows 10 will automatically download and install drivers in Windows Update when they become available. However, by enabling Specify Search Order For Device Driver Source Locations and then selecting Do Not Search Windows Update from the Device Installation settings in a Group Policy object (GPO), Windows Update will not be searched for device drivers. By enabling Do Not Include Drivers With Windows Updates from the Windows Update settings in a Group Policy object (GPO), this will prevent the system from searching Windows Update for device drivers.

28. B. Windows Deployment Services (WDS) is a suite of components that allows you to install Windows 10 remotely on client computers. You can configure WDS on a Windows Server computer by using the Windows Deployment Services Configuration Wizard or by using the `wdsutil.exe` command-line utility.

29. B. The Windows Analytics service was retired on January 31, 2020, and it was replaced with Desktop Analytics. Desktop Analytics is a cloud-based service that integrates with Configuration Manager. The service allows you to make informed decisions regarding the update readiness of your Windows clients. Use Desktop Analytics with Configuration Manager to do the following:

- Assess app compatibility with the latest Windows 10 feature updates.

- Create an inventory of apps running in an organization.

- Create pilot groups that represent the entire application and driver estate across a minimal set of devices.

- Deploy Windows 10 to pilot and production-managed devices.

- Identify compatibility issues and receive mitigation suggestions based on cloud-enabled data insights.

30. C. Volume license customers whose licenses have expired will need to change the edition of Windows 10 to an edition with an active license. Switching to a downgraded edition of Windows 10 is possible using the same method that was used to perform the edition upgrade. If the downgrade path is supported, then the apps and settings can be migrated from the current edition. If a path is not supported, then a clean install will be required. Downgrading from any edition of Windows 10 to Windows 7, 8, or 8.1 by providing a different product key is not supported. It is also not feasible to downgrade from a later version to an earlier version of the same edition (for example, Windows 10 Pro 1709 to 1703) unless the rollback process is used.

31. D. You can upgrade devices by using a device configuration profile. The option that you'd want to configure is Edition Upgrade. Edition Upgrade allows you to upgrade Windows 10 (and later) devices to a newer version of Windows. To create the profile, do the following:

1. Sign in to the Microsoft Endpoint Manager admin center.

2. Select Devices ➤ Configuration Profiles ➤ Create Profile.

3. Enter the following properties:

    Name: Enter a descriptive name for the new profile.

    Description: Enter a description for the profile.

> **Platform:** Select Windows 10 and later.
>
> **Profile Type:** Select Edition Upgrade.
>
> **Settings:** Enter the settings you want to configure.

4. Click OK to save the profile settings.

32. C. For existing computers currently running Windows 7, Windows 8, or Windows 8.1, the recommended path for organizations deploying Windows 10 is to use the Windows installation program, `setup.exe`, to perform an in-place upgrade. Performing an in-place upgrade will preserve all data, settings, applications, and drivers from the existing operating system version. This will require the least administrative effort, since there is no need for any complex deployment infrastructure.

33. D. Windows Autopilot profiles allow an administrator to choose how the Windows 10 system will be set up and configured on Azure AD and Intune. The Windows Autopilot simplifies enrolling devices in Intune. With Windows Autopilot and Microsoft Intune, you can give new devices to end users without the need to build, maintain, and apply custom operating system images. When you use Intune to manage Autopilot devices, you can manage policies, profiles, apps, and more.

34. B. If you install a feature update and it is not as you expected, you can roll back the update. Previously, Windows 10 had a 30 day roll back. Now, however, you have only 10 days to roll back an update.

35. A. Windows 10 deployment rings are a method used to separate computers into a deployment timeline. They are a collection of settings that configure when Windows 10 updates get installed. You can specify the number of days from 0 to 30 for which Quality Updates are deferred. This number of days is in addition to any deferral period that is part of the service channel selected. The deferral period initiates when the policy is received by the device. Quality Updates are usually fixes and improvements to existing Windows functionality. In this question, Computer1 is a member of Group1 and Ring1 is applied to Group1, so the quality deferral will be 3 days.

36. A. Windows 10 deployment rings are a method used to separate computers into a deployment timeline. They are a collection of settings that configure when Windows 10 updates get installed. You can specify the number of days from 0 to 30 for which Quality Updates are deferred. This number of days is in addition to any deferral period that is part of the service channel selected. The deferral period initiates when the policy is received by the device. Quality Updates are usually fixes and improvements to existing Windows functionality. In this question, Computer1 and Computer2 are members of Group1 and Ring1 is applied to Group1, so the quality deferral will be 3 days.

37. D. Delivery Optimization is used to reduce bandwidth usage by sharing the work of downloading these packages using multiple devices. Delivery Optimization is a self-organizing distributed cache that allows clients to download packages from alternate sources. It allows updates from other clients that connect to the Internet using the same public IP. Delivery Optimization is enabled by default in the Windows 10 Enterprise, Professional, and Education editions. In this case, Computer1 can only use the computers from its own

subnet to download the upgrades. So, all of the devices must use the same Network Address Translation (NAT), but it can be configured differently by using Group Policies and Mobile Device Management (MDM) solutions such as Microsoft Intune.

38. C. You should recommend using Windows Configuration Designer to create a provisioning package (.ppkg) that contains the customized settings. The provisioning package can be applied to a device running Windows 10 or Windows 10 Mobile. Use Windows Configuration Designer to create a provisioning package to upgrade a desktop edition or mobile edition of Windows 10. Windows Configuration Designer can be installed from the Microsoft Store. To create a provisioning package for upgrading desktop editions of Windows 10, select Runtime Settings ➢ EditionUpgrade ➢ UpgradeEditionWithProductKey in the Available Customizations panel in Windows ICD and enter the product key for the upgraded edition. To create a provisioning package for upgrading mobile editions of Windows 10, select Runtime Settings ➢ EditionUpgrade ➢ UpgradeEditionWithLicense in the Available Customizations panel in Windows ICD and enter the product key for the upgraded edition.

39. B. By using Windows provisioning, it is easier for an administrator to configure end-user devices without using imaging. By using Windows provisioning, an administrator can specify desired configurations and settings to enroll devices and then apply the configurations to the target device. A provisioning package (.ppkg) is a collection of configuration settings. With Windows 10, an administrator can create provisioning packages that allow them to configure a device quickly without having to install a new image. A provisioning package can be:

- Installed by using removable media
- Attached to an email
- Downloaded from a network share
- Deployed in NFC tags or barcodes

40. B. Windows PowerShell is a Windows command-line shell designed especially for system administrators. By using the `Get-AzureADPolicy` command, this allows an Azure administrator to view an Azure AD policy.

41. A, C. Use the Windows Configuration Designer tool to create provisioning packages to configure devices running Windows 10. The ConnectivityProfiles settings are used to configure profiles that a user will use to connect with, such as an email account or VPN profile. The Policies settings allow you to configure provisioning package policies. You can set ApplicationManagement within the Policies settings.

42. A, D. Windows Autopilot makes enrolling devices in Intune easy. With Microsoft Intune and Autopilot, an administrator can give new devices to end users without the need to build, maintain, and apply custom operating system images. When using Intune to manage Autopilot devices, you can manage policies, profiles, apps, and more. Autopilot deployment profiles are used to configure the Autopilot devices. You can create up to 350 profiles per tenant. If you want to create a group that includes all of the Autopilot devices, type (**device.devicePhysicalIDs -any _ -contains "[ZTDId]"**). The ZTDId tag is applied to all Windows Autopilot devices, and it is a unique value assigned to all imported Windows Autopilot devices.

43. C. The scanstate command is used with the User State Migration Tool (USMT) to scan the source computer, collect the files and settings, and create a store. The scanstate command's syntax is as follows:

```
scanstate [StorePath] [/apps]
        [/ppkg:FileName] [/i:[Path\]FileName] [/o] [/v:VerbosityLevel]
        [/nocompress] [/localonly] [/encrypt
        /key:KeyString|/keyfile:[Path\]FileName] [/l:[Path\]FileName]
        [/progress:[Path\]FileName] [/r:TimesToRetry] [/w:SecondsBeforeRetry]
        [/c] [/p] [/all] [/ui:[DomainName|ComputerName\]UserName]
        [/ue:[DomainName|ComputerName\]UserName]
        [/uel:NumberOfDays|YYYY/MM/DD|0] [/efs:abort|skip|decryptcopy|copyraw]
        [/genconfig:[Path\]FileName[/config:[Path\]FileName] [/?|help]
```

The command that you'd like to run to meet your requirements includes the following:

/i:[Path]FileName: Specifies an .xml file that contains rules that define what user, application, or system state to migrate. This option can be specified multiple times to include all of your .xml files.

/genconfig:[Path]FileName: Generates the optional Config.xml file, but does not create a migration store.

/nocompress: Disables compression of data and saves the files to a hidden folder named File at StorePath\USMT. Compression is enabled by default.

/ui:<DomainName>\<UserName> or /ui:<ComputerName>\<LocalUserName>: Migrates the specified users. By default, all users are included in the migration. DomainName and UserName can contain the asterisk (*) wildcard character.

44. C. A multivariant provisioning package is a single provisioning package that can work with multiple conditions. To provision multivariant settings, use the Windows Configuration Designer to create a provisioning package that contains all the wanted customization settings to be applied. Next, manually edit the .xml file for that project to define each set of devices (a *target*). For each target, specify at least one condition with a value. Then, for each target, provide the customization settings to be applied. For the steps on creating a provisioning package with multivariant settings, check out the following Microsoft website:

docs.microsoft.com/en-us/windows/configuration/provisioning-packages/ provisioning-multivariant#create-a-provisioning-package-with- multivariant-settings-1

45. B. Deployment Image Servicing and Management (DISM) is a command-line utility that allows an administrator to manipulate a Windows image. DISM works along with the Sysprep utility to create and manage Windows 10 image files for deployment. DISM is included with Windows 10, and it is installed in the %WINDIR%\system32\DISM folder. The parameter /get-drivers will display the basic information regarding the driver packages in the online or offline image.

46. B. `ComputerAccount` specifies the settings that you can configure when joining a device to a domain, including the computer name and the account to use for joining the computer to the domain. Use these settings to join a device to an Active Directory domain or an Azure Active Directory tenant or to add local user accounts to the device. Using %RAND% will create a random number between 0–9, allowing you to create 10 unique values and to run the package on 10 devices.

47. C. The Password Reset section allows an administrator to control if they want to enable self-service password reset (SSPR). If you enable this feature, then users will be able to reset their own passwords or unlock their accounts. An administrator can allow all accounts to use SSPR, or they can just choose certain groups to have the ability to do SSPR.

48. D. The Custom Domain Names section allows an administrator to add and verify new domain names. When the Azure subscription is first built, it comes with an Azure AD tenant that originates with an initial domain name. Administrators cannot change or delete the initial domain name once it's been created. However, they can add a domain name to the list of supported names.

49. D. The `/unattend` option can be used with the `setup.exe` command to initiate an unattended installation of Windows 10. The `/unattend` parameter enables you to use an answer file with Windows Setup. The `<answer_file>` is the file path and filename of the answer file. The syntax is `setup /unattend:<answer_file>`.

50. B. Windows 10 and Windows 7 no longer use a `boot.ini` file to control the boot order. The Boot Configuration Data (BCD) store contains boot information parameters. To edit the boot options in the BCD store, you need to use the command-line utility, `bcdedit.exe`, from the command prompt. Using the `bcdedit /default` command allows you to configure Windows 7 as the default operating system.

51. C. Windows Autopilot is a way to set up and preconfigure devices. You can use Windows Autopilot to reset, repurpose, and recover devices. Windows Autopilot user-driven mode is designed to enable Windows 10 devices to be converted from their initial state into a ready-to-use state without an administrator working on the device. You can add Windows Autopilot devices by importing a CSV file with their information. To import the CSV using the Microsoft Endpoint Manager admin center, do the following:

1. Navigate to choose Devices ➢ Windows ➢ Windows Enrollment ➢ Devices (under Windows Autopilot Deployment Program ➢ Import).

2. Under Add Windows Autopilot Devices, browse to a CSV file listing the devices that you want to add.

3. Choose Import to start importing the device information. Importing can take several minutes.

4. After import is complete, choose Devices ➢ Windows ➢ Windows Enrollment ➢ Devices (under Windows Autopilot Deployment Program ➢ Sync). A message is displayed to inform you that the synchronization is in progress and may take a few minutes to complete.

5. To see the new devices, refresh the view.

52. C. Windows Autopilot is a way to set up and preconfigure devices. Administrators can use Windows Autopilot to reset, repurpose, and recover devices. Windows Autopilot user-driven mode is designed to enable new Windows 10 devices to be transformed from their initial state to a ready-to-use state without requiring the IT department to touch the device. Because this is a user-driven deployment, the user needs to enter their Azure AD credentials in order to join the device to Azure AD. When the Windows Autopilot profile is applied to the computer, it will be registered in Azure AD and not joined.

53. C. Windows Autopilot user-driven mode is designed to enable new Windows 10 devices to be transformed from their initial state to a ready-to-use state without requiring the IT department to touch the device. The end user will do the following:

- Unbox the device, plug it in, and turn it on.

- Choose a language, locale, and keyboard layout.

- Connect it to a network (wireless or wired) with Internet access. If wireless, the user must establish the Wi-Fi connection.

- Specify their organizational account email address and password.

As soon as the Windows Autopilot is complete, the user can see their desktop and will only be able to modify the desktop settings for themselves.

54. C. Windows Autopilot user-driven mode is designed to enable new Windows 10 devices to be transformed from their initial state to a ready-to-use state without requiring the IT department to touch the device. The end user will do the following:

- Unbox the device, plug it in, and turn it on.

- Choose a language, locale, and keyboard layout.

- Connect it to a network (wireless or wired) with Internet access. If wireless, the user must establish the Wi-Fi connection.

- Specify their organizational account email address and password.

The user can configure their keyboard layout during the deployment.

55. B. When you're installing or upgrading Windows 10, the version of Windows 10 that is installed must match the CPU version. So, if a system is a 32-bit system, you must use a 32-bit version of Windows 10. If a system is a 64-bit system, you can install either the 32-bit or 64-bit version of Windows 10. For computers running Windows 7, Windows 8, or Windows 8.1, the recommended path to deploy Windows 10 is by using the Windows installation program, setup.exe, to perform the in-place upgrade. Using the in-place upgrade preserves all data, settings, applications, and drivers from the existing operating system version. In this example, Computer2 is running 64-bit, so it is the only computer that can be upgraded to Windows 10 64-bit.

56. B. An answer file is an XML-based file that has the setting definitions and values that will be used during Windows Setup. In an answer file, an administrator will specify several setup options. These options include how to partition disks, where to locate the Windows image to be installed, and what product key will be applied. An administrator can specify the values that will apply to the Windows installation, such as the names of user accounts and display settings. The answer file is usually called unattend.xml. During a DVD-based setup, an answer file can be used to automate the installation process. The Windows Setup program searches for an answer file in several locations, including the root of the DVD.

57. D. Windows System Image Manager (SIM) is the tool that you should use to create unattended Windows Setup answer files in Windows 10. It uses a GUI-based interface to set up and configure the more common options that are used in an answer file. Answer files are .xml files that are used with Windows Setup, Sysprep, Deployment Image Servicing and Management (DISM), and other deployment tools. You can access Windows SIM by searching for Windows System Image Manager on a computer.

58. A. Run sysprep.exe to prepare a Windows installation to be captured. The sysprep.exe /generalize command removes system-specific information from the Windows installation so that it can be reused on different computers. There are many options that can be used with the sysprep.exe command. To see a complete list, type **sysprep.exe /?** at a command-line prompt.

59. B. Azure AD Connect is a Microsoft utility that allows an administrator to set up a hybrid design between Azure AD and an onsite AD. It allows both versions of Active Directory to connect to each other. Azure AD Connect provides the following features:

- Federation integration
- Health monitoring
- Pass-through authentication
- Password hash synchronization
- Synchronization

60. B. Azure Active Directory (Azure AD) simplifies the way that you manage your applications by providing a single identity system for your cloud and on-premises apps. Administrators can use the Get-AzureADApplicationPolicy command to view an Azure AD application policy.

61. B. Azure Active Directory (Azure AD) simplifies the way that you manage your applications by providing a single identity system for your cloud and on-premises apps. Administrators can use the Get-AzureADDirectorySetting command to get the directory setting from Azure AD.

62. A. After you install the Windows 10 operating system, the next step will be to load all updates and patches. You can download these patches from Microsoft's website by using Windows Update. Windows Update is a free service offered by Microsoft that is used to provide updates such as service packs and patches for the Windows operating system and other Microsoft software. Windows Update can also be used to update drivers for hardware devices. Patches and other security updates are regularly released on the second Tuesday of every month. This is referred to as *Patch Tuesday.*

63. C. Windows Autopilot is a collection of technologies used to set up and pre-configure new devices, getting them ready for productive use. It is a zero-touch, self-service Windows deployment platform introduced with Windows 10. You can also use Windows Autopilot to reset, repurpose, and recover devices. Windows Autopilot allows you to do the following:

- Auto-enroll devices into MDM services, such as Microsoft Intune.

- Automatically join devices to Azure Active Directory (Azure AD) or Active Directory (via Hybrid Azure AD Join).

- Create and auto-assign devices to configuration groups depending on the device's profile.

- Customize Out of Box Experience (OOBE) content specific to the organization.

- Restrict the Administrator account creation.

64. A, B. Windows Update allows you to check for new updates and change the active hours. Active hours lets Windows know when you are usually at your computer. That information is used to schedule updates and restarts when the computer is not being used. There are two ways to set active hours in Windows 10: you can have Windows automatically adjust active hours depending on the device's activity, or you can select your own active hours.

65. D. Windows System Image Manager (SIM) is a graphical utility that can be used to create an answer file. Answer files can be used to automate the installation routine so that no user interaction is required. The first step in using an answer file with Windows SIM is to create a catalog file. The catalog file contains a writable version of the `install.wim` file from the Windows install media that the administrator can use to install the operating system. It also displays all of the Windows image's configurable settings and the information on the current status of the settings. An administrator can then create an answer file by selecting File ➢ New Answer File.

66. B. Azure AD Identity Protection allows an Azure administrator to use the same type of _protection that Microsoft uses to protect and secure user identities. Identity Protection allows an administrator to control the Windows Hello for Business experience on Windows 10 and Windows 10 Mobile devices. You can use Identity Protection settings to configure options for devices, such as PINs and gestures for Windows Hello for Business.

67. D. A provisioning package (`.ppkg`) is a container for a collection of configuration settings. Administrators can create provisioning packages that let them quickly and efficiently configure a device without having to install a new image. Administrators can use the Windows Configuration Designer (WCD), which has the tools that allow an administrator to create a provisioning package easily.

68. D. A provisioning package is created by using the Windows Configuration Designer (WCD) and can be used to send one or more configurations to applications and settings on a device. You use Windows Configuration Designer to create a provisioning package (`.ppkg`) that contains customization settings. A provisioning package can be applied to a device running Windows 10 or Windows 10 Mobile. For the steps on creating a provisioning package for Windows 10, check out the following Microsoft website:

`docs.microsoft.com/en-us/windows/configuration/provisioning-packages/provisioning-create-package`

69. D. Windows Hello is a two-factor biometric authentication mechanism built into Windows 10. Windows Hello for Business is the enterprise version of Windows Hello that allows users to authenticate to Active Directory or Azure AD and permits them to access network resources. You can configure Windows Hello for Business by using Group Policy or by using a mobile device management (MDM) policy. Windows Hello for Business uses certificate-based or asymmetric (public/private key) authentication.

70. A. A provisioning package (.ppkg) is a container for an assembly of configuration settings. You can create provisioning packages that allow you to configure a device quickly without having to install a new image. You can deploy the provisioning package to users by using email, by using physical media, or by sharing the file. The settings are applied to the target device using one of the following methods:

- By running the .ppkg file

- By using the Settings app to add the provisioning package

- By using the Add-ProvisioningPackage Windows PowerShell command

71. B. Companies with enterprise agreements (EAs) can use volume activation methods that provide tools and services that allow the activation to be automated and deployed on a larger scale. These tools and services include the following:

- Active Directory–based activation

- Key Management Service (KMS)

- Multiple Activation Key (MAK)

However, in this question, you are specifically being asked about the Key Management Service (KMS). KMS is an automated service that is hosted on a computer in a domain-based network, and all volume editions of Windows 10 intermittently connect to the KMS host to request activation. KMS allows organizations to activate systems within their own network, removing the need for individual computers to connect to Microsoft for product activation.

72. B. Deployment Image Servicing and Management (DISM) is a command-line tool that is used to mount and service Windows images before deployment. Use DISM to work with provisioning packages (.ppkg) files. The syntax is as follows:

```
DISM.exe <image location> /Add-ProvisioningPackage /PackagePath:<package_
path> [/CatalogPath:<path>]
```

73. B. There are a number of system requirements that must be met prior to installing Windows 10. However, to meet your deployment requirements, you must have the following:

- Miracast requires a display adapter that supports Windows Display Driver Model (WDDM) 1.3, and a Wi-Fi adapter that supports Wi-Fi Direct.

- BitLocker Drive Encryption requires a Trusted Platform Module (TPM) 1.2 or higher.

- Windows Hello requires a camera configured for near infrared (IR) imaging or fingerprint reader for biometric authentication.

In examining the requirements needed to install Windows 10, only Computer2 fits the necessary requirements.

74. A, C. You can upgrade to Windows 10 from Windows 7 or a later operating system. The easiest path to upgrade computers that are currently running Windows 7, Windows 8, or Windows 8.1 to Windows 10 is through an in-place upgrade. Since this question states that you will be using an in-place upgrade, we can only upgrade to the same bit architecture. So, you can only perform an in-place upgrade on the 32-bit version of Windows 10 Professional and Windows 10 Enterprise.

75. B. Windows PE (WinPE) for Windows 10 is a small operating system used to install, deploy, and repair Windows 10 for desktop editions (Home, Pro, Enterprise, and Education), Windows Server, and other Windows operating systems. To upgrade the Windows 8 machines to Windows 10, you should start the computers from Windows PE and then run `setup.exe` from a network share that contains the Windows 10 installation source files.

76. D. There are three types of updates that Windows Update for Business manages for Windows 10 devices: Quality Updates, Feature Updates, and Non-Deferrable Updates. The update that is being discussed is the Quality Update. Quality Updates are typically released on the second Tuesday of each month and include security, critical, and driver updates. Quality Updates are cumulative in that they supersede all previous updates. Updates for Microsoft products are also categorized as Quality Updates.

77. D. While all of the listed options are important to the troubleshooting process, the objective of ensuring that Windows Autopilot has Internet access falls within the network connectivity troubleshooting process. Windows Autopilot requires Internet access to work. Windows Autopilot has a few network configuration requirements, such as the devices must have Internet access, and the devices must be able to access the cloud services that are utilized by Autopilot, such as DNS name resolution, and firewall access through HTTP port 80, HTTPS port 443, and UDP/NTP port 123.

78. D. Windows Autopilot Reset removes personal files, applications, and settings and returns a device's original settings, while keeping its identity connection to Azure AD and its management connection to Intune. The Windows Autopilot Reset process retains information from the existing device, such as the following:

- The region, language, and keyboard values
- Wi-Fi connection information
- Any provisioning packages that were previously applied to the device
- Azure Active Directory (Azure AD) device membership and mobile device management (MDM) enrollment information

79. B. A private store is a feature in Microsoft Store for Business that companies obtain during the signup process. When you add apps to the private store, all corporate personnel can view and download the apps. The private store is available as a tab in the Microsoft Store app, and it is typically named for your company. Only apps with online licenses can be added to the private store. To claim an app from the private store, an employee should do the following:

1. Sign in to their computer using their Azure Active Directory (AD) credentials and start the Microsoft Store app.

2. Click the Private Store tab.

3. Click the app to be installed and then click Install.

80. D. A provisioning package (.ppkg) is a container for a set of configuration settings. You can create provisioning packages that let you configure a device without having to install a new image. A provisioning package can perform a variety of tasks, such as the following:

- Adding computers onto a domain
- Adding files
- Configuring computer names and user accounts
- Configuring network connectivity settings
- Configuring the Windows user interface
- Implementing security settings
- Installing applications
- Installing certificates
- Removing installed software
- Resetting Windows 10
- Running Windows PowerShell scripts
- Upgrading between Windows 10 versions, provided the path is supported

In this question, the option is to downgrade from Enterprise to Home. Downgrading from Enterprise to Home is not supported.

81. D. Azure Active Directory (Azure AD) simplifies the management of applications by providing a single identity system for cloud and on-premises apps. Administrators can use the `Set-AzureADPolicy` Windows PowerShell command to update a policy.

82. D. Azure Active Directory (Azure AD) simplifies the management of applications by providing a single identity system for cloud and on-premises apps. Administrators can use the `New-AzureADPolicy` command to create a policy.

83. C. The System Preparation Tool (Sysprep) is used to prepare a computer for disk imaging, and the disk image can then be captured using Deployment Image Servicing and Management (DISM). The DISM tool is included with Windows 10. Sysprep is a free utility that comes with all Windows operating systems. By default, the `sysprep.exe` utility can be found on Windows 10 operating systems in the `Windows\system32\sysprep` directory.

84. A. Administrators can use the Custom Domain Names section of Azure AD to add an organization's new or existing domain names to the list of supported names. The Custom Domain Names section allows an administrator to add and verify new domain names. When the Azure subscription is first created, it comes with an Azure AD tenant that has an initial domain name. Administrators cannot change or delete the initial domain name once it has been created, but you can add a domain name to the list of supported names. For the steps on how to add a custom domain name to Azure AD, check out the following Microsoft website:

docs.microsoft.com/en-us/azure/active-directory/fundamentals/add-custom-domain#add-your-custom-domain-name-to-azure-ad

85. B. In Configuration Manager, client and site server components record process information in individual log files. An administrator can use the information in these logs to help with troubleshooting. By default, Configuration Manager enables logging for client and server components. All Configuration Manager log files are plain text, so they can be viewed with any text reader such as Notepad. The log type being discussed is `PolicyAgentProvider` `.log`, which records policy changes.

86. B. Use the Windows Configuration Designer (WCD) tool to create provisioning packages to configure devices running Windows 10. All of the statements are true except that you cannot run multiple instances of Windows Configuration Designer (WCD) on a computer simultaneously.

87. B. Windows Update for Business allows administrators to use the cloud-based Windows Update service to deploy and manage Windows Updates. The feature being discussed in the question is the Internal Deployment Groups, which allows you to assign Windows 10 devices into groups and then specify the order in which they receive updates.

88. A. Microsoft offers both a 32-bit version and a 64-bit version of Windows 10. To install Windows 10 successfully, the system must meet or exceed certain minimum hardware requirements. The minimum requirements are as follows:

CPU (processor): 1 GHz or faster processor or system-on-a-chip (SoC)

Memory (RAM): 1 GB for 32-bit or 2 GB for 64-bit

Hard disk: 16 GB for 32-bit OS or 20 GB for 64-bit OS

Video adapter: DirectX 9 or later with WDDM 1.0 driver

Optional drive: DVD-R/W drive

Network device: Compatible network interface card

In this question, since you have only a 15 GB hard drive, this does not meet the requirement to install the 64-bit versions. So, given the options, you can only install the 32-bit version of Windows 10 Enterprise.

89. D. You can use the User State Migration Tool (USMT) to automate migration during large deployments of the Windows operating system. USMT uses configurable migration rule (`.xml`) files to control precisely what user accounts, files, operating system configurations, and application settings are migrated and how they are migrated. There are a large number of items that can be migrated; however, you cannot migrate the following using USMT:

- Customized shortcut icons
- Device drivers

- Files and settings if a foreign language is installed
- Local printers and hardware-related configurations
- Passwords
- Shared folder permissions

90. B. There are three types of updates that Windows Update for Business manages for Windows 10 devices: Quality Updates, Feature Updates, and Non-Deferrable Updates. The update that is being discussed are Non-Deferrable Updates. Non-Deferrable Updates include anti-malware and anti-spyware definition updates that are used by Windows Security components, such as Windows Defender. These types of updates cannot be deferred. Definition updates will be installed immediately regardless of any deferral settings.

91. C. When an Update Compliance is added to a Log Analytics workspace, you can start enrolling your devices into your organization by using the CommercialID. A CommercialID is a globally unique identifier that is assigned to a specific Log Analytics workspace. The CommercialID is copied to a Mobile Device Management (MDM) or Group Policy object, and it is used to identify devices within your environment. To find your CommercialID within Azure, perform the following:

   1. Navigate to the Solutions tab for your workspace and then select the WaaSUpdateInsights solution.

   2. Select the Update Compliance Settings page on the navigation bar.

   The CommercialID will be available on the settings page.

92. C. Deployment scenarios are assigned to one of three categories. The categories include modern, dynamic, and traditional. Dynamic deployment methods enable an administrator to configure applications and settings for specific use cases. Dynamic deployment scenarios include Subscription Activation, Azure Active Directory Join (Azure AD) with Automatic Mobile Device Management (MDM), and Provisioning Packages. Windows 10 Subscription Activation allows an administrator to upgrade devices automatically with Windows 10 Professional to Windows 10 Enterprise without needing to enter a product key or perform a restart.

93. C. Using the Windows Configuration Designer (WCD), a provisioning package can be created and can be used to send one or more configurations to applications and settings on a device. The WCD is included in the Windows Assessment and Deployment Kit (Windows ADK). You can also download the stand-alone WCD app from the Microsoft Store.

94. A. Provisioning packages can be deployed to users in a variety of ways, including by email, by physical media, or by sharing the file using OneDrive for Business. Settings can be applied to the target device in a number of methods. Some of these methods include the following:

- By running the .ppkg file
- By using the Settings app to add the provisioning package
- By using the Add-ProvisioningPackage Windows PowerShell cmdlet

The `Add-ProvisioningPackage` cmdlet will apply a provisioning package. The syntax is as follows:

```
Add-ProvisioningPackage [-Path] <string> [-ForceInstall] [-LogsFolder
<string>] [-QuietInstall] [-WprpFile <string>] [<CommonParameters>]
```

95. C. You should perform a pilot deployment prior to performing a full rollout. The pilot deployment will involve rolling out the new software to a select group of users within the company. The pilot deployment is important because it can ensure compatibility with any existing hardware, applications, and infrastructure. You can then review and implement any feedback that is received from users.

96. C. Desktop Analytics is a replacement of Windows Analytics, which was retired on January 31, 2020. The functions of Windows Analytics are combined in the Desktop Analytics service. Desktop Analytics is integrated with Configuration Manager. Desktop Analytics provides several benefits. Some include the following:

    Device and software inventory: This is the inventory of key factors such as apps and versions of Windows.

    Pilot identification: This is the identification of factors that focus on the key aspects to the pilot deployment of Windows upgrades and updates.

    Issue identification: This service uses collected market data along with your data to predict potential issues. It will then suggest potential mitigations.

    In this question, the benefit of issue identification is being discussed.

97. C. If you have deployed a `.ppkg` file and then have issues, you should first inspect the provisioning package. You can locate the project file by opening the file with the `.icdproj` in the file extension. Open it using the Windows Configuration Designer (WCD). You should then review the settings and confirm that they are correct. Once the customization settings have been confirmed as correct, you should export the package again. Increase the version number to avoid confusion with the previous version. Packages with the same versioning number will not be applied to the same target device twice.

98. C. Windows Autopilot is a way to set up and preconfigure devices. You can use Windows Autopilot to reset, repurpose, and recover devices. Windows Autopilot self-deploying mode is used for converting Windows 10 devices that will be automatically configured for use as a kiosk terminal, as a shared computer, or as a digital signage device.

99. A. There are several requirements and prerequisites that must be met to use Windows Autopilot with your Windows 10 devices. The devices must have an Internet connection. If Internet access is not available, then you will need to use an alternative deployment method. The devices also need to use DNS for name resolution and must have firewall access for HTTP port 80, HTTPS port 443, and UDP/NTP port 123.

100. B. Prior to deploying a device using Windows Autopilot, the device must be registered with the Windows Autopilot deployment service. This is typically performed by the original equipment manufacturer (OEM), reseller, or distributor. However, an organization can perform this task by collecting the hardware identity and uploading it manually. You can collect the hardware ID from an existing device by using Windows PowerShell. You can use the `Get-WindowsAutoPilotInfo.ps1` PowerShell script. This script has been published to the PowerShell Gallery website at `www.powershellgal-lery.com/packages/Get-WindowsAutoPilotInfo`. For more information on how to collect the hardware ID from existing devices by using Windows PowerShell, check out the following Microsoft website:

`docs.microsoft.com/en-us/windows/deployment/windows-autopilot/add-devices`

101. A. Using Configuration Manager, you can extract the hash information and put it into a `.csv` file. Use Configuration Manager to collect and report the device information that is needed by Intune. This information contains the device serial number, the Windows product identifier, and a hardware identifier. This information is used to register the device in Intune to support Windows Autopilot. To create the report, perform the following steps:

1. In the Configuration Manager console, go to the Monitoring workspace, expand the Reporting node, expand Reports, and select the Hardware – General node.

2. Run the report, Windows Autopilot Device Information, and review the results.

3. In the report viewer, select the Export icon and choose the CSV (comma-delimited) option.

4. After saving the file, upload the data to Intune.

102. B. When using Windows Autopilot and an issue occurs, an error code will be generated. Some error codes are seen on the device when an issue occurs, and some error codes can be viewed using the Event Trace for Windows tool. The error `0x801c0003` indicates that the Azure AD join failed. The error will read "Something went wrong." If you are receiving error `801c0003` when joining a computer to Azure Active Directory, you may need to modify the default device settings in Azure AD. To correct the issue, log onto the Azure AD portal at `portal.azure.com`, navigate to Azure Active Directory ➤ Devices, and confirm the device settings.

103. B. The Windows Analytics service was retired on January 31, 2020, and was replaced with Desktop Analytics. Desktop Analytics is a cloud-based service that integrates with Configuration Manager. The service allows you to make informed decisions regarding the update readiness of your Windows clients. Use Desktop Analytics with Configuration Manager to do the following:

- Assess app compatibility with the latest Windows 10 feature updates.

- Create an inventory of apps running in an organization.

- Create pilot groups that represent the entire application and driver estate across a minimal set of devices.

- Deploy Windows 10 to pilot and production-managed devices.

- Identify compatibility issues and receive mitigation suggestions based on cloud-enabled data insights.

- Deploy Windows 10 to pilot and production-managed devices.

104. C. The Windows Analytics service was retired on January 31, 2020. Desktop Analytics is the replacement of Windows Analytics. If your Configuration Manager site had a connection to Upgrade Readiness, you need to remove it and reconfigure clients. To remove the Upgrade Readiness connection, do the following:

1. Open the Configuration Manager console as an administrator.

2. Go to the Administration workspace, expand Cloud Services, and select the Azure Services node.

3. Delete the Windows Analytics service.

For eligible Windows Analytics customers, a data migration option exists to help with onboarding to Desktop Analytics. For additional information, go to the following Microsoft website:

docs.microsoft.com/en-us/mem/configmgr/core/clients/manage/upgrade-readiness

105. C. You can use the User State Migration Tool (USMT) to automate migration during Windows deployments. USMT uses configurable migration rule (.xml) files to control what user accounts, user files, operating system settings, and application settings are migrated. You can use USMT for either side-by-side migrations, where one piece of hardware is being replaced, or wipe-and-load (or refresh) migrations, when only the operating system is being upgraded. A side-by-side migration is used when the source and destination computers for the upgrade are different machines. You install Windows 10 on a new computer and then migrate the data and user settings.

106. D. The User State Migration Tool (USMT) uses configurable migration rule (.xml) files to control what user accounts, user files, operating system settings, and application settings are migrated. They can be written to improve efficiency, and it can be customized with settings and rules. USMT migration XML files include the following:

- MigApp.xml

- MigDocs.xml

- MigUser.xml

- Custom XML files that are created

107. D. The User State Migration Tool (USMT) is included with the Windows Assessment and Deployment Kit (Windows ADK) for Windows 10. USMT consists of several command-line tools and configuration files that use XML files to store customizations. The usmtutils.exe file is used to compress, encrypt, and validate the migration store files.

108. D. You can use the User State Migration Tool (USMT) to automate migration during Windows deployments. USMT uses configurable migration rule (.xml) files to control what user accounts, user files, operating system settings, and application settings are migrated. You can use USMT for either side-by-side migrations, where one piece of hardware is being replaced, or wipe-and-load (or refresh) migrations, when only the operating system is being upgraded. A wipe-and-load migration is where the source and destination computer are the same. You back up the user data and settings to an external location and then install Windows 10. Then you restore the user data and settings.

109. A. You configure Delivery Optimization settings by using Group Policy. The GPO settings are found at Computer Configuration ➤ Administrative Templates ➤ Windows Components ➤ Delivery Optimization. Download Mode is the setting used to configure the use of Windows Update Delivery Optimization for downloads of Windows Updates, apps, and app updates. There are six Download Mode options. They are as follows:

- Bypass

- Group

- HTTP Only

- Internet

- LAN

- Simple

The Group mode is HTTP downloading and peering in the same private group on a local LAN.

110. C. Windows 10 implements the Windows Update for Business service for organizations to update devices, and it uses the concept of update branches with different tracks that allow an administrator to fine-tune the management of updates. The Windows Update for Business service provides the tools required to configure Windows 10 update settings using either Group Policy or Microsoft Intune. The Maintenance windows feature allows administrators to specify when the updates will be applied to devices.

111. A. Windows Update for Business manages three types of updates for Windows 10 devices. They are as follows:

- Feature Updates

- Non-Deferrable Updates

- Quality Updates

The update type that is being discussed in this question is Feature Updates. Feature Updates are updates that include all previous security and quality updates and introduces new operating system features and changes. These updates include a change in the Windows 10 version and are released twice a year (usually in March and September).

112. D. You can configure Windows Update for Business by using Group Policy. The settings are located at Computer Configuration ➢ Administrative Templates ➢ Windows Components ➢ Windows Update ➢ Windows Update For Business. The Select When Quality Updates Are Received setting allows an administrator to specify when to receive quality updates and to defer receiving quality updates for up to 30 days. An administrator can also temporarily pause quality updates up to 35 days.

113. C. While Windows Analytics was retired on January 31, 2020, support for Update Compliance has continued through the Azure Portal. Update Compliance enables organizations to do the following:

- Check bandwidth savings acquired across multiple content types by using Delivery Optimization.

- Monitor security, quality, and feature updates for the Windows 10 Professional, Education, and Enterprise editions.

- View a report of device and update compliance issues that require attention.

Use Update Compliance to monitor your device's Windows updates and Windows Defender Antivirus status.

114. B. While Windows Analytics was retired on January 31, 2020, support for Update Compliance has continued through the Azure Portal. Update Compliance is used to monitor a device's Windows updates and Windows Defender Antivirus status. The Update Compliance overview blade summarizes all of the data Update Compliance provides. There are different sections available in Update Compliance. The section being discussed in the question is the Need Attention! section. The Need Attention! section is the default section of the Update Compliance workspace. It provides a summary of the different update-related issues encountered by devices.

115. A. Azure Active Directory (Azure AD) includes features such as Azure Multifactor Authentication (Azure MFA) and Azure AD Self-Service Password Reset (SSPR). These allow an administrator to protect their organizations and users with secure authentication methods. The use of security questions is available only in Azure AD SSPR. If security questions are used, Microsoft recommends that they be used in conjunction with another security method. Security questions are stored privately and securely on a user object in the directory, and they can only be answered by users during registration. There is no way for an administrator to read or modify a user's questions or answers.

116. B. For this question, the best option is to tell your colleague is that multifactor authentication is using smart cards and PINs. Multifactor authentication (MFA) is a security system that requires more than one method of authentication from separate categories of credentials to verify the user's identity for a login or other transaction. The authentication categories are as follows:

- Something you know

- Something you have

- Something you are

117. B. In this scenario, you and your colleague are discussing something you have. Physical objects may be used as authentication mechanisms. If an organization is looking to protect sensitive information and critical resources, then they should implement multifactor authentication. Multifactor authentication implementations combine two or more authentication mechanisms from different authentication categories. The authentication categories are something you know, something you have, and something you are.

118. A. Azure Multifactor Authentication (Azure MFA) provides companies with a two-step verification solution that can be used to maintain access to data and applications, and it provides users with a simple sign-in process. By enabling Azure AD Identity Protection, this method uses an Azure AD Identity Protection risk policy to enforce two-step verification for sign-in to all cloud applications. For the steps on how to enable the user risk and sign-in risk policies, visit the following Microsoft website:

docs.microsoft.com/en-us/azure/active-directory/identity-protection/
howto-identity-protection-configure-risk-policies#enable-policies

119. C. As an administrator, you may want to prevent users from associating their Microsoft accounts with a device and to block users from accessing personal cloud resources by using their Microsoft accounts. To achieve this, you can configure Microsoft account restrictions using two GPOs. They are Block All Consumer Microsoft Account User Authentication and Accounts: Block Microsoft Accounts. In this question, you want to prevent users from using Microsoft accounts for authentication for applications or services, so you will be utilizing Block All Consumer Microsoft Account User Authentication. Using this setting can prevent users from using Microsoft accounts for authentication for applications or services. It is recommended to enable this setting prior to a user signing into a device to prevent cached tokens from being present. This GPO is located at Computer Configuration\Administrative Templates\Windows Components\Microsoft Account.

120. D. In Windows 10, Windows Hello for Business replaces passwords with strong two-factor authentication on computers and mobile devices. This consists of user credentials that are linked to a device, and it uses a biometric or PIN. An administrator can create policies to manage Windows Hello for Business that are used on the Windows 10 devices that connect to the network. In this question, you are connecting the new computer to an Azure AD, so the machine would need to be upgraded to Windows 10 Enterprise.

121. B. You can sign in to a computer using a picture password. You can select a picture and three gestures that will be used to create a customized password. Once you have chosen a picture, you can draw with the mouse, with a touchpad, or on a touchscreen to create a combination of circles, straight lines, and taps. The size, position, and direction of the drawn gestures become part of the picture password. To access a picture password, go to Sign-in Options by going to Start ➤ Settings ➤ Accounts ➤ Sign-in Options. On the Sign-in Options page, the following sign-in methods are available:

- Windows Hello Face
- Windows Hello Fingerprint
- Windows Hello PIN

- Security key
- Password
- Picture Password

Click Picture Password and then click Add and follow the prompts.

122. D. Windows Hello is a biometrics system integrated into Windows. Windows Hello is a Microsoft account that can be used to authenticate to a domain, a cloud-based domain, or a computer. To do this, you need to link your Microsoft account to your Windows 10 system. When you set up Windows Hello on a device, you can set up the system to use Windows Hello or a personal identification number (PIN). To configure Windows Hello options, select Start ➤ Settings ➤ Accounts. Windows Hello for Business is a newer credential in Windows 10 that helps increase security when accessing corporate resources. Windows Hello for Business replaces passwords with strong two-factor authentication on computers and mobile devices. This authentication consists of a user credential that is linked to a device and uses a biometric or PIN.

123. C. Windows 10 gives you the ability to set up a logon with a picture. If you want to use a picture for authentication, you first choose a picture, and then you add three gestures onto the picture. These gestures can be straight lines, circles, squares, or anything you want. Then, when you log on to the system, you just re-create the gestures on the picture and the system will log you in.

124. D. When securing Windows 10 with Windows Hello for Business, you can increase the level of security by using a personal identification number (PIN). A PIN can require or block special characters, uppercase characters, lowercase characters, and digits. The maximum length that can be set for a PIN is 127 characters.

125. B. Windows 10 can use other devices that are paired with a computer to detect when you walk away and lock the computer after the paired device is out of Bluetooth range. This makes it harder for an individual to access a device if they step away from the computer and forget to lock it. You utilize Bluetooth to pair a device with a computer. Follow these steps to set up a dynamic lock:

1. On a Windows 10 computer, select Start ➤ Settings ➤ Accounts ➤ Sign-in Options.

2. Under Dynamic Lock, select the Allow Windows To Automatically Lock Your Device When You're Away checkbox.

Then, take the Bluetooth device with you when you move away from the computer. This will automatically lock a minute or so after you're out of Bluetooth range. Just note that the Bluetooth range is different depending on the device. You can configure dynamic lock functionality for devices by using the Configure Dynamic Lock Factors GPO settings as well. This policy can be located at `Computer Configuration\Administrative Templates\Windows Components\Windows Hello for Business`.

Chapter 6: Manage Policies and Profiles

1. A. Microsoft Intune includes many built-in settings to control different features on a device. You can also create custom profiles, which are created similar to built-in profiles. Custom profile settings allow an Intune administrator to configure options that are not automatically included with Intune. For example, an administrator can set a custom profile that allows you to create ADMX-backed policy or even enable self-service password resets. For more information on how to create a custom policy, check out the following Microsoft website:

   docs.microsoft.com/en-us/mem/intune/configuration/custom-settings-configure#create-the-profile

2. A. A conditional access policy specifies the app or services that you want to protect, so you control the devices and apps that can connect to your email and company resources. There are two types of conditional access with Intune: device-based and app-based. For the steps on how to create a conditional access policy, check out the following Microsoft website:

   docs.microsoft.com/en-us/mem/intune/protect/create-conditional-access-intune#create-conditional-access-policy

3. B. Device compliance policies are a key feature when using Intune to protect an organization's resources. In Intune, you create rules and settings that devices must meet to be considered compliant. You can integrate Microsoft Defender Advanced Threat Protection (Microsoft Defender ATP) with Microsoft Intune as a Mobile Threat Defense solution. Microsoft Defender ATP works with devices that run Windows 10 or later and with Android devices. You can use a device compliance policy to set the level of risk you want to allow. Risk levels are reported by Microsoft Defender ATP. Devices that exceed the allowed risk level are identified as noncompliant. Intune device compliance policies are used to classify devices with a Medium or High level of risk as noncompliant. The compromised device is classified as noncompliant. For the steps on how to create a device compliance policy, check out the following Microsoft website:

   docs.microsoft.com/en-us/mem/intune/protect/advanced-threat-protection#create-and-assign-the-compliance-policy

4. D. This cannot be done. The feature called hybrid mobile device management is now deprecated. Hybrid MDM is not the same as co-management. Support for Hybrid MDM ended on September 1, 2019, and new customers can no longer create a hybrid connection. If your Configuration Manager site has a Microsoft Intune subscription listed, you need to remove it. To remove hybrid MDM, perform the following steps:

   1. In the Configuration Manager console, go to the Administration workspace. Expand Cloud Services ➤ Microsoft Intune Subscription. Delete the existing Intune Subscription.

   2. In the Remove Microsoft Intune Subscription Wizard, select the option Remove Microsoft Intune Subscription from Configuration Manager and then click Next.

   3. Complete the wizard.

5. B. One advantage of utilizing Azure is the ability to protect corporate data by making sure that users and devices meet certain requirements. When using Intune, this is known as *compliance policies*. Compliance policies are rules and settings that users and devices must follow to connect and access In-tune. Compliance reports allow you to review device compliance and troubleshoot any compliance-related issues. To open the compliance dashboard, perform the following steps:

   1. Sign in to the Microsoft Endpoint Manager admin center.

   2. Select Devices ➤ Overview and go to the Compliance status tab.

   The device compliance shows the compliance states for all Intune-enrolled devices. The device compliance states are kept in two different databases: Intune and Azure Active Directory. The different device compliance policies are as follows:

   - Compliant
   - In-grace period
   - Not evaluated
   - Not compliant
   - Device not synced

6. A. Windows Known Folder Move (KFM) for OneDrive is a feature that automatically redirects a user's personal folders and important files to their OneDrive for Business account stored on the Microsoft cloud. This allows users to access their files across different devices and applications. There are two primary advantages of moving or redirecting Windows known folders to OneDrive:

   - Your users can continue using the folders they're familiar with. They don't have to change their work habits to save files to OneDrive.
   - Saving files to OneDrive backs up your users' data in the cloud and gives them access to their files from any device.

   The folders that are redirected as part of the Windows known folders feature include the following:

   - Camera Roll
   - Desktop
   - Documents
   - Pictures
   - Screenshots

7. C. Azure Active Directory (Azure AD) Terms of Use provide a method that you can use to present information to end users. Azure AD Terms of Use are in PDF format. The PDF file can be any content, such as existing contract documents, that allows you to collect end-user agreements during the user sign-in process. To add a Terms of Use document, check out the following Microsoft website:

   docs.microsoft.com/en-us/azure/active-directory/conditional-access/
   terms-of-use#add-terms-of-use

8.   B. Mobile device management (MDM) solutions help guard corporate data by requiring that users and devices meet certain requirements. In Intune, this feature is called *compliance policies*. Compliance policies define the rules and settings that users and devices must meet to be compliant. When combined with conditional access, an administrator can block users and devices that don't meet the rules. For this question, DeviceB will not be compliant because its IP address is on is not on NetworkA, which is required under the compliance policy.

9.   B. Folder Redirection allows users and administrators to redirect the path of a known folder to a new location, manually or by using Group Policy. The new location can be a folder on the local computer or a directory on a file share. Users interact with files in the redirected folder as if it still existed on the local drive. The AppData folder contains application settings, files, and data specific to the application on a Windows computer. Because both the Desktop folder and the `AppData\Roaming` folder have been redirected, the user will be able to see the created document, the screen saver settings, the desktop background, and the default save location for Word.

10.   D. There are two types of computer hard disks: basic disks and dynamic disks. Basic disks are usually used as storage media with Windows that contains partitions such as the primary partitions and logical drives. Dynamic disks provide the ability to create fault-tolerant volumes that can span multiple disks. Dynamic disks allow you to create simple volumes, extended volumes, spanned volumes, mirrored volumes, and striped volumes.

11.   A, B. Folder Redirection allows users and administrators to redirect the path of a known folder to a new location manually, or by using Group Policy. The new location can be a folder on the local computer or a directory on a file share. Users interact with files in the redirected folder as if it still existed on the local drive. To configure the Folder Redirection feature, do the following:

   1.   Open the Group Policy object where the Folder Redirection policy is set.

   2.   Under User Configuration, double-click Windows Settings.

   3.   Double-click Folder Redirection.

   4.   Click the folder to be configured, right-click the folder, and then click Properties.

   5.   Select the Settings property page, click to clear the Grant The User Exclusive Rights To My Documents checkbox, and then click OK.

   6.   Close all windows.

On the Settings tab of the Properties dialog box for a folder, you can also enable or disable Policy Removal. There are two options available under Policy Removal. They are Redirect The Folder Back To The User Profile Location When Policy Is Removed and Leave The Folder In The New Location When Policy Is Removed. In this question, the option Leave The Folder In The New Location When Policy Is Removed is enabled. You want to instead enable Redirect The Folder Back To The User Profile Location When Policy Is Removed. This way, the folder remains at its redirected location, and the contents remain at the redirected location. The user continues to have access to the contents in the redirected folder.

12. B. Windows Hello is a two-factor biometric authentication mechanism that is built into Windows 10. Windows Hello for Business is the enterprise implementation of Windows Hello. It allows users to authenticate to Active Directory or Azure Active Directory (Azure AD) and enables users to access network resources. You can configure Windows Hello for Business by using Group Policy objects (GPOs) or by using mobile device management (MDM) policies. To create a Windows Hello for Business policy in Intune, check out the following Microsoft website:

docs.microsoft.com/en-us/mem/intune/protect/windows-hello#create-a-windows-hello-for-business-policy

In this question, the options are Windows 8.1, Windows 10 or later, and macOS. Windows Hello for Business can be run in a hybrid deployment; however, Windows 10 is the only platform listed that can support Windows Hello for Business.

13. C. Windows Hello is a two-factor biometric authentication mechanism that is built into Windows 10. Windows Hello for Business is the enterprise implementation of Windows Hello. It allows users to authenticate to Active Directory or Azure Active Directory (Azure AD) and enables users to access network resources. You can configure Windows Hello for Business by using Group Policy objects (GPOs) or by using mobile device management (MDM) policies. With Intune, you can use device configuration profiles to manage common endpoint protection security features on devices, including the following:

- Firewall

- BitLocker

- Allowing and blocking apps

- Microsoft Defender and encryption

So, since you want to create an Intune profile to configure Windows Hello for Business, you should use endpoint protection.

14. B. An administrator can implement conditional access policies from Azure Active Directory (Azure AD), Intune, or the Microsoft 365 Device Management console. Conditional access policies allow an administrator to control access automatically to cloud apps and corporate data depending upon the defined conditions. An administrator can assign conditional access policies to users and groups, cloud apps, and devices. The device state condition can be used to exclude devices that are hybrid Azure AD–joined and/or devices marked as compliant with a Microsoft Intune compliance policy from an organization's conditional access policies.

15. A. With Windows 10, Azure Active Directory (Azure AD) users can synchronize their user settings and application settings data to the cloud. Enterprise State Roaming provides users with a unified experience across their Windows devices. By using Enterprise State Roaming, the desktop background, the Favorites folder, and the browsing history will be available on the new computers.

16. B. When you have new Windows 10 devices that will be joined to Azure AD and automatically enrolled into Intune, you will want to install the Configuration Manager client to reach a co-management state. Configuration Manager is used to collect and report the device information required by Intune. This information contains the device serial number, the Windows product identifier, and a hardware identifier. For Internet-based devices, you will need to create an app in Intune and deploy the app to the Windows 10 devices that aren't already Configuration Manager clients.

17. A. With co-management, you can maintain your established processes for using Configuration Manager to manage your network's computers. Configuration Manager includes a single primary site with all site system roles located on the same server. It is called the *site server*. When you enable co-management, you will assign a collection as a Pilot group. This is a group that contains a small number of clients to test the co-management configurations. So, you should configure a device collection in Configuration Manager.

18. A. One of the options that you can set in device configuration profiles is the ability to set up custom profiles. Custom profile settings allow an Intune administrator to configure options that are not automatically included with Intune. An administrator can set a custom profile that allows you to create ADMX-backed policy or even enable self-service password resets. For the steps on how to create a custom device configuration profile, check out the following Microsoft website:

    docs.microsoft.com/en-us/mem/intune/configuration/custom-settings-configure#create-the-profile

19. C. Device identity management in Azure Active Directory (Azure AD) ensures that the users accessing resources meet your standards for security and compliance. The Azure AD portal offers a central location to manage device identities. The Devices page enables you to do the following:

    - Configure the device settings.
    - Locate devices.
    - Perform device identity management tasks.
    - Review device-related audit logs.

    You can access the Devices page by performing the following steps:

    1. Sign into the Azure portal.
    2. Browse to Azure Active Directory ➤ Devices.

    To manage device identities using the Azure AD portal, the devices either need to be registered or joined to Azure AD. The device settings page enables an administrator to configure settings related to device identities, shown in the following graphic.

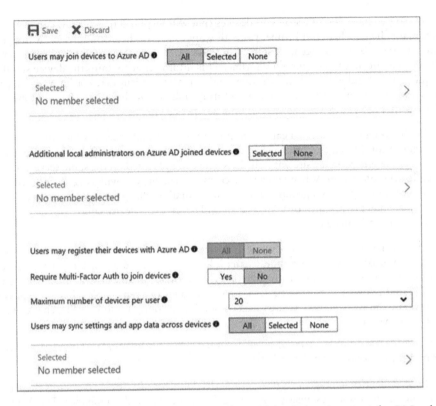

20. B. Endpoint protection allows you to set Windows 10 (and above) options for BitLocker and Windows Defender settings. You can set Windows Defender for a threat score setting so that if a device has a High threat score rating, then you can stop the device from accessing your network resources.

21. E. The Office Deployment Tool (ODT) is a command-line tool that can be used to download and deploy Microsoft 365 Apps to client computers. It controls Office installations. You can define the installed products and languages, how the products are updated, and if the install experience is displayed to the users. You can download the ODT from the Microsoft Download Center. After the file is downloaded, run the self-extracting executable file called setup.exe and a sample configuration file called configuration.xml.

22. D. File systems are used to track the storage of files on a hard drive in a way that is understood by end users while allowing the operating system the ability to retrieve the requested files. In this case, both Windows 10 and Windows XP Professional support FAT32 and NTFS, so both file systems will be viewable on both operating systems. Microsoft recommends that you use the NTFS file system with Windows 10 since it will allow you to take advantage of features such as local security, file compression, and file encryption. You should choose the FAT32 file system only if you want to dual-boot a computer with a version of Windows that does not support NTFS since it is backward compatible.

23. B. Windows Hello for Business is a method for signing in to Windows devices by replacing passwords, smart cards, and virtual smart cards. Intune includes built-in settings so that Administrators can configure and use Windows Hello for Business. You can use these settings to do the following:

- Enable Windows Hello for Business for devices and users.

- Set device PIN requirements, including a minimum or maximum PIN length.

- Allow gestures, such as a fingerprint, that users can (or can't) use to sign in to devices.

So, to ensure that the users are prompted to set up a six-digit pin when they join, you need to configure automatic mobile device management (MDM) enrollment from the Azure Active Directory admin center. Then, from the Device Management admin center, configure the Windows Hello for Business enrollment options. The setting to configure is Minimum PIN Length, which will allow an administrator to specify a minimum PIN length for devices. Windows device defaults are 6 characters, but this setting can enforce a minimum of 4 to 127 characters.

24. B. With Windows 10, Azure Active Directory (Azure AD) users have the ability to securely synchronize their user and application settings data to the cloud. Enterprise State Roaming provides users with a combined experience across their Windows devices and decreases the time required for configuring a new device. Enterprise State Roaming offers enhanced security in that data is automatically encrypted prior to leaving the user's Windows 10 device by using Azure Rights Management (Azure RMS) and that the data also stays encrypted in the cloud. All content stays encrypted at rest in the cloud.

25. C. The Disk Defragmenter utility is used to rearrange files so that they are stored contiguously on the disk. This enhances access to those files. Optimizing your drives can help a computer run better and boot faster. To defragment a Windows 10 computer, do the following:

   1. Select the search bar on the taskbar and enter **defrag**.

   2. Select Defragment And Optimize Drives.

   3. Select the disk drive to be optimized.

   4. Click the Optimize button.

26. D. File systems are used to track the storage of files on a hard drive in a way that is understood by end users while allowing the operating system the ability to retrieve the requested files. Microsoft recommends that you use the NTFS file system with Windows 10 since it allows you to take advantage of features such as local security, file compression, and file encryption. You should use NTFS when formatting the new disk. NTFS supports both file encryption and file compression. Both Windows 7 and Windows 10 can access NTFS partitions.

27. C. You can upgrade devices by using a device configuration profile. The option that you want to configure is Edition Upgrade. Edition Upgrade allows you to upgrade Windows 10 (and later) devices to a newer version of Windows. To create a profile that will upgrade the computers, do the following:

   1. Sign in to the Microsoft Endpoint Manager admin center.

   2. Select Devices ➤ Configuration Profiles ➤ Create Profile.

3. Enter the following properties:

   Name: Enter a descriptive name for the new profile.

   Description: Enter a description for the profile.

   Platform: Select Windows 10 and later.

   Profile type: Select Edition Upgrade.

   Settings: Enter the settings that you want to be configured.

4. Click OK and then Create to save the changes.

28. B. Profiles work like policies since they are a way to put rules onto Intune devices. Microsoft Intune, along with Device Configuration profiles, allows you to configure settings and features that can be enabled or disabled on the different devices. One of the options that you can set in Device Configuration profiles is the ability to set up custom profiles. Custom profile settings allow you to configure options that are not automatically included with Intune, such as the ability to enable self-service password resets.

29. A. Windows Known Folders include the following folders:

    - Camera Roll
    - Desktop
    - Documents
    - Pictures
    - Screenshots

    There are two advantages of moving or redirecting Windows Known Folders to OneDrive:

    - The users can continue using the folders with which they are familiar.
    - Saving files to OneDrive backs up the users' data in the cloud and gives them access to those files from any device.

30. D. Co-management is a way to attach your existing Configuration Manager deployment to the Microsoft 365 cloud. It helps unlock additional cloud-powered capabilities like conditional access. Co-management enables you to manage Windows 10 devices concurrently by using both Configuration Manager and Microsoft Intune. However, in this question, it states that the forest and the domain are Windows Server 2012 R2 with several hundred Windows 10 computers. In this case, the first thing that you will need to do is to upgrade Configuration Manager to Current Branch. To upgrade to Configuration Manager Current Branch, do an in-place upgrade.

31. C. The Azure AD portal provides an administrator with a central location to manage device identities. You can access it either by going to the direct link or by doing the following:

    1. Sign in to the Azure portal.

    2. Browse to Azure Active Directory ➤ Devices.

The Devices page enables you to do the following:

- Configure the device settings.

- Locate devices.

- Perform device identity management tasks.

- Review device-related audit logs.

32. D. Intune supports the use of the Simple Certificate Enrollment Protocol (SCEP) to authenticate connections to apps and corporate resources. SCEP uses the Certification Authority (CA) certificate to secure the exchange of messages for the Certificate Signing Request (CSR). The Network Device Enrollment Service (NDES) allows software on routers and other network devices to obtain certificates based on the SCEP. The NDES performs the following functions:

- Generates and provides one-time enrollment passwords to administrators

- Submits enrollment requests to the CA

- Retrieves enrolled certificates from the CA and forwards them to the network device

In this case, you should select Server4 because it is the Network Device Enrollment Service (NDES) server, and the question states that NDES issues the certificates from the subordinate CA.

33. A. Azure AD Connect is a Microsoft utility that allows an administrator to set up a hybrid design between Azure AD and an onsite AD. Azure AD Connect allows both versions of Active Directory to connect to each other. An advantage of the Azure AD Connect section is that it allows an administrator to download and install Azure AD Connect by using the Download link. Azure AD Connect allows corporate users to be more productive by giving those users access to both cloud and on-premises resources by using a common user account for accessing both networks.

34. B. You can upgrade devices by using a device configuration profile. The option that you want to configure is Edition upgrade. Edition upgrade allows you to upgrade Windows 10 (and later) devices to a newer version of Windows. For the steps on how to create a device configuration profile to perform an Edition upgrade, visit the following Microsoft website:

docs.microsoft.com/en-us/mem/intune/configuration/edition-upgrade-configure-windows-10#create-the-profile

35. D. On Windows 10 devices, use Intune to run devices as a kiosk. This is also sometimes called *dedicated devices*. A device in kiosk mode can run one app or run many apps. You can display a customized Start menu, add different apps including Win32 apps, add a specific home page to a web browser, and more. Kiosk settings allow an administrator to configure a Windows 10 (and later) device to run a single application or run many applications. Kiosk systems are normally designed to be in a location where many people can use the same device, and that device will run only limited applications. For the steps on how to create a profile using kiosk, check out the following Microsoft website:

docs.microsoft.com/en-us/mem/intune/configuration/kiosk-settings#create-the-profile

36. B. On Windows 10 devices, use Intune to run devices as a kiosk. This is also sometimes called *dedicated devices*. A device in kiosk mode can run one app or run many apps. You can display a customized Start menu, add different apps including Win32 apps, add a specific home page to a web browser, and more. Kiosk settings allow an administrator to configure a Windows 10 (and later) device to run a single application or run many applications. Kiosk systems are normally designed to be in a location where many people can use the same device, and that device will run only limited applications.

37. A. Windows Known Folder Move (KFM) for OneDrive is a feature that will automatically redirect a user's personal folders and important files to their OneDrive for Business account stored on the Microsoft cloud. This allows users to access their files across different devices and applications. The folders that are redirected as part of the Windows known folders feature include the following:

- Camera Roll
- Desktop
- Documents
- Pictures
- Screenshots

38. A. A selective wipe will remove apps and associated data installed by Configuration Manager. It will uninstall apps and remove any sideloading keys. It will revoke the encryption key for apps, and the data will no longer be accessible. Selective wipes will also remove company data managed by Intune, leaving personal data intact. The type of company data removed will vary depending on the platform, and it includes profiles, applications, policies, and the Intune Endpoint Protection software.

39. C. Co-management enables an administrator to manage Windows 10 devices concurrently by using both Configuration Manager and Microsoft Intune. When concurrently managing Windows 10 devices with both Configuration Manager and Microsoft Intune, this configuration is called *co-management*. When you manage devices with Configuration Manager and enroll the devices to a third-party MDM service, this configuration is called *coexistence*.

40. C. The Configuration Manager console has the following four workspaces:

- Administration
- Assets and Compliance
- Monitoring
- Software Library

In Configuration Manager, an administrator can view a dashboard with information regarding co-management. The dashboard helps an administrator review machines that are co-managed in the environment. The graphs can help identify devices that might need attention. To monitor co-management in Configuration Manager, go to the Monitoring workspace and select the Co-management node.

41. D. In Configuration Manager, an administrator can view a dashboard with information regarding co-management. The dashboard helps an administrator review machines that are co-managed in the environment. The graphs identify devices that may require attention. To monitor co-management in Configuration Manager, go to the Monitoring workspace and select the Co-management node. The dashboard displays the following:

Co-managed devices: Shows the percentage of co-managed devices throughout the environment

Client OS distribution: Shows the number of client devices per OS by version

Co-management status (donut): Shows the breakdown of device success or failure in the following categories:

> **Success:** Hybrid Azure AD Joined
>
> **Success:** Azure AD Joined
>
> **Failure:** Auto-enrollment failed

Co-management status (funnel): A funnel chart that shows the number of devices with the following states from the enrollment process:

- Eligible devices
- Scheduled
- Enrollment initiated
- Enrolled

Co-management enrollment status: Shows the breakdown of device status

Workload transition: Displays a bar chart with the number of devices that have been transitioned to Microsoft Intune for the available workloads

Enrollment errors: Displays enrollment errors, if any occur.

42. B. The Known Folder Move Group Policy object (GPO) consists of several settings that can selected. These include the following:

Prompt Users To Move Windows Known Folders To OneDrive: Use this setting to give the users a call to action to move their Windows known folders.

Silently Move Windows Known Folders To OneDrive: Use this setting to redirect known folders to OneDrive without any user interaction.

Prevent Users From Redirecting Their Windows Known Folders To Their PC: Use this setting to force users to keep their known folders directed to OneDrive.

Prevent Users From Moving Their Windows Known Folders To OneDrive: This setting prevents users from moving their Documents, Pictures, and Desktop folders to any OneDrive account.

To use these Group Policy objects, you need the OneDrive sync build 18.111.0603.0004 or later. You can view the build number on the About tab in OneDrive settings. Microsoft recommends upgrading to the latest available build prior to deploying to prevent deployment issues. Known Folder Move does not work for users syncing OneDrive files in SharePoint Server.

43. B. There are many mobile device management (MDM) solutions that will help a company protect their data by requiring that users and devices meet certain requirements. In Intune, these are called *compliance policies*. Compliance policies define the set of rules and settings that users and devices must meet to be compliant. When combined with conditional access, administrators can block users and devices that don't meet the requirements.

44. A. Conditional access is the feature used by Azure Active Directory (Azure AD) to bring together signals, to make decisions, and to enforce organizational policies. Conditional access policies are basically "if-then" statements: if a user wants to access a resource, then they must complete an action. By using conditional access policies, an administrator can apply the precise access controls needed to keep the organization secure. Conditional access takes into account signals when making a policy decision.

45. B. You can use the Intune Management Extension to upload PowerShell scripts into Intune and then run these scripts on your devices. For the steps on how to create a script policy and assign it in Intune, check out the following Microsoft website:

docs.microsoft.com/en-us/mem/intune/apps/intune-management-extension#create-a-script-policy-and-assign-it

46. B. Device profiles allow an administrator to add and configure settings and then push those settings to devices within the organization. Profiles are created in the Microsoft Endpoint Manager admin center. In this admin center, select Devices. An administrator will have the following profile options:

- By platform
- Monitor
- Overview
- Policy

The profile option being discussed is the Monitor profile option. It allows an administrator to check the status of their profiles for success or failure and also view logs on their profiles.

47. C. Windows 10 allows devices to be registered in Azure ActiveDirectory (Azure AD) and enrolled into mobile device management (MDM) automatically. Automatic enrollment lets users enroll their Windows 10 devices in Intune. To enroll, users add their work account to their personally owned devices or join corporate-owned devices to Azure AD. To configure automatic MDM enrollment, sign in to the Azure portal.

48. D. Automatic enrollment lets users enroll their Windows 10 devices in Intune. To enroll, users add their work account to their personally owned devices or join corporate-owned devices to Azure Active Directory (Azure AD). To configure automatic MDM enrollment, perform the following steps:

1. Sign in to the Azure portal, and select Azure Active Directory.

2. Select Mobility (MDM and MAM) and then select Microsoft Intune.

3. Configure MDM User scope by specifying which users' devices should be managed by Microsoft Intune. These Windows 10 devices can automatically enroll for management with Microsoft Intune.

None: MDM automatic enrollment is disabled.

Some: Selects the groups that can automatically enroll their Windows 10 devices.

All: All users can automatically enroll their Windows 10 devices.

4. Use the default values for the following URLs:

- MDM terms of use URL

- MDM discovery URL

- MDM compliance URL

5. Click Save.

49. A. Group Policy will take priority over the mobile device management (MDM) policy when both policies are applied. Starting with Windows 10 version 1803 and later, Intune includes a configuration service provider (CSP) setting called `ControlPolicyConflict` that includes the `MDMWinsOverGP` policy. This policy allows administrators to configure a preference for which policy triumphs when both Group Policy and its equivalent MDM policy are configured to apply to the device. The `ControlPolicyConflict` policy default value is 0. These are the supported values:

0: The default setting.

1: The MDM policy is used, and the GP policy is blocked.

50. D. Administrators can use a local tool to help evaluate existing Group Policies to decide whether they are suitable candidates for migration to Microsoft Intune. The MDM Migration Analysis Tool (MMAT) is used to evaluate which Group Policies have been set for a target user/device and to cross-reference against a built-in list of supported Intune policies. You can download the latest MDM Migration Analysis Tool (MMAT) at `github.com/WindowsDeviceManagement/MMAT`.

51. D. Once the tool is run on a device, the MDM Migration Analysis Tool (MMAT) will generate both an XML report and an HTML report. These reports will indicate the level of support for all Group Policies that have been received from the device and whether MDM provides an equivalent policy. The MDMMigrationAnalysis.xml is an XML report that contains information regarding policies for the target user and computer and how they map to MDM, if applicable. The MDMMigrationAnalysis.html report is an HTML representation of the XML report.

52. C. Co-management is one of the primary means to attach an existing Configuration Manager deployment to the Microsoft 365 cloud. Co-management enables an administrator to manage Windows 10 devices concurrently by using both Configuration Manager and Microsoft Intune. With co-management, Configuration Manager and Intune balance the workloads to make sure that there are no conflicts. Some benefits that can be obtained with devices in a co-management state consist of the following:

- Centralized visibility of device health
- Conditional access with device compliance
- Intune-based remote actions, such as restart, remote control, or factory reset
- Using Azure Active Directory (Azure AD) to link users, devices, and apps
- Using Windows Autopilot for modern provisioning
- Remote actions

53. A. Conditional access policies are basically "if-then" statements: if a user wants to access a resource, then it must complete an action. When a client device requests access to corporate resources such as information contained in a controlled application, then Azure AD will first check whether any conditional access policies are in place with Intune and if a conditional access policy defines a condition that has not been met. For example, if a device must be encrypted, then the device can be denied access to the resource. If the device is compliant, then access will be granted.

54. C. A conditional access policy is an if-then statement of assignments and access controls. Within a conditional access policy, an administrator can make use of signals from conditions. Conditional access policies can have a number of conditions. Some of these conditions include the following:

Client Apps: By default, conditional access policies apply to browser apps, mobile apps, and desktop clients that support modern authentication. This condition allows conditional access policies to target specific client applications that are not using modern authentication.

Device Platforms: Companies with multiple device operating system platforms can enforce specific policies on different platforms. You can specify the device platforms to which you want this policy to apply.

Device State: This condition is used to apply or exclude devices that are hybrid Azure AD–joined or marked as compliant in Intune. So, you can choose to apply or exclude specific device states.

Locations: Location data is provided by IP geolocation data. Administrators can choose to define locations and choose to mark some as trusted. You can specify whether the policy applies to trusted network locations.

55. B, D. To use co-management, the device needs to be managed by both Configuration Manager and Intune. You can choose one of two main paths available for your clients.

Existing Configuration Manager clients: Windows 10 devices managed using Configuration Manager already have the Configuration Manager client installed. You can enroll the device into Intune once you have set up hybrid Azure AD by using Azure AD Connect.

New Internet-based devices: New Windows 10 devices will join Azure AD and be automatically enrolled into Intune. To allow the device to be co-managed, you need to install the Configuration Manager client.

56. D. The access controls portion of the conditional access policy controls how a policy is imposed. Grant provides administrators with a means of policy enforcement where they can block or grant access. Access controls allow you to grant or block access to enforce the controls. For this question, since you'd like to require multifactor authentication (Azure Multi-Factor Authentication), you will need to select Grant Access. If you choose Grant Access, you can choose one or more of the following:

- Require approved client app
- Require app protection policy
- Require device to be marked as compliant (Intune)
- Require Hybrid Azure AD–joined device
- Require multifactor authentication (Azure Multi-Factor Authentication)

57. B. Conditional access policies use conditions and controls that can be used to create the rules that will be evaluated by Azure Active Directory (Azure AD) to determine access to corporate resources. The access controls portion of the conditional access policy controls how a policy is imposed. Within a conditional access policy, an administrator can make use of Session controls to enable experiences within a specific cloud application. In this question, you are discussing the Conditional Access App Control. This uses a reverse proxy architecture and is uniquely integrated with Azure AD conditional access.

58. B. Intune uses Azure Active Directory (Azure AD) for authentication, and if the network already has a local Active Directory Domain Services (AD DS) environment, you can connect the two services using a tool called Azure AD Connect. Azure AD Connect helps you incorporate your on-premises Active Directory with Azure AD.

59. A. Conditional access policies use conditions and controls that are used to build the rules that will be evaluated by Azure Active Directory (Azure AD) when determining access to resources. Access controls define the actions that are allowed or disallowed when a condition is met. Access controls include the following:

- Allowing access
- Blocking access

60. C. Conditional access policies use conditions and controls that are used to build the rules that will be evaluated by Azure Active Directory (Azure AD) when determining access to resources. Assignments are the rules that are checked in accordance with conditional access requirements, such as device encryption or password requirements. Some conditions are based upon the following:

- The client apps that are used to access the data
- The client browser type
- The device platform being used
- The location where the data is being accessed

61. C. Device profiles allow you to add and configure settings and then push these settings to devices in your organization. When creating a profile, you can choose from a wide variety of profile types. The profile type being discussed in this question is Kiosk. On Windows 10 devices, use Intune to run devices as a kiosk, sometimes known as a *dedicated device*. Kiosk allows an administrator to configure a device to run one or more apps, such as a web browser. This feature supports Windows 10, and kiosk settings are also available as device restrictions for Android, Android Enterprise, and iOS devices.

62. B. With Windows 10, Azure Active Directory (Azure AD) users have the ability to securely synchronize their user settings and application settings data to the cloud using Enterprise State Roaming. Enterprise State Roaming provides users with a unified experience across their Windows devices and diminishes the time required for configuring a new device. To enable Enterprise State Roaming, perform the following steps:

1. Sign in to the Azure AD admin center.
2. Select Azure Active Directory ➢ Devices ➢ Enterprise State Roaming.
3. Select Users May Sync Settings And App Data Across Devices.

When an administrator enables Enterprise State Roaming, their organization is automatically granted a free, limited-use license for Azure Rights Management protection from Azure Information Protection.

63. B. When implementing a transition to co-management, organizations are encouraged to deploy a phased approach that will allow administrators to roll out features and functionality to an increasing number of devices over a period of time. With a staged rollout, issues and feedback can be gathered and used to develop the process for future user groups and devices. This question discusses the extended pilot group. After a successful pilot rollout, an administrator can choose to roll out co-managing to an extended pilot group. This rollout incorporates the devices, findings, and feedback from the initial pilot group and then applies them to a larger number of devices and users.

64. A. You can implement conditional access policies from Azure AD, Intune, or the Microsoft 365 Device Management console. Conditional access policies allow an administrator to control access automatically to cloud apps and corporate data depending upon the conditions that have been defined. An administrator can assign conditional access policies to the following types of objects: Users and Groups, Cloud Apps or Actions, and Conditions. Access controls are not part of the Assignments section of the conditional access policy. Access controls control how a policy is enforced.

65. A, B. Administrative Templates files are divided into `.admx` files and language-specific `.adml` files to be used by Group Policy administrators. Windows uses a Central Store to store Administrative Templates files. To create a Central Store for `.admx` and `.adml` files, create a new folder that is named `PolicyDefinitions` in File Explorer. ADMX policies offer administrators the ability to implement GPO settings through Intune for both user and device targets.

66. B. The system creates a user profile the first time that a user logs on to a computer. At successive logins, the system will load the user's profile and other system components to configure the user's environment based on the information in the profile. A user profile consists of the following two elements:

- The registry hive is the file `ntuser.dat`. The hive is loaded by the system at user logon, and it is mapped to the `HKEY_CURRENT_USER` registry key.

- A set of profile folders stored in the file system. User-profile files are stored in the `Profiles` directory on a folder per-user basis.

67. D. Using Intune, deployment of PowerShell scripts is supported for all enrolled Windows 10 devices that are Azure AD–joined, Hybrid Azure AD domain–joined, or co-managed. An administrator can upload PowerShell scripts in Intune and then run those scripts on Windows 10 devices. When choosing to run a PowerShell script using Intune, there are three script settings to choose from. This question is discussing Run This Script Using The Logged-On Credentials. By selecting Yes, this will run the script with the user's credentials on the device. By selecting No (default), it will run the script in the system context.

68. A. Using Intune, deployment of PowerShell scripts is supported for all enrolled Windows 10 devices that are Azure AD–joined, Hybrid Azure AD domain–joined, or co-managed. An administrator can upload PowerShell scripts in Intune and then run those scripts on Windows 10 devices. When choosing to run a PowerShell script using Intune, there are three script settings to choose from. This question is discussing Enforce Script Signature Check. By selecting Yes, the script must be signed by a trusted publisher. By selecting No (default), there isn't a requirement for the script to be signed.

69. B. There are several types of user profiles. These include the following:

- Local user profiles

- Mandatory user profiles

- Roaming user profiles

- Super-mandatory user profiles

- Temporary user profiles

In this question, you are discussing mandatory user profiles, which are fixed profiles. If a user changes the desktop settings, they will be lost when the user logs off. Only system administrators can make changes to mandatory user profiles. To create a mandatory user profile, an administrator should first configure a roaming user profile, modify the profile settings as required, and then rename the `ntuser.dat` file (the registry hive) to `ntuser.man`. The `.man` extension creates the read-only mandatory profile, and all user modifications to the profile will not be saved.

70. B. Azure Active Directory (Azure AD) Identity Protection is a tool that allows a company to achieve these three key tasks:

- Automate the detection and remediation of identity-based risks.
- Investigate risks using data in the portal.
- Export risk detection data to third-party utilities for further analysis.

Azure AD Identity Protection identifies risks. The risk signals that can trigger remediation efforts may include requiring users to perform Azure Multi-Factor Authentication, requiring users to reset their password by using self-service password reset, or blocking until an administrator takes action.

71. C. An administrator can use the Microsoft Intune Management Extension to upload PowerShell scripts into Intune to run on Windows 10 devices. The management extension enhances Windows 10 mobile device management (MDM). Once an administrator has uploaded a PowerShell script to Intune, the management extension client checks with Intune to see whether there are any new PowerShell scripts or changes that have been made. This check is done once every hour and after every reboot. After the PowerShell script is executed on a targeted device, then the PowerShell script is not executed again unless here has been a change in the script or the policy.

72. C. There are several types of user profiles. These include the following:

- Local user profiles
- Mandatory user profiles
- Roaming user profiles
- Super-mandatory user profiles
- Temporary user profiles

In this question, you are discussing a roaming user profile. A roaming user profile is a copy of the local profile that has been copied to and stored on the network. Each time that the user logs on to a device on the network, this profile is used. If the profile has been modified since the last logon, Windows will download the latest profile from the network location. Changes made to a roaming user profile are synchronized with the network copy of the profile each time the user logs off. Roaming user profiles allow the user to use their personalized environment and system settings on each computer they use on a network.

73. D. Scope tags are used to assign and filter policies to specific groups. An administrator can also use scope tags to provide just the right amount of access and visibility to objects in Intune. Scope tags can be applied to different objects on Azure and Intune. The tag is basically a unique identifier. To add a scope tag, do the following:

1. As a global administrator, sign into the Intune portal at devicemanagement.microsoft.com.

2. Select Roles.

3. Under Manage, select Scope (Tags).

4. On the Intune Roles-Scope (Tags) blade, click + Create.

5. On the Create Scope Tag blade, enter the name for the tag and, if wanted, a description.

6. Click Create. Once the scope tag is created, it will appear on the list.

74. B. Folder Redirection allows users and administrators to redirect the path of a known folder to a new location, manually or by using Group Policy. The new location can be a folder on the local computer or a directory on a file share. Users can then work with documents as if they were on the local drive but are available to the user from any computer on the network. Folder Redirection can be found under Windows Settings in the console tree by editing domain-based Group Policy via the Group Policy Management Console (GPMC).

75. A. Some issues that may be encountered are issues with the policies and profiles and possible conflicts and Azure AD enrollment. When two profile settings are applied to the same device, the most restrictive value will be applied. Any settings that are identical in each policy will be applied as configured. If a policy has been deployed to a device and is active and then a second policy is deployed, the first policy will take precedence.

76. A. Each time a user logs onto a Windows 10 computer, the system checks to see whether they have a local user profile in the Users folder. The first time a user logs on, they receive a default user profile. A folder that matches the user's logon name is created for the user in the Users folder. The user profile folder that is created holds a file called `ntuser.dat` as well as subfolders that contain directory links to the user's desktop items. A mandatory profile is stored in a file named `ntuser.man`. To create a mandatory profile, just change the user's profile extension from `.dat` to `.man`. In this question, you are changing from a mandatory profile, so you need to change the extension back to `.dat`.

77. B. For this question, the answer that is incorrect is that the configuration profile settings will take priority over compliance policy settings. The actual way that these two policies would interact is that the compliance policy settings will take priority over configuration profile settings. If you have a compliance policy and it includes the same settings that are found in another compliance policy, then the most restrictive setting will be applied. If you have a configuration policy setting that clashes with the setting in another configuration policy, then the issue will be displayed in Intune, and the administrator will need to resolve the issue manually.

78. A. Quotas provide the ability to limit the amount of hard disk space that a user can have on a volume or partition. By default, quotas are disabled. To enable quotas, select the Enable Quota Management checkbox. An example of the Quota tab of the volume's properties dialog box is shown in the following graphic.

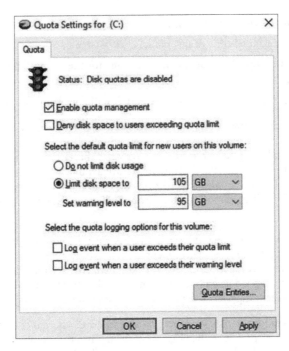

79. A. OneDrive is a Microsoft cloud storage service that allows users to store their personal files in one location, share them with others, and obtain them from any device that is connected to the Internet. For most subscription plans, the default storage space for each user is 1 TB. Depending on the plan and the number of licensed users, this can be increased to 5 TB for storage.

80. C. As an administrator, you may need to troubleshoot a device if you have a policy that is not being applied or a PowerShell script that is set to be run but is not being started by Intune. You should first perform a full reboot of the device by holding down the Shift key and then selecting Shutdown from the Start menu. Once the device is powered off, you can then power the device back on. After turning the device back on, the built-in Windows 10 Intune client will determine whether there are any new policies or changes available. Make sure to give the service enough time after rebooting to sync with Intune and receive any changes.

81. D. The What If tool in Conditional Access is a wonderful tool when determining why a policy was or wasn't applied to a user under specific circumstances or why a policy would apply in a known state. The What If tool is located in the Azure portal by selecting Azure Active Directory ➤ Conditional Access ➤ What If. Some companies may create a policy based upon a network's location to permit trusted locations and block other locations. To confirm that a configuration has been set up correctly, you can use the What If tool to mimic access from a location that should be permitted and from a location that should be denied access.

82. D. By redirecting the profile folders, you can redirect specific folders to be stored at a location outside the user profile. These can be stored on a shared location on a file server or sent to OneDrive for Business. For domain users, an administrator can configure Folder Redirection and a variety of other settings that include setting quotas to limit the size of redirected folders by using Group Policy.

83. D. Folder Redirection enables users and administrators to redirect the path of a known folder to a new location. This can be done manually or by using Group Policy objects. The new location can be a folder on the local device or a directory on a file share. To administer Folder Redirection, you must be signed in as a member of the Domain Administrators, Enterprise Administrators, or Group Policy Creator Owners.

84. D. When setting Sync settings, you can choose to sync the theme, passwords, language preferences, Ease of Access, and other Windows settings. Some of the categories and common Sync settings that are included on a Windows 10 device include the following:

Theme: Background, system color, system sounds, screen saver, slideshow wallpaper, and taskbar settings

Passwords: Windows Credential Manager, including Wi-Fi profiles

Language Preferences: Spelling dictionary and system language settings

Ease of Access: Narrator, On-screen Keyboard, and Magnifier

Other Windows Settings: Device settings for items such as printers and mouse options, File Explorer settings, and notification preferences

To find the Sync settings, select Start ➢ Settings ➢ Accounts ➢ Sync.

85. C. With OneDrive for Business, you can store and access files from all your devices. Users can use OneDrive to store and protect files and access them using multiple devices when signed in using their Azure AD credentials. OneDrive for Business offers a large list of features. The feature that is being discussed is OneDrive Files On-Demand. This feature enables users to view, search for, and interact with files stored in OneDrive using File Explorer without downloading the files to their device. This feature allows you to work with files without taking up space on the local hard drive.

86. C. Conditional access is a feature used by Azure Active Directory (Azure AD) to bring signals together, to make decisions, and to enforce policies. To manage conditional access abilities, you should assign the Conditional Access Administrator role. Users that have the Conditional Access Administrator role have permissions to view, create, modify, and delete conditional access policies. The Conditional Access Administrator can perform the following tasks in Azure Active Directory (Azure AD):

Create: Create conditional access policies

Read: Read conditional access policies

Update: Update conditional access policies

Delete: Delete conditional access policies

87. A. When setting Sync settings, you can choose to sync the theme, passwords, language preferences, Ease of Access, and other Windows settings. Some of the categories and common Sync settings that are included on a Windows 10 device include the following:

Theme: Background, system color, system sounds, screen saver, slideshow wallpaper, and taskbar settings

Passwords: Windows Credential Manager, including Wi-Fi profiles

Language Preferences: Spelling dictionary and system language settings

Ease of Access: Narrator, on-screen keyboard, and magnifier

Other Windows Settings: Device settings for items such as printers and mouse options, File Explorer settings, and notification preferences

To find the Sync settings, select Start ➤ Settings ➤ Accounts ➤ Sync. Using the Ease Of Access ➤ Keyboard settings, a user can do the following:

- Turn on/off on-screen keyboard.
- Turn on sticky keys (off by default).
- Turn on filter keys (off by default).
- Turn on toggle keys (off by default).

88. C. You cannot recover a corrupted file directly from Windows 10. You would want to use OneDrive to recover the file. You can utilize Version History in OneDrive. Version History allows you to see and restore older versions of all your files in OneDrive. Using Version History is fairly simple: just navigate to your OneDrive account, right-click the file to be restored or to view a previous version of, and then select Version History.

89. C. Because this user only cleared the Recycle Bin on the local machine, you should restore the files using OneDrive for Business's Recycle Bin. When synchronized files are deleted locally, it also triggers the delete operation on OneDrive for Business and on all machines connected to the same share. To restore the files, perform the following steps:

1. Go to the OneDrive website and sign in.
2. In the navigation pane, select Recycle Bin.
3. Select the files or folders to be restored by pointing to each item and clicking the circle checkbox that appears. Then click Restore.

90. C. The Health Insurance Portability and Accountability Act of 1996 (HIPPA) is U.S. legislation that requires data privacy and security provisions for safeguarding medical information. The law has emerged into greater importance recently with the explosion of health data breaches caused by cyberattacks and ransomware attacks on health insurers and providers.

91. B. With OneDrive for Business, you can store and access files from all your devices. Users can use OneDrive to store and protect files and access them using multiple devices when signed in using their Azure AD credentials. OneDrive for Business offers a large list of features. The feature that is being discussed is Windows Known Folder Move (KFM) for OneDrive. This feature automatically redirects a user's personal folders and important files to their OneDrive for Business account, and the files are stored in the cloud. This redirect will give the users the ability to access their files while using different devices and applications.

92. D. Windows Known Folder Move (KFM) for OneDrive is a feature that automatically redirects a user's personal folders and important files to their OneDrive for Business account stored on the Microsoft cloud. This allows users to access their files across different devices and applications. To configure OneDrive Known Folder Move using Group Policy, you need to ensure that the following requirements are met:

- OneDrive sync build 18.111.0603.0004 or later must be installed on client devices.

- Any existing Windows Folder Redirection Group Policy settings used within the domain need to be removed.

- Move users' OneNote notebooks out of their known folders because known folders, which include OneNote notebooks, won't be moved.

If users have OneNote notebooks in their known folders, the known folders won't be moved. You will need to move the OneNote to OneDrive prior to doing the KFM. To check which version of OneDrive you are using, perform the following:

1. Click the OneDrive cloud icon in the notification area and select More ➢ Settings.

2. Select the About tab to see the version number under About Microsoft OneDrive.

93. C. There are several GPO settings that an administrator can use to refine the configuration of OneDrive Known Folder Move. The setting being discussed is Prompt Users To Move Windows Known Folders To OneDrive. This setting will show the users a pop-up notification that they can use to protect their files by automatically moving their Windows known folders to OneDrive. If the user dismisses the prompt, then a reminder notification will appear in the Activity Center until they complete the move. If the user has already redirected their known folders to a different OneDrive account, the prompt will request to direct the folders to your organization's OneDrive account.

94. B. The Gramm-Leach-Bliley Act (GLBA) is also known as the Financial Modernization Act of 1999. It is a U.S. federal law that requires financial institutions to explain how they share and protect their customers' private information.

95. D. There are several GPO settings that an administrator can use to refine the configuration of OneDrive Known Folder Move. The setting being discussed is Silently Move Windows Known Folders To OneDrive. This setting will redirect the user's known folders to OneDrive without user interaction. Once this setting is configured, it will redirect the known folder content to OneDrive. An administrator can choose to display a notification to the users that their folders have been redirected.

96. B. To use the OneDrive GPO settings, you will first need to import the `.adml` and `.admx` files from a client and add them to your domain's GPO Central Store in this location: `\sysvol\domain\Policies\PolicyDefinitions`. Administrative Template files are divided into `.admx` files and `.adml` files for use by Group Policy administrators. Windows uses a Central Store to store Administrative Templates files. To create a Central Store for `.admx` and `.adml` files, create a new folder that is named `PolicyDefinitions` in File Explorer.

97. B. If a device that is unenrolled tries to gain access to corporate resources, then it will be deemed as noncompliant and access will be blocked. There are a few actions that you can configure for noncompliance. The setting being discussed in this question is Mark Device Non-Compliant. Using this setting, the noncompliant device will be allowed access to resources as long as the device is made compliant within a specified amount of time, known as the *grace period*. After the time has expired, the noncompliant device will be blocked. By default, this action is set for each compliance policy and has a schedule of zero days, marking devices as noncompliant immediately.

98. B. Within a conditional access policy, an administrator can make use of signals from conditions such as risk, device platform, or location to enhance their policy decisions. When accessing an application, an administrator may factor sign-in risk information from Azure AD Identity Protection and location into their access decision in addition to other controls, such as multifactor authentication (MFA). When configuring location as a condition, you can choose to include or exclude locations. These locations may include the public IPv4 network information, country or region, or even unknown areas that don't map to specific countries or regions. Only IP ranges can be marked as a trusted location.

99. A. Devices that are Azure AD–registered are usually personally owned or mobile devices and are signed in with a personal Microsoft account or another local account. Azure AD–joined devices are owned by the company and are signed in with an Azure AD account belonging to that organization. They exist only in the cloud. With Windows 10, Azure Active Directory (Azure AD) users gain the ability to synchronize their user settings and application settings data to the cloud. Enterprise State Roaming provides users with a unified experience across all of their Windows devices. In this case, since the machines are enrolled using Enterprise State Roaming, regardless of what device the user logs into will change the desktop settings, and the settings will appear on all of the users' devices.

100. C. With Windows 10, Azure Active Directory (Azure AD) users can synchronize their user settings and application settings data to the cloud. Enterprise State Roaming provides users with a unified experience across their Windows devices. By using Enterprise State Roaming, the desktop background, Favorites folder, and browsing history will be available on the new computers. The requirements of Enterprise State Roaming are as follows:

- The device must be installed with Windows 10, with the latest updates, and a minimum version 1511 (OS Build 10586 or later).

- The device is Azure AD–joined or hybrid Azure AD–joined.

- Enterprise State Roaming must be enabled for the tenant in Azure AD.

- The user is assigned an Azure Active Directory (Azure AD) Premium license.

- The device must be restarted, and the user must sign in again to access Enterprise State Roaming features.

In this question, only User2 has Enterprise State Roaming enabled. Computer 2 is only running Windows 8.1. So, the only option that will work that meets the Enterprise State

Roaming requirements will be if User2 modifies the desktop icons on Computer1. The changes will be available when the user signs into Computer3.

101. C. Data that is synced to the Microsoft cloud using Enterprise State Roaming is retained until it is manually deleted or until the data is determined to be stale. Explicit deletion is when an Azure admin deletes a user or a directory or requests that data is to be deleted. The setting being discussed is On Request Deletion. If the Azure AD admin wants to delete a specific user's data or settings data manually, the admin can request a ticket with Azure support.

102. B. Data that is synced to the Microsoft cloud using Enterprise State Roaming is retained until it is manually deleted or until the data is determined to be stale. The setting being discussed is Stale Data Deletion. Stale data deletion is data that has not been accessed for one year (the retention period). It will be treated as stale and may be deleted from the Microsoft cloud. The retention period may change, but it will not be less than 90 days.

103. A. An administrator can deploy a compliance policy to users in user groups or devices in device groups. When a compliance policy is deployed to a user, all of the user's devices are checked for compliance. Intune also has a set of built-in compliance policy settings. The setting being discussed in this question is Compliance Status Validity Period (Days). An administrator will enter the time period that devices report the status for all received compliance policies. Devices that do not return their status within the given time period are treated as noncompliant. The default value is 30 days. The maximum value is 120 days. The minimum value is 1 day.

104. C. Intune uses different refresh cycles to check for updates to compliance policies. Whenever a device has a compliance policy assigned, a compliance status will be determined. If a device has multiple compliance policies and the device has different compliance statuses for two or more of the assigned compliance policies, then a single compliance status is assigned. This assignment is based upon the severity level assigned to each compliance status. Each compliance status has the following severity level:

Unknown: 1

NotApplicable: 2

Compliant: 3

InGracePeriod: 4

NonCompliant: 5

Error: 6

The severity is reported to Microsoft Intune and is used to determine access to corporate resources. When a device has multiple compliance policies, then the highest severity level of all the policies is assigned to the device. If a device has two policies applied and one is compliant and the other is noncompliant, the status for the device will be noncompliant.

This setting shows as the Is Active default compliance policy found in Devices ➤ Monitor ➤ Setting Compliance.

105. C. Intune informs the device to check in with the Intune service. The notification times differ, from occurring immediately or up to a few hours. If a device does not check in to get the policy or profile after the first notification, then Intune will make three more attempts. Devices connect to Intune on a periodic basis, and the compliance status is checked. For Windows 10 computers enrolled as a device, the refresh cycle time is every 3 minutes for 15 minutes, then every 15 minutes for 2 hours, and then around every 8 hours. At any time, a user can open the Company Portal app and select Settings ➤ Sync to check for policy or profile updates.

106. A. With device identity management in Azure Active Directory (Azure AD), an administrator can ensure that the users are accessing resources from devices that meet corporate standards for security and compliance. The Azure AD portal provides a central location to manage device identities. You can manage device identities by using a direct link or by performing the following steps:

1. Sign in to the Azure portal.

2. Browse to Azure Active Directory ➤ Devices.

The Devices page enables an administrator to do the following:

- Configure device settings.

- Locate devices.

- Perform device identity management tasks.

- Review device-related audit logs.

107. B. A mandatory user profile is a special type of preconfigured roaming user profile that administrators use to specify settings for users. Mandatory profiles cannot be modified by users. Mandatory profiles can only be managed by members of the Administrators group, and they must be associated with a roaming profile and not a local profile. User profiles become mandatory profiles when the administrator renames the ntuser.dat file (the registry hive) on the server to ntuser.man. The .man extension causes the user profile to be a read-only profile.

108. C. Microsoft Intune is included with Microsoft 365. Microsoft Intune is a cloud-based service that focuses on mobile device management (MDM) and mobile application management (MAM). With Intune, an administrator can do the following:

- With Intune, choose to be 100 percent cloud or be co-managed with Configuration Manager and Intune.

- Set rules and configure settings on devices to access data and networks.

- Deploy and authenticate apps on devices.

- Protect corporate information by managing the way a user accesses and shares information.

- Ensure that devices and apps are compliant with security requirements.

109. D. Administrators can use a local tool to help evaluate existing Group Policies to decide whether they are suitable candidates for migration to Microsoft Intune. The MDM Migration Analysis Tool (MMAT) is used to evaluate which Group Policies have been set for a target user/device and to cross-reference against a built-in list of supported Intune policies. You can download the latest MDM Migration Analysis Tool (MMAT) at github.com/WindowsDeviceManagement/MMAT.

110. A. Azure AD Connect is a Microsoft utility that allows an administrator to set up a hybrid design between Azure AD and an on-site AD. Azure AD Connect allows both versions of Active Directory to connect to each other. An advantage of the Azure AD Connect section is that it allows an administrator to download and install Azure AD Connect by using the Download link. Azure AD Connect allows corporate users to be more productive by giving those users access to both cloud and on-premises resources by using a common user account for accessing both networks.

111. D. When implementing a transition to co-management, organizations are encouraged to deploy a phased approach that will allow administrators to roll out features and functionality to an increasing number of devices over a period of time. With a staged rollout, issues and feedback can be gathered and used to develop the process for future user groups and devices. So, you should recommend creating a rollout group for staging co-management.

112. C. Mobile device management (MDM) is built into Microsoft 365. It helps an administrator secure and manage the users' mobile devices such as iPhones, iPads, Androids, and Windows phones. An administrator can create and manage device security policies, remotely wipe a device, and view detailed device reports. The recommended way to enable and use Azure Multi-Factor Authentication is by using conditional access policies. Conditional access lets you create and define policies that react to sign-in events and requests additional actions prior to the user being granted access to an application or service. So, for this question, you should include a multifactor authentication conditional access policy that can be used with supported cloud-based apps.

113. C. Within a conditional access policy, an administrator can make use of signals from conditions such as risk, device platform, or location to enhance their policy decisions. For this question, you should implement a conditional access policy that uses a location-based condition. When configuring location as a condition, organizations can choose to include or exclude locations. With Azure Active Directory (Azure AD) conditional access, you can control how authorized users can access cloud apps. The location condition of a conditional access policy enables you to link access controls settings to the network locations of your users.

114. C. When configuring location as a condition, you can choose to include or exclude locations. These locations may include the public IPv4 network information, country or region, or even unknown areas that don't map to particular countries or regions. Only IP ranges can be marked as a trusted location. When including a location, this option includes any IP address on the Internet, not just configuring the named locations. When selecting any location, you can choose to exclude all trusted or selected locations. So, for this question, you would need the employee to provide you with the IP address of their home network.

115. B. When planning a conditional access deployment, it is imperative to achieve the organization's access strategy for apps and resources. When new policies are ready for the environment, deploy them in phases in the production environment. First apply a policy to a small set of users in a test environment and then verify that the policy behaves as expected. So, for this question, you should suggest a conditional access test plan. First, test the policies in a nonproduction environment or with a pilot group to ensure that the results of the policies are as expected.

Chapter 7: Manage and Protect Devices

1. C. Microsoft Intune includes settings and features that an administrator can enable or disable on different devices. These settings and features are added to a configuration profile. You can create profiles for different devices and different platforms. The Password Reset section allows an administrator to control if they want to enable self-service password reset (SSPR). If this feature is enabled, then users will be able to reset their own passwords or unlock their accounts. To create a device configuration policy in Intune, perform the following:

1. Sign in to the Azure portal and click Intune.

2. Create a new device configuration profile by going to Device Configuration ➢ Profiles ➢ Create Profile.

3. Configure Settings.

4. Click Create.

5. This policy can then be assigned to specific users, devices, or groups.

2. A. An administrator can set up Intune to enroll iOS/iPadOS devices purchased through Apple's Automated Device Enrollment (ADE). This was formerly known as Device Enrollment Program (DEP). ADE lets an administrator enroll large numbers of devices without ever touching them. Just note that Apple recently changed from using the DEP to ADE. At the time of this writing, Intune is still updating the Intune user interface to reflect the change, so until the changes take effect, users will continue to see Device Enrollment Program in the Intune portal. For the steps on how to enroll iOS/iPadOS devices automatically, check out the following Microsoft website:

docs.microsoft.com/en-us/mem/intune/enrollment/device-enrollment-program-enroll-ios

3. A. Azure Monitor is software that runs as a service (SaaS). All of the supporting infrastructure runs in Azure and is handled by Microsoft. It was created to perform analytics, diagnostics, and monitoring. Azure Monitor maximizes the availability and performance of applications and services by delivering a complete solution for collecting, analyzing, and acting on telemetry from your cloud and on-premises environments. All data collected by Azure Monitor falls into one of two categories: metrics and logs.

4. D. A Log Analytics workspace is a unique environment for Azure Monitor log data. Each workspace has its own configuration and data repository. A Log Analytics workspace is used for collecting the following data sources:

    ▪ Your Azure subscription resources

    ▪ On-premises computers monitored by System Center Operations Manager

    ▪ Configuration Manager device collections

    ▪ Azure storage diagnostics or log data

    To create a workspace, perform the following steps:

    1. Sign in to the Azure portal at `portal.azure.com`.

    2. In the Azure portal, click All Services. In the list of resources, type **Log Analytics**.

    3. Click Add and then select the choices you'd like.

    4. After providing the required information on the Log Analytics Workspace pane, click OK.

5. D. To monitor and manage physical computers or virtual machines with Azure Monitor, an administrator needs to deploy the Microsoft Monitoring Agent (MMA) (also called a *Log Analytics agent*) and configure it to report to one or more Log Analytics workspaces. The MMA service gathers events from log files and Windows event logs, performance data, and other information. For additional information on Microsoft Monitoring Agent Setup, check out Microsoft's website at `docs.microsoft.com/en-us/services-hub/health/mma-setup`.

6. C. Microsoft Defender is built in to Windows 10, and it is an application that protects the system from viruses and spyware. It is included for free with the operating system. Microsoft Defender offers Always-On Protection, which consists of real-time protection, behavior monitoring, and heuristics to recognize malware based upon known malicious activity. For the steps on how to enable and configure Always-On Protection using Group Policy, check out the following Microsoft website:

    `docs.microsoft.com/en-us/windows/security/threat-protection/windows-defender-antivirus/configure-real-time-protection-windows-defender-antivirus#enable-and-configure-always-on-protection-in-group-policy`

    For this question, since Computer1 is not providing any real-time protection, this indicates that Microsoft Defender has been disabled and needs to be turned back on.

7. A. Microsoft Defender Application Guard is designed for Windows 10 and Microsoft Edge. Application Guard uses an approach that performs hardware isolation. This allows untrusted site navigation to launch inside a container. Hardware isolation allows companies to protect their network and corporate data just in case a user visits a site that is compromised or is malicious. An administrator can define what sites are trusted, cloud resources, and internal networks. If something is not trusted, it is considered untrusted, and these sites will be isolated from the network and corporate data on the user's device.

8. A, C, E. An administrator can set up Intune to enroll iOS devices automatically, which are purchased through Apple's Automated Device Enrollment (ADE). ADE was formerly called Device Enrollment Program (DEP). ADE allows you to enroll a large number of devices. The administrator gives users access to the Company Portal app on an ADE device. Before a device can be enrolled with ADE, you need to get an ADE token (.p7m) file from Apple. This token lets Intune sync information about the ADE devices, permits Intune to upload enrollment profiles to Apple, and assigns devices to those profiles. Once the token is installed, you then create an enrollment profile for the ADE devices. An Apple enrollment profile defines the settings applied to a group of devices during enrollment. Then you need to assign the enrollment profile to the devices. To see all of the steps and how to enroll iOS devices automatically with Apple's ADE, go to the following Microsoft website:

docs.microsoft.com/en-us/mem/intune/enrollment/device-enrollment-program-enroll-ios

9. A. Windows Event logs are a common source for collecting data since many applications write to the Windows event log. Log queries help an administrator use the data collected in Azure Monitor Logs. All data collected in Azure Monitor Logs is able to obtain and analyze in log queries. The Event query retrieves all records from the Event table. The pipe (|) character separates commands, so the output of the first command is the input of the next command. So, in this question, a way for the administrator to view the events collected from a specific computer in Azure is to run a query in the Logs Analytics. Administrators can run the following query:

Event | where Computer = = "ComputerName"

10. C. Desktop Analytics is a cloud-based service that works with Configuration Manager. Desktop Analytics provides insights so that you can make more informed decisions regarding the update readiness of your Windows clients. Device profiles allow an administrator to add and configure settings and then push those settings to devices within the corporate environment. Device configuration profiles allow an administrator to configure settings and features that can be enabled or disabled. Device configuration profile settings and features are added to your configuration profiles. You can build these profiles for devices and platforms, including iOS, Android, and Windows. After these profiles are built, an Intune administrator can apply or assign these profiles to their devices.

11. B. Microsoft Defender Credential Guard is a virtualization-based security tool to help isolate critical files so that only system software that is privileged can access those critical files. Once enabled, a Windows 10 machine that is part of Active Directory or Azure Active Directory (Azure AD) will have the systems credentials protected by Microsoft Defender Credential Guard. Microsoft Defender Credential Guard can be enabled by using Group Policy, the registry, or the Hypervisor-Protected Code Integrity (HVCI) and Microsoft Defender Credential Guard hardware readiness tool.

12. A. Microsoft Defender Credential Guard is a virtualization-based security to help isolate critical files so that only system software that is privileged can access those critical files. To enable Microsoft Defender Credential Guard using Intune, perform the following steps:

1. Sign in to Microsoft Intune.

2. Click Device Configuration.

3. Click Profiles ➤ Create Profile ➤ Endpoint Protection ➤ Microsoft Defender Credential Guard.

13. A. Microsoft Intune includes settings and features that allow you to enable or disable features for different devices. These settings and features are added to configuration profiles. Once you create a configuration profile, you will then use Intune to assign the profile to the devices. There are several profile types. Administrative templates include hundreds of settings that can be configured for Microsoft Edge, Internet Explorer, OneDrive, Remote Desktop, Word, Excel, and more. These templates provide an administrator with a simplified view of settings similar to Group Policy, and they are all cloud-based.

14. C. Microsoft Defender Exploit Guard helps protect systems from common malware attacks that use executable files and scripts that will attack applications. Microsoft Defender Exploit Guard also looks for suspicious scripts or behavior that is not normal on the Windows 10 system. Microsoft Defender Exploit Guard helps protect Windows 10 systems from malware, ransomware, and other types of attacks. It reduces the device attack surface.

15. C. Performance Monitor is designed to allow users and system administrators to monitor performance statistics for various operating system parameters. It allows an administrator to collect data from local computers or remote Windows 10 machines. It also allows for the collection of data from either a single computer or multiple computers concurrently. An administrator can view data as it is being collected in real time or historically from collected data. An administrator has full control over what data can be collected by selecting specific objects and counters.

16. A, D. As an Intune administrator, you can create and manage enrollment restrictions that define what devices can enroll into management with Intune. You can create multiple restrictions and apply them to different user groups. You can set the priority order for your different restrictions. For the steps on how to create a device type restriction, check out the following Microsoft website:

docs.microsoft.com/en-us/mem/intune/enrollment/enrollment-restrictions-set

17. B. Microsoft Intune includes many built-in settings to control different device features. An administrator can also create custom profiles. Custom profiles are for when you want to use device settings and features that are not built into Intune. Windows 10 custom profiles use Open Mobile Alliance Uniform Resource Identifier (OMA-URI) settings to configure different features. These settings are used by mobile device manufacturers to control device features. In Intune, use the OMA-URI settings of a custom policy to configure the commercial ID. The OMA-URI is a case-sensitive path for configuring the commercial ID. The path is as follows:

./Vendor/MSFT/DMClient/Provider/MS DM Server/CommercialID

For the steps on how to create a custom profile, check out the following Microsoft website:

docs.microsoft.com/en-us/mem/intune/configuration/custom-settings-configure

18. C. Microsoft Defender Exploit Guard helps protect systems from common malware attacks that use executable files and scripts that will attack applications. Microsoft Defender Exploit Guard also looks for suspicious scripts or behavior that are not normal on the Windows 10 system. Microsoft Defender Exploit Guard helps protect Windows 10 systems from malware, ransomware, and other types of attacks. It reduces the device attack surface.

19. B. Inbound and outbound rules consist of many preconfigured rules that can be enabled or disabled. Inbound rules monitor inbound traffic, while outbound rules monitor outbound traffic. To configure Microsoft Defender Firewall to allow SMTP inbound and outbound traffic, you would configure TCP port 25. TCP port 20 is for FTP data, UDP port 53 is for DNS, and TCP port 80 is for HTTP.

20. D. To review a policy report on the deployment status for a Windows 10 update ring, perform the following:

1. Sign in to the Microsoft Endpoint Manager admin center.

2. Select Devices ➤ Overview ➤ Software Update Status. You can view general information regarding the status of any assigned update rings.

3. To view additional details, select Monitor. Below Software Updates, select Per Update Ring Deployment State and choose the deployment ring to review.

In the Monitor section, you can choose from the following reports:

Device status: Shows the device configuration status

User status: Shows the username, status, and last report date

End-user update status: Shows the Windows device update state

21. A. App protection policies (APPs) are rules that make sure that the company data stays safe or contained within a managed app. A policy is a set of rules that are either enforced or prohibited. In this question, the app protection policy is applied to all devices in Group1 and Group2 and is excluded from any device in Group3, unless those devices are also members of Group1 or Group2. So, in this case, only Device1, Device2, Device4, and Device5 can apply the app protection policy.

22. B. Desktop Analytics is a cloud-based service that works with Configuration Manager. Microsoft uses a unique CommercialID to map information from the user computers to the Azure workspace. A CommercialID is a globally unique identifier that is assigned to a specific Log Analytics workspace. The CommercialID is copied to a mobile device management (MDM) or Group Policy object and is used to identify devices within the environment. To find your CommercialID within Azure, perform the following:

1. Navigate to the Solutions tab for your workspace and then select the WaaSUpdateInsights solution.

2. Select the Update Compliance Settings page on the navigation bar.

3. The CommercialID is available on the settings page.

4. Copy the CommercialID key and deploy it to user computers.

23. A. Microsoft created the Microsoft Defender Application Control (WDAC) to help stop data attacks through applications. WDAC was introduced with Windows 10, and it allows an administrator to regulate what drivers and applications can run on their Windows 10 clients. Administrators can use WDAC to ensure that only applications that are specifically allowed can run on the Windows 10 computers.

24. A, B. Intune Managed Browser is an approved client app for conditional access. This allows an administrator to restrict mobile browser access to Azure AD–connected web apps where users can only use the Managed Browser. This will block access from other unprotected browsers. To restrict Azure AD–connected web apps to use the Intune Managed Browser on mobile platforms, an administrator can create a conditional access policy requiring approved client applications. For the steps on how to create conditional access for protected browsers, visit the following Microsoft website:

docs.microsoft.com/en-us/mem/intune/apps/app-configuration-managed-browser#conditional-access-for-protected-browsers

25. C. To monitor and manage virtual machines or physical computers on a local data center or a cloud environment with Azure Monitor, an administrator needs to deploy the Log Analytics agent. This is also called the Microsoft Monitoring Agent (MMA). The MMA is configured to report to one or more Log Analytics workspaces. On a monitored Windows computer, the agent is shown as the Microsoft Monitoring Agent service. The MMA service collects log file events and Windows event logs, performance data, and other telemetry.

26. A. Microsoft Defender Advanced Threat Protection (Microsoft Defender ATP) is designed to help prevent, detect, investigate, and respond to advanced threats. Microsoft Defender ATP includes a configuration score that can help assess the security state of an enterprise network, identify any unprotected systems, and take recommended actions to improve corporate security. The Microsoft Secure Score is visible in the Threat & Vulnerability Management dashboard of the Microsoft Defender Security Center. The higher the configuration score, the better the endpoints are. The endpoints will be more resistant to cybersecurity threat attacks. The score is based on the collective security configuration state of machines, and it looks at the following categories:

- Accounts
- Application
- Network
- Operating System
- Security Controls

27. C. TrueType fonts (TTFs) are the basic fonts created by Apple and Microsoft. In this case, since you want to protect the system, you will use Microsoft Defender Exploit Guard. This helps protect systems from common malware attacks, which use executable files and scripts that will attack applications. Microsoft Defender Exploit Guard looks for suspicious scripts or behaviors that are not normal on the Windows 10 system. Microsoft Defender Exploit Guard helps protect Windows 10 systems from malware, ransomware, and other types of attacks. It reduces the device attack surface.

28. C. Microsoft Defender Credential Guard is a Windows 10 Enterprise and Windows Server 2016 and newer security feature that uses virtualization-based security to protect credentials. Hyper-V is Microsoft's hardware virtualization product that allows you to create and run a software version of a computer, called a virtual machine. For Microsoft Defender Credential Guard to provide protection, the computers must meet certain hardware, firmware, and software requirements. To provide basic protection, Microsoft Defender Credential Guard uses the following:

- Secure boot (required)
- Support for virtualization-based security (required)
- TPM 1.2 or 2.0 (preferred)
- UEFI lock (preferred)

Virtualization-based security requires the following:

- 64-bit CPU
- CPU virtualization extensions plus extended page tables
- Windows hypervisor (Hyper-V)

29. C. Use the Microsoft Azure IoT Central applications to monitor devices and change settings. Azure IoT Central applications are hosted by Microsoft, which decreases the administrative overhead of managing applications. Azure IoT Central Applications is an Internet of Things (IoT) application platform that reduces the load and cost of developing, managing, and maintaining IoT solutions.

30. D. Windows 10 Performance Monitor includes data collector sets. Data collector sets work with performance logs. Data collector sets are groups of performance counters, event logs, and system information that can be used to collect multiple datasets, on-demand or over a period of time. They are used to collect data into a log so that the data can be reviewed. You can view the log files with Performance Monitor. Data collector sets are broken down into two categories:

User-defined data collector sets: Created and configured by an administrator. They are custom sets that contain counters, event logs, and trace information.

System data collector sets: Automatically created and defined by the operating system, applications, and components.

31. B. Microsoft Defender Application Guard was designed for Windows 10 and Microsoft Internet browsers (Edge and Internet Explorer). Application Guard works with Edge to isolate untrusted websites, which protects your network and data while users are on the Internet. You can pick and choose which websites have been defined as trusted sites. These sites can be internal or external websites, corporate websites, or cloud-based organizations. If a site is not on the trusted list, it will be considered untrusted and automatically be isolated whenever a user visits the site. Microsoft Defender Application Guard is disabled by default.

32. B, C. Microsoft Intune includes a wide variety of settings to help protect your devices. These settings are created in an endpoint protection configuration profile in Intune to control security. Microsoft Defender Exploit Guard is used to manage and reduce the attack surface of apps. The Block Office Communication Application From Creating Child Processes rule prevents Outlook from creating child processes while still allowing valid functions. The Microsoft Defender Firewall blocks unauthorized network traffic moving into or out of the local device. In this case, it will block the FTP traffic.

33. C. An administrator can create and manage enrollment restrictions that define what devices can enroll into management with Intune. You can define the number of devices allowed and which operating systems and versions are allowed. For the steps on how to create a device type restriction, check out the following Microsoft website:

docs.microsoft.com/en-us/mem/intune/enrollment/enrollment-restrictions-set#create-a-device-type-restriction

If an administrator blocks personally owned Windows devices from enrollment, Intune will check to ensure that each new Windows enrollment request has been authorized. Unauthorized enrollments will be blocked.

34. C. Microsoft Intune includes settings and features that allow you to enable or disable features for different devices. These settings and features are added to configuration profiles. Once you create a configuration profile, you will then use Intune to assign the profile to the devices. There are several profile types. Custom profiles allow an administrator to assign device settings that are not built into Intune. As an example, on an Android device, you can enter OMA-URI values, and for iOS/iPadOS devices, you can import a configuration file that was created using the Apple Configurator.

35. C. Microsoft Defender Application Guard was designed for Windows 10 and Microsoft Edge. It uses a hardware isolation approach. This lets untrusted site navigation launch inside a container, thus safeguarding corporate networks and data. The administrator determines which sites are trusted sites, cloud resources, and internal networks. Anything that is not on the trusted sites list is considered untrusted. If a user goes to an untrusted site through either Microsoft Edge or Internet Explorer, Microsoft Edge opens the site in an isolated Hyper-V-enabled container, which is separate from the host operating system. To use Microsoft Defender Application Guard, the environment has a few hardware requirements that must be met. These include the following:

64-Bit CPU: A 64-bit computer with minimum four cores (logical processors) is required for hypervisor and virtualization-based security (VBS).

CPU virtualization extensions: Extended page tables, also called Second Level Address Translation (SLAT), and either one of these virtualization extensions for VBS: VT-x (Intel) or AMD-V.

Hardware memory: Microsoft requires a minimum of 8GB RAM.

Hard disk: 5 GB free space, solid-state disk (SSD) recommended.

Input/Output Memory Management Unit (IOMMU) support: Not required but recommended.

36. C. Microsoft Defender Credential Guard is virtualization-based security that helps isolate critical files so that only system software that is privileged can access them. Once enabled, a Windows 10 machine that is part of Active Directory or Azure Active Directory (Azure AD) will have the system credentials protected by Microsoft Defender Credential Guard. After you enable Microsoft Defender Credential Guard, the Local Security Authority (LSA) process in the operating system works with a new component named the isolated LSA. The isolated process stores and protects the critical data.

37. D. Microsoft Defender Firewall with Advanced Security is a tool that provides detailed control over the Microsoft Defender Firewall rules. An administrator can view the rules that are used by Microsoft Defender Firewall, change the properties, create new rules, or disable existing rules. Microsoft Defender Firewall with Advanced Security is a host firewall that helps secure a device. It can filter the network traffic permitted to enter the device from the network and control what network traffic the device is allowed to send to the network. So, Microsoft Defender Firewall with Advanced Security allows you to set up inbound and outbound rules used by Windows Firewall. Inbound rules monitor inbound traffic, while outbound rules monitor outbound traffic.

38. C. Inbound and outbound rules consist of many preconfigured rules that can be enabled or disabled. Inbound rules monitor inbound traffic, while outbound rules monitor outbound traffic. To configure your Windows Firewall to allow DNS inbound and outbound traffic, you would configure UDP port 53. TCP port 20 is for FTP data, TCP port 25 is for SMTP (mail), and TCP port 80 is for HTTP.

39. D, E. Microsoft Defender Antivirus helps protect devices by dynamically detecting spyware, malware, and viruses. Microsoft Defender runs in the background and automatically installs new definitions once they become available. An administrator can use Microsoft Defender Antivirus manually to check for malware or can set up various scan options. If real-time protection is enabled, then files and scripts are scanned prior to them being accessed and executed. Microsoft Defender SmartScreen protects devices against phishing or malware websites and applications, and by not allowing the downloading of possible malicious files. Microsoft Defender SmartScreen determines whether a site is possibly malicious by doing the following:

- Analyzing visited web pages checking for indications of suspicious behavior
- Checking the visited web pages against a dynamic list of reported phishing sites and malicious software sites

40. A, D. The first thing that an administrator would want to do is to reset the user's password. Then perform a wipe of the user's laptop. By using the Retire or Wipe action, an administrator can remove devices from Intune that are no longer needed, being given to another user, or stolen/missing. Users can also issue a remote command from the Intune Company Portal to devices that are enrolled in Intune. The Wipe action restores a device to its factory default settings. The user data can be kept if you choose the Retain Enrollment State And User Account checkbox. Otherwise, all data, apps, and settings will be removed. As long as the sales staff-owned laptop is being managed by the management infrastructure agent, then the administrator can use the remote wipe feature.

41. B. Inbound and outbound rules consist of many preconfigured rules that can be enabled or disabled. Inbound rules monitor inbound traffic, while outbound rules monitor outbound traffic. To configure your Microsoft Defender Firewall to allow FTP traffic, you would configure TCP port 20 and TCP port 21. TCP port 25 is for mail, and UDP port 53 is for DNS. TCP port 80 is for HTTP, and TCP port 443 is for HTTPS.

42. A. Windows 10 Task Manager provides a quick overview of important system performance statistics without requiring any configuration. There are several ways to access Task Manager. These include the following:

- Right-click the Windows Taskbar and then click Task Manager.
- Press Ctrl+Alt+Del and then select Task Manager.
- Press Ctrl+Shift+Esc.
- Type **Taskman** in the Windows search box.

The Details tab shows all of the applications that are running on the Windows 10 machine. From here, an administrator can stop an application from running by right-clicking the application and selecting Stop.

43. C. Event Viewer is a tool used for monitoring network information. An administrator can use the logs to view any information, warnings, or alerts related to the functionality of the network. You can access Event Viewer by selecting Windows Administrative Tools ➤ Event Viewer or by right-clicking the Start button and selecting Event Viewer. Event Viewer can display hundreds of events. In this case, you would want to create a custom view to achieve your requirements. You would not be able to use the Administrative Events view, which is the default view because it also includes all warnings. This question states that you want to see Critical and Error events only. Custom Views allow you to filter events to create your own customized look and to filter events by event level (critical, error, warning, and so forth), by logs, and by source.

44. C. The graphic shown is an example of a Line view output. The three options are Line view, Histogram Bar view, and Report view. The Line view is the default display that is presented when you first access Performance Monitor. The chart displays values using the vertical axis and time using the horizontal axis. This view is useful if you want to display values over a period of time or see the changes in values over a period of time. Each point that is plotted on the graph is based on an average value calculated during the sample interval for the measurement being made.

45. B. Windows 10 Performance Monitor is designed to allow users and administrators to monitor performance statistics for various operating system parameters. You can collect, store, and analyze information about the CPU, memory, disk, and network resources. By collecting and analyzing performance values, this allows you to identify potential problems. You should monitor the Memory counters. If a computer does not have enough memory, this can cause excessive paging, which can be observed as a disk subsystem bottleneck.

46. A. Microsoft Defender Application Guard was designed for Windows 10 and Microsoft Edge. It uses a hardware isolation approach. This lets untrusted site navigation launch inside a container, thus safeguarding corporate networks and data. The administrator determines which sites are trusted sites, cloud resources, and internal networks. Anything that is not on the trusted sites list is considered untrusted. If a user goes to an untrusted site through either Microsoft Edge or Internet Explorer, the site will open in an isolated Hyper-V-enabled container, which is separate from the host operating system. To use Microsoft Defender Application Guard, the environment has a few hardware requirements that must be met, which include the following:

64-Bit CPU: A 64-bit computer a minimum of four cores (logical processors) is required for hypervisor and virtualization-based security (VBS).

CPU virtualization extensions: Extended page tables, also called Second Level Address Translation (SLAT), and either one of these virtualization extensions for VBS: VT-x (Intel) or AMD-V.

Hardware memory: Microsoft requires a minimum of 8 GB RAM.

Hard disk: 5 GB free space, solid-state disk (SSD) recommended.

Input/Output Memory Management Unit (IOMMU) support: Not required but recommended.

47. C. Microsoft Defender Credential Guard can be enabled by using Group Policy, the registry, or the Hypervisor-Protected Code Integrity (HVCI) and the Microsoft Defender Credential Guard hardware readiness tool. You can use Group Policy to enable Microsoft Defender Credential Guard. This will add and enable the virtualization-based security features. To enable Microsoft Defender Credential Guard by using Group Policy, perform the following steps:

   1. From the Group Policy Management Console, go to Computer Configuration ➤ Administrative Templates ➤ System ➤ Device Guard.

   2. Double-click Turn On Virtualization Based Security and then click the Enabled option.

   3. In the Select Platform Security Level box, choose Secure Boot or Secure Boot And DMA Protection.

   4. In the Credential Guard Configuration box, click Enabled With UEFI lock and then click OK. If you want to be able to turn off Microsoft Defender Credential Guard remotely, choose Enabled Without Lock.

   5. In the Secure Launch Configuration box, choose Not Configured, Enabled, or Disabled.

   6. Close the Group Policy Management Console.

48. A. Fresh Start allows an administrator to perform a clean reinstallation and update of Windows while maintaining the personal data and keeping most Windows settings intact. To use Fresh Start, select Start ➤ Settings ➤ Update & Security ➤ Microsoft Defender ➤ Device Performance & Health. Under Fresh Start, select Additional Info ➤ Get Started. Please note that Fresh Start will remove most of the apps, including Microsoft 365, third-party antivirus software, and desktop apps that came pre-installed on a device. You will not be able to recover removed apps, and you will manually need to reinstall these apps later. You may also lose the digital licenses and digital content associated with apps, which could affect your ability to use the apps or app-related content that has already been paid for.

49. B. Windows 10 includes Windows Security. Windows Security provides the latest antivirus protection. Devices will be actively protected from the moment Windows 10 is started. Windows Security constantly scans for malware, viruses, and security threats. To help keep devices secure, Windows Security will monitor devices for security issues and provides a health report. This health report appears on the Device Performance & Health page. The Health report alerts an administrator to common issues with the system and offers recommendations on how to fix them. To view the health report for a device in Windows Security, perform the following:

   1. In the search box on the taskbar, type **Windows Security** and then select it from the results.

   2. Select Device Performance & Health. What is displayed in the report will vary, depending on the Windows version, device, permissions, and the issues that are found.

50. B. There are several management features available on Configuration Manager. Each feature has its own prerequisites and how each might influence the design and implementation of the Configuration Manager hierarchy. Company Resource Access allows you to give users in your organization access to data and applications from remote locations. This feature includes Wi-Fi, VPN, email, and certificate profiles.

51. D. Microsoft Defender Exploit Guard helps protect Windows 10 devices against malware, ransomware, and other types of attacks. It does this by reducing the attack surface of a device. There are a number of ways that an administrator can turn on Microsoft Defender Exploit Guard. It can be enabled by using the Microsoft Defender Security Center, a Group Policy object, System Center Configuration Manager (SCCM), or Mobile Device Management (MDM) using Microsoft Intune. Microsoft Defender Exploit Guard is part of Microsoft Defender Advanced Threat Protection. Microsoft Defender Exploit Guard consists of four components:

   - Attack surface reduction rules

   - Controlled folder access

   - Exploit protection

   - Network protection

   In this question, network protection is being discussed. It extends Microsoft Defender SmartScreen protection in Microsoft Edge to other applications to prevent access to Internet domains that may host phishing scams, exploits, and other malicious content.

52. D. Microsoft Defender SmartScreen protects against phishing or malware websites and applications and the downloading of potentially malicious files. Microsoft Defender SmartScreen works with Intune, Group Policy, and mobile device management (MDM) settings to help manage organizational computer settings. SmartScreen helps administrators protect users when they attempt to visit websites that have previously been reported as phishing or malware websites, or if a user tries to download a potentially malicious file.

53. A. Mobile device management (MDM) enrollment is the first phase of enterprise management. During the enrollment process, devices need to be configured to communicate with the MDM server using security precautions. The enrollment service will verify that only authenticated and authorized devices can be managed. So, in this question, since you are purchasing new Apple iOS 9.0 and macOS 10.9 devices, you need to obtain an Apple Push Notification service certificate. This will enable Intune to communicate securely with the devices.

54. A. The Apple mobile device management (MDM) push certificates are valid for one year and must be renewed to maintain iOS and macOS device management. If a certificate expires, enrolled devices cannot be contacted or managed. Apple MDM push certificates, MDM server tokens, and VPP tokens expire 365 days after they are created. If the Apple MDM certificate expires or is deleted, you will need to reset and re-enroll the devices with a new certificate. For the steps on renewing an Apple MDM certificate, go to the following Microsoft website:

docs.microsoft.com/en-us/intune-education/renew-ios-certificate-token#renew-apple-mdm--certificate

55. B. Microsoft Defender Advanced Threat Protection (Microsoft Defender ATP) is designed to help enterprise networks prevent, detect, investigate, and respond to advanced threats. Microsoft Defender ATP has a number of built-in features and capabilities. These include the following:

- Automated Investigation and Remediation
- Attack Surface Reduction
- Configuration Score
- Endpoint Detection and Response
- Microsoft Threat Experts
- Next Generation Protection
- Threat & Vulnerability Management

Endpoint Detection and Response capabilities are put in place to detect, investigate, and respond to advanced threats. Advanced hunting provides a query-based threat-hunting tool that allows an administrator to proactively find breaches and create custom detections.

56. B. Intune allows an administrator to manage devices and apps and how those devices access company data. To use mobile device management (MDM), the devices must first be enrolled in the Intune service. When a device is enrolled, it's issued an MDM certificate that is used to communicate with the Intune service. By default, devices for all platforms are allowed to enroll in Intune. The method being described in the question is bring your own device (BYOD). BYOD includes personally owned phones, tablets, and computers. Users install and run the Company Portal app to enroll BYODs. This allows users to access company resources such as email.

57. B. Microsoft Defender Antivirus can help protect devices by actively detecting spyware, malware, and viruses on both operating systems and Windows 10 installed on Hyper-V virtual machines. It runs in the background and installs new definitions automatically as they are released. Microsoft Defender Antivirus can manually scan for malware using the Microsoft Defender scan options. The scan options include the following:

- Custom

- Full

- Quick

- Microsoft Defender Offline Scan

In this question, you are discussing a full scan, which will scan all of the files on a hard disk and scan all of the running programs for spyware, malware, and viruses.

58. A. The Device Enrollment Manager (DEM) is a special user account that is used to enroll and manage multiple corporate-owned devices. If you want to enroll a large number of devices into your organization, you can use the DEM account in Microsoft Intune. The DEM allows you to enroll up to 1,000 devices. A standard user can manage and enroll up to 15 devices. For security reasons, the DEM should not also be an Intune administrator.

To add a DEM, perform the following steps:

1. Sign in to the Microsoft Endpoint Manager admin center, and choose Devices ➢ Enroll Devices ➢ Device Enrollment Managers.

2. Select Add.

3. On the Add User blade, enter a user principal name (UPN) for the DEM user and select Add. The DEM user is added to the list of DEM users.

59. A. On Windows 10, Performance Monitor is used to analyze data, such as hard drive, memory, processor, and network usage. Since you want to collect data regarding the processor utilization, you need to monitor the Process performance object. Performance Monitor is used for viewing real-time statistics. By default, only one counter is selected; the %Processor Time counter. There are several ways to open Performance Monitor:

- Open Start and search for *Performance Monitor*. Then click the result.

- Use the Windows key+R keyboard shortcut to open the Run command, type **perfmon**, and click OK.

- Use the Windows key+X keyboard shortcut to open the Power User menu, select Computer Management, and click Performance.

The Add Counters window of Performance Monitor shows the counters and options that are available for a process. The list on the left lists all the available counters for a process that can be selected. The list on the right shows all the instances of a process object that can be selected for monitoring.

60. A. Automatic enrollment allows users enroll their Windows 10 devices in Intune. To enroll, users add their company account to their personally owned devices or join corporate-owned devices to Azure Active Directory (Azure AD). To configure automatic enrollment for Windows devices, perform the following steps:

1. Select the Device Enrollment node.

2. Select Windows Enrollment ➢ Automatic Enrollment.

3. On the Configure blade, select one of the MDM User Scope options. Select either None, Some, or All. If you selected Some, then click Select Groups to browse for and select the wanted groups that will have automatic enrollment privileges.

4. Click Save.

61. B. Microsoft Defender Exploit Guard helps protect Windows 10 devices against malware, ransomware, and other types of attacks. It does this by reducing the attack surface of a device. There are a number of ways that an administrator can turn on Microsoft Defender Exploit Guard. It can be enabled by using the Microsoft Defender Security Center, a Group Policy object, System Center Configuration Manager (SCCM), or Mobile Device Management (MDM) using Microsoft Intune. Microsoft Defender Exploit Guard is part of Microsoft Defender Advanced Threat Protection. Microsoft Defender Exploit Guard consists of four components.

- Attack surface reduction rules

- Controlled folder access

- Exploit protection

- Network protection

In this question, controlled folder access is being discussed. This helps protect against ransomware and malware by stopping changes to files in protected folders if the app attempting to make changes is malevolent or exhibits malicious behavior.

62. C. To manage devices in Intune, they must first be enrolled. Both personally owned and corporate-owned devices can be enrolled. There are two ways to get devices enrolled in Intune:

- Administrators can configure policies to force automatic enrollment without any user intervention.

- Users can self-enroll their devices.

Users can self-enroll their Windows device by using any of the following methods:

- Autopilot

- Azure Active Directory (Azure AD) join

- Bring your own device (BYOD)

- MDM-only enrollment

The method being discussed in the question is bring your own device (BYOD). A user can enroll their personally owned devices by choosing to connect a Work and School account from Settings of the device. This process will register the device with Azure AD to obtain access to corporate resources and will enroll the device in Intune as a personally owned device (BYOD).

63. C. The Performance Monitor is a Windows 10 utility for monitoring computer performance in real time or from a log. It collects data from a local computer or remote Windows 10 machine. Data can be collected from a single computer or from multiple computers at the same time. It allows you to view data collected in real time or historically from collected data.

64. B. Windows 10 includes Windows Security. Windows Security provides the latest antivirus protection. Devices will be actively protected from the moment Windows 10 is started. Windows Security constantly scans for malware, viruses, and security threats. The App & Browser Control section covers the Microsoft Defender SmartScreen settings and Exploit protection mitigations. To access Windows Security and review the Microsoft Defender SmartScreen settings, perform the following:

1. In the search box on the taskbar, type Windows Security and then select it from the results.

2. Select App & Browser Control.

65. C. By default, licensed users can add up to 15 devices to their accounts. Device administrators have the ability to add devices to Intune, but users do have the ability to enroll 15 devices on their own. Unless there is an enrollment restriction in place, then users can manage and enroll up to 15 devices.

66. C. To manage devices in Intune, they must first be enrolled. Both personally owned and corporate-owned devices can be enrolled. There are two ways to get devices enrolled in Intune:

- Administrators can configure policies to force automatic enrollment without any user intervention.

- Users can self-enroll their devices.

Users can self-enroll their Windows device by using any of the following methods:

- Autopilot

- Azure Active Directory (Azure AD) join

- Bring your own device (BYOD)

- MDM-only enrollment

The method being discussed in the question is Azure Active Directory (Azure AD) join. This method joins the device with Azure AD, and it enables users to sign in to Windows with their Azure AD credentials. If Auto Enrollment is enabled, the device is automatically enrolled in Intune. The device is marked as a corporate-owned device in Intune.

67. B. Windows Security constantly scans for malware, viruses, and security threats. The App & Browser Control section covers the Microsoft Defender SmartScreen settings and Exploit Protection mitigations. Exploit Protection helps to protect users' devices against malware that uses exploits to sweep through your corporate network. Exploit Protection consists of a number of specific mitigations that must be separately enabled and configured. By default, Exploit Protection already enables several mitigations that apply to the operating system and to specific apps. To access Windows Security and review the Microsoft Defender Exploit Protection settings, perform the following:

1. In the search box on the taskbar, type Windows Security and then select it from the results.

2. Select App & Browser Control.

68. B. The Windows Analytics service was retired on January 31, 2020, and it was replaced with Desktop Analytics. Desktop Analytics is a cloud-based service that works in conjunction with Configuration Manager. This service allows you to make informed decisions regarding the update readiness of your Windows clients. Use Desktop Analytics with Configuration Manager to do the following:

- Assess app compatibility with the latest Windows 10 feature updates.
- Create an inventory of apps running in an organization.
- Create pilot groups that represent the entire application and driver estate across a minimal set of devices.
- Deploy Windows 10 to pilot and production-managed devices.
- Identify compatibility issues and receive mitigation suggestions based on cloud-enabled data insights.

69. C. Enroll a personal or corporate-owned Android device to obtain secure access to corporate email, apps, and data. The Company Portal app supports Android devices, including Samsung Knox, running Android 4.4 and later. Install the Intune Company Portal app from Google Play. For the complete set of steps on how to enroll an Android device, check out the following Microsoft website:

docs.microsoft.com/en-us/mem/intune/user-help/enroll-device-android-company-portal#enroll-device

70. C. While Windows Analytics was retired on January 31, 2020, support for Update Compliance has continued through the Azure portal. Update Compliance enables you to do the following:

- Check bandwidth savings acquired across multiple content types by using Delivery Optimization.
- Monitor security, quality, and feature updates for the Windows 10 Professional, Education, and Enterprise editions.
- View a report of device and update compliance issues that require attention.

Use Update Compliance to monitor your device's Windows updates and Microsoft Defender Antivirus status.

71. C. Log Analytics is the primary tool in the Azure portal for writing log queries and analyzing the results. You can start Log Analytics from several places within the Azure portal. The scope of the data available is determined by how you start Log Analytics. You can do the following:

- Select Logs from the Azure Monitor menu or Log Analytics workspaces menu.
- Select Logs from the Overview page of an Application Insights application.
- Select Logs from the menu of an Azure resource.

72. A. Microsoft Intune offers the ability to obtain reports covering a wide variety of items. The Intune reports help an administrator monitor the status of enrolled devices and to check if there are any problems that need to be addressed. The reports allow you to examine both the hardware and software inventory. To access the different reports available in Intune, open the Intune Management Console and click the Reports link on the left side. There are a number of reports that can be run. Some of these reports are as follows:

- Computer Inventory Reports
- Detected Software Reports
- License Installation Reports
- License Purchase Reports
- Mobile Device Inventory Reports
- Terms and Conditions Reports
- Update Report

The report type being discussed in this question is Computer Inventory Reports. These reports will help you obtain detailed information regarding the managed computers in the company. You can use them for planning hardware purchases and to get an overview of the hardware needs of the users.

73. C. The Microsoft Windows Performance Monitor is a tool that you can use to examine how programs run on a computer and how those programs affect the computer's performance. The tool can be used in real time and can also be used to collect information in a log to analyze the data at a later time. With Performance Monitor, you can set up counter logs and alerts. All performance statistics fall into three main categories that you can measure: performance objects, counters, and instances.

74. C. Intune reports let you monitor the health and activity of endpoints across the corporate network and provide other reporting information. You can see reports regarding device compliance, device health, and trends. You can also create custom reports. Report types are organized into four focus areas as follows:

Operational: Provides timely and targeted data that helps you focus and take action

Organizational: Provides a wider summary of the overall view, such as the device management state

Historical: Provides patterns and trends over a period of time

Specialist: Allows you to use raw data to create your own customized reports

75. A. Microsoft Defender Exploit Guard helps protect Windows 10 devices against malware, ransomware, and other types of attacks. It does this by reducing the attack surface of a device. There are a number of ways that an administrator can turn on Microsoft Defender

Exploit Guard. It can be enabled by using the Microsoft Defender Security Center, a Group Policy Object, System Center Configuration Manager (SCCM), or Mobile Device Management (MDM) using Microsoft Intune. Microsoft Defender Exploit Guard is part of Microsoft Defender Advanced Threat Protection. Microsoft Defender Exploit Guard consists of four components:

- Attack surface reduction rules
- Controlled folder access
- Exploit protection
- Network protection

In this question, attack surface reduction rules are being discussed. Attack surface reduction rules use rules to help prevent attack vectors that are applied by scripts, email, and Office-based malware.

76. A. To access device inventory reports, select the Devices node. You will see an overall summary of enrolled devices. To view additional information regarding enrolled devices, click the All Devices tab. You can also perform the following tasks to customize the view to meet your needs:

- Refresh
- Filter
- Columns
- Export

The option being discussed in this question is the Columns button. You can determine exactly what information is being displayed. Select from the available columns and click Apply. There is a large list of options that allow you to customize the view to what you want to see displayed. In this question, you are looking to see the Device Name, Managed By, and OS Version information. These will be displayed in columns.

77. B. The Windows Analytics service was retired on January 31, 2020, and it was replaced with Desktop Analytics. Desktop Analytics is a cloud-based service that integrates with Configuration Manager. The service allows you to make knowledgeable decisions regarding the update readiness of your Windows clients. Use Desktop Analytics with Configuration Manager to do the following:

- Assess application compatibility with the latest Windows 10 feature updates.
- Create an inventory of applications running in an organization.
- Create pilot groups that represent the entire application and driver estate across a minimal set of devices.
- Deploy Windows 10 to pilot and production-managed devices.
- Identify compatibility issues and receive mitigation suggestions based on cloud-enabled data insights.

78. B, D. You configure Exploit Protection settings by using the Windows Security app on an individual machine and then exporting the configuration as an XML file that can be deployed to other devices. You can use Group Policy to distribute the XML file to multiple devices at once. You can also configure the mitigations using PowerShell. There are two PowerShell cmdlets used for setting Exploit Protection:

- ```Get-ProcessMitigation```
- ```Set-ProcessMitigation```

Using ```Get``` will list the current configuration status of any mitigations that have been enabled on the device. Use ```Set``` to configure each mitigation. The syntax for using ```Set-ProcessMigration``` is as follows:

```
Set-ProcessMitigation -<scope> <app executable> -<action> <mitigation or
options>,<mitigation or options>,<mitigation or options>
```

79. C. Microsoft Intune offers the ability to obtain reports covering a wide variety of items. The Intune reports help an administrator to monitor the status of enrolled devices and to check whether there are any problems that need to be addressed. The reports allow you to examine both the hardware and software inventories. To access the different reports available in Intune, open the Intune Management Console and click the Reports link on the left side. There are a number of reports that can be run, including the following:

- Computer Inventory Reports
- Detected Software Reports
- License Installation Reports
- License Purchase Reports
- Mobile Device Inventory Reports
- Terms and Conditions Reports
- Updates Reports

The report being discussed in this question is a License Installation Report. This report allows you to compare installed software with your current license agreement coverage.

80. A. Attack surface reduction rules help prevent software that may abuse or compromise devices on your network. You can customize attack surface reduction rules by excluding files and folders or by adding custom text to the notification alert that appears on a user's device. Excluding files and folders from being evaluated by attack surface reduction rules means that even if an attack surface reduction rule detects that the file may be malicious, the file will not be blocked from running. You can specify individual files, folder paths, or the fully qualified domain name (FQDN). There are 15 attack surface reduction rules. The rule being discussed in this question is Block Executable Content From Email Client and Webmail—BE9BA2D9-53EA-4CDC-84E5-9B1EEEE46550. For a complete list of attack surface reduction rules and their corresponding GUIDs, check out the following Microsoft website:

docs.microsoft.com/en-us/windows/security/threat-protection/microsoft-defender-atp/attack-surface-reduction#attack-surface-reduction-rules

If you are configuring the rules using Group Policy or PowerShell, you will need to know the associated GUID. If you are using Microsoft Endpoint Configuration Manager or Microsoft Intune, you do not need the GUIDs.

81. C. To access device inventory reports, select the Devices node. You will see an overall summary of enrolled devices. To view additional information regarding enrolled devices, click the All Devices tab. You can also perform the following tasks to customize the view to meet your needs:

- Refresh
- Filter
- Columns
- Export

The option being discussed in this question is the Filter option. Using Filter allows you to display only certain devices depending upon the options chosen to filter for. There is a large list of options that can be chosen to filter for. Some of the options include filtering for devices that are managed by a specific user, ownership, compliance, operating system, phone number, and so forth. When filtering, only the devices that meet the specified filters will be shown.

82. C. Desktop Analytics is a replacement of Windows Analytics, which was retired on January 31, 2020. The functions of Windows Analytics are combined in the Desktop Analytics service. Desktop Analytics is integrated with Configuration Manager. Desktop Analytics provides several benefits, including the following:

Device and software inventory: The inventory of key factors, such as apps and versions of Windows.

Pilot identification: The identification of factors that focus on the key aspects of the pilot deployment of Windows upgrades and updates.

Issue identification: Uses collected market data along with your data to predict probable issues and then suggest possible mitigations.

Configuration Manager integration: A service cloud that enables your existing on-premises infrastructure. You use this data and analysis to deploy and manage Windows on your devices.

In this question, the benefit of issue identification is being discussed.

83. D. Network protection helps prevent users from using any apps to access a domain that may be hosting a phishing scam, an exploit, or other malicious content over the Internet. You can enable network protection by using any of the following:

- Group Policy
- Microsoft Endpoint Configuration Manager
- Microsoft Intune

- Mobile Device Management (MDM)
- PowerShell

To configure network protection by using Intune, perform the following:

1. Sign in to the Azure portal and open Intune.
2. Click Device Configuration ➤ Profiles ➤ Create Profile.
3. Name the profile, choose Windows 10 And Later, and choose Endpoint Protection.
4. Click Configure ➤ Microsoft Defender Exploit Guard ➤ Network Filtering ➤ Enable.
5. Click OK to save each open blade and click Create.
6. Click the Profile Assignments, assign to All Users & All Devices, and click Save.

84. B. Intune reports let you monitor the health and activity of endpoints across the corporate network and provide other reporting information. You can see reports regarding device compliance, device health, and trends. You can also create custom reports. Report types are organized into four focus areas.

Operational: Provides timely and targeted data that helps you focus and take action

Organizational: Provides a wider summary of the overall view, such as the device management state

Historical: Provides patterns and trends over a period of time

Specialist: Allows you to use raw data to create your own customized reports

85. C. Microsoft Defender Antivirus can help protect devices by actively detecting spyware, malware, and viruses on both operating systems and Windows 10 installed on Hyper-V virtual machines. It runs in the background and installs new definitions automatically as they are released. Microsoft Defender Antivirus can manually scan for malware using the Microsoft Defender scan options. The scan options include the following:

- Custom
- Full
- Quick
- Microsoft Defender Offline Scan

In this question, you are discussing a quick scan that will scan the most likely areas on a hard disk where spyware, malware, and viruses are commonly known to infect.

86. C. Microsoft Defender Exploit Guard helps protect Windows 10 devices against malware, ransomware, and other types of attacks. It does this by reducing the attack surface of a device. There are a number of ways that an administrator can turn on Microsoft Defender Exploit Guard. It can be enabled by using the Microsoft Defender Security Center, a Group Policy object, System Center Configuration Manager (SCCM), or Mobile Device

Management (MDM) using Microsoft Intune. Microsoft Defender Exploit Guard is part of Microsoft Defender Advanced Threat Protection. Microsoft Defender Exploit Guard consists of the following four components:

- Attack surface reduction rules
- Controlled folder access
- Exploit protection
- Network protection

In this question, exploit protection is being discussed. Exploit protection uses Microsoft Defender Antivirus or, if installed, a third-party antivirus software to help exploit techniques used against corporate apps.

87. C. Microsoft Defender Application Guard was designed for Windows 10 and Microsoft Edge. Application Guard helps by protecting the corporation while users browse the Internet by segregating untrusted sites. You can configure Microsoft Defender Application Guard in one of two modes:

Stand-alone mode: In stand-alone mode, users can use hardware-isolated browsing sessions without any administrative or management policy configurations.

Enterprise mode: In enterprise mode, an administrator defines the company limitations by adding trusted domains and by customizing Application Guard to meet and enforce the needs on the users' devices.

88. C. Network protection helps prevent users from using any apps to access a domain that may be hosting a phishing scam, an exploit, or other malicious content over the Internet. You can enable network protection by using any of the following:

- Group Policy
- Microsoft Endpoint Configuration Manager
- Microsoft Intune
- Mobile Device Management (MDM)
- PowerShell

To enable network protection by using PowerShell, perform the following:

1. Type **powershell** in the Start menu, right-click Windows PowerShell, and click Run As Administrator.

2. Enter this cmdlet: **Set-MpPreference -EnableNetworkProtection Enabled**.

The Set-MpPreference cmdlet configures the preferences for Microsoft Defender scans and updates. An administrator can modify exclusion filename extensions, paths, or processes and specify the default action for high, moderate, and low threat levels.

89. C. Intune allows an administrator to manage devices and apps and how those devices access company data. To use this mobile device management (MDM), the devices must first be enrolled in the Intune service. When a device is enrolled, it's issued an MDM certificate that is used to communicate with the Intune service. By default, devices for all platforms are allowed to enroll in Intune. The method being described in the question is corporate-owned device (COD), which include phones, tablets, and computers that are owned by the company and distributed to the users. COD enrollment supports scenarios such as automatic enrollment, shared devices, or pre-authorized enrollment requirements.

90. B. Microsoft Defender Advanced Threat Protection (Microsoft Defender ATP) is designed to help enterprise networks prevent, detect, investigate, and respond to advanced threats. Microsoft Defender ATP has a number of built-in features and capabilities, including the following:

- Automated Investigation and Remediation
- Attack Surface Reduction
- Configuration Score
- Endpoint Detection and Response
- Microsoft Threat Experts
- Next Generation Protection
- Threat & Vulnerability Management

Microsoft Defender ATP includes a configuration score that helps assess the security state of a corporate network, identify unprotected systems, and take recommended actions to improve the overall corporate security.

91. B. To access device inventory reports, select the Devices node. You will see an overall summary of enrolled devices. To view additional information regarding enrolled devices, click the All Devices tab. You can also perform the following tasks to customize the view to meet your needs:

- Refresh
- Filter
- Columns
- Export

The option being discussed in this question is Export. Once you have filtered the devices in the list, click the Export button. When prompted, click Save. This will create a CSV file that can be opened in Microsoft Excel to review the information.

92. C. Microsoft Defender Application Guard functionality is turned off by default. You can quickly install it on a user's device using the Control Panel, using PowerShell, or using your mobile device management (MDM) solution. To install Microsoft Defender Application Guard by using the Control Panel, perform the following steps:

1. Open the Control Panel, click Programs And Features, and then click Turn Windows Features On Or Off.

2. Select the checkbox next to Microsoft Defender Application Guard and then click OK.

3. Click OK. You will be prompted to restart the computer.

93. D. Microsoft Intune allows you to manage a wide variety of devices by enrolling them into the service. You can enroll some device types yourself, or users can enroll using the Company Portal app. Enrolling allows them to browse and install apps, make sure that devices are compliant with company policies, and contact their IT support, if needed. To enable device enrollment, click Device Enrollment in the Microsoft Intune Navigation pane. Under Device Enrollment there are several options that can be managed, including the following:

- Apple Enrollment
- Android Enrollment
- Windows Enrollment
- Terms and Conditions
- Enrollment Restrictions
- Device Categories
- Corporate Device Identifiers
- Device Enrollment Managers

This question is discussing the Windows Enrollment option. From this blade, you can access a number of settings. Some of these settings include the following:

- Automatic Enrollment
- CNAME Validation
- Enrollment Status Page
- Intune Connector for Active Directory
- Windows Autopilot
- Windows Autopilot deployment profiles
- Windows Hello for Business

94. A. An important facet of monitoring performance is that it should be performed over a period of time. This is called a *baseline*. Many performance problems cannot be identified simply by looking at performance at a quick glance. Instead, you need a baseline so that you can analyze the performance. Then, when a problem arises, you can compare the current performance to the baseline to see what the differences are. Since performance can also change over time, it is recommended that you create a baseline regularly so that you can chart the performance measures and identify trends.

95. B. To use Microsoft Defender Application Guard in stand-alone mode, while using Microsoft Edge, click the ellipsis button (...). The steps on how to open a New Application Guard window are as follows:

1. Open Microsoft Edge.

2. Click the Settings And More (...) menu on the right side and click New Application Guard Window.

3. You may see a splash screen, and then a new instance of Microsoft Edge will open with Microsoft Defender Application Guard enabled.

4. You can now enter any website address in the address bar to visit, and that session will be isolated.

96. A. Audit logs include a record of events that generate a change in Intune. Actions such as create, update (edit), delete, assign, and remote actions all create audit events that can be reviewed. By default, auditing is enabled for all users and cannot be disabled. To audit logs for Intune workloads, perform the following steps:

1. Sign in to the Microsoft Endpoint Manager admin center.

2. Select Tenant Administration ➢ Audit Logs.

3. To filter the results, select Filter and refine the results using the following options:

   Category: Such as Compliance, Device, and Role.

   Activity: The options listed here are restricted by the option chosen under Category.

   Date range: You can choose logs for the previous month, week, or day.

4. Choose Apply.

5. Select an item in the list to see the activity details.

97. D. Microsoft Defender Advanced Threat Protection (Microsoft Defender ATP) allows an administrator to use the Microsoft Defender Security Center portal to manage Microsoft Defender ATP settings and to view reports and alerts. You can access the portal at `securitycenter.windows.com`. Enterprise security teams can use the portal to monitor and assist in responding to alerts or data breaches. You can use the Microsoft Defender Security Center to do the following:

- Change Microsoft Defender ATP settings, including time zone and review licensing information.

- Search for more information on observed indicators, such as files and IP addresses.

- View, sort, and triage alerts from the endpoints.

When you open the portal, you will see the following:

- Navigation pane (select the horizontal lines at the top of the navigation pane to show or hide it)

- Search, Community Center, Localization, Help and Support, and Feedback

98. C. Microsoft Intune allows you to manage a wide variety of devices by enrolling them into the service. You can enroll some device types yourself, or users can enroll them using the company portal app. Enrolling allows users to browse and install apps, make sure that devices are compliant with company policies, and contact their IT support, if needed. To enable device enrollment, click Device Enrollment in the Microsoft Intune Navigation pane. Under Device Enrollment there are several options that can be managed, including the following:

- Apple Enrollment
- Android Enrollment
- Windows Enrollment
- Terms and Conditions
- Enrollment Restrictions
- Device Categories
- Corporate Device Identifiers
- Device Enrollment Managers

This question is discussing the device categories. Device categories allow you to create device categories that users must choose during device enrollment. Device categories help when you are using the reporting tools. Users can select an appropriate category during enrollment. You can filter reports and create Azure Active Directory device groups based on device categories. To create a device category, click the + Create option and follow the steps.

99. A. Azure Monitor was created to perform analytics, diagnostics, and monitoring. The core components consist of collectors, metrics and logs store, and analytics. Azure Monitor maximizes the availability and performance of apps and services by delivering a solution for collecting, analyzing, and acting on telemetry from your cloud and on-premises environments. The following is a list of a few things that can be done with Azure Monitor:

- Compare infrastructure issues for VMs and Azure Monitor for Containers.
- Create visualizations using Azure dashboards and workbooks.
- Detect and diagnose issues across applications and dependencies with Application Insights.
- Monitor data using Log Analytics for diagnostics and troubleshooting.
- Support operations at scale using smart alerts and automated actions.

100. A. Microsoft Defender Application Control (WDAC) was introduced with Windows 10, and it allows companies to control what drivers and applications are permitted to run on their Windows 10 clients. It does this by blocking any unsigned apps and scripts. WDAC is ideal when:

- You are adopting application control mainly for security reasons.
- Your application control policy can be applied to all users on the managed computers.
- All of the devices to be managed are running Windows 10.

Administrators can configure WDAC through the use of a Group Policy object or by using mobile device management (MDM) and Microsoft Intune. After Microsoft Defender Application Control is set up, administrators can create and configure policies by using GPOs or Intune.

101. C. You can deploy Intune terms and conditions to user groups to describe how enrollment, access to corporate resources, and the Company Portal app will affect their devices. As an Intune admin, you can require that users accept the terms and conditions prior to using the Company Portal app to enroll their devices or to access resources such as company apps and email. There are two ways to create terms and conditions:

- By using Intune
- By using the Azure Active Directory Terms Of Use feature

To create terms and conditions, perform the following tasks:

1. Sign in to the Microsoft Endpoint Manager admin center and choose Tenant Administration ➤ Terms And Conditions.
2. Click Create.
3. On the Basics page, specify information such as the name and description.
4. Click Next to go to the Terms page and provide information such as the title, the terms and conditions, and the summary of terms.
5. Click Next to go to the Scope Tags page.
6. Choose Select Scope Tags, select the scope tags to be assigned to the terms and conditions, and then choose Select.
7. Click Next to go to the Assignments page and choose either All Users or Select Groups.
8. Click Next ➤ Create.

102. A. Microsoft Defender Application Guard was designed for Windows 10 and Microsoft Edge. Application Guard helps by protecting the corporation while users browse the Internet by segregating untrusted sites. You can configure Microsoft Defender Application Guard in one of two modes.

Stand-alone mode: In stand-alone mode, users can use hardware-isolated browsing sessions without any administrative or management policy configurations.

Enterprise mode: In enterprise mode, an administrator defines the company limitations by adding trusted domains and by customizing Application Guard to meet and enforce the needs on the users' devices.

103. A, D. All of the data that is collected by Azure Monitor fits into one of two fundamental types:

- *Metrics* are numerical values that express a piece of the system at a specific point in time. They are capable of supporting real-time scenarios.
- *Logs* contain other kinds of data that is arranged into records with different sets of properties for each type.

The data collected by Azure Monitor will appear on the right side on the Overview page in the Azure portal. You may see several charts that display the performance metrics. If you click any of the graphs, it will open the data in Metrics Explorer.

104. C. As an Intune administrator, you can create and manage enrollment restrictions that limit what devices can enroll into management with Intune, including the following:

- Number of devices allowed

- Which operating systems and versions are allowed

You can create multiple restrictions and apply them to different user groups, or you can set the priority order for different restrictions. For the steps on how to create a device limit restriction, check out the following Microsoft website:

docs.microsoft.com/en-us/mem/intune/enrollment/enrollment-restrictions-set#create-a-device-limit-restriction

The device limit restriction can be set to any number between 1 and 15, with 15 being the default number of devices that a user can enroll.

105. C. Microsoft Defender Antivirus is the next-generation protection component of Microsoft Defender Advanced Threat Protection (Microsoft Defender ATP). An administrator can manage and configure Microsoft Defender Antivirus by using the following:

- Group Policy

- Microsoft Endpoint Configuration Manager

- Microsoft Intune

- PowerShell cmdlets

- The mpcmdrun.exe utility

- Windows Management Instrumentation (WMI)

You can perform a variety of Microsoft Defender Antivirus functions with the dedicated command-line tool mpcmdrun.exe. This utility is useful when you want to automate Microsoft Defender Antivirus. You can find the utility in %ProgramFiles%\Microsoft Defender\mpcmdrun.exe. This must be run from a command prompt. The syntax is as follows:

mpcmdrun.exe [command] [-options]

106. B. To help keep a device secure, Windows Security monitors devices for security issues and delivers a health report. The health report appears on the Device Performance & Health page. The health report alerts you to issues with a system and provides recommendations on how to fix them. Windows Security constantly scans for malware, viruses, and security threats. To view the health report for a device in Windows Security, perform the following:

1. Go to Start ➤ Settings ➤ Windows Security.

2. Select Device Performance & Health. The report display will vary depending on the Windows version, device, permissions, and issues that are found.

107. C. Device Security provides a report in greater detail regarding the security features that are integrated into a Windows device. The Device Security page provides you with status reporting and management of security features. What you see displayed will depend on the device's built-in security features. One of the following messages will be seen, depending upon the device's system configuration:

- Your device meets the requirements for standard hardware security.

- Your device meets the requirements for enhanced hardware security.

- Your device exceeds the requirements for enhanced hardware security.

- Standard hardware security is not supported.

The available features of Device Security include the following:

- Core isolation

- Memory integrity

- Secure boot

- Security processor

To view the device security report for a device in Windows Security, perform the following steps:

1. Go to Start ➤ Settings ➤ Windows Security.

2. Select Device Security. The report display will vary depending on the device's built-in security features.

108. B. Device Guard is a built-in feature of Windows 10 Enterprise that prevents the execution of unwelcome code and applications. Device Guard can be configured using two rule actions—allow and deny.

Allow: Limits execution of applications to an allowed list of code or trusted publisher and blocks everything else.

Deny: Blocks the execution of specific applications.

You can manage Device Guard by using group policies, the Microsoft System Center Configuration Manager (SCCM), Windows PowerShell, and Microsoft Intune.

109. A. Desktop Analytics is a cloud-based service that works with Configuration Manager. The process used to sign into Desktop Analytics and configure your subscription is called Initial Onboarding. This procedure is a one-time process used to set up Desktop Analytics for your company. For the steps on how to perform Initial Onboarding, visit the following Microsoft website:

docs.microsoft.com/en-us/mem/configmgr/desktop-analytics/set-up#initial-onboarding

110. D. Microsoft Defender Antivirus provides real-time protection against software threats such as viruses, malware, and spyware across email, apps, the cloud, and the web. Microsoft Defender Antivirus regularly scans devices to keep them safe. An administrator can schedule Microsoft Defender Antivirus to scan at any time and frequency. To schedule a scan in Microsoft Defender Antivirus, perform the following steps:

1. In the search box on the taskbar, enter `Task Scheduler` and open the app.

2. In the left pane, expand the Task Scheduler Library ➤ Microsoft ➤ Windows, and then scroll down and select the Microsoft Defender folder.

3. In the top center pane, double-click Microsoft Defender Scheduled Scan.

4. In the Microsoft Defender Scheduled Scan Properties (Local Computer) window, select the Triggers tab, go to the bottom of the window, and then select New.

5. Specify how often you want scans to run and when you'd like them to start.

Chapter 8: Manage Apps and Data

1. D. A Configuration Manager application outlines the metadata regarding an application. An application can have one or more deployment types that can include the installation files and information on how software on devices is to be installed. A deployment type incudes rules that identify when and how the client installs the software. Before an application can be deployed, you need to create at least one deployment type for the application. To deploy an application, perform the following:

1. In the Configuration Manager console, go to the Software Library workspace, select Application Management, and select either the Applications or Application Groups node.

2. Select an application or application group from the list to deploy. Then click Deploy.

So, for this question, to meet the requirements you need to create an application deployment from Configuration Manager and then copy the Microsoft 365 Apps for Enterprise distribution files to a Configuration Manager distribution point in each office. Distribution points host the content files that will be deployed to devices and users. When a new distribution point is installed, you use the installation wizard that will walk you through the available settings.

2. B. When you sideload an application, this means you are loading an application that is already owned, or one that the company has created into a delivery system such as Intune, Microsoft Store, or images. Sideloading in Windows 10 is different than in earlier versions of Windows. Sideloading in Windows 10 enables the following:

- Devices do not have to be joined to a domain.

- License keys are not required.

- You can unlock a device for sideloading by using an enterprise policy or by using the Settings app.

To turn on sideloading for managed devices, deploy an enterprise policy. To turn on sideloading for unmanaged devices, perform the following steps:

1. Open Settings.

2. Click Update & Security ➤ For Developers.

3. On Use Developer Features, select Sideload Apps.

3. B. To sideload an application, you need to do the following:

   - Turn on sideloading by pushing a policy with a mobile device management (MDM) provider, or use the Settings app.

   - Trust the app by importing the security certificate to the local device.

   - Install the app by using PowerShell to install the app package.

   To install the app, you need to go to the folder with the AppX package and then run the PowerShell Add-AppxPackage command.

4. D. You must enroll devices into Intune. To enroll clients into Intune, you need to download the Intune client software onto the devices to be enrolled. If the device is an Apple iOS, then an Apple Push Notification service (APNs) certificate must be imported from Apple so that you can manage the iOS devices. This certificate allows an administrator to manage iOS. APNs is a platform service created by Apple that allows third-party applications developers to send push notifications to iOS users. Administrators need to open the Microsoft Intune administration portal and then go to Administration ➤ Mobile Device Management ➤ iOS And Mac OS X ➤ Download The APNs Certificate Requests. Then you need to save the certificate signing request (.csr) file locally. The .csr file is used to request a trust relationship certificate from the Apple Push Certificates Portal. The administrator then needs to click Upload The APNs Certificate.

5. B. App protection policies (APPs) are rules that make sure that corporate data remains safe. A policy can be a rule that enforces or prohibits actions within an app. There are different APPs depending on the type of device. For APP settings for iOS/iPadOS devices, the policy settings can be configured on the Settings pane in the Azure portal. There are three of policy settings: Data Relocation, Access Requirements, and Conditional Launch. Configure Conditional Launch settings to set sign-in security requirements. By default, there are several settings that are provided with preconfigured values and actions. Some of the Conditional Launch settings include the following:

Min OS version: This specifies a minimum iOS/iPadOS operating system to use the app.

Max PIN attempts: This specifies the number of attempts a user has to enter the PIN successfully before the configured action is taken.

Offline grace period: This specifies the number of minutes that Mobile Application Management (MAM) apps can run offline.

Jailbroken/rooted devices: There is no value to set for this setting. Actions can include blocking access or wiping data.

Min app version: This specifies a value for the minimum operating system value.

Min SDK version: This specifies a minimum value for the Intune SDK version.

Device model(s): This specifies a semicolon-separated list of model identifier(s).

Max allowed device threat level: This specifies a maximum threat level acceptable to use the app.

6. A. App protection policies (APPs) are rules that make sure that corporate data remains safe. A policy can be a rule that enforces or prohibits actions within an app. There are different APPs depending on the type of device. For APP settings for iOS/iPadOS devices, the policy settings can be configured on the Settings pane in the Azure portal. There are three categories of policy settings: Data Relocation, Access Requirements, and Conditional Launch. There are several Access Requirements settings, including the following:

PIN for access: Select Require to require a PIN to use this app.

PIN type: Set a requirement for either numeric or passcode type PINs before accessing an app that has app protection policies applied.

Simple PIN: Select Allow to allow users to use simple PIN sequences such as 1234, 1111, abcd, or aaaa. Select Block to prevent users from using simple sequences.

Select minimum PIN length: Specify the minimum number of digits in a PIN sequence.

Touch ID instead of PIN for access (iOS 8+): Select Allow to allow a user to use Touch ID instead of a PIN for app access.

Override Touch ID with PIN after timeout: To use this setting, select Require and then configure an inactivity timeout.

7. B. To configure the update restart prompt setting, you must configure the Microsoft Intune Agent Settings policy. Setting the Prompt User To Restart Windows During Intune Client Agent Mandatory Updates to No will stop the users from receiving restart prompts after mandatory updates. To configure update policy settings, perform the following steps:

   1. In the Microsoft Intune administration console, choose Policy ➢ Overview ➢ Add Policy.

   2. Configure and deploy a Microsoft Intune Agent Settings policy for the update settings. In this case, you will want to set Prompt User To Restart Windows During Intune Client Agent Mandatory Updates to No.

8. D. PowerShell is designed for managing and administering resources from the command line. PowerShell cmdlets follow a standard naming convention: verb-noun. The verb describes the action such as New, Get, Set, or Remove, and the noun describes the resource type. The New-AzureADApplication command allows an administrator to create a new application in Azure.

9. D. On Windows 10 devices, use Intune to run devices as a kiosk. These are also sometimes called *dedicated devices*. A device in kiosk mode can run one app or run many apps. You can display a customized Start menu, add different apps, including Win32 apps, add a specific home page to a web browser, and more. Kiosk settings allow an administrator to configure a Windows 10 (and later) device to run a single application or run many applications. Kiosk systems are normally designed to be in a location where many people can use the same device, and that device will only run limited applications. For the steps on how to create a profile using kiosk, check out the following Microsoft website:

docs.microsoft.com/en-us/mem/intune/configuration/kiosk-settings#create-the-profile

10. B. Before an administrator can configure, assign, protect, or monitor apps, they must add them to Microsoft Intune. To deploy the application to computers, make sure that the application content is copied to a distribution point. Devices access the distribution point to install the application. To add the application content to a distribution point, perform the following steps:

1. In the Configuration Manager console, choose Software Library.

2. In the Software Library workspace, expand Applications. Then, in the list of applications, select the application.

3. On the Home tab, in the Deployment group, choose Distribute Content.

4. On the General page of the Distribute Content Wizard, check that the application name is correct and then choose Next.

5. On the Content page, review the information to be copied to the distribution point and then choose Next.

6. On the Content Destination page, choose Add to select one or more distribution points, or distribution point groups, on which to install the application content.

7. Complete the wizard.

An administrator can check that the application content was copied successfully to the distribution point from the Monitoring workspace under Distribution Status ➤ Content Status.

11. C. A line-of-business (LOB) app is one that an administrator adds from an app installation file. This kind of app is typically written in-house. To select the app type, perform the following steps:

1. Sign in to the Microsoft Endpoint Manager admin center.

2. Select Apps ➤ All Apps ➤ Add.

3. In the Select App Type pane, under Other App Types, select Line-Of-Business App.

4. Click Select. The Add App steps are displayed.
   For steps on how to deploy an application, check out the following Microsoft website:

   docs.microsoft.com/en-us/mem/configmgr/apps/get-started/create-and-deploy-an-application#deploy-the-application

12. D. Tethering allows users to use their Windows 10 mobile device through their mobile phones. If you have a Windows 10 mobile device and want it to access the Internet, you can go through your cell coverage to get online. Tethering can also connect one mobile device to another mobile device for gaining access to the Internet. Since mobile phones have Internet access, they need to have the cellular hotspots enabled. This way, the tablet can connect to the mobile phone to access the Internet.

13. B. Before an administrator can configure, assign, protect, or monitor apps, the app must first be added to Microsoft Intune. You need to determine which apps are needed and then consider the groups of users and the apps they need. After you add an app, you need to assign a group of users that can use the app. First, determine which group should have access to the app. You may need to include or exclude certain types of roles. For steps on how to assign an app, check out the following Microsoft website:

docs.microsoft.com/en-us/mem/intune/apps/apps-deploy#assign-an-app

14. C. The Intune Company Portal app is used to enroll Android, iOS, macOS, and Windows devices. Enroll personal or corporate-owned iOS and Android devices to acquire secure access to corporate email, apps, and data. The Company Portal supports Android devices, including Samsung Knox, running Android 4.4 and later. For the steps on how to enroll a device using the Intune Company Portal app, check out the following Microsoft website:

docs.microsoft.com/en-us/mem/intune/user-help/enroll-device-android-company-portal#enroll-device

After the devices are enrolled, they become managed devices.

15. C. The Intune Company Portal app is used to enroll Android, iOS, macOS, and Windows devices. Go to the App Store to download and install the Intune Company Portal app onto the devices. You will need to make sure to maintain a Wi-Fi connection and have access to Safari during enrollment. For the steps on how to enroll the iOS device, check out the following Microsoft website:

docs.microsoft.com/en-us/mem/intune/user-help/enroll-your-device-in-intune-ios#enroll-your-ios-device

16. C. PowerShell is designed for managing and administering resources from the command line. PowerShell cmdlets follow a standard naming convention: verb-noun. The verb describes the action such as New, Get, Set, or Remove, and the noun describes the resource type. The Set-AzureADApplication PowerShell command allows an administrator to update an application.

17. C. When you sideload an application, this means that you are loading an application that is already owned, or one that the company has created into a delivery system such as Intune, Microsoft Store, or images. Sideloading in Windows 10 is different than in earlier versions of Windows. Sideloading in Windows 10 enables the following:

- Devices do not have to be joined to a domain.
- License keys are not required.
- You can unlock a device for sideloading by using an enterprise policy or by using the Settings app.

To turn on sideloading for managed devices, deploy an enterprise policy. To turn on sideloading for unmanaged devices, perform the following steps:

1. Open Settings.

2. Click Update & Security ➤ For Developers.

3. On Use Developer Features, select Sideload Apps.

18. A. Microsoft uses Intune to safeguard proprietary data that users access from their corporate-owned and personal mobile devices. Intune contains device and app configuration policies, software update policies, and installation statuses to help an administrator secure and monitor data access. App protection policies (APPs) are rules that ensure that corporate data remains safe in a managed app. A policy can be a rule that enforces or prohibits actions within an app. A managed app is an app that has an APP applied to it and can be maintained using Intune.

19. D. Windows Information Protection (WIP) was formerly known as Enterprise Data Protection (EDP). WIP helps protect against potential data leakage and helps protect enterprise apps and data against an accidental data leak on corporate-owned devices and personal devices. An administrator can set a WIP policy to use one of four protection and management modes. The protection and management modes are Block, Allow Overrides, Silent, and Off. Silent WIP runs silently, logging inappropriate data sharing without stopping anything that would have been prompted for user interaction while in Allow Overrides mode. Unallowed actions, such as apps improperly trying to access a network resource or WIP-protected data, are still stopped.

20. B. Microsoft Intune uses Azure Active Directory (Azure AD) groups to manage devices and users. As an Intune admin, you can set up groups to meet your corporate needs. Create groups to organize users or devices by geographic location, department, or hardware characteristics. When creating a new group in Intune, you can enter a membership type. The membership types include the following:

Assigned: Administrators manually assign users or devices to this group and manually remove users or devices.

Dynamic User: Administrators create membership rules to add and remove members automatically.

Dynamic Device: Administrators create dynamic group rules to add and remove devices automatically.

In this question, you are discussing the Dynamic Device membership type.

21. B. To determine the Enterprise Context of an app running in Windows Information Protection (WIP), use Task Manager. Task Manager will determine whether an app is considered work, personal, or exempt. You can see the WIP settings in the apps in real time. To view the Enterprise Context column, open Task Manager, go to the Details tab, and add the column for Enterprise Context. To add the Enterprise Context column to Task Manager, perform the following steps:

1. Open the Task Manager (taskmgr.exe), click the Details tab, right-click in the column heading area, and click Select Columns. The Select Columns box appears.

2. Scroll down and check the Enterprise Context option and then click OK to close the box. The Enterprise Context column should now be available in Task Manager.

The Enterprise Context column shows an administrator what each app can do with your enterprise data:

- Domain will show the employee's work domain. This app is considered work-related, and it can open work data and resources.

- Personal will show the text *Personal*. This app is considered non–work-related, and it can't open any work data or resources.

- Exempt will show the text *Exempt*. WIP policies don't apply to these apps.

22. C. The Sync device action forces the selected device to check in immediately with Intune. When a device checks in, it immediately receives any pending actions or policies that have been appointed. To force a sync between Intune and Microsoft Store for Business, perform the following steps:

1. Sign in to Azure Portal as Intune Admin.

2. Select All Services ➢ Intune. Intune is in the Monitoring + Management section.

3. In the Intune pane, select Client Apps and then select Microsoft Store for Business.

4. Select Enable to sync the Microsoft Store for Business apps with Intune.

23. D. PowerShell is designed for managing and administering resources from the command line. PowerShell cmdlets follow a standard naming convention: verb-noun. The verb describes the action such as New, Get, Set, or Remove, and the noun describes the resource type. The Remove-AzureADApplicationPasswordCredential PowerShell command allows an administrator to remove the password credentials from an application.

24. A. An administrator can monitor the status of the app protection policies (APPs) that have been applied to users from the Intune App Protection pane in the Azure portal. An administrator can also find information regarding the users who may be affected by app protection policies, policy compliance status, and any issues that a user may be encountering. There are three different places to monitor app protection policies:

- Summary view

- Detailed view

- Reporting view

To take a look at the Summary view, perform the following steps:

1. Sign in to the Microsoft Endpoint Manager admin center.

2. Select Apps ➢ Monitor ➢ App Protection Status.

25. A. Administrators have the ability to limit and monitor network usage by configuring the network as a metered network. Network metering allows network downloading to be watched or metered, and then administrators can charge users or departments for the network usage. When setting up your company's Internet connection, the ISP has the ability to charge by the amount of data used. That's called a *metered Internet connection*. If you have a metered Internet connection, setting the network connection to metered in Windows can help reduce the amount of data sent and received. To set this up in Windows, perform the following steps:

1. Click Start ➤ Settings, and then select Network & Internet.

2. Tap or click the Wi-Fi link and then, under Metered Connection, turn Set As A Metered Connection on or off.

26. A, B. If using Configuration Manger, an administrator can configure it to manage mobile devices. To do this, it requires the administrator to create a Windows Intune subscription and use a connector to synchronize user accounts. Configuration Manager allows an administrator to perform some of the following tasks:

- Deploy corporate operating systems, applications, and updates.
- Monitor and fix computers for compliance requirements.
- Monitor hardware and software inventory.
- Remotely administer devices.

The Intune Connector for Active Directory creates autopilot-enrolled computers in the on-premises Active Directory domain. The computer that hosts the Intune Connector must have the rights to create computer objects within the domain.

27. A. After you have added an application into Intune, you can assign the app to users and devices. You can assign an app to a device whether or not the device is managed by Intune. When assigning the app to a group, you can select an assignment type. These assignment types include the following:

Available For Enrolled Devices: This option allows you to assign the app to groups of users who can install the app from the Company Portal app or website.

Available With Or Without Enrollment: This option allows you to assign the app to groups of users whose devices are not enrolled with Intune; however, the users must still be assigned an Intune license.

Required: This option allows for the app to be installed on devices in the selected groups.

Uninstall: This option will uninstall the app from devices in the selected groups if Intune has previously installed the application onto the device by using the Available For Enrolled Devices or Required assignment types.

For the steps on how to assign an application to Intune, check out the following Microsoft website:

docs.microsoft.com/en-us/mem/intune/apps/apps-deploy#assign-an-app

28. A. Microsoft Intune supports a variety of app types and deployment scenarios for Windows 10 devices. After an app has been added to Intune, you can assign the app to users and devices. For Windows 10 devices, Intune provides line-of-business (LOB) apps and Microsoft Store for Business apps. These are the app types that are supported for Windows 10 devices. The file extensions for Windows apps include `.msi`, `.appx`, and `.appxbundle`. The application type that is being discussed in this question is Windows 10 LOB apps. You can assign and upload Windows 10 LOB apps to the Intune admin console. These can include modern apps, such as Universal Windows Platform (UWP) apps and Windows App Packages (AppX), as well as Win 32 apps, such as Microsoft Installer package files (MSI). You must manually upload and deploy updates to LOB apps. These updates are automatically installed on user devices that have installed the application with no user intervention required. Users have no control over updates.

29. A. After you have added an app to Microsoft Intune, you can assign the application to groups of users or devices. Here are the steps on how to assign an application to a group:

1. Sign in to Intune as a Global administrator or an Intune Service administrator.

2. In Intune, select Apps ➤ All Apps.

3. Select the app that you want to assign to a group.

4. Select Assignments ➤ Add Group to display the Add Group pane.

5. In the Assignment Type drop-down box, select Available For Enrolled Devices.

6. Select Included Groups ➤ Select Groups To Include and then select the group you want.

7. Click Select, click OK twice, and then click Save to assign the group.

30. B. Intune mobile application management (MAM) refers to a suite of Intune management features that allows an administrator to publish, push, configure, secure, monitor, and update mobile apps. MAM allows you to manage and protect corporate data within an app. Intune MAM supports two configurations.

- Intune MDM + MAM

- MAM without device enrollment

In this question, the configuration being discussed is Intune MDM + MAM. This allows you to manage apps only using MAM and app protection policies on devices that are enrolled with Intune mobile device management (MDM). To manage apps using MDM + MAM, customers should use the Intune console in the Azure portal at portal.azure.com.

31. B. Office 365 ProPlus is being renamed to Microsoft 365 Apps for Enterprise. The new name will appear in Version 2004 and beyond, starting April 21, 2020. Starting with Version 2005, you go to Control Panel ➤ Programs ➤ Programs And Features, and you will see Microsoft 365 for Enterprise – en-us.

32. A. You and your colleague are discussing the App Protection Policies option, which is found in the Client Apps section. This option is used to configure policies that help protect against data leakage from deployed apps. Settings include Data Protection, Access Requirements, and Conditional Launch Properties. To view the app protection policies, perform the following steps:

1. Sign in to Intune.

2. Select Client Apps ➢ Manage ➢ App Protection Policies.

The options found in the Client Apps node include the following:

- Apps
- App Protection Policies
- App Configuration Policies
- App Selective Wipe
- iOS App Provisioning Profiles

33. A. Intune's mobile application management (MAM) refers to the suite of Intune management features that allows an administrator to publish, push, configure, secure, monitor, and update mobile apps for users. The advantage to using MAM is that you have the ability to manage and protect your corporate data from within the application that the user is using.

34. B. You and your colleague are discussing the Audit Logs option, which is found in the Client Apps section. This option allows you to view the app-related activity for all Intune administrators. To view the Audit Logs, perform the following steps:

1. Sign in to Intune.

2. Select Client Apps ➢ Monitor ➢ Audit Logs.

The options found in the Monitor include the following:

- App Licenses
- Discovered Apps
- App Install Status
- App Protection Status
- Audit Logs

35. B. Intune provides a list of detected apps on the Intune enrolled devices in your tenant. To view the list, perform the following steps:

1. Sign in to Intune.

2. Select Client Apps ➢ Monitor ➢ Discovered Apps.

The Discovered Apps option will be found under the Monitor heading. Discovered Apps will display information about apps that are assigned by Intune or installed on devices.

36. B. Microsoft Intune supports a variety of app types and deployment scenarios for Windows 10 devices. After an app has been added to Intune, you can assign the app to users and devices. For Windows 10 devices, Intune provides line-of-business (LOB) apps and Microsoft Store for Business apps. These are the app types that are supported for Windows 10 devices. The file extensions for Windows apps include `.msi`, `.appx`, and `.appxbundle`. The application type that is being discussed in this question is Microsoft Store for Business apps. These are modern apps that have been purchased from the Microsoft Store for Business admin portal. They are then synced to Microsoft Intune for management. The apps can be either online or offline licensed. The Microsoft Store manages any updates, with no additional administrator action required. You can also prevent updates to specific apps by using a custom Uniform Resource Identifier (URI). Users also have the ability to disable updates for all Microsoft Store for Business apps on devices.

37. D. Windows Information Protection (WIP) was formerly known as Enterprise Data Protection (EDP). WIP is a built-in Windows 10 feature that allows an administrator to maintain and monitor company data from any personal data that is on a user's device. WIP also helps to protect corporate apps and data against accidental data leak on corporate-owned devices and personal devices. An administrator can set a WIP policy to use one of four protection and management modes. The protection and management modes are Block, Allow Overrides, Silent, and Off.

38. C. Microsoft Intune allows you to create and deploy a Windows Information Protection (WIP) policy. You can select which apps to protect, the level of protection, and how to find corporate data on the network. Devices can be managed by mobile device management (MDM) or managed by mobile application management (MAM). Before you can create a WIP policy using Intune, you need to configure an MDM or MAM provider in Azure Active Directory (Azure AD). To configure the MDM or MAM provider, perform the following steps:

1. Sign in to the Azure portal.

2. Select Azure Active Directory ➤ Mobility (MDM and MAM) ➤ Microsoft Intune.

3. Click Restore Default URLs or enter the settings for MDM or MAM user scope and click Save.

39. C. Intune mobile application management (MAM) refers to a suite of Intune management features that allows an administrator to publish, push, configure, secure, monitor, and update mobile apps. MAM allows you to manage and protect corporate data within an app. Intune MAM supports two configurations:

▪ Intune MDM + MAM

▪ MAM without device enrollment

In this question, the configuration being discussed is MAM without device enrollment. MAM without device enrollment allows you to manage apps using MAM and app protection policies on devices not enrolled with Intune MDM. This means that apps can be managed by Intune on devices enrolled with third-party Enterprise Mobility Management (EMM) providers. To manage these apps, users should use the Intune console in the Azure portal at `portal.azure.com`.

40. C. Depending on the app type, you can install an app on a Windows 10 device in one of two ways: User Context and Device Context. In this question, User Context is being discussed. User Context is when the app is installed for a user on a device when the user signs into the device. Modern line-of-business (LOB) apps and Microsoft Store for Business apps (both online and offline) can be deployed in user context.

41. B. Windows Information Protection (WIP) is a built-in Windows 10 feature that allows an administrator to control and manage corporate data independently from personal data on your users' devices. To create a WIP policy, perform the following steps:

1. Sign in to the Azure portal.

2. Open Microsoft Intune, select Client Apps ➤ App Protection Policies, and click the + Create Policy button.

3. On the App Policy screen, click Add A Policy, and then fill out the fields, such as Name, Description, Platform, and Enrollment State.

4. Click Protected Apps, and then click Add apps.

You can add the following types of apps:

- Desktop apps
- Recommended apps
- Store apps

42. A. Intune mobile application management (MAM) refers to a suite of Intune management features that allows an administrator to publish, push, configure, secure, monitor, and update mobile apps. MAM allows you to manage and protect corporate data within an app. You can create an app protection policy in Intune either with device enrollment for MDM or without device enrollment for MAM.

- MAM supports only one user per device.
- MAM has added Access settings for Windows Hello for Business.
- MAM can selectively wipe corporate data from a user's personal device.
- MAM requires an Azure Active Directory (Azure AD) Premium license.

43. D. You can use Microsoft Intune to manage the client apps that your corporate users use. You can find most app-related information in the Apps workload. You can access the Apps workload by performing the following:

1. Sign in to the Microsoft Endpoint Manager admin center.

2. Select Apps.

The apps workload provides links to access common app information and functionality. To view the tenant name, the MDM authority, the tenant location, the account status, the app installation status, and the app protection policy status, you should go to the Overview section.

44. A. Windows Information Protection (WIP) is a built-in Windows 10 feature that allows an administrator to maintain and monitor company data from any personal data that is on a user's device. WIP also helps to protect corporate apps and data against accidental data leakage on corporate-owned devices and personal devices. An administrator can set a WIP policy to use one of four protection and management modes. The protection and management modes are Block, Allow Overrides, Silent, and Off. In this question, the Allow Overrides management mode is being discussed. Allow Overrides looks for inappropriate data sharing, warning users if they do something considered potentially unsafe. This management mode allows the user to override the policy and share the data, but this action will log the event to an audit log.

45. A. After you have created a Windows Information Protection (WIP) policy, you will need to deploy it to your corporate-enrolled devices. Enrollment can be completed for corporate or personal devices, which will allow the devices to use your managed apps and to sync with your managed content and information. To deploy a WIP policy, perform the following steps:

1. Sign in to Intune.

2. On the App Protection Policies pane, click the newly created policy, click Assignments, and then select the groups to include or exclude from the policy.

3. Choose the group that you want your policy to apply to, and then click Select to deploy the policy.

The policy is now deployed to the selected users' devices.

46. B. A line-of-business (LOB) app is one that an administrator adds from an app installation file. This kind of app is typically written in-house. To select the app type, perform the following steps:

1. Sign in to the Microsoft Endpoint Manager admin center.

2. Select Apps ➢ All Apps ➢ Add.

3. In the Select App Type pane, under Other App Types, select the Line-Of-Business app.

4. Click Select. The Add App steps are displayed.

For steps on how to deploy an application, check out the following Microsoft website.

docs.microsoft.com/en-us/mem/configmgr/apps/get-started/create-and-deploy-an-application#deploy-the-application

47. B. Before signing up for Microsoft Store for Business, you need to make sure that you are the Global Administrator for your company. Users who are assigned to the Global Administrator role can read and modify every administrative setting in an Azure AD organization. By default, the person who signs up for an Azure subscription is assigned the Global Administrator role for the Azure AD organization. Only Global Administrators and Privileged Role administrators can delegate administrator roles. Then you will need to sign up to use Microsoft Store for Business to be able to deploy and manage apps. To sign up for Microsoft Store for Business, perform the following steps:

1. Open a web browser, navigate to www.microsoft.com/business-store, and click Sign Up.

Note: If you start the Microsoft Store sign-up process and you don't have an Azure Active Directory (Azure AD) directory for your company, Microsoft will help create one. If you do already have an Azure AD directory, then you will sign in to Store for Business and accept the Store for Business terms.

48. B. Windows Information Protection (WIP) classifies apps into two categories: Enlightened and Unenlightened. In this question, you are discussing Enlightened apps. Enlightened apps can differentiate between corporate and personal data and correctly determine which apps to protect depending upon the policies. For a list of Enlightened Microsoft apps, check out the following Microsoft website:

docs.microsoft.com/en-us/windows/security/information-protection/ windows-information-protection/enlightened-microsoft-apps-and- wip#list-of-enlightened-microsoft-apps

49. A. The first person to sign into Microsoft Store for Business must be a Global Administrator of the Azure Active Directory (Azure AD) tenant. Once the Global Administrator has signed in, they can assign permissions to other users. Although you can administer everything in Microsoft Store for Business using the Azure AD Global Administrator account, you can assign administrative roles to corporate users. Some of the roles that can be assigned are as follows:

Billing Account Owner: Can perform all tasks

Billing Account Contributor: Can manage the store account and sign agreements

Billing Account Reader: Can only view the account information

Signatory: Can sign agreements for the company

Purchaser: Can obtain and distribute products for your company

Basic Purchaser: Can obtain and distribute products they own

To assign roles to personnel, perform the following steps:

1. Open a web browser, navigate to www.microsoft.com/business-store, and sign in as the Global Administrator, or as a Billing Account Owner, to access the Permissions section.

2. Select Manage and then select Permissions.

3. On Roles, or Purchasing Roles, select Assign Roles.

4. Enter a name, select the role that you want to assign, and click Save. If you don't find the name you are looking for, you may need to add it to the Azure AD directory.

50. C. The Private Store is a feature in Microsoft Store for Business that companies receive when they set up Microsoft Store for Business. When an administrator adds apps to the Private Store, the corporate users can view and download the apps. Only online-licensed apps can be distributed from the Private Store. The name of the Private Store is shown on a tab in Microsoft Store app or on Microsoft Store for Business. To change the name of your Private Store, perform the following steps:

1. Sign in to the Microsoft Store for Business.
2. Click Settings and then click Distribute.
3. In the Private Store section, click Change.
4. Type a new display name for the Private Store and click Save.

51. C. For a user to install and use an app, the app must be licensed. The Microsoft Store for Business supports two options to license apps: Online and Offline. This question is discussing Online licensing. Online licensing is the default licensing model. Online licensed apps require that users and devices connect to the Microsoft Store services to acquire an app and its license.

52. C. You and your colleague are discussing the App Selective Wipe option. This option allows you to remove corporate data from a device's apps. To access the App Selective Wipe, perform the following steps:

1. Sign in to Intune.
2. Select Client Apps ➤ Manage ➤ App Selective Wipe.

The options found in the Client Apps node include the following:

- Apps
- App Protection Policies
- App Configuration Policies
- App Selective Wipe
- iOS App Provisioning Profiles

53. B. The Private Store is a feature in Microsoft Store for Business that companies receive when they set up Microsoft Store for Business. When an administrator adds apps to the Private Store, the corporate users can view and download the apps. Only online-licensed apps can be distributed from the Private Store. The name of the Private Store is shown on a tab in Microsoft Store app or on Microsoft Store for Business. To change the name of your Private Store, perform the following steps:

1. Sign in to the Microsoft Store for Business.
2. Click Settings and then click Distribute.
3. In the Private Store section, click Change.
4. Type a new display name for the Private Store and click Save.

54. A. Some apps are free, and some apps have an associated cost. Apps can be bought from the Microsoft Store using a credit card. Credit card information can be entered on the Account Information page or when an app is purchased. Administrators can enable the Allow Users To Shop setting. This setting controls the shopping capability in Microsoft Store for Business. When this setting is enabled, Purchasers and Basic Purchasers can purchase products and services. To manage the Allow Users To Shop setting, perform the following steps:

1. Sign in to Microsoft Store for Business.

2. Select Manage and then select Settings.

3. On the Shop page, under Shopping Behavior, turn on or turn off Allow Users To Shop by using the toggle switch.

55. A. App protection policies (APPs) can be applied to apps running on devices that may or may not be managed by Intune. The APP data protection structure is organized into three different configuration levels, with each level building off the previous level. The levels are as follows:

- Enterprise basic data protection (Level 1)

- Enterprise enhanced data protection (Level 2)

- Enterprise high data protection (Level 3)

The level being discussed in this question is Enterprise basic data protection. Enterprise basic data protection (Level 1) makes sure that apps are protected using a PIN, are encrypted, and perform selective wipe operations.

56. B. Once an app is in your Private Store, people in your company can install the app on their devices. To add an app into your Private Store, perform the following steps:

1. Sign in to Microsoft Store for Business.

2. Click Manage and then choose Apps & Software.

3. Use Refine Results to search for online-licensed apps under License Type.

4. From the list of online-licensed apps, click the ellipsis for the app you want and then choose Add To Private Store.

The value under Private Store for the app will change to Pending. It may take about 36 hours before the app will become available in the Private Store.

57. D. Sideloading is the process of installing a line-of-business (LOB) app in Windows 10 without requiring the use of the Microsoft Store for Business to deploy the app to users' devices. By default, the sideloading option in Windows 10 is disabled. You can enable sideloading through using a Group Policy object (GPO) or through the Settings app. To sideload apps using the Settings app, perform the following:

1. Open Settings.

2. Click Update & Security ➤ For Developers.

3. On Use Developer Features, select Sideload Apps.

4. Click Yes in response to any security warning message.

After sideloading is enabled, any line-of-business (LOB) Microsoft Store app that is signed by a certification authority (CA) that the computer trusts can be installed.

58. A. Sideloading is the process of installing a line-of-business (LOB) app in Windows 10 without requiring the use of the Microsoft Store for Business to deploy the app to users' devices. By default, the sideloading option in Windows 10 is disabled. You can enable sideloading through using a Group Policy object (GPO) or through the Settings app. You can use gpedit.msc to set the group policies to enable devices. To enable sideloading using a Group Policy setting so that computers can accept and install sideloaded apps, perform the following:

1. Run gpedit.msc.

2. Go to Local Computer Policy\Computer Configuration\Administrative Templates\Windows Components\App Package Deployment.

3. To enable sideloading, edit the policies by double-clicking Allow All Trusted Apps To Install.

59. C. You and your colleague are discussing the Windows Enterprise Certificate option, which is found in the Client Apps ≻ Setup section. This option enables an administrator to view and apply code-signing certificates. This certificate is used to distribute line-of-business (LOB) apps to managed Windows devices. To view the Windows Enterprise Certificate, perform the following steps:

1. Sign in to Intune.

2. Select Client Apps ≻ Setup ≻ Windows Enterprise Certificate.

The options found in the Setup include the following:

- iOS VPP Tokens
- Windows Enterprise Certificate
- Windows Symantec Certificate
- Microsoft Store for Business
- Windows Side Loading Keys
- Branding And Customization
- App Categories
- Managed Google Play

60. A. If you want to sideload apps to more than one computer, you can use Deployment Image Servicing and Management (DISM) commands to manage app packages in a Windows image. When you use DISM to provision app packages, those packages are added to a Windows image and are installed for the chosen users when they log on to their computers.

DISM is a command-line tool that is used to create and manage Windows 10 image (.wim) files. The syntax to service an app package (.appx or .appxbundle) for an offline image is as follows:

```
dism.exe /Image:<path_to_image_directory> [/Get-ProvisionedAppxPackages
| /Add-ProvisionedAppxPackage | /Remove-ProvisionedAppxPackage | /Set-
ProvisionedAppxDataFile]
```

61. D. You can use the Windows Configuration Designer (WCD) tool to create provisioning packages to configure Windows 10 devices. WCD is designed to be used by users who need to provision bring your own device (BYOD) and business-supplied devices. You can install the WCD app on devices running Windows 10 from the Microsoft Store.

62. A. Mobile application management (MAM) is part of Intune, and it is a suite of administrator management tools that allow you to manage, configure, publish, update, and monitor applications for your mobile devices. An advantage to using MAM is that an administrator has the ability to manage and protect the company's data from within the application that the user is using. For a complete list of applications that Intune and MAM can support, check out the following Microsoft website:

docs.microsoft.com/en-us/intune/apps-supported-intune-apps

63. C. Kiosk settings allow you to configure a Windows 10 device to run a single application or run many applications. Kiosk systems are typically designed to be in a location where many people can use the same device, and that device will run only a limited amount of applications. You can also customize other features including a start menu and a web browser. There are two types of profiles that you can specify in the XML:

A lockdown profile: Users who have been assigned a lockdown profile will see the desktop in tablet mode with the specific apps on the Start screen.

A kiosk profile: Users assigned a kiosk profile will not see the desktop, but only the kiosk app running in full-screen mode.

<Config> that specify group accounts cannot use a kiosk profile, only a lockdown profile. If a group is configured to a kiosk profile, the CSP will reject the request. The group accounts are specified using <UserGroup>. Nested groups are not supported. So, in this question, the only user who will have the lockdown profile applied will be User3.

64. B. A kiosk (also known as Assigned Access) is a feature that allows you to configure a computer or a kiosk device to serve a specific purpose. If you set up a kiosk using Settings for Windows 10, you create the kiosk user account at the same time. To set up assigned access in Settings, perform the following:

1. Go to Start ➢ Settings ➢ Accounts ➢ Other Users.

2. Select Set Up A Kiosk ➢ Assigned Access and then select Get Started.

3. Enter a name for the new account.

4. Choose the app that will run when the kiosk account signs in. Only apps that can run above the lock screen will be available in the list of apps from which to choose.

5. Select Close.

65. D. Microsoft recommends using the Readiness Toolkit for Office add-ins and VBA as a basic solution for application compatibility and readiness assessment. This tool can help identify compatibility issues with Microsoft Visual Basic for Applications (VBA) macros and add-ins that are used with Microsoft 365 Apps for Enterprise. The Readiness Toolkit contains the Readiness Report Creator, which creates an Excel report with VBA macro compatibility and add-in readiness information to help a company assess its readiness to transition to Microsoft 365 Apps for Enterprise. Office 365 ProPlus was renamed to Microsoft 365 Apps for Enterprise. You can download the Readiness Toolkit for free from the Microsoft Download Center or by visiting this website:

www.microsoft.com/en-us/download/details.aspx?id=55983

66. D. Mobile application management (MAM) in Intune is designed to protect corporate data at the application level, including custom apps and store apps. App management can be used on corporate-owned devices and personal devices. When apps are managed in Intune, administrators can do the following:

- You can add and assign mobile apps to user groups and devices, including users and devices in specific groups.

- You can configure apps to start and run with specific settings enabled and update existing apps that are already on a device.

- You can perform a selective wipe by removing only corporate data from apps.

- You can view reports on which apps are used and track their usage.

67. B. To create a readiness report, you first need to select what information to use to create the report. Microsoft provides several report options. The report option being discussed in this question is Most Recently Used Office Documents And Installed Add-ins On This Computer. With this report, the Readiness Report Creator only scans Office documents that are in the user's list of most recently used files. This lets you focus on just scanning the documents that a user accesses regularly. The Readiness Report Creator will also look for any add-ins for Office that are installed on the computer on which the Readiness Report Creator is run.

68. A. You can use Microsoft Intune to manage the client apps that your corporate users use. You can find most app-related information in the Apps workload. You can access the Apps workload by performing the following:

1. Sign in to the Microsoft Endpoint Manager admin center.

2. Select Apps.

The apps workload provides links to access common app information and functionality. To display a list of all available apps, as well as the ability to add additional apps, you should go to the All Apps section. This section also lets you see the status of each app as well as whether each app is assigned.

69. D. Enable mobile application management (MAM) for Windows 10 by setting the MAM provider in Azure Active Directory (Azure AD). This allows you to define the enrollment state when creating a new Windows Information Protection (WIP) policy with Intune. The enrollment state can be either MAM or mobile device management (MDM). To configure the MAM provider, perform the following steps:

1. Sign in to the Microsoft Endpoint Manager admin center.

2. Select All Services and choose M365 Azure Active Directory to switch dashboards.

3. Select Azure Active Directory.

4. Choose Mobility (MDM and MAM) in the Manage group.

5. Click Microsoft Intune.

6. Configure the settings in the Restore Default MAM URLs group on the Configure pane. Options include the following:

   ▪ MAM Compliance URL

   ▪ MAM Discovery URL

   ▪ MAM Terms Of Use URL

   ▪ MAM User Scope

7. Click Save.

This question is discussing MAM User Scope. This setting uses MAM auto-enrollment to manage enterprise data on your users' Windows devices. MAM auto-enrollment will be configured for bring-your-own-device (BYOD) scenarios. Settings include None, Some, and All. By setting the All setting, this will allow all users to be enrolled in MAM.

70. B. The Readiness Report Creator creates a readiness report as an Excel .xls file. The information presented in the report depends on what information served as the basis for your report, as well as whether you chose to create a basic or advanced report. Microsoft recommends using the Advanced reports, since they provide more complete information on which to base your decisions. Each report will start with an Overview page, which provides high-level information regarding the results, and links to the reports. The report spreadsheet will be made up of a number of worksheets. Each worksheet contains information about different aspects of the existing devices' compatibility.

71. D. Windows Information Protection (WIP) is a built-in Windows 10 feature that allows an administrator to maintain and monitor company data from any personal data that is on a user's device. WIP also helps to protect corporate apps and data against accidental data leakage on corporate-owned devices and personal devices. An administrator can set a WIP policy to use one of four protection and management modes. The protection and management modes are Block, Allow Overrides, Silent, and Off. In this question, the Silent mode will be running silently, logging any inappropriate data sharing without blocking anything. Actions that are not allowed can include apps inappropriately trying to access network resources or WIP-protected data, which will be stopped.

72. A. Windows 10 comes with two Internet browsers. They are Internet Explorer and Microsoft Edge. However, not all websites can function properly when opened with Edge. To help with this issue, you can use Internet Explorer Enterprise Mode. This allows you to define which browser to use when opening specific websites. Internet Explorer Enterprise Mode is a compatibility mode that runs on Internet Explorer 11, allowing websites to use a modified browser configuration that has been designed to imitate an earlier version of Internet Explorer. To use Internet Explorer Enterprise Mode, you need to download and install the Enterprise Mode Site List Manager tool. This can be obtained from the following Microsoft website:

www.microsoft.com/en-us/download/details.aspx?id=49974

73. B. You and your colleague are discussing the Branding And Customization option, which is found in the Client Apps ➤ Setup section. This option allows you to customize the Intune Company Portal app. Since this is usually the first thing a user with an enrolled device will see, you want to make sure to configure your corporate branding. To view the Branding And Customization, perform the following steps:

1. Sign in to Intune.

2. Select Client Apps ➤ Setup ➤ Branding And Customization.

The following options are found in the Setup:

- iOS VPP Tokens
- Windows Enterprise Certificate
- Windows Symantec Certificate
- Microsoft Store for Business
- Windows Side Loading Keys
- Branding And Customization
- App Categories
- Managed Google Play

74. D. In many companies, it is common to allow users to use both Intune Mobile Device Management (MDM) managed devices, such as corporate-owned devices, and unmanaged devices protected with only Intune app protection policies. Unmanaged devices are often known as bring your own device (BYOD). The Intune device types include the following:

Android Device Administrator: These are Intune-managed devices using the Android Device Administration API.

Android Enterprise: These are Intune-managed devices using Android Enterprise work profiles or Android Enterprise Full Device Management.

Intune Managed Devices: Managed devices are managed by Intune MDM.

Unmanaged: Unmanaged devices are devices where Intune MDM management has not been detected. This includes devices managed by third-party MDM vendors.

75. C. The Office Telemetry Dashboard is an Excel workbook that shows compatibility and inventory, usage, and health data regarding Office files, Office add-ins, and Office solutions that are used in your company. This tool is an on-premises tool. The data is mainly created to help your company with application compatibility testing. At a minimum, Office Telemetry Dashboard requires one database and one processor and shared folder pair. These can be hosted on the same computer. Microsoft recommends using the Office Telemetry Dashboard only if you need specific usage and health information. Office Telemetry Dashboard gathers an inventory of add-ins and Office files as they are being used. Since this inventory is gathered through usage, you need to collect inventory over a period of time, such as at least 30 days.

76. C. App protection policies (APPs) can be applied to apps running on devices that may or may not be managed by Intune. The APP data protection structure is organized into three different configuration levels, with each level building off the previous level. The levels are as follows:

- Enterprise basic data protection (Level 1)
- Enterprise enhanced data protection (Level 2)
- Enterprise high data protection (Level 3)

The level being discussed in this question is Enterprise high data protection (Level 3). This level introduces advanced data protection mechanisms, enhanced PIN configuration, and APP Mobile Threat Defense. This configuration is desired for users who are accessing high-risk data.

77. A. In many companies, it is common to allow users to use both Intune Mobile Device Management (MDM) managed devices, such as corporate-owned devices, and unmanaged devices protected with only Intune app protection policies. Unmanaged devices are often known as bring your own device (BYOD). The Intune device types include the following:

Android Device Administrator: These are Intune-managed devices using the Android Device Administration API.

Android Enterprise: These are Intune-managed devices using Android Enterprise work profiles or Android Enterprise Full Device Management.

Intune Managed Devices: Managed devices are managed by Intune MDM.

Unmanaged: Unmanaged devices are devices where Intune MDM management has not been detected. This includes devices managed by third-party MDM vendors.

78. A. Depending on the app type, you can install an app on a Windows 10 device in one of two ways: User Context and Device Context. In this question, Device Context is being discussed. Device Context is when the managed app is installed directly to the device by Intune. Only modern line-of-business (LOB) apps and offline licensed Microsoft Store for Business apps can be deployed in Device Context.

79. D. Windows Information Protection (WIP) classifies apps into two categories: Enlightened and Unenlightened. In this question, you are discussing Unenlightened apps. Unenlightened apps consider all data as corporate and encrypts everything. Usually, you can tell an unenlightened app because:

- Windows Desktop shows it as always running in enterprise mode.
- Windows Save As experiences only allow you to save your files as enterprise.

80. A. When troubleshooting mobile application management (MAM), there are a number of issues that may arise. If the Office app policy is not being applied and the app protection policies are not applying to any supported Office apps for any user, then you will want to confirm that the user is licensed for Intune and that the Office apps are targeted by a deployed app protection policy. It may take up to eight hours for a newly deployed app protection policy to be applied.

81. C. You and your colleague are discussing the App Protection Status option that is found in the Client Apps section. This option displays information regarding the status of the app protection policy. The options found in the Monitor include the following:

- App Licenses
- Discovered Apps
- App Install Status
- App Protection Status
- Audit Logs

You can use this section to validate an app protection policy that has been set up in Microsoft Intune. To configure the user app protection status, perform the following steps:

1. Sign in to the Microsoft Endpoint Manager admin center.
2. Select Apps ➢ Monitor ➢ App Protection Status and then select the Assigned Users tile.
3. On the App Reporting page, choose Select User to show a list of users and groups.
4. Search for and select a user from the list and then choose Select User. At the top of the App Reporting pane, you will see whether the user is licensed for app protection.

82. D. The Private Store is a feature in Microsoft Store for Business that companies receive during the sign-up process. When an administrator adds apps to the Private Store, then all corporate users can view and download the apps. The Private Store is available as a tab in the Microsoft Store app and is typically named for the company. Only apps with online licenses can be added to the Private Store. To obtain an app from the Private Store, perform the following steps:

1. Sign into a computer with their Azure Active Directory (AD) credentials and starts the Microsoft Store app.
2. Click the Private Store tab.
3. Click the app to be installed and then click Install.

83. D. To create a readiness report, you first need to select what information to use to create the report. Microsoft provides several report options. The report option being discussed in this question is Previous Readiness Results Saved Together In A Local Folder Or Network Share. This option allows you to create a consolidated report composed of individual readiness results from multiple stand-alone computers. For example, you may want to run the Readiness Report Creator on all the computers in the Marketing department and save the results of each scan to a network share. Then you can use this option to create a consolidated report for the department.

84. B. The device state condition can be used to exclude devices that are hybrid Azure AD–joined and/or devices that are marked as compliant with a Microsoft Intune compliance policy. A Hybrid Azure AD join takes precedence over the Azure AD registered state. This condition allows you to include or exclude device states.

85. C. Azure Information Protection provides protection of information by helping classify, label, and protect documents and emails. Azure Information Protection is an Azure service, and it is a cloud-based solution that requires no on-premises infrastructure. This uses the Azure Rights Management (Azure RMS) technology to allow administrators to set rules and conditions. Azure Information templates are also called Rights Management templates. Note that the Azure Information Protection client (classic) and Label Management in the Azure Portal are being deprecated as of March 31, 2021. This timeframe will allow all current Azure Information Protection customers to transition to a unified labeling solution by using the Microsoft Information Protection Unified Labeling platform.

86. B. For a user to install and use an app, the app must be licensed. The Microsoft Store for Business supports two options to license apps: Online and Offline. This question is discussing Offline Licensing. Offline Licensing allows corporations to cache apps and their licenses to deploy within their network.

87. B. Intune provides several ways to monitor the properties of apps that you manage and to manage app assignment status. To monitor app information and assignments using Microsoft Intune, perform the following steps:

1. Sign in to the Microsoft Endpoint Manager admin center.

2. Select Apps ➢ All Apps.

3. In the list of apps, select an app to monitor. You will see the app pane, which includes an overview of the device status and the user status.

The All Apps overview pane shows the following sections:

- Device And User Status Graphs
- Device Install Status
- Essentials
- User Install Status

This question is discussing Device Install Status. The device status list is displayed when you select Device Install Status in the Monitor section, and it has the following columns:

- Device name
- User name
- Platform
- Version
- Status
- Status details
- Last check-in

88. C. The first person to sign into Microsoft Store for Business must be a Global Administrator of the Azure Active Directory (Azure AD) tenant. Once the Global Administrator has signed in, they can assign permissions to other users. Although you can administer everything in Microsoft Store for Business using the Azure AD Global Administrator account, you can assign administrative roles to corporate users. Some of the roles that can be assigned are as follows:

Billing Account Owner: Can perform all tasks

Billing Account Contributor: Can manage the store account and sign agreements

Billing Account Reader: Can only view the account information

Signatory: Can sign agreements for the company

Purchaser: Can obtain and distribute products for your company

Basic Purchaser: Can obtain and distribute products they own

To assign roles to personnel, perform the following steps:

1. Open a web browser, navigate to www.microsoft.com/business-store, and sign in as the Global Administrator or as a Billing Account Owner
2. Select Manage and then select Permissions.
3. On Roles, or Purchasing Roles, select Assign Roles.
4. Enter a name, select the role you want to assign, and click Save. If you don't find the name you are looking for, you may need to add it to the Azure AD directory.

89. C. In many companies, it is common to allow users to use both Intune Mobile Device Management (MDM) managed devices, such as corporate-owned devices, and unmanaged devices protected only with Intune app protection policies. Unmanaged devices are often known as bring your own device (BYOD). The Intune device types include the following:

Android Device Administrator: These are Intune-managed devices using the Android Device Administration API.

Android Enterprise: These are Intune-managed devices using Android Enterprise work profiles or Android Enterprise Full Device Management.

Intune Managed Devices: Managed devices are managed by Intune MDM.

Unmanaged: Unmanaged devices are devices where Intune MDM management has not been detected. This includes devices managed by third-party MDM vendors.

90. C. When troubleshooting mobile application management (MAM), there are a number of issues that may arise. If user accounts are missing from app protection policy reports and the Admin console reports do not show the user accounts for an app protection policy was recently deployed, then you need to check to see whether the user is newly targeted by an app protection policy. It can take up to 24 hours for that user to show up in reports as a targeted user.

91. D. Intune provides several ways to monitor the properties of apps that you manage and to manage app assignment status. To monitor app information and assignments using Microsoft Intune, perform the following steps:

1. Sign in to the Microsoft Endpoint Manager admin center.

2. Select Apps ➤ All Apps.

3. In the list of apps, select an app to monitor. You will see the app pane, which includes an overview of the device status and the user status.

The All Apps overview pane shows the following sections:

- Device And User Status Graphs
- Device Install Status
- Essentials
- User Install Status

This question is discussing User Install Status. The user status list is displayed when you select User Install Status in the Monitor section, and it has the following columns:

- Name
- User Name
- Installations
- Failures
- Not Installed

92. B. App protection policies (APPs) can be applied to apps running on devices that may or may not be managed by Intune. The APP data protection structure is organized into three different configuration levels, with each level building off the previous level. The levels are as follows:

- Enterprise basic data protection (Level 1)
- Enterprise enhanced data protection (Level 2)
- Enterprise high data protection (Level 3)

The level being discussed in this question is Enterprise enhanced data protection (Level 2). This level introduces APP data leakage prevention mechanisms and minimum OS requirements. This is the configuration that is applicable to most mobile users accessing work or school data.

93. D. To protect sensitive corporate data, Power Automate provides the ability to create and enforce policies that define which consumer connectors can access and share business data. These policies define how data can be shared and are referred to as *data loss prevention (DLP) policies*. Power Automate is a public cloud service to help individuals and teams to set up automated workflows between their favorite apps and services to synchronize, get notifications, collect data, and more. There are two possible ways for users to sign up for Power Automate through the web portal:

Option 1: Users can sign up by going to flow.microsoft.com, selecting Sign Up Free, and then completing the sign-up process for Power Automate through admin.microsoft .com or signup.live.com.

Option 2: Users can sign up by going to flow.microsoft.com, selecting Sign In, signing in with their email, and accepting the Power Automate terms of use.

94. A. A company's data is crucial for its success. Corporate data needs to be available for decision-making, but it needs to be secure so that it is not shared with people who shouldn't have access to it. To create a DLP policy, you must have permissions to at least one environment through either environment admin or tenant admin permissions. For the steps on how to create a DLP policy that prevents data loss, check out the following Microsoft website:

docs.microsoft.com/en-us/power-automate/prevent-data-
loss#prerequisites-for-creating-dlp-policies

95. A. Security groups define who can access resources and are recommended. Microsoft Intune does not allow you to change a security group parent. When you delete a group, the users are not deleted. So, the only way to change a group's parent group is to create the security group under the parent. In this question, Group3 needs to be re-created under Group2, and then the users need to be re-added.

96. A. Microsoft Intune uses Azure Active Directory (Azure AD) groups to manage devices and users. As an Intune admin, you can set up groups to meet your corporate needs. Create groups to organize users or devices by geographic location, department, or hardware characteristics. When creating a new group in Intune, you can enter a membership type. The membership types include the following:

Assigned: Administrators manually assign users or devices to this group and manually remove users or devices.

Dynamic User: Administrators create membership rules to add and remove members automatically.

Dynamic Device: Administrators create dynamic group rules to add and remove devices automatically.

In this question, you are discussing the Assigned membership type.

97. C. Microsoft Intune uses Azure Active Directory (Azure AD) groups to manage devices and users. As an Intune admin, you can set up groups to meet your corporate needs. Create groups to organize users or devices by geographic location, department, or hardware characteristics. When creating a new group in Intune, you can enter a membership type. The membership types include the following:

Assigned: Administrators manually assign users or devices to this group and manually remove users or devices.

Dynamic User: Administrators create membership rules to add and remove members automatically.

Dynamic Device: Administrators create dynamic group rules to add and remove devices automatically.

In this question, you are discussing the Dynamic User membership type.

98. C. Windows Information Protection (WIP) helps protect against potential data leakage and helps protect enterprise apps and data against accidental data leakage on corporate-owned devices and personally owned devices. WIP helps tackle the everyday challenges in the enterprise. Benefits include the following:

- WIP helps stop enterprise data leaks, even on personally owned devices that can't be locked down.

- WIP reduces user frustration due to the restrictive data management policies on corporate-owned devices.

- WIP helps maintain the ownership and control of your corporate data.

- WIP helps control network and data access and data sharing for apps that are not enterprise aware.

99. A. There are several ways to add apps. A user can add an app package, which will make the app available to just that user. Or, the app can be installed in the Windows image, which will make the app available to every user of the Windows image at first logon or at the next logon if the user account is already created. This is called *provisioning an app package*. After sideloading is enabled, you can install an app package (.appx or .appxbundle) on a per-user basis by using the Add-AppxPackage PowerShell cmdlet. There is no limit to the number of LOB apps that you can add for each user.

100. A. Protection settings for Azure Information Protection are saved in protection templates. Everything that you can do in the Azure portal to create and manage protection settings, you can do from the command line by using PowerShell. The Add-AipServiceTemplate cmdlet creates a protection template for Azure Information Protection with the specified name, description, and policy and sets the status of the template to archived or published. To learn more about the different switches and how to work with this PowerShell cmdlet, go to the following Microsoft website:

docs.microsoft.com/en-us/powershell/module/aipservice/add-aipservicetemplate?view=azureipps

Chapter 9: Practice Exam 1: MD-100

1. B. When performing a clean install to the same partition as an existing version of Windows, then the contents of the existing Users (or Documents And Settings), Program Files, and Windows directories will be placed in a directory called C:\Windows.old. The old operating system will no longer be available.

2. D. Deployment Image Servicing and Management (dism.exe) is a command-line tool that can be used to create and manage Windows images, including those used for Windows PE, Windows Recovery Environment (Windows RE), and Windows Setup. DISM can be used to service a Windows image (.wim) or a virtual hard disk (.vhd or .vhdx). You can configure a reference installation as desired and then use DISM to create an image of the installation that can be deployed to the remaining computers.

3. A. If you are moving from Windows Vista, Windows XP, or earlier editions of Windows to Windows 10, then you must perform a clean installation. If any of the following conditions exist, then you must perform a clean installation:

   - There currently is no operating system installed on the machine.

   - You currently have an operating system installed that does not support an in-place upgrade to Windows 10. These earlier versions include DOS, Windows 9x, Windows NT, Windows ME, Windows 2000 Pro, Windows Vista, and Windows XP.

   - You want to install from scratch without keeping any of the existing preferences.

   - You want to be able to dual-boot between Windows 10 and a previous operating system.

4. A. The requirements for Windows 10 are as follows:

   Processor: 1 gigahertz (GHz) or faster processor

   RAM: 1 gigabyte (GB) for 32-bit or 2 GB for 64-bit

   Hard disk space: 16 GB for 32-bit OS or 20 GB for 64-bit OS

   Graphics card: DirectX 9 or later with WDDM 1.0 driver

   Display: 800 x 600

5. A. The Registry is a database used by the operating system to store configuration information. You can edit the Registry in Windows 10 by using regedit.exe or regedt32.exe. However, always use caution when editing the Registry because any misconfigurations can cause the computer to fail to boot. You can just use the Control Panel if you don't want to open the Registry directly but you still want to perform some Registry changes. The Control Panel is a set of GUI utilities allowing you to configure Registry settings without the need to use the Registry Editor.

6. A. Windows 10 regularly checks for new updates automatically. To check for updates, go to Settings ➤ Update And Security ➤ Windows Update and click the Check For Updates button. When you click this button, Windows Update will retrieve a list of all the available updates. You can then click View Available Updates to see what updates are available. Updates are marked as Important, Recommended, or Optional.

7. C. Once the reference computer is set up and installed, you can use the System Preparation Tool (Sysprep) to prepare the computer to be used with disk imaging. Image Capture Wizard is a utility that can be used to create a disk image after it is prepared using the Sysprep utility. The image can then be transported to the destination computer(s).

8. C. Windows Update allows you to check for new updates and to change settings. To configure Windows Update, do the following:

1. Select Start ➤ Settings ➤ Update And Security.

2. Configure the options that you want to use for Windows Update by clicking the Advanced Options link. You can access the following options from Windows Update:

   ▪ Give me updates for other Microsoft products

   ▪ Choose when updates are installed

   ▪ Pause updates

   ▪ Delivery Optimization

   ▪ Privacy settings

9. C. Windows Deployment Services (WDS) is a suite of components that allows you to install Windows 10 remotely on client computers. You can configure WDS on a computer by using the Windows Deployment Services Configuration Wizard or by using the wdsutil.exe command-line utility. The /initialize-server switch initializes the configuration of the WDS server.

10. D. An administrator can add an input language, set a display language, or install a language pack in Settings ➤ Time & Language. This allows you to change the language being used on Windows 10, applications, and websites. Adding an input language lets you set a language-preference order for websites and apps, as well as change the keyboard language. To change the system language on Windows 10, close any running app and then follow these steps:

1. Open Settings ➤ Time & Language ➤ Language.

2. Under the Preferred Languages section, click the Add A Preferred Language button.

3. Search for the language you want.

4. Select the language package from the result and click Next.

5. Check the Set As My Display Language option.

    6. Check the Install Language Pack option.

    7. Check or clear the additional language features as needed.

    8. Click the Install button, click Yes, and then click the Sign Out Now button.

    9. Sign back into the Windows 10 account.

11. C. You can sign onto a computer by using a picture password. You can select a picture and three gestures that will be used to create a customized password. Once you have chosen a picture, you can draw with the mouse, with the touchpad, or on a touchscreen to create a combination of circles, straight lines, and taps. The size, position, and direction of the drawn gestures become part of the picture password. To access a picture password, go to Sign-in Options. Go to Start ➤ Settings ➤ Accounts ➤ Sign-in Options. On the Sign-in Options page, the following sign-in methods are available:

- Windows Hello Face
- Windows Hello Fingerprint
- Windows Hello PIN
- Security Key
- Password
- Picture Password

Click Picture Password, click Add, and then follow the prompts.

12. B. Microsoft Edge gives users a new way to find pages and read and write on the web, plus get help from Cortana. Microsoft Edge is the default browser for all Windows 10 devices, and it is built to be compatible with the modern web. Edge brings Microsoft's digital assistant, Cortana, to the desktop. Using Cortana with Edge allows you to pull up pictures, explanations, and search results easily on any word or link while browsing, just by right-clicking and selecting Ask Cortana.

13. A. The Background setting allows a user to pick their Desktop background. The background wallpaper can be either a picture or an HTML document. Setting up a desktop background can be as simple as picking a solid color and placing a favorite picture on top of it. To configure the Windows Desktop and how it looks, right-click the Desktop and select Personalize. When you choose to personalize the Desktop, there are several different settings that can be configured. These include Background, Colors, Lock Screen, Themes, Fonts, Start, and Taskbar.

14. B. The default shared permission for Administrators is Full Control. The shared permissions from lowest to highest are Read, Change, Full Control, and Deny. Share permissions can be applied only to folders.

15. A. Permissions are additive among themselves. This means you get the highest level of permissions among the group membership. In this question, the user is a member of three different groups, which consist of Read, Modify, and Deny. Since the permissions are additive and the user will get the highest level of permission, the user's effective permission will be Deny. Because the user has been denied access through the HR membership, the deny permissions override the allowed permissions.

16. B. Using the `diskpart.exe` command helps to manage a computer's drives (disks, partitions, volumes, or virtual hard disks). Using the `/create` switch creates a partition on a disk, a volume on one or more disks, or a virtual hard disk (VHD). The syntax is as follows:

`/create partition`

`/create volume`

`/create vdisk`

To create a partition, make sure that you are using unallocated disk space. So, to create a partition, enter **diskpart /create partition primary size=<partitionsize>**. You will see a message that states that `diskpart.exe` succeeded in creating the specified partition.

17. C. Windows 10 gives you the ability to set up a logon with a picture. If you want to use a picture for authentication, first you choose a picture, and then you add three gestures onto the picture. These gestures can be straight lines, circles, squares, or anything you want. Then, when you log on to the system, you just re-create the gestures on the picture and the system will log you in.

18. B. BitLocker requires that you have a hard disk with at least two NTFS partitions. One partition will be utilized as the system partition that will be encrypted, and the other partition will be the active partition that is used to start the computer. This partition will remain unencrypted.

19. D. To restrict the amount of disk space used by users on the network, administrators can establish disk quotas. By default, Windows 10 supports disk quota restrictions at the volume level. This allows you to restrict the amount of storage space that a specific user can use on a single disk volume. You can set up disk quotas based on volume or on users.

20. B, D. Permissions are cumulative among themselves. This means that you will obtain the highest level of permissions. But when the two permissions meet, the most restrictive set of permissions will apply. Shared folder permissions apply only across the network (remotely), and they can be placed only on folders. NTFS permissions can apply locally and remotely and can be placed on files or folders.

21. A. If you want to convert an existing partition from FAT or FAT32 to NTFS, you must to use the `convert` command-line utility and insert the drive letter to be converted. The syntax is as follows: `convert [drive:]/fs:ntfs`.

22. B. The Encrypting File System (EFS) is a component of the NTFS file system. It enables transparent encryption and decryption of files by using cryptographic algorithms. Any individual or program that doesn't have the appropriate cryptographic key cannot read the encrypted data. EFS allows a user or administrator to secure files or folders by using encryption. The encryption uses the user's security identifier (SID) number to secure the file or folder. To implement encryption, open the Advanced Attributes dialog box for a folder and select the Encrypt Contents To Secure Data checkbox.

23. D. The Profile tab of the user's properties dialog box allows you to customize the user's environment. You can specify the Home Folder, Logon script, and User profile path. Users typically store their personal files and information in a private folder called a *Home Folder*. One reason that you would assign your users Home Folders on a server is because the servers are normally the only machines that get backed up. If the Home Folder that you are specifying does not exist, Windows 10 will create the folder for you. You can also use the variable %username% in place of a specific user's name. This variable will automatically change to the name of the user on which you are currently working.

24. D. Windows Hello is a biometrics system integrated into Windows. Windows Hello is a Microsoft account that can be used to authenticate to a domain, a cloud-based domain, or a computer. To do this, you need to link your Microsoft account to your Windows 10 system. When you set up Windows Hello on a device, you can set up the system to use Windows Hello or a personal identification number (PIN). To configure Windows Hello options, click Start ➤ Settings ➤ Accounts. Windows Hello for Business is a newer credential in Windows 10 that helps increase security when accessing corporate resources. Windows Hello for Business replaces passwords with strong two-factor authentication on computers and mobile devices. This authentication consists of a new type of user credential that is tied to a device and uses a biometric or PIN.

25. A. The Modify permission allows the following:

- Changing the attributes of a file or folder
- Creating new files and writing data to the files
- Creating new folders and changing data to the files
- Deleting files
- Listing the contents of a folder and reading the data in a folder's files
- Navigating folders and executing files in the folders
- Seeing the attributes of a file or folder

If the Modify permission is selected, the Read & Execute, List Folder Contents, Read, and Write permissions will be checked by default and cannot be unchecked. So, by assigning the Allow Modify permission, this will meet the requirements set out in the new corporate policy.

26. C. Microsoft Defender Firewall helps secure Windows devices by filtering what network traffic is permitted to enter or exit the device. To configure the Windows Firewall to allow Domain Name System (DNS) inbound and outbound traffic, you would configure UDP port 53. TCP port 20 and port 21 are for File Transfer Protocol (FTP) data, TCP port 25 is for Simple Mail Transfer Protocol (SMTP), TCP port 80 is for Hypertext Transfer Protocol (HTTP), and TCP port 443 is for Hypertext Transfer Protocol Secure (HTTPS).

27. A. When you look at an IPv6 address, the first sections tell you the IPv6 address space prefix. fd00:: /8 is the unique local unicast prefix that allows the server to communicate with all local machines within your intranet.

28. C. Remote Desktop Connection (RDC) allows a local computer to connect to and control a remote computer over a network or the Internet. From the Local Resources tab, you can configure remote audio settings, keyboard settings, and local device and resource access. The options include Remote Audio, the Apply Windows Key Combinations drop-down list, and Local Devices And Resources.

29. C. The CIDR /29 tells you that 29 1s are turned on in the subnet mask. Twenty-nine 1s equals 11111111.11111111.11111111.11111000. This would then equal 255.255.255.248.

30. B. Network prefixes are determined directly from the subnet mask of the network. A Class B subnet mask would be 255.255.0.0. To determine the network prefix on a Class B subnet, you would need to convert each octet of the subnet mask to a binary value. So, for a Class B subnet, it would be 11111111.11111111.00000000.00000000. Count the consecutive 1s to determine the prefix. Thus, the answer would be /16.

31. B. The Domain Name System (DNS) turns a hostname into an IP address so that you can connect to a computer by the computer name. If you can connect to a computer by using the TCP/IP address but not the name, then the issue is with the DNS. DNS is a name-resolution service that resolves a hostname to a TCP/IP address. DNS also has the ability to resolve a TCP/IP address to a name. In this question, the DNS server in the ping results is listed as 127.0.0.1. This is the loopback diagnostic address and cannot be used for the IP configuration.

32. D. Packet Internet Groper (`ping`) is a diagnostic tool that tests the connection between two nodes or devices across a network. It verifies if a network data packet is able to be distributed to an address without errors. You can ping your own computer by using the loopback address, also known as the *local loopback*. Every Windows computer gets this address automatically; it's 127.0.0.1. You can enter **ping localhost**, **ping loobback**, or **ping 127.0.0.1**. The loopback address is used as a way of testing the functionality of a network adapter. The results in this question have failed, and the packets are being lost.

33. C. The `ipconfig` results are showing that this is a Class A address that is being used as a Class C network. On a Class C network, you *cannot* use the first or last number in the IP range (0 and 255). The first number of any range represents the network ID. The last number of any range represents the broadcast ID (255). So, having the default gateway set as 10.254.254.255 is not correct. The highest number on a Class C network that can be issued to a device is 254.

34. A. Most routers and other wireless access points (WAPs) communicate their network name (SSID) automatically every few seconds. SSID broadcasting makes it so that wireless users can see and connect to the network. In this question, you want to make the WLAN more secure, so you should disable SSID broadcasting. When SSID broadcast is disabled, the wireless network cannot be automatically detected until it is manually configured to connect.

35. A. Every NIC card has a hardware address known as a Media Access Control (MAC) address associated with it. The MAC address is assigned to a network adapter when it's manufactured. The Address Resolution Protocol (ARP) is a communication protocol that is used to discover the link layer address, such as a MAC address. Using arp with the -a switch will display all the MAC addresses of recently resolved IP addresses.

36. C. Before you can connect a Windows 10 machine to the domain, you must set up the network interface card (NIC). The NIC is a hardware component that is used to connect computers or other devices to the network to allow the machine to communicate on the network. NICs are responsible for providing the physical connection that recognizes the physical address (MAC address) of the device.

37. B. A Remote Desktop Gateway (RD Gateway) enables authorized remote users to connect to resources on an internal corporate or private network from anywhere using the Internet. You can create and manage your gateways using the Remote Desktop client. You will need to deploy Remote Desktop Gateway in the corporate office, and the remote users will then be able to connect to their work computers by using the Remote Desktop client from their home computers. The home computers need to be configured with the IP address of the Remote Desktop Gateway.

38. A. Administrators have the ability to limit and monitor network usage by configuring the network as a metered network. Network metering allows network downloading to be watched or metered, and then administrators can charge individuals or departments for the network usage. A metered connection is an Internet connection that has a data limit associated with it. Cellular data connections are set as metered by default. By default, Wi-Fi and Ethernet networks are not metered. To set a Wi-Fi network connection as metered, perform the following steps:

1. Select Start ➢ Settings ➢ Network & Internet ➢ Wi-Fi ➢ Manage Known Networks.

2. Select the Wi-Fi network, select Properties, and turn on Set As Metered Connection.

39. D. wbadmin.exe allows an administrator to back up and restore an operating system, volumes, files, folders, and applications while using the command prompt. The wbadmin.exe command replaces the ntbackup.exe command that was released with previous versions of Windows. To run the wbadmin.exe command, you must start it from an elevated command prompt.

40. B. By default, Microsoft's OneDrive is built into Windows 10, and it is a cloud-based storage system that corporate or home users can use to store their data on the cloud. OneDrive allows users to use up to 5 GB of cloud storage for free without a subscription. Users can obtain more cloud-based storage by purchasing a higher subscription. Users can store and then access those documents from anywhere in the world using Internet access.

41. C. The Startup Repair tool can be used if a computer will not boot into Safe Mode. This tool can be used to replace corrupted system files. If there are any hardware errors, then this option will not help. If a computer will not boot due to a missing or corrupted system file, then this tool will fix the issues. Startup Repair cannot be used to recover personal files that have become corrupted, damaged by viruses, or deleted. If this tool is unable to fix the issue, you may need to reinstall Windows 10, but this should be a last resort. This is why it is so important to perform regular backups of your Windows 10 machines.

42. B. Windows PowerShell is a task-based command-line utility designed especially for system administration. The `powershell.exe` command-line tool starts a Windows PowerShell session in a Command Prompt window. Windows 10 has a wide variety of PowerShell configuration commands that can be used to manage and configure a Windows 10 machine. By using the `Get-ControlPanelItem` command, this allows an administrator to find Control Panel items on a local computer by name, category, or description. The syntax for using this command is as follows: PS C:\> Get-ControlPanelItem -Name "<ITEM WANTED>" | Show-ControlPanelItem.

43. D. Restore points allow an administrator to bring a system back to a previous point in time. Restore points are snapshots of the Windows 10 system that can be used to revert to another snapshot. Restore points contain Registry and system information as it was at a certain point in time. Restore points are automatically generated when you install a new app, driver, or Windows update, and they are generated when you manually create a restore point. Using a restore point will not affect the personal files in the %UserProfile% folder, but it can remove apps, drivers, and updates that were installed after a restore point was created. If a system restore doesn't provided the expected results, then you can undo the restore point to return the system to how it was before doing the system restore.

44. C. System Protection creates and saves information about drivers, programs, system files, and settings. Windows will create restore points automatically. System Protection saves multiple previous versions of saved configurations rather than just overwriting them. This makes it possible to return to multiple configurations in your Windows 10 history, known as *restore points*. These restore points are created before most significant events, such as installing a new driver. Restore points are created automatically every seven days. System Protection is turned on by default in Windows 10 for any drive formatted with NTFS.

45. C. The Windows 10 Security And Maintenance window is used as a troubleshooting tool. If it discovers an issue that requires immediate attention, you will see a red circle with a white X in it.

46. B. Microsoft typically releases product updates on Tuesdays. So, this day was given the nickname of Patch Tuesdays. Updates are tested prior to being released to the public. With Windows 10, Microsoft has introduced new ways to service updates. Microsoft's new servicing options are referred to as Semi-Annual Channel, Long-Term Servicing Channel (LTSC), and Windows Insider.

47. C. Boot logging creates a log file that tracks the loading of drivers and services. When you choose the Enable Boot Logging option from the Advanced Boot Options menu, Windows 10 loads normally, not in Safe Mode. This allows you to see all the processes that take place during a normal boot sequence. This log file can be used to troubleshoot the boot process. When logging is enabled, the log file is written to \Windows\Ntbtlog.txt. This option will not fix any issues on a device, but it can be used to analyze what could be preventing a machine from loading properly.

48. B. OneDrive is free online storage that comes with a Microsoft account. If you save files into OneDrive folders, you can access them from any computer, tablet, or phone. To access files in OneDrive, open File Explorer. Click a OneDrive folder (it will have a cloud icon), and you will be able to see the files within the folder. If you want to view a OneDrive folder or file online, right-click it and select View Online. If you see an icon showing two blue arrows forming a circle, then the file or folder is in the process of syncing.

49. C. Delivery Optimization is a peer-to-peer distribution method used in Windows 10. Users can obtain content from other devices on the local network that have already downloaded the updates or from peers over the Internet. Delivery Optimization can be used for Windows Update, Windows Update for Business, and Windows Server Update Services (WSUS). Delivery Optimization reduces the amount of network traffic to external Windows Update sources as well as the time it takes for users to obtain the updates.

50. B. Windows 10 Performance Monitor is designed to allow users and administrators to monitor performance statistics for various operating system parameters. You can collect, store, and analyze information about items such as CPU, memory, disk, and network resources. By collecting and analyzing performance values, this allows you to identify potential issues. You should also monitor the Memory counters. If a computer does not have enough memory, this can cause excessive paging, which can be observed as a disk subsystem bottleneck.

Chapter 10: Practice Exam 2: MD-101

1. D. When safeguarding Windows 10 with Windows Hello for Business, an administrator can increase the level of security by using a personal identification number (PIN). A PIN may require or block certain special characters, uppercase and lowercase characters, and digits. The maximum length that can be set for a PIN is 127 characters.

2. D. Windows Hello is a biometrics system built into Windows. It is a Microsoft account that can be used to authenticate to a domain, a cloud-based domain, or a computer. To do this, you need to link your Microsoft account to your Windows 10 system. When you set up Windows Hello on a device, you can set up the system to use Windows Hello or a personal identification number (PIN). To configure Windows Hello options, click Start ➤ Settings ➤ Accounts. Windows Hello for Business is a newer credential in Windows 10, and it helps increase security when accessing corporate resources. This replaces passwords with strong two-factor authentication on computers and mobile devices. This consists of a user credential that is linked to a device and uses biometrics or a PIN.

3. A. Azure Multi-Factor Authentication (Azure MFA) provides businesses with a two-step verification solution that can be used to maintain access to data and applications and provide users with a simple sign-in process. By enabling Azure AD Identity Protection, this method uses an Azure AD Identity Protection risk policy to enforce two-step verification for signing into all cloud applications.

4. B. Multi-Factor Authentication (MFA) is a security system that requires more than one method of authentication from separate categories of credentials to verify the user's identity for a login or other transaction. The authentication categories are as follows:

    - Something you know

    - Something you have

    - Something you are

    For this question, the best option to tell your colleague is that MFA is using smart cards and PINs.

5. D. You can configure Windows Update for Business by using Group Policy objects (GPOs). The settings are located at Computer Configuration ➤ Administrative Templates ➤ Windows Components ➤ Windows Update ➤ Windows Update For Business. The Select When Quality Updates Are Received setting allows you to specify when to receive quality updates and to defer receiving quality updates for up to 30 days. You can also temporarily pause quality updates for up to 35 days.

6. A. You configure Delivery Optimization settings by using Group Policy. The GPO settings are found at Computer Configuration ➤ Administrative Templates ➤ Windows Components ➤ Delivery Optimization. Download Mode is the settings used to configure the use of Windows Update Delivery Optimization for downloads of Windows Updates, apps, and app updates. There are six Download Mode options:

    - Bypass

    - Group

    - HTTP Only

    - Internet

    - LAN

    - Simple

    In this question, the Group mode is being discussed. When Group mode is set, the group is automatically selected depending upon the device's Active Directory Domain Services (AD DS) site or the domain the device is authenticated to.

7. D. You can use the User State Migration Tool (USMT) to automate migration during Windows deployments. USMT uses configurable migration rule (.xml) files to control what user accounts, user files, operating system settings, and application settings are migrated. You can use USMT either for side-by-side migrations, where one piece of hardware is being replaced, or for wipe-and-load (or refresh) migrations, when only the operating system is being upgraded. A wipe-and-load migration is where the source and destination computer are the same. You back up the user data and settings to an external location and then install Windows 10. Then you restore the user data and settings.

8. D. The User State Migration Tool (USMT) uses configurable migration rule (.xml) files to control what user accounts, user files, operating system settings, and application settings are migrated. They can be written to improve productivity, and can be customized with settings and rules. USMT migration XML files include the following:

- `MigApp.xml`
- `MigDocs.xml`
- `MigUser.xml`
- Custom XML files that are created

9. C. The Windows Analytics service was retired as of January 31, 2020. Desktop Analytics is the replacement of Windows Analytics. If your Configuration Manager site had a connection to Upgrade Readiness, you need to remove it and reconfigure clients. To remove the Upgrade Readiness connection, do the following:

1. Open the Configuration Manager console as an administrator.
2. Go to the Administration workspace, expand Cloud Services, and select the Azure Services node.
3. Delete the Windows Analytics service.

10. A. Provisioning packages can be deployed to users in a variety of ways including by using email, by using physical media, or by sharing the file using OneDrive for Business. Settings can be applied to the target device in a number of methods. Some of these methods include the following:

- By running the `.ppkg` file
- By using the Settings app to add the provisioning package
- By using the `Add-ProvisioningPackage` Windows PowerShell cmdlet

The `Add-ProvisioningPackage` cmdlet will apply a provisioning package. The syntax is as follows:

```
Add-ProvisioningPackage [-Path] <string> [-ForceInstall] [-LogsFolder
<string>] [-QuietInstall] [-WprpFile <string>] [<CommonParameters>]
```

11. D. You can use the User State Migration Tool (USMT) to automate migration during large deployments of the Windows operating system. USMT uses configurable migration rule (.xml) files to control what user accounts, files, operating system configurations, and application settings are migrated and how they are migrated. There are several items that can be migrated; however, you cannot migrate the following using USMT:

- Customized shortcut icons
- Device drivers
- Files and settings if a foreign language is installed
- Local printers and hardware-related configurations
- Passwords
- Shared folder permissions

12. A. Microsoft offers both a 32-bit version and a 64-bit version of Windows 10. To install Windows 10 successfully, the system must meet or exceed certain minimum hardware requirements. The minimum requirements are as follows:

CPU (processor): 1 GHz or faster processor or system-on-a-chip (SoC)

Memory (RAM): 1 GB for 32-bit or 2 GB for 64-bit

Hard disk: 16 GB for 32-bit OS or 20 GB for 64-bit OS

Video adapter: DirectX 9 or later with WDDM 1.0 driver

Optional drive: DVD-R/W drive

Network device: Compatible network interface card

In this question, since you have only a 15 GB hard drive, this does not meet the requirement to install the 64-bit versions. So, given the options, you can install only the 32-bit version of Windows 10 Enterprise.

13. C. The System Preparation Tool (`sysprep`) is used to prepare a computer for disk imaging, and the disk image can then be captured using Deployment Image Servicing and Management (DISM). The DISM tool is included with Windows 10. `sysprep` is a free utility that comes with all Windows operating systems. By default, the `sysprep` utility can be found on Windows 10 operating systems in the `Windows\system32\sysprep` directory.

14. D. Azure Active Directory (Azure AD) simplifies the management of applications by providing a single identity system for cloud and on-premises apps. You can use the `Set-AzureADPolicy` PowerShell command to update a policy.

15. C. A conditional access policy is an `if-then` statement of Assignments and Access controls. Within a conditional access policy, an administrator can make use of signals from conditions. Conditional access policies can have a number of conditions. Some of these conditions include the following:

- Client Apps
- Device Platforms
- Device State
- Locations

In this question, you are discussing Device State. Device State is used to apply or exclude devices that are hybrid Azure AD joined or marked compliant in Intune. So, you can choose to apply or exclude specific device states.

16. A. Windows known folder move (KFM) for OneDrive is a feature that automatically redirects a user's personal folders and important files to their OneDrive for Business account stored on the Microsoft Cloud. This allows users to access their files across different devices and applications. There are two primary advantages of moving or redirecting Windows known folders to OneDrive.

- Users can continue using the folders with which they are familiar. They don't have to change their work habits to save files to OneDrive.
- Saving files to OneDrive backs up the users' data in the cloud and gives them access to their files from any device.

The folders that are redirected as part of the Windows known folders feature are the Camera Roll, Desktop, Documents, Pictures, and Screenshots folders.

17. D. When implementing a transition to co-management, companies are encouraged to deploy a phased approach that will allow them to roll out features and functionality to an increasing number of devices over a period of time. With a staged rollout, issues and feedback can be gathered and used to develop the process for future user groups and devices. So, you should first recommend creating a rollout group for staging co-management.

18. A. With Windows 10, Azure Active Directory (Azure AD) users can synchronize their user settings and application settings data to the cloud. Enterprise State Roaming provides users with a unified experience across their Windows devices. When you use Enterprise State Roaming, the desktop background, Favorites folder, and browsing history will be available on the new computers.

19. A. With device identity management in Azure Active Directory (Azure AD), you can ensure that the users are accessing resources from devices that meet corporate standards for security and compliance. The Azure AD portal provides a central location to manage device identities. You can manage device identities by using a direct link or by performing the following steps:

1. Sign in to the Azure portal.

2. Browse to Azure Active Directory ➢ Devices.

The Devices page enables an administrator to do the following:

- Configure device settings.
- Locate devices.
- Perform device identity management tasks.
- Review device-related audit logs.

20. B. To use the OneDrive GPO settings, you will first need to import the .adml and .admx files from a client and add them to your domain's GPO Central Store in the following location: \sysvol\domain\Policies\PolicyDefinitions. Administrative template files are divided into .admx files and .adml files for use by Group Policy administrators. Windows uses a Central Store to store administrative templates files. To create a Central Store for .admx and .adml files, create a new folder that is named PolicyDefinitions in File Explorer.

21. B. The Gramm-Leach-Bliley Act (GLBA) is also known as the Financial Modernization Act of 1999. It is a U.S. federal law that requires financial institutions to explain how they share and protect their customers' private information.

22. A. When setting Sync settings, you can choose to sync the theme, passwords, language preferences, Ease of Access, and other Windows settings. Some of the categories and common Sync settings that are included on a Windows 10 device include the following:

Theme: Background, system color, system sounds, screen saver, slideshow wallpaper, and taskbar settings

Passwords: Windows Credential Manager, including Wi-Fi profiles

Language Preferences: Spelling dictionary and system language settings

Ease of Access: Narrator, on-screen keyboard, and magnifier

Other Windows Settings: Device settings for items such as printers and mouse options, File Explorer settings, and notification preferences

To find the Sync settings, select Start ➤ Settings ➤ Accounts ➤ Sync. Using the Ease Of Access ➤ Keyboard settings, a user can do the following:

- Turn on/off on-screen keyboard.
- Turn on sticky keys (off by default).
- Turn on filter keys (off by default).
- Turn on toggle keys (off by default).

23. D. By redirecting the profile folders, you can redirect specific folders to be stored in a location outside of the user profile. These can be stored in a shared location on a file server or sent to OneDrive for Business. For domain users, an administrator can configure Folder Redirection and a variety of other settings, including setting quotas, to limit the size of redirected folders by using Group Policy.

24. B. Folder Redirection allows users and administrators to redirect the path of a known folder to a new location, manually or by using Group Policy. The new location can be a folder on the local computer or a directory on a file share. Users can then work with documents as if they were on the local drive but are available to the user from any computer on the network. Folder Redirection can be found under Windows Settings in the console tree by editing domain-based Group Policy via the Group Policy Management Console (GPMC).

25. D. Scope tags are used to assign and filter policies to specific groups. An administrator can also use scope tags to provide just the right amount of access and visibility to objects in Intune. Scope tags can be applied to different objects on Azure and Intune. The tag is basically a unique identifier.

26. B. The system creates a user profile the first time that a user logs on to a computer. At successive logins, the system will load the user's profile and other system components to configure the user's environment based on the information in the profile. A user profile consists of the following two elements:

- The registry hive, which is the file `ntuser.dat`. The hive is loaded by the system at user logon, and it is mapped to the `HKEY_CURRENT_USER` registry key.
- A set of profile folders stored in the file system. User-profile files are stored in the Profiles directory on a folder per-user basis.

27. B. Intune uses Azure Active Directory (Azure AD) for authentication, and if the network already has a local Active Directory Domain Services (AD DS) environment, you can connect the two services together using a tool called Azure AD Connect. Azure AD Connect helps you join your on-premises Active Directory with Azure AD.

28. A. Desktop Analytics is a cloud-based service that works with Configuration Manager. The process used to sign into Desktop Analytics and configure your subscription is called Initial Onboarding. This procedure is a one-time process used to set up Desktop Analytics for your company.

29. B. To help keep a device secure, Windows Security monitors devices for security issues and delivers a health report. The health report appears on the Device Performance & Health page. The health report alerts you to issues with a system, and it provides recommendations on how to fix them. Windows Security constantly scans for malware, viruses, and security threats.

30. A. Microsoft Defender Application Guard was designed for Windows 10 and Microsoft Edge. Application Guard helps by protecting the corporation while users browse the Internet by segregating untrusted sites. You can configure Microsoft Defender Application Guard in one of two modes: stand-alone mode or enterprise mode. In this question, enterprise mode is being discussed. Enterprise mode is when an administrator defines the company limitations by adding trusted domains and by customizing Application Guard to meet and enforce the corporation's needs on the users' devices.

31. A. Microsoft Defender Application Control (WDAC) was introduced with Windows 10, and it allows companies to control what drivers and applications are allowed to run on their Windows 10 clients. It does this by blocking any unsigned apps and scripts. WDAC is ideal in the following situations:

- You are adopting application control for security reasons.

- Application control policy can be applied to all users on the managed computers.

- All of the devices are running Windows 10.

Administrators can configure WDAC through the use of a Group Policy object or by using mobile device management (MDM) and Microsoft Intune. After Microsoft Defender Application Control is set up, administrators can create and configure policies by using GPOs or Intune.

32. C. Microsoft Intune allows you manage a wide variety of devices by enrolling them into the service. You can enroll some device types yourself, or users can enroll using the Company Portal app. Enrolling allows them browse and install apps, make sure that devices are compliant with company policies, and contact support, if needed. To enable device enrollment, click Device Enrollment in the Microsoft Intune Navigation pane. Under Device Enrollment there are several options that can be managed. These options include the following:

- Apple Enrollment

- Android Enrollment

- Windows Enrollment

- Terms and Conditions
- Enrollment Restrictions
- Device Categories
- Corporate Device Identifiers
- Device Enrollment Managers

This question is discussing the device categories. Device categories allow you to create a device category that users must choose during device enrollment. Device categories help when you are using the reporting tools. Users can select an appropriate category during enrollment. You can filter reports and create Azure Active Directory device groups based on device categories. To create a device category, click the + Create option and follow the steps.

33. A. An important feature of monitoring performance is that it should be performed over a period of time. This is called a *baseline*. Many performance problems cannot be identified simply by looking at performance at a quick glance. Instead, you need a baseline so that you can analyze the performance. Then, if a problem arises, you can compare the current performance to the baseline to see the differences. Since performance can also change over time, it is recommended that you create a baseline regularly so that you can chart the performance measures to identify trends.

34. C. Microsoft Defender Application Guard functionality is turned off by default. You can quickly install it on users' devices either through the Control Panel using PowerShell or with your mobile device management (MDM) solution. To install Microsoft Defender Application Guard by using the Control Panel, perform the following steps:

    1. Open the Control Panel, click Programs And Features, and then click Turn Windows Features On Or Off.

    2. Select the checkbox next to Microsoft Defender Application Guard and then click OK.

    3. Click OK. You will be prompted to restart the computer.

35. C. Intune allows an administrator to manage devices and apps and how those devices access company data. To use this mobile device management (MDM), the devices must first be enrolled in the Intune service. When a device is enrolled, it is issued an MDM certificate that is used to communicate with the Intune service. By default, devices for all platforms are allowed to enroll in Intune. The method being described in the question is corporate-owned device (COD), which include phones, tablets, and computers that are owned by the company and distributed to the users. COD enrollment supports scenarios such as automatic enrollment, shared devices, or pre-authorized enrollment requirements.

36. C. Microsoft Defender Antivirus can help protect devices by actively detecting spyware, malware, and viruses on both operating systems and Windows 10 installed on Hyper-V virtual machines. It runs in the background and installs new definitions automatically as they are released. Microsoft Defender Antivirus can manually scan for malware using the Microsoft Defender scan options. The scan options include Custom, Full, Quick, and Microsoft Defender Offline Scan. In this question, you are discussing a quick scan, which will scan the most likely areas on a hard drive where spyware, malware, and viruses are commonly known to infect.

37. C. The Microsoft Windows Performance Monitor is a tool that you can use to examine how programs run on a computer and how those programs affect the computer's performance. The tool can be used in real time, and it can also be used to collect information in a log to analyze the data at a later time. With Performance Monitor, you can set up counter logs and alerts. All performance statistics fall into three main categories that you can measure: performance objects, counters, and instances.

38. C. Log Analytics is the primary tool in the Azure portal for writing log queries and analyzing the results. You can start Log Analytics from several places within the Azure portal. The scope of the data available is determined by how you start Log Analytics. You can do the following:

- Select Logs from the Azure Monitor menu or Log Analytics Workspaces menu.
- Select Logs from the Overview page of an Application Insights application.
- Select Logs from the menu of an Azure resource.

39. C. By default, licensed users can add up to 15 devices to their accounts. Device administrators have the ability to add devices to Intune, but users do have the ability to enroll 15 devices on their own. Unless there is an enrollment restriction in place, then users can manage and enroll up to 15 devices.

40. A. Automatic enrollment allows users enroll their Windows 10 devices in Intune. To enroll, users add their company account to their personally owned devices or join corporate-owned devices to Azure Active Directory (Azure AD).

41. A. There are several ways to add apps. A user can add an app package, which will make the app available to just that user. Or, the app can be installed in the Windows image, which will make the app available to every user of the Windows image at first logon or at the next logon, if the user account is already created. This is called *provisioning* an app package. After sideloading is enabled, you can install an app package (.appx or .appxbundle) on a per-user basis by using the Add-AppxPackage PowerShell cmdlet. There is no limit to the number of LOB apps that you can add for each user.

42. C. Microsoft Intune uses Azure Active Directory (Azure AD) groups to manage devices and users. As an Intune admin, you can set up groups to meet your corporate needs. Create groups to organize users or devices by geographic location, department, or hardware characteristics. When creating a new group in Intune, you can enter a membership type. The membership types include Assigned, Dynamic User, and Dynamic Device. In this question, you are discussing the Dynamic User membership type. The Dynamic User membership type allows an administrator to create membership rules to add and remove members automatically.

43. B. App protection policies (APPs) can be applied to apps running on devices that may or may not be managed by Intune. The APP data protection structure is organized into three different configuration levels, with each level building off the previous level. The levels are as follows:

- Enterprise basic data protection (Level 1)
- Enterprise enhanced data protection (Level 2)
- Enterprise high data protection (Level 3)

The level being discussed in this question is Enterprise enhanced data protection (Level 2). This level introduces APP data leakage prevention mechanisms and minimum OS requirements. This is the configuration that is applicable to most mobile users accessing work or school data.

44. C. The first person to sign into Microsoft Store for Business must be a Global Administrator of the Azure Active Directory (Azure AD) tenant. Once the Global Administrator has signed in, they can assign permissions to other users. Although you can administer everything in Microsoft Store for Business using the Azure AD Global Administrator account, you can assign administrative roles to corporate users. Some of the roles that can be assigned are as follows:

- Billing Account Owner

- Billing Account Contributor

- Billing Account Reader

- Signatory

- Purchaser

- Basic Purchaser

In this question, the Billing Account Reader role is being discussed. This role can only view the account information.

45. B. The device state condition can be used to exclude devices that are hybrid Azure AD joined and/or devices that are marked as compliant with a Microsoft Intune compliance policy. A Hybrid Azure AD join takes precedence over the Azure AD registered state. This condition allows you to include or exclude device states.

46. D. Windows Information Protection (WIP) classifies apps into two categories: Enlightened and Unenlightened. In this question, you are discussing Unenlightened apps. Unenlightened apps consider all data as corporate and encrypt everything. Usually, you can tell an unenlightened app because of the following:

- Windows Desktop shows it as always running in enterprise mode.

- Windows Save As only allows you to save your files as enterprise.

47. A. Windows 10 comes with two Internet browsers: Internet Explorer and Microsoft Edge. However, not all websites can function properly when opened with Edge. To help with this issue, you can use Internet Explorer Enterprise mode. This allows you to define which browser to use when opening specific websites. Internet Explorer Enterprise mode is a compatibility mode that runs on Internet Explorer 11, allowing websites to use a modified browser configuration that has been designed to imitate an earlier version of Internet Explorer.

48. D. Windows Information Protection (WIP) is a built-in Windows 10 feature that allows an administrator to maintain and monitor company data from any personal data that is on a user's device. WIP also helps to protect corporate apps and data against accidental data leaks on corporate-owned and personal devices. An administrator can set a WIP policy to use one of four protection and management modes. The protection and management modes are Block, Allow Overrides, Silent, and Off. In this question, the Silent mode will be running silently, logging any inappropriate data sharing without blocking anything. Actions that are not allowed can include apps inappropriately trying to access network resources or WIP-protected data, which will still be stopped.

49. A. You can use Microsoft Intune to manage the client apps that your corporate users use. You can find most app-related information in the Apps workload. You can access the Apps workload by performing the following:

1. Sign in to the Microsoft Endpoint Manager admin center.

2. Select Apps.

The Apps workload provides links to access common app information and functionality. To display a list of all available apps, as well as the ability to add additional apps, you should go to the All Apps section. This section also lets you see the status of each app, as well as whether each app is assigned.

50. D. You can use the Windows Configuration Designer (WCD) tool to create provisioning packages to configure Windows 10 devices. WCD is designed to be used by users who need to provision a bring your own device (BYOD) type of device and business-supplied devices. You can install the WCD app on devices running Windows 10 from the Microsoft Store.

Index

K

T

X–Y–Z

Comprehensive Online Learning Environment

Register to gain one year of FREE access after activation to the online interactive learning environment and test bank to help you study for your MCA Modern Desktop certification exam—included with your purchase of this book!

The online test bank includes **Practice Test Questions** to reinforce what you've learned.

Go to www.wiley.com/go/sybextestprep to register and gain access to this comprehensive study tool package.

Register and Access the Online Test Bank

To register your book and get access to the online test bank, follow these steps:

1. Go to bit.ly/SybexTest.
2. Select your book from the list.
3. Complete the required registration information, including answering the security verification to prove book ownership. A PIN code will be emailed to you.
4. Follow the directions in the email or go to www.wiley.com/go/sybextestprep.
5. Enter the PIN code you received and click the Activate PIN button.
6. On the Create An Account Or Login page, enter your username and password, and click Login. A message that says "Thank you for activating your PIN!" will appear on your screen. If you don't have an account already, create a new account.
7. Click the Go To My Account button to add your new book to the My Products page.